Computational Economics: A Perspective from Computational Intelligence

Shu-Heng Chen
National Chengchi University, Taipei, Taiwan

Lakhmi Jain
University of South Australia, Adelaide, Australia

Chung-Ching Tai
National Chengchi University, Taipei, Taiwan

IDEA GROUP PUBLISHING
Hershey • London • Melbourne • Singapore

Acquisitions Editor:	Michelle Potter
Development Editor:	Kristin Roth
Senior Managing Editor:	Amanda Appicello
Managing Editor:	Jennifer Neidig
Copy Editor:	Becky Shore
Typesetter:	Diane Huskinson
Cover Design:	Lisa Tosheff
Printed at:	Integrated Book Technology

Published in the United States of America by
Idea Group Publishing (an imprint of Idea Group Inc.)
701 E. Chocolate Avenue, Suite 200
Hershey PA 17033
Tel: 717-533-8845
Fax: 717-533-8661
E-mail: cust@idea-group.com
Web site: http://www.idea-group.com

and in the United Kingdom by
Idea Group Publishing (an imprint of Idea Group Inc.)
3 Henrietta Street
Covent Garden
London WC2E 8LU
Tel: 44 20 7240 0856
Fax: 44 20 7379 3313
Web site: http://www.eurospan.co.uk

Library of Congress Cataloging-in-Publication Data

Computational economics : a perspective from computational intelligence / Shu-Heng chen and Lakhmi Jain, editors.
p. cm.
Summary: "This book identifies the economic as well as financial problems that may be solved efficiently with computational methods and explains why those problems should best be solved with computational methods"--Provided by publisher.
Includes bibliographical references and index.
ISBN 1-59140-649-8 (hardcover) -- ISBN 1-59140-650-1 (softcover) -- ISBN 1-59140-651-X (ebook)
1. Economics--Data processing. 2. Economics, Mathematical. 3. Finance--Data processing. I. Chen, Shu-Heng, 1959- II. Jain, L. C.
HB143.5.C663 2006
330'.0285--dc22
2005020633

Computational Economics: A Perspective from Computational Intelligence is part of the Idea Group Publishing series named *Computational Intelligence and Its Applications Series*.

British Cataloguing in Publication Data
A Cataloguing in Publication record for this book is available from the British Library.

Computational Economics:
A Perspective from Computational Intelligence

Table of Contents

Preface

MAIN IDEA OF THE BOOK

Computational Economics: The Old Style

The attempt to make economics computational is not new, given that economics is by nature both mathematical and quantitative. The use of computational models is so prevalent that one can hardly see the need to disentangle a field called *computational economics* from other branches of economics, let alone even bother to ask *what it is*. On their Web site, the Society of Computational Economics provides us with a simple description: "Computational economics explores the intersection of economics and computation." However, what is this intersection? Which parts do they intersect? Do they change over time, and what is the significance of these changes? These questions are not easy to answer without first making an effort to delineate what computational economics is. For most people most of the time, however, it is nothing more than using computing tools or algorithms to solve economic problems, when they become analytically intractable. This is what we may regard as old-style computational economics.

In old-style computational economics, computing resources, be they software or hardware, are basically viewed as ancillary to economic theory. They at best serve merely as a refinement to the already well-established theory, instead of being the core itself. A quick review of the past can help us recall what this old-style computational economics has been up to. In the 1970s, the development of *computational general equilibrium models* provided numerical algorithms to solve already well-formalized Walrasian general equilibrium structures, pioneered in the 1950s by two Nobel Laureates, namely Kenneth Arrow and Gerard Debreu. Computational economics at this stage sought to provide a numerical realization of Brouwer's or Kakutani's *fixed point theorem* to economic models.

In addition, in the 1970s, viewing the whole economy as following a law of motion and having its associated dynamics became somewhat standard in economic theory. With the advent of the *era of economic dynamics*, computational economics embarked upon new missions. First, it enhanced the application of optimal control theory to large Keynesian macroeconomic models. Led by a few economists, such as Robert Pindyck, David Kendrick, and Gregory Chow, computational economic models were further extended from conventional static temporal optimization to dynamical intertemporal optimization problems. Numerical algorithms involving computer simulation were used in solving these dynamic economic models to help in designing the optimal macroeconomic policy.

Second, in the late 1970s, the then dominant Keynesian view of the world was challenged by the *rational expectations revolution*. The former treats the economy more or less as a system of controllable objects constantly following a time-invariant rule (consumption functions, investment functions, ..., and so on.), whereas the latter attempts to acknowledge the ability of humans to change behavior when they expect economic policies to change. When the view of the world changes, the techniques for generating solutions also have to change accordingly. Therefore, in the 1980s and 1990s, one evidenced a great amount of effort being devoted to solving for linear or non-linear rational expectations equilibria, which, from a mathematical viewpoint, once again gave rise to a fixed point problem.

Coming as a result of the rational expectations revolution is a new interpretation of business cycles, known as *real-business cycle theory*, which was pioneered in the early 1980s by another two Nobel Laureates, Finn Kydland and Edward Prescott. The real-business cycle theory postulates that business cycles are created by *rational agents* responding *optimally* to *real shocks,* such as fluctuations in productivity growth, preferences, government purchases, and import prices. In a sense, the real-business cycle theory is under the joint influence of general equilibrium models and rational expectations; therefore, it is also commonly referred to as a *dynamic general equilibrium model* or a *stochastic dynamic general equilibrium model*.

The real-business cycle model per se is very computational. Real-business cycle theorists actually evaluate the model's suitability for describing reality by using a quantitative technique known as *calibration*. If the calibrated model can fit the real data well, then one should take its quantitative policy implications seriously. So, from the late 1980s until the present, working on the numerical aspect of the real-business cycle model has become another major activity of computational economics.

This review intends to be brief, and hence not exhaustive. However, the point here is to highlight the essential feature of the old-style computational economics or, at least, one aspect of computational economics, namely, using numerical methods to solve or optimize already established economic models, when the embedded theoretical environment is complicated by dynamics, nonlinearity and uncertainty. This volume, however, shares a different aspect of computational economics.

Computational Economics: Legacy of Herbert Simon

We do not treat computational economics as only a collection of numerical recipes. Instead, for us, computational economics comprises the economic models *built* and *solved* computationally. The role that computation plays is not just to solve or optimize something already established, but, what is more important, *to define and model what the problem itself is*. Therefore, it is not just ancillary to economic models, but can be the core itself. To distinguish our vision from the old style, we call this approach to computational economics *a perspective from computational intelligence*.

We shall elaborate on the reason why the term *computational intelligence* (CI) is preferred here (see also Chen, 2005).

The idea of looking at computational economics from the perspective of computational intelligence arises essentially from acknowledging the legacy of Herbert Simon to economics. Herbert Simon, the only person to win the Nobel Memorial Prize in Economics, the Turing Award of the ACM and the ORSA/TIMS von Neumann Prize, initiated the interdisciplinary research field and broke down the conventional distinctions among economics, computer science and cognitive psychology. The latter two played almost no role in the early days of Herbert Simon, but have now proved to be an indispensable part of computational economics, in particular, when *agent-based computational economics* emerges as an integration of the originally disparate research on experimental economics, behavioral finance and economics with heterogeneous interacting agents. The increasingly enlarged interdisciplinary framework really leads us to an even richer environment than in the days of Herbert Simon.

The idea behind computational intelligence is basically to model the intelligent behavior observed from linguistic behavior, biology, insects (swarm intelligence), neural sciences, and immune systems, just as it is said "natural does it all." This is different from the classical AI, which was mainly motivated by and built upon mathematical logic. It is also different from the conventional models of learning which are mainly based upon probability and statistics. However, modeling intelligence observed from natural behavior often leads us to computationally intensive models because the subjects that we are trying to model are by no means simple as in the classical dynamic systems. It is our anticipation that if we can model this observed behavior successfully, we can then have a better chance of understanding the operation of the economic system as a complex adaptive system, which is already a research target of many well-known research institutes.

With this anticipation in mind, we attempt in this volume to present chapters on novel economic and financial applications of computational intelligence. We began from those basic tools that every standard CI textbook should cover, namely, fuzzy logic, artificial neural networks, and evolutionary computation. Nevertheless, the ever-increasing interdisciplinary network makes us quickly realize that it would be meaningless to draw a clear line like this in such a complex, dynamically evolving scientific environment. Although intelligent behavior (and learning behavior as a part of it) is still one focus of this volume, we do not necessarily restrict this volume to computational intelligence only, be it narrowly defined or broadly defined. Chapters that introduce novel ideas motivated by computational theory, statistics, econometrics, physics, mathematics, and psychology are also included.

The second focus of this volume is on the application of CI to modeling the autonomous agents in agent-based computational models of economics and finance. Thus, agent-based computational economics and finance have become another broadly defined interest of this volume. Since agent-based modeling has now also become a very popular tool in the management sciences, we also prepare chapters on agent-based models of management in this volume. While CI is a key weapon for agent engineering, other approaches, such as the formal approach or the analytical approach to agent-based modeling, are also considered in this volume. In fact, the most striking example is the approach coming from *Econphysics*.

MAKING OF THE BOOK

The making of the book is based on the working guideline prepared by the IGI publisher. All papers are subjected to a peer-review process. We first send out call for papers to a selection of participants who presented their papers at the Third Workshop on Computational Intelligence in Economics and Finance (CIEF'2003), held at Cary, North Carolina, September 26-30, 2003. There were 72 papers out of 84 accepted by CIEF'2003, but only about 45 papers were in the invitation list. By the deadline, we had received 27 submissions. Each of these was sent to two to three referees, and the authors of each paper were asked to revise their drafts by taking the referees' comments into account. Authors who failed to do this or were unable to meet the deadline were eventually not accepted. In the end, we published a total of 15 chapters in this book.

CONTRIBUTORS TO THE BOOK

Before we go further into the main body of the book, a few things should also be said about the book's contributors. First, readers may find that there is a great variety in the authorss backgrounds. Table 1 enumerates all the associated academic departments or organizations that they belong to. The diversity in their background says something about the essential feature of computational methods in the social sciences—its diverse constituent techniques and wide applicability. A solid knowledge of both natural sciences and humanities is needed and fused in this research regime. Second, by probing deeper, it can be found that the authors of five co-authored chapters come from both the natural and social sciences, which is very typical, just as we should expect from a fast-growing interdisciplinary research community.

Third, in addition to the scientific background, Table 2 provides the authors' geographical background. While the sample is pretty small, it still reveals some stylized

Table 1. Authors' background

Division	Department/Classification	Author(s)
Academic Institution	Economics	7
	Finance	1
	Financial Economics	1
	Management	2
	Management Science and Engineering	1
	Information Sciences	1
	Information & Decision Sciences	2
	Computer Science	3
	Computer Software	1
	Computer Sciences & Engineering	1
	System Information Engineering	1
	Electrical Engineering	2
	Physics & Complex Systems	1
	Mathematics / Psychology	1
Company	Scientific Research & Application Company	3
Others	Research Institution	1
	US NASA	1

Table 2. Authors' geographical relationships

Continent	Geographical Region	Author(s)
Asia	Japan	5
	Taiwan	2
Europe	France	1
	United Kingdom	2
America	Argentina	2
	United States	17
Oceania	Australia	1

facts. The United States still plays the dominant role in research of this kind, and Japan has already taken the lead in Asia in this area for more than a decade.

CI TECHNIQUES

As the subtitle of this book suggests, the main methodology adopted in this book is computational intelligence. Table 3 reveals the specific CI techniques used by the authors. Among the many existing CI techniques, fuzzy logic, artificial neural networks, and evolutionary computation (specifically, genetic algorithms) are the three most popular ones. In addition to these three, other techniques used in this book are wavelets, Bayesian networks, and reinforcement learning. What is particularly striking here is that many authors use more than one CI technique, and make them work together as a hybrid system, which has been a research direction in CI for many years. Chapters I, II and IX are illustrations of why and how these CI techniques can be hybridized and used more efficiently.

A major methodologically distinguishing feature that readers may find interesting in this book is agent-based modeling. Agent-based modeling is a button-up method used to construct a system such as an organization, a market, or even an economy. In an agent-based model, economic individuals or members of organizations could be constructed heterogeneously by CI algorithms or by encoding with computer languages. The idea of modeling in this way follows people's knowledge of complex adaptive systems (CAS). In a complex adaptive system, individuals interact and form the macro results in a nonlinear way, and they also face an environment that is constantly changing and in which decision-making becomes a more sophisticated problem. The recogni-

Table 3. CI approaches adopted in this book

Chapter	CI techniques
I	Artificial Neural Networks + Genetic Algorithms
II	Wavelets + Artificial Neural Networks + Genetic Algorithms
III	Bayesian Networks
V	Genetic Algorithms
VII	Reinforcement Learning
VIII	Reinforcement Learning
IX	Artificial Neural Networks + Fuzzy Inference System
XI	Fuzzy Sets

tion of nonlinearity in complex adaptive systems, together with the aggregation problem in representative agent models, provides the basis for agent-based modeling. Chapters I, IV, V, VI, VIII, XII, XIV in this book employ agent-based models or similar settings.

Apart from computational intelligence, some chapters in this book also employ analytical methods borrowed from computer science or physics to facilitate their respective studies. Simulation plays an important role in such research due to the complexity of the specific problems looked into.

STRUCTURE AND CHAPTER HIGHLIGHTS

The formulation of a taxonomy of chapters in an edited volume like this one is not easy and definitely not unique. Depending on how this book is to be used, there are always different taxonomies. Nevertheless, only one can be considered here, and the criterion used here to divide these 15 chapters into sections discussing their major associated application domains. Based on this criterion, this book is composed of six sections, namely, financial modeling of investment and forecasting, market making and agent-based modeling of markets, game theory, cost estimation and decision-support systems, policy appraisal, and organizational theory and interorganizational alliances. We shall present a highlight of each chapter below.

Section I of this book, Financial Modeling of Investment and Forecasting, demonstrates some novel applications of CI techniques for tackling issues related to financial decisions, including financial pattern detection, financial time series forecasting, option pricing, portfolio selection, and so on. In Chapter I, Financial Modeling and Forecasting with Evolutionary Artificial Neural Network, Serge Hayward uses artificial neural networks to search for optimal relationships between the profitability of trading decisions and investors' attitudes towards risk, which serve as an appropriate loss function minimization in the learning process. A dual network structure is then designed accordingly, and genetic algorithms are employed to search for the best topology of the network.

In Chapter II, Pricing Basket Options with Optimum Wavelet Correlation Measures, Christopher Zapart, Satoshi Kishino, and Tsutomu Mishina introduce a new approach for dealing with correlations between financial time series. By transforming time series data into time-frequency domains via wavelets, and by using two versions of wavelet models (i.e., static and dynamic models), the authors overcome the limitations of existing methods and find that their outcomes are superior to those resulting from standard linear techniques in out-of-sample tests.

In Chapter III, Influence Diagram for Investment Portfolio Selection, Chiu-Che Tseng applies Bayesian networks to construct an influence diagram for investment portfolio selection by inheriting the concepts of Bayesian theory. The resultant influence diagram is able to provide decision recommendations under uncertainty. The author finds that the system outperforms the leading mutual fund by a significant margin for the years from 1998 to 2002.

Section II of this book, Market Making and Agent-Based Modeling of Markets, is concerned with the operation of the market mechanism and connects the observed aggregate phenomena to the interactions among agents at the micro level of the markets. In Chapter IV, Minimal Intelligence Agents in Double Auction Markets with Speculators, Senlin Wu and Siddhartha Bhattacharyya study the potential impact of the intelligence of individual market participants on the aggregate market efficiency in a double auction setting. They extend some early studies on this issue to an interesting case of asymmetric markets with speculators. They find that under various market conditions with speculators, ZI-C (zero-intelligence with constraints) traders, who shout prices uniformly but not beyond their own reservation prices, are incapable of making the market price converge to the equilibrium level. They also observe that, when there are not too many speculative activities in the market, ZIP (zero-intelligence plus) traders, who are able to learn by altering their profit margin, are sufficiently capable of driving market price to the equilibrium.

In Chapter V, Optimization of Individual and Regulatory Market Strategies with Genetic Algorithms, Lukas Pichl and Ayako Watanabe delineate the limitations of static portfolio optimization models, and propose agent-based modeling methodology as a promising alternative. They employ genetic algorithms as the agent engineering technique, and then build a model to demonstrate the distinguishing feature of complex adaptive systems, namely, co-evolutionary dynamics. In addition to the bottom-up behavioral modeling, they also consider a Kareken-Wallace setting to study the policy optimization problem for the social planner from a top-down perspective.

In Chapter VI, Fundamental Issues in Automated Market Making, Yuriy Nevmyvaka, Katia Sycara, and Duane J. Seppi provide a rich overview concerning fundamental issues of market making. This chapter provides an excellent tutorial for readers who want to have a quick grasp of this research area. They also set up an electronic environment that can merge real data with artificial data to run market experiments. The decision process of a dealer is formalized. Statistical techniques are used to discern possible structures of the data, and dealers' optimal responses are then discussed. Borrowing from their experience in robotics, they present an appropriate experimental environment and all the necessary tools for real implementations in the future.

Section III of this book, Games, addresses game-theoretic issues. Game theory in economics has a long and active history and has received very intensive treatment in terms of CI methodology. Chapter VII, Slow Learning in the Market for Lemons: A Note on Reinforcement Learning and the Winner's Circle, by Nick Feltovich, deals with the famous issue in auctions known as the *winner's curse*. Due to asymmetric information, a bidder may systematically bid more than the optimal amount, and this raise the question of why people make the same mistake in this area over and over again. The author of this chapter tries to propose a more persuasive reason for this phenomenon—that human-bounded rationality causes people to learn in a way that could be described as reinforcement learning. The author finds that results can conform qualitatively to the typical experimental results observed from laboratories with human participants.

Chapter VIII, Multi-Agent Evolutionary Game Dynamics and Reinforcement Learning Applied to Online Optimization for the Traffic Policy, by Yuya Sasaki, Nicholas S. Flann, and Paul W. Box, studies Nash equilibria and evolutionarily stable strategy profiles of traffic flow. The choice of routes to a destination becomes a typical game when the number of people on the road starts to have a negative effect on everyone's access to and the quality of the transportability. Instead of a standard static method, Sasaki et al. also adopt reinforcement learning to model their agents in the complex traffic network problem. They identify the equilibria of the game. They further validate their method using geographic information systems to a complex traffic network in the San Francisco Bay area.

Section IV of this book, Cost Estimation and Decision-Support Systems, should interest those readers who would like to see CI applied to operations research or engineering economics. Chapter IX, Fuzzy-Neural Cost Estimation for Engine Tests, by Edit J. Kaminsky, Holly Danker-McDermot, and Freddie Douglas, III, attempts to perform the tough task of cost estimation. Cost estimation is never easy since it is highly uncertain, especially in a huge project like the engine testing conducted by NASA. Besides relying upon past experiences, several software systems have been developed in the past to perform the cost estimation for NASA. Even so, they require either detailed data or data that are rarely available. Therefore, the authors propose a hybrid system that combines fuzzy logic and artificial neural networks in order to build an adaptive network-based fuzzy inference system. They show that the system can work even with a small set of data, and the accuracy of the predicted cost is enhanced as the complexity of the system increases.

In uncertain circumstances, the cost estimation and decision making of software development projects also pose difficult problems for small IT companies. The complexity in the interactions among project tasks, resources, and the people involved usually makes the estimate of the project factors very crude, which can lead to very harmful decisions. In Chapter X, Computer-Aided Management of Software Development in Small Companies, Lukas Pichl and Takuya Yamano tackle this issue by developing a customizable, object-oriented software project simulation environment that facilitates duration and cost estimates and supports decision making. They run simulations both to optimize the project structure and to determine the effects of stochastic variables in certain fixed structures. As a result, an online Java program is devised as a tool for software project management simulations.

In Chapter XI, Modern Organizations and Decision-Making Processes: A Heuristic Approach, Ana Marostica and Cesar Briano propose a hybrid decision support system that deals with several important topics in decision-making processes. The authors provide detailed definitions, principles, and classes for each element in a decision-support system: utility, subjective beliefs, rationality, and algorithms that can cope with ambiguity and vagueness. They also point out a hybrid decision-support system in which there is an embodiment relationship between the user and the computer program, and therefore make it applicable to multiagent systems.

Section V of this book, Policy Appraisal, includes chapters that contribute to the application of CI techniques to policy appraisal issues. Chapter XII, An Application of Multi-Agent Simulation to Policy Appraisal in the Criminal Justice System, by Seán Boyle, Stephen Guerin, and Daniel Kunkle, illustrates an interesting case of the criminal justice system in England. In an intricate system such as the CJS in England, three distinct departments are involved in these affairs. The diverse government bodies have reciprocal influences on each other and therefore any policy taken by one of them will have complex impacts on the system. Hence Boyle et al. have developed an agent-based program to simulate the whole system, and on assessment of the impact across the whole justice system of a variety of policies is thus possible.

Chapter XIII, Capital Controls and Firm's Dynamics, by Alexei G. Orlov, illustrates another hot topic in economic policy, namely, capital controls. The issue of capital controls in multinational enterprises is always debatable. Evaluating the effectiveness of capital restrictions is a daunting task, let alone political or other debates. Orlov overcomes the time-series difficulties of evaluating exchange controls by examining transitional dynamics in a model of a multinational enterprise. He constructs a model of a multinational enterprise to quantify the effects of various exchange control policies on the capital stocks, debt positions, innovations and outputs of the headquarters and its subsidiary. The simulation results show that lifting exchange controls produces an inflow of capital into the less developed countries, and not an outflow as the governments sometimes fear.

Section VI, Organizational Theory and Inter-Organizational Alliances, extends the applications of CI to organization theory and management sciences. Chapter XIV, A Physics of Organizational Uncertainty: Perturbations, Measurement, and Computational Agents, by William F. Lawless, Margo Bergman, and Nick Feltovich, is a theoretic work in which two contradictory approaches to organizations are discussed and compared. The authors then point out the dangers of a subjective approach to multiagent systems and provide a model with the mathematical physics of uncertainty borrowed from quantum theory. This chapter could be viewed as having a goal of revising the rational theory of multiagent systems.

Chapter XV, Reducing Agency Problem and Improving Organizational Value-Based Decision-Making Model of Inter-Organizational Strategic Alliance, by Tsai-Lung Liu and Chia-Chen Kuo, is also an attempt to refine past theories and to explore the impact of interorganizational strategic alliances on organizational value-based decision-making processes. The authors attempt to solve the agency problem due to asymmetric information, specifically, asymmetric uncertain information. The authors combine past theories and accordingly form propositions as well as a conceptual model.

REFERENCES

Chen, S.-H. (2005). Computational intelligence in economics and finance: Carrying on the legacy of Herbert Simon. *Information Sciences, 170,* 121-131.

Section I

Financial Modeling of Investment and Forecasting

Chapter I

Financial Modeling and Forecasting with an Evolutionary Artifical Neural Network

Serge Hayward
Ecole Supérieure de Commerce de Dijon, France

ABSTRACT

In this chapter, I consider a design framework of a computational experiment in finance. The examination of statistics used for economic forecasts evaluation and profitability of investment decisions, based on those forecasts, reveals only weak relationships between them. The "degree of improvement over efficient prediction" combined with directional accuracy are proposed in an estimation technique, as an alternative to the conventional least squares. Rejecting a claim that the accuracy of the forecast does not depend upon which error-criteria are used, profitability of networks trained with L_6 *loss function appeared to be statistically significant and stable. The best economic performances are realized for a 1-year investment horizon with longer training not leading to enhanced accuracy. An improvement in profitability is achieved for models optimized with genetic algorithm. Computational intelligence is advocated for searching optimal relationships among economic agents' risk attitude, loss function minimization in the learning process, and the profitability of trading decisions.*

INTRODUCTION

A significant part of the financial research deals with identifying relationships among observed variables. Conventional financial modeling decided upon a mechanism (form, size, etc.) and searches for parameters that give the best fit between the observed values and the model's solutions. Econometrics is supposed to direct the choice of the model's functional form. Nevertheless, density assumption rests as a controversial and problematic question. Computational intelligence (CI[1]) provides a general data mining structure, particularly suitable for complex nonlinear relationships in financial data, without a need to make assumptions about the data generating mechanism. Tailoring the desired output to the given input, CI tools determine the functional form of the model. However, CI tools are often viewed as "black-box" structures. Unlike the well-established statistical foundation of econometrics, a search for the foundation of CI tools in finance is in its early stages. This research is a step in the direction of examining the set-up of an artificial neural network (ANN).

Similarly, problems with applications of evolutionary computation (EC) in economics and finance are often due to the lack of common methodology and statistical foundations of its numerous techniques. These deficiencies sometimes cast doubt on conjectured results and conclusions. At the same time, relationships between summary statistics used for predictions' evaluation and profitability of investment decisions based on these predictions are not straightforward in nature. The importance of the latter is particularly evident for applications of an evolutionary artificial neural network (EANN) under supervised learning, where the process of network training is based on a chosen statistical criterion, but when economic performance is an overall objective.

The relationship between agents' utility functions and optimal investment decisions[2] is a long-standing issue in financial research. Recent development in computational economics and finance (CEF) allows me to address this question from a new perspective. This chapter aims to examine how investors' preferences affect their behavior.

Advances in CEF also stimulate investigation of the relationship between investors' time horizons and their actions. To date, most research considering time horizons in CEF deal with memory length. Agents' time horizon heterogeneity with back and forward time perspectives has not yet been systematically examined. I examine how investors' time horizons affect stock trading strategies.

Financial assets' prices often exhibit nonstationarity, autocovarience and frequent structural breaks, posing problems for their modeling. This research also investigates how data mining benefits from genetic algorithm (GA) model discovery, performance surface optimization, pre- and postprocessing, thus improving predictability and profitability or both.

ECONOMIC AGENTS' PREFERENCES AND INVESTMENT DECISIONS

It is common in analytical research to relate economic agents' risk preferences and their decisions. This general approach has different realizations in supporting various "optimal" utility functions. It is often stated that for long-time investment it is optimal to maximize the geometric mean in each period, which implies a logarithmic utility function. Blume and Easley (1992) claimed that agents' fitness in terms of long-term survival is a function of appropriate (logarithmic) preferences, but not at all a function of an accurate prediction. This leads to a conclusion that even perfect foresight might not help agents with nonlog utilities to survive.

Merton and Samuelson (1974) criticized the geometric mean utility function, yet they use the power utility function (which includes the log utilities as a special case). With these preferences the investment policy in each period is independent of the number of periods. Thus, investors are considered to be myopic, maximizing one period ahead expected utility.

Chen and Huang (2003) in the computational experiment found that long-term survivals are traders with constant relative risk aversion (CRRA). A key factor of CRRA agents' dominance is the stability of their saving rate. Simulation demonstrates that for traders with very low saving rates, there exist situations, leading to a significant decrease in wealth. After a while this might result in the disappearance of those agents from the market. Only traders with CRRA are uninhibited from relative risk aversion approaching zero. They never choose a saving rate too low and, therefore, will survive. This outcome makes the authors largely support Blume and Easley's (1992) assertions.

This research is motivated by the results of Chen and Huang (2003) that agents' optimal investment actions are a function of risk aversion through saving decisions, rather than a function of an accurate prediction through portfolio decision. In this investigation I approach the subject from a different perspective. First , I examine the mapping of traders' risk attitude into their predictions. Second, bearing in mind that stock trading models' time horizons do not typically exceed 1 to 2 years, I can limit my investigation to short-medium term analysis. Third, considering an environment with agents possessing an optimal stable saving rate (e.g., locked-up saving contracts), allows me to focus on trading decisions, examining the profitability of actions over short and long terms.

The second motivation for this research comes from Leitch and Tanner (2001), arguing that traditional summary statistics are not closely related to a forecast's profit. As I consider the effect of agents' risk attitude on their actions' profitability through loss functions (and associated errors) minimization, this relationship is particularly important. If agents' preferences have an impact on their wealth, there should be a statistically significant relationship between forecasts' errors and actions' profitability, in order to investigate it under a supervised learning paradigm.

In this chapter I search for optimal (if any) relationships between agents' attitude towards risk, a (appropriate) loss function minimization in learning the surrounding environment and the profitability of trading decisions. Specifically, I consider the following questions:

1. What are the relationships among risk aversion coefficients, conventional loss functions, and common error measures?
2. Conditioning on an optimal saving rate; what is the wealth distribution among agents with heterogeneous risk preferences?
3. How significant (statistically) is the relationship between error measures (used to train a forecasting ANN) and trading profitability (based on that forecast)?

Utility Functions

Consider a few risk preferences assumptions common in finance. $U(W) = W - \rho W^2$, the quadratic function, where ρ is a risk aversion coefficient[3]. The quadratic utility is appealing as it permits mean-variance analysis, disregarding higher moments of return distribution. On the other hand, for some critical value it results in U' < 0. This utility function is characterized by increasing absolute risk aversion (IARA) and increasing relative risk aversion (IRRA), with a coefficient of relative risk aversion approaching to zero when the return on investment falls.

One of the attractions of the negative exponential utility function, $U(W) = -e^{-\rho W}$ is its convenience for analytical analysis. Constant absolute risk aversion (CARA) characterizes these risk preferences and appeals to advocates of such underlying behavior in the financial markets. In CEF, negative exponential utility function was adopted in Arthur, Holland, LeBaron, Palmer, and Taylor (1997); Chen and Yeh (2001b); Hommes (2001); and Lettau (1997). This utility function is also described by IRRA preferences.

$U(W) = W^{1-\rho} / 1-\rho$, the power utility function is characterized by CRRA and became particularly popular after Merton and Samuelson (1974). An attractive feature of CRRA for CEF is that it allows wealth to enter into the demand function, which corresponds to the actual financial markets behavior, where wealthier traders have more impact on prices.

Laboratory results of Gordon, Paradis, and Rorke (1972) suggested that ρ in the power utility function, is in the range [0.6,1.4]. Estimations by Friend and Blume (1975) asserted that ρ is in the range [1.0, 2.0]. Chen and Huang (2003) examined a particular form of the power utility with ρ equal to 0.5: $U(W) = \sqrt{W}$ and found that reducing the value of ρ decreases traders' survivability.

$U(W) = ln(W)$, logarithmic risk preferences were advocated by Hakansson (1971), Kelly (1956), Latane (1959), and Markowitz (1976). In Chen and Huang (2003) agents with log utility in survivability came only second to traders with the square root function. Testing agents' fitness in response to a slow step increase in the risk aversion coefficient, particularly in the region [0.6, 1.0], might reveal some optimal level. For comparison I also consider an optimization without formulating a utility function explicitly, such as the "worst case" objective.

Notice a recent trend in the choice of risk preferences in CEF. CARA preferences traditionally are a common option, probably, following and by influence of some seminal works, such as Arthur et al. (1997) and Chen and Yeh (2001a). CRRA become more used in computational modeling since its early applications by Levy, Levy, and Solomon (1994). It is noteworthy that LeBaron after 1997 (LeBaron, 2001a, 2001b, 2002) moved from CARA to CRRA in his research. Similarly, Chen, who used to assume CARA in Chen and Yeh (2001a, 2001b) proved the long-term dominance of traders with CRRA in Chen and Huang (2003).

TIME HORIZONS

Stylized facts often suggest that financial asset prices exhibit nonstationary behavior with profound structural breaks. Thus, in a market, with a frequently changing data-generating mechanism, it could be advantageous to look at the limited past. In designing an experiment, a model with short-term training is more likely to over-fit the data, whereas training a model over the long term could result in overlooking potentially useful (even if incipient) contemporary relationships. In alternative computational settings, I test the conclusion that, as longer validation periods get agents' beliefs closer to the true process, portfolio strategy's accuracy increases with the memory length (Chen & Huang, 2003). I also explore experimentally a supposition made in LeBaron (2001b) that in a highly dynamic environment the general behavior over long time might be unobtainable.

A trading strategy choice (with respect to the time horizons) is a function of market conditions that are themselves functions of strategies used by the agents who populate this market. In these settings, market conditions (or the strategies used by the dominant type of trader) determine the optimal memory length. This approach moves towards considering the market environment endogenously within financial data mining.

METHODOLOGY

For my experiment, I build ANN forecasts and generate a posterior optimal rule. The rule, using future information to determine the best current trading action, returns a buy/sell signal (B/S) today if prices tomorrow have increased/decreased. Since the posterior optimal rule signal (PORS) looks into the future, it cannot be employed for trading or as an input for a prediction. Nevertheless, PORS can be used as the desired output of a prediction to model trading activity.

PORS is then modeled with ANN forecasts, generating a trading B/S signal. Combining a trading signal with a strategy warrants a position to be taken. I consider a number of market timing strategies, appropriate for different strengths of the B/S signal. If I have a buy (sell) signal on the basis of prices that are expected to increase (decrease), then I enter a long (short) position. When prices are expected to increase (decrease), although not sufficiently to enter a long (short) position, an exit short (long) position is taken, implying buying the shares at the current price to replace those that were borrowed (selling the shares currently owned). If the size of an expected price movement is unknown or predicted not to be worth trading against, the hold position is taken. Note that my approach is different from the standard B/S signal generation by a technical trading rule. In the latter, it is only a signal from a technical trading rule that establishes that prices are expected to increase/decrease. In my model, I link a signal's expectations of price change (given by PORS) to a time-series forecast.

PORS is a signal based on a trading strategy[4], a minimum profit, and a number of periods into the future. Stepping forward one period at a time, the potential profit is examined. If the expected profit exceeds the minimum profit after transaction costs (TC), a PORS is generated. The direction of PORS is governed by the direction of the price movement. Normally, the strength of the signal reflects the size of underlying price changes, although, I also examine signals without this correlation to identify when profit-generating conditions begin. Last, I consider those PORS generated only at the points of highest profit to establish the maximum profit available. However, such a signal may be the most difficult to predict since it delays entry into profitable situations until the highest profit can be achieved. It is also the most vulnerable to everyday noise in financial data.

To apply my methodology, I develop a dual network structure, presented in Figure 1. The forecasting network feeds into the acting network, from which the information set

Figure 1. Dual ANN: (1) forecasting network; (2) acting network

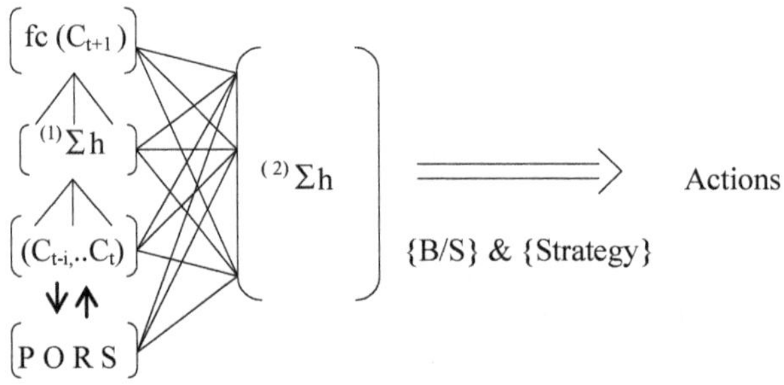

C_{t-i}... C_t: price time-series; $fc(C_{t+1})$: next-period's forecast; PORS: posterior optimal rule signal; B/S: buy/sell signal; $^{(1)}\Sigma$: forecasting network; $^{(2)}\Sigma$: acting network.

includes the output of the first network and PORS, as well as the inputs used for forecasting, in order to relate the forecast to the data upon which it was based.

This structure is an effort to relate an action's profitability to forecasting quality, examining this relationship in a computational setting. The model is evolutionary in the sense that it considers a population of networks (individual agents facing identical problems/instances) that generate different solutions, which are assessed and selected on the basis of their fitness. Backpropagation is used in the forecasting net to learn to approximate the unknown conditional expectation function (without the need to make assumptions about a data-generating mechanism and beliefs formation). It is also employed in the acting net to learn the relationship between the statistical characteristics of the forecasts and the economic characteristics of the actions. Finally, agents discover their optimal settings with a GA. Such a basis for the ANN model discovery makes technical decisions less arbitrary. The structure seems to be intuitive, and it is simple to generate results independent from a chosen architecture. The results are sufficiently general, showing stability over multiple independent runs with different random seeds for the dual forecasting/acting net and a single forecasting net.

DESCRIPTION OF THE ENVIRONMENT

Let Y be a random variable defined on a probability space $(\Omega, \mathcal{F}, P)$. Ω is a space of outcomes, $\mathcal{F}$ is a σ-field and P is a probability measure. For a space $(\Omega, \mathcal{F}, P)$, a conditional probability $P[A|\mathcal{F}]$ for a set A, defined with respect to a σ-field $\mathcal{F}$, is the conditional probability of the set A, being evaluated in light of the information available in the σ-field $\mathcal{F}$. Suppose economic agents' utility functions are given by a general form:

$$U(W_{t+s}) = g(Y_{t+s}, \delta(fc_{t+s})). \qquad (1)$$

According to (1), an agent's utility depends on a target variable Y_{t+s} and a decision/strategy variable, $\delta(fc_{t+s})$, which is a function of the forecast, fc_{t+s}, where $s \geq 1$ is a forecasting horizon. Setting the horizon equal to *1*, I examine the next period's forecast (when this simplification does not undermine the results for $s \geq 1$). A reward variable W_{t+s} is sufficiently general to apply to different types of economic agents and includes wealth, reputation, and the like. $w_{t+1}(y_{t+1}, fc_{t+1})$ is the response function, stating that, at time $t+1$, an agent's reward w_{t+1} depends on the realization of the target variable y_{t+1} and on the target's forecast, fc_{t+1}. Forecasting is regarded as a major factor in a decision rule, which is close to reality in financial markets. Also, it has an established statistical foundation in econometrics, allowing its application in computational settings.

The overall number of periods is $n+1$ and the number of observations available to produce the first forecast is t. Thus, forecasting starts at $t+1$ and ends at $n+1$, with the total forecasts available equal to $T \equiv n+1-t$. In such a scheme, $\{fc_{t+s}\}_{t \leq t+s < T+t}$, agents recursively learn the parameters of the forecasting model, using all the information presented prior to the period of the forecast.

Let $fc_{t+1} = \theta' X_t$ be a forecast of Y_{t+1} conditional on the information set $\mathcal{F}_t$, with an unknown m-vector of parameters, $\theta \in \Theta$, (Θ compact in $\mathbf{R}^k$) and an n-vector of variables, X_t, observable at time t. X_t is $\mathcal{F}_t$–measurable and might include some exogenous variables, indicators, lags of Y_t, and the like. An optimal forecast does not exclude model misspecification, which can be due to the form of fc_{t+1} or a failure to include all relevant information in X_t. With imperfect foresight, the response function and, therefore the utility function, are negatively correlated with the forecast error, $\varepsilon_{t+1} \equiv y_{t+1} - fc_{t+1}$; $|\varepsilon_{t+1}| > 0$. A mapping of the forecast into a strategy rule, $\delta(fc_{t+1})$ (combined with elements of X_t) determines a predictive density g_y, which establishes agents' actions.

In this setting, maximizing expected utility requires me to find an optimal forecast, $\hat{fc}_{t+1}$, and to establish an optimal decision rule, $\hat{\delta}(fc_{t+1})$. Note that optimality is with respect to a particular utility function, implemented through a loss function, in the sense that there is no loss (cost or disutility) for a correct decision and a positive loss for an incorrect one. Given a utility function, expected utility maximization requires minimization of the expected value of a loss function, representing the relationship between the size of the forecast error and the economic loss incurred because of that error. A strategy evolution (mapping of the forecast into a decision rule) is another way to minimize the expected value of a loss function.

In an experimental design problem, where the exact functional form of the mapping $f: X \rightarrow \mathbf{R}^k$ is unknown and a measurement of $f(x)$ for any given $x \in X$ is noisy and costly, $f(x)$ is approximated for a final sample $\{x_1, \ldots x_n\}$. Points, x_i that provide the maximum information about the function f, need to be determined. With the aim of identifying the function $f(x)$ the learning system considers input-target pairs (x, y) and generates the output $\Phi = f''(x, \psi)$, determining appropriate weights, ψ to minimize discrepancy with the target. ANN approximation of Y with Φ is effectively an approximation of $f(x)$ with input-target map $f''(x, \psi)$. To make this optimization problem operational the objective function has to be defined explicitly.

Given some characteristic moments, an objective function is the distance between empirical moments of the real market data and simulated data. The parameters of the model are estimated by minimizing the objective function. Without prior knowledge about the functional form of f, an objective function, permitting an analytical solution for the optimization, might be unobtainable. Facing continuous but non-convex optimization, minimization of a stochastic approximation of the objective function might be addressed with some heuristic algorithms.

A loss function, $L: \mathbf{R} \rightarrow \mathbf{R}^+$, related to some economic criteria or a statistical measure of accuracy, takes a general form:

$$L(p, \alpha, \varepsilon) \equiv [\alpha + (1-2\alpha)1(\varepsilon < 0)]\varepsilon^p, \tag{2}$$

where p is a coefficient of absolute risk aversion (related to a coefficient of relative risk aversion, ρ through some function h, $p = h(\rho)$); ε is the forecast error; $\alpha \in [0,1]$ is the degree of asymmetry in the forecaster's loss function, and 1 in $1(\varepsilon<0)$ is the indicator function.

Economic agents' marginal utility is a function of their degree of asymmetry in the loss function. If $\alpha < 1$, more weight is given to negative forecast, cost of negative error exceeds the cost of positive error. If $\alpha > 1$, cost of positive error exceeds the cost of negative error. If $\alpha = \frac{1}{2} \Rightarrow \alpha/1 - \alpha = 1$ is the symmetry[5].

$L(p, \alpha, \varepsilon)$ is $\mathcal{F}_t$–measurable and also presented as

$$L(p, a, \theta) \equiv [a + (1-2a)1(Y_{t+1} - fc_{t+1}(\theta) < 0)]\left|Y_{t+1} - fc_{t+1}(\theta)\right|^p, \tag{3}$$

where α and $p\,(\rho)$ are shape parameters of a loss function; vector of unknown parameters, $\theta \in \Theta$. Order of the loss function is determined by p. Setting agents' attitude towards risk, p to different values, allows me to identify the main loss function families. Consider some families and their popular representatives:

1. $L(1, [0,1], \theta)$ – piecewise linear family "Lin-Lin" or "Tick" Function.
   - $L(1, 1/2, \theta) = |Y_{t+1} - fc_{t+1}|$ – absolute value loss function or mean absolute error (MAE) loss function, $L(\varepsilon_{t+1}) = |\varepsilon_{t+1}|$. This loss function determines the error measure, defined as:

$$MAE = T^{-1}\sum_{s=1}^{T}\left|\varepsilon_{t+s}\right|. \tag{4}$$

2. $L(2, [0,1], \theta)$ – piecewise quadratic family "Quad-Quad."
   - $L(2, 1/2, \theta) = (Y_{t+1} - fc_{t+1})^2$ – squared loss function or mean squared error (MSE) loss function, $L(\varepsilon_{t+1}) = \varepsilon^2_{t+1}$. Appropriate for this loss function error measure is defined as:

$$MSE = T^{-1}\sum_{s=1}^{T}\varepsilon^2_{t+s}. \tag{5}$$

The choice of a loss function is influenced by the object of analysis. In this chapter, loss functions that are not directly determined by the value of risk aversion coefficient are limited out. For given values of p and α, an agent's optimal one-period forecast is

$$\min_{\theta \in \Theta} E[L(\rho, \alpha, \theta)] = E[L(Y_{t+1} - fc_{t+1})] = E[L(\varepsilon_{t+1})]. \quad (6)$$

Traders' utility maximization depends on their attitude towards risk (given by a coefficient of risk aversion) and the attitude towards costs of +/- errors (given by a degree of asymmetry in the loss function). Note that a degree of asymmetry is itself a function of a coefficient of risk aversion. Therefore, economic agents' utility maximization is uniquely determined by their attitude towards risk. In a multi-period forecast, in addition to the choice of the form of loss function, agents decide on the appropriate time horizon.

Training ANN with different loss functions (validation and testing durations), allows me to examine how agents' statistical and economic performances relate to risk preferences (past and forward time horizons). Similarly, training EANN with different settings allows me to investigate how the model's operation relates to the topology choice, as well as to consider the effect of GA optimization on its performance.

EXPERIMENTAL DESIGN

I use ANN with GA optimization for the building/evolution of price forecasts and the development/evolution of trading strategies based on relevant forecasts. Being consistent with the characteristics that are normally attributed to the cognitive boundaries of traders' learning process, the mechanism appears to be an intuitive way to deal with agents' cognitive limits in forecasting and optimizing, modeling the traders' learning process to approximate an unknown conditional expectation function[6]. It also provides a natural procedure to consider heterogeneous decisions made by agents viewing similar information. A single hidden layer ANN is deemed to be sufficient for my problem, particularly considering the universal approximation property of feedforward nets (Hornik, Stinchcombe, & White, 1989)[7].

Through the nature inspired evolutionary processes, GA enhances ANN generalization[8], and adds additional explanatory power to the analysis. Selecting candidates for the current stage with a probability proportional to their contributions to the objective function at a previous stage, GA reproduces the "fittest individuals" from a population of possible solutions. As a result, the best suited to performing specific task settings are identified.

Learning Paradigm

To learn a mapping $\mathbf{R}^d \rightarrow \mathbf{R}$ an input/output training set $D_I = \{x_i, y_i\}_{i=1}^{I}$ is presented to the network. $x_i \in \mathbf{R}^d$ is assumed to be drawn from a continuous probability measure with compact support. Learning entails selecting a learning system $L = \{H, A\}$, where the set H is the learning model and A is a learning algorithm. From a collection of candidate functions, H (assumed to be continuous) a hypothesis function h is chosen by learning algorithm A: $D_I \rightarrow H$ on the basis of a performance criterion.

Learning law is a systematic way of changing the network parameters (weights) in an automated fashion, such that the loss function is minimized. One of the most common algorithms used in supervised learning is backpropagation. Being simple and computationally efficient, the search here, nevertheless, can get caught in local minima. Backpropagation is also often criticized for being noisy and slow to converge. To improve the original gradient learning, particularly its slowness of convergence, I examine a number of alternatives (presented in Appendix A1).

ANN Architecture

I consider that ANN architecture is application-dependent. Maximum information available about the problem needs to be built into the network to achieve good learning abilities. At the same time capacity parsimonious structure is required for good generalization. I construct and modify architectures incrementally, identifying optimal settings for modeling financial data. Furthermore, GA is applied to search for optimal structures. Appendix A2 presents network topologies popular for modeling and forecasting the financial time series.

PERFORMANCE EVALUATION

The framework of performance evaluation includes evaluation criteria and benchmarks. Evaluation criteria, given in terms of a fitness function, can take various forms, which are determined by agents' preferences and their objectives. For forecasting evaluation, a fitness function often chosen is an accuracy measure, using some error statistics, such as MSE, MAE, Theil U, the Pesaran-Timmermann test, or the Diebold-Mariano test. As agents' actions have an effect on their wealth, criteria evaluating traders' decisions should be related to wealth. For strategy evaluation a popular fitness function is profit, given by some wealth measure, such as mean annual (total) return. I consider different evaluation criteria to examine the relationship between predictive accuracy and profitability.

Regarding a choice of a benchmark, for forecasting evaluation, common options are random walk (RW) or linear time series models (e.g., ARIMA). For trading strategy evaluation, typical benchmarks are buy-and-hold strategy (B/H), financial indexes, technical trading rules or filter rules.

Evaluation Criteria

The performance surface of ANN (given by errors versus weights[9]) is governed by a choice of the cost function:

$$C = \sum_{i=1}^{I} f(\mathrm{Y_i}, \Phi_i), \tag{7}$$

where Y_i and Φ_i are a desired and the network's outputs respectively, and I is the number of observations. The function L is minimized when $Y_i = \Phi_i = \psi_{i,j} X_i$, where X_i is the input vector, $\psi_{i,j}$ weights connecting I inputs of the input layer with J neurons of the hidden layer.

Under the standard gradient descent algorithm, weights, ψ_{ij} are changed by an amount $\Delta\psi_{ij}$ proportional to the gradient of L at the present location:

$$\Delta\psi_{i,j} = \eta \frac{\partial L}{\partial \psi_{i,j}} = \eta \sum (Y_i - \Phi_i) X_i, \tag{8}$$

where η is the learning rate. The measure of ANN performance is given by the sensitivity of a cost function with respect to the network's output:[10]

$$\frac{\partial C}{\partial \Phi_i} \equiv \varepsilon_i \equiv Y_i - \Phi_i. \tag{9}$$

Recall the l_p norm of a vector $x \in l_p$, defined for the class of measurable functions by $\|x\|_p = (\sum_{i=1}^{\infty} |x_i|^p)^{\frac{1}{p}}$; $for\ 1 \le p < \infty$ and consider a loss function of order p:

$$L_P = I^{-1} \sum_{i=1}^{I} (Y_i - \Phi_i)^p, \tag{10}$$

where p is a user-defined constant. Since ANN weights' modification depends on the order of a loss function, different values of p produce dissimilar learning and solutions to the optimization problem. By examining a slow step increase in the value of p, the behavior of the model with different objective functions is investigated. For comparison I consider L_∞ loss function in the nonlinearly constrained min-max problem[11].

At p value equal to 1 and 2 common L_1 and L_2 loss functions are observed. L_1, absolute value or MAE loss function takes the form:

$$L_1 = I^{-1} \sum_{i=1}^{I} |Y_i - \Phi_i|. \tag{11}$$

The error function used to report to the supervised learning procedure is the sign of the difference between the network's output and desired response: $\varepsilon_i = -\text{sgn}(Y_i - \Phi_i)$. The cost returned is the accumulation of the absolute differences between the ANN output and the desired response. L_1 gives equal weights to large and small errors, weighting the differences proportionally to their magnitude. Learning under L_1 loss function deemphasizes outliers and rare large discrepancies have less influence on results than learning under its main competitor, L_2 function. For that reason L_1 is sometimes viewed as a more robust norm, compared to L_2.

L_2, quadratic or MSE loss function takes the form:

$$L_2 = I^{-1} \sum_{i=1}^{I} (Y_i - \Phi_i)^2. \tag{12}$$

The error function is the squared Euclidean distance between the network's output and the target : $\varepsilon_i = -(Y_i - \Phi_i)^2$. The cost returned is the accumulation of the squared errors. Quadratic performance surface is particularly appropriate for linear systems. With L_2 loss function the equations to be solved for computing the optimal weights are linear for the weights in linear networks, giving closed form solutions. L_2 function is also attractive for giving probabilistic interpretation of the learning output, but might be inappropriate for highly non-Gaussian distributions of the target. Minimizing quadratic loss function corresponds and would be particularly appropriate for agents with a quadratic utility function (characterized by IARA and IRRA). Minimizing the error power, L_2 weights significantly the large errors. ANN trained with L_2 function assign more weight to extreme outcomes and focus on reducing large errors in the learning process.

Under MSE and MAE loss functions all errors are considered symmetrically. Since conventional investment behavior implies putting more effort into avoiding large losses, i.e. pursuing an asymmetric target, L_1 and L_2 loss functions might be less appropriate for agents with these risk preferences. ANN trained under symmetry tends to follow risky solutions[12].

Generally, for $p > 1$, the cost will always increase at a faster rate than the instantaneous error. Thus, larger errors receive progressively more weight under learning with higher order L_p functions. The upper limit here is given by L_∞ function, where all errors are ignored, except the largest. The L_∞ loss function is an approximation of the l_∞ norm, $\|x\|_\infty = \sup\{|x_1|,\ldots,|x_n|,\ldots\}$. Notice that l_∞ norm is essentially different from l_p norm in the behavior of its tails. L_∞ allows me to minimize the maximum deviation between the target and the net's output:

$$L_\infty = \sum_{i=1}^{I} \left|\tan(Y_i - \Phi_i)\right|. \tag{13}$$

L_∞ locally emphasizes large errors in each output, rather than globally searching the output for the maximum error. The error function is the hyperbolic tangent of the difference between the network's output and the target: $\varepsilon_i = \left|\tan(Y_i - \Phi_i)\right|$. The cost returned is the accumulation of the errors for all output neurons.

On another extreme the performance surface with $p = 0$ is presented. Considering only the sign of the deviations, it is viewed as equivalent to the performance surface optimized solely for directional accuracy (DA). In this research, $L\varpi$ loss (a variant of the L_2 function that weight various aspects of [time-series] data differently) is considered:

$$L\varpi = I^{-\varpi} \sum_{i=1}^{I} (Y_i - \Phi_i)^2, \tag{14}$$

where ϖ is the weighting factor. Errors are scaled (with a user-defined scale factor) according to the following criteria: DA; recency of observations and magnitude of change.

Preliminary, asymmetric higher order L_p functions seem to be attractive for minimizing large losses. At the same time, stability and robustness of learning under higher order loss functions need to be investigated. Furthermore, it is expected that paying less attention to small errors might have adverse effect on the boundary decisions. Thus a search for the optimal performance surface is viewed as a crucial step in ANN set-up.

PERFORMANCE MEASURES

The internal error, associated with a chosen cost function, presents the comparison of the output of the ANN to the desired response. In price forecasting, the target is the next-day's closing price, whereas in signal modeling, the target is the current strategy. Achieving an accurate representation of the mapping between the input and the target might not necessarily lead to an exploitable forecast or allow a strategy using that forecast to be profitable.

I require that the evaluation criteria measure not so much the absolute effectiveness of the model with respect to the environment[13], as its relative effectiveness with respect to other models. Although I train ANN so as to minimize an internal error function, networks are tested and optimized by comparing their performance to a benchmark, an efficient prediction (EP)[14]. When forecasting future prices, the EP is the last available price[15], while for predicting strategies, it is the B/H strategy. The degree of improvement over the efficient prediction (IEP) is calculated as an error from a de-normalized value of the ANN and a desired output, and then normalizing the result with the difference between the target and EP value.

Making a prediction using a change or a percentage change, the value of IEP is particularly significant. IEP around 1, implying that the ANN predicted a change or a percentage change of zero, indicates that the network does not have adequate information to make a valid prediction. So, it ends up predicting the mean of all changes, zero. Predicting two samples or more in advance, one can obtain a reduced value of IEP (in comparison to one sample prediction). This does not mean that there is an improvement, since the change in the desired value is typically larger for a longer prediction. I classify my results using the following scale: IEP $< 0.8 \Rightarrow$ excellent; IEP $< 0.85 \Rightarrow$ very good; IEP $< 0.9 \Rightarrow$ good; IEP $< 0.95 \Rightarrow$ satisfactory; IEP $\geqslant 0.95 \Rightarrow$ weak.

Profitability as Performance Measure

To make the final goal meaningful in economic terms, I use profitability as a measure of overall success. In CEF absolute wealth as actions' evaluation criteria has some potential problems for modeling, particularly if prices are exogenous. This is because final wealth largely depends on prices of the last simulation. Because strategy evaluation criteria should measure its relative effectiveness, relative wealth is often used as an evaluation criteria. A ratio of final and initial wealth overcomes the dependence on the final prices. Although, relative wealth evaluation criteria introduces another dependence (i.e., on initial wealth).

Absolute or relative wealth on its own as an evaluation criterion largely ignore risk aversion, and favor riskier strategy with higher return. For modeling risk-averse traders in computational settings, a composite index, combining wealth and risk, was proposed. For example, Beltratti, Margarita and Terna (1996) mix the change in wealth and the sum of the absolute values of the exposure to risky assets.

Similar to the performance evaluation criteria of investment managers (total realized returns adjusted for the riskness) evaluation criteria for trading rules, developed under evolutionary learning, present the realized total continuously compounded returns (LeBaron, 1991) or continuously compounded excess returns (Allen & Karajalainen, 1999). Unlike case-by-case evaluation of actions of portfolio managers, decisions of evolutionary agents are assessed on aggregate, over the entire trading period. Therefore, in computational modeling, process/means used by agents need to be explicitly evaluated. Under continuously compounded reinvestment of realized returns, strategies with a higher number of trades and lower returns per trade receive greater fitness. Bhattacharyya and Mehta (2002) demonstrated that strategies with the lowest mean returns and variances per trade could be evaluated as best.

Simple aggregate realized returns overcome problems with frequent trading. Although, the number of trades minimization favors infrequent but prolonged positions. More important, realized returns ignore opportunity costs (nonrealized losses from missing profitable opportunities), incurred maintaining a certain market position. A proposed solution here is to use nonrealized simple aggregate returns (Bhattacharyya & Mehta, 2002; Pictet, Docorogna, Choparad, Shirru, & Tomassini, 1995).

Nonsynchronous trading of securities expected to cause daily portfolio returns to be autocorrelated (Fisher, 1966; Scholes & Williams, 1977). This index phenomenon referred to as the Fisher effect, after Lawrence Fisher, hypothesized its probable cause. Observed security price changes occur at different times throughout the trading day. Reported daily returns reflect only the last trade that took place. Thus, there is often a substantial divergence between reported transaction-based returns and true returns, especially for less active issues. In this case, the use of reported daily returns as a proxy for true returns may result in the econometric problem of measurement errors. One solution to a nonsynchronous trading bias of return measurement is to simulate trading rules on trades with a delay of one day. This approach was used in Pereira (2002), removing a first-order autocorrelation, as well as evidence of predictive ability and profitability of the model. To overcome the Fisher effect, I also consider trading positions with a 1-day delay.

I examine the following forms of cumulative and individual trade-return measures: nonrealized simple aggregate return, profit/loss factor[16], average, and maximum gain/loss. In addition I estimate exit efficiency, measuring whether trades may have been held too long relative to the maximum amount of profit to be made, as well as the frequency and the length of trades, including out-of-market positions. To assess risk exposure, I adopt common "primitive" statistics, the Sharpe ratio[17] and the maximum drawdown. The latter, calculating the percentage loss (relative to the initial investment) for the period, measures the largest loss that occurred during open trades. It demonstrates how resistant a strategy is to losses.

Computational models without TC included in the learning structure tend to favor decisions with frequent trading. Profitability of such models usually changes dramatically after TC is incorporated. Typically computational models with TC either adjust prices or introduce a penalty based on the number of trades.

TC is assumed to be paid both when entering and exiting the market, as a percentage of the trade value. TC accounts for broker's fees, taxes, liquidity cost (bid-ask spread), as well as costs of collecting/analysis of information and opportunity costs. According to Sweeney (1988), TC reasonably range from a minimum of 0.05% for floor traders to somewhat over 0.2% for money managers getting the best prices. TC in this range is often used in computational models (Allen & Karajalainen, 1999; Neely & Weller, 1999; Pereira, 2002). Because TC would differ for heterogeneous agents, I report the break-even TC that offsets trading revenue with costs leading to zero profits.

Thus, profitability is a function of return, risk and transaction costs. The classification of the ANN output as different types of B/S signals determines the capability of the model to detect the key turning points of price movements. Evaluating the mapping of a forecast into a strategy, $\delta(fc_{t+1})$, assesses the success in establishing a predictive density, g_y, that determines agents' actions.

Trading Strategy Styles

Both long and short trades are allowed in the simulation. Having invested total funds for the first trade, subsequent trades (during a year) are made by reinvesting all of the money returned from previous trades. If the account no longer has adequate capital to cover TC, trading stops.

With regard to investment horizons, I examine the behavior of short-term speculating traders, defined by a 1 year forward period and long-term investing traders, defined by a 3 years forward horizon. Long-term traders are represented by three types: those who make investment decisions once every 3 years; those who make only portfolio decisions at the end of each year, reinvesting all the capital generated from a yearly trading; and those who make portfolio and saving decisions at the end of each year, with reinvestment equal to $w_t(1-v_t)$, where w_t is wealth, accumulated at the end of trading period t and v_t is the saving rate.

In Chen and Huang (2003), the optimal agents saving rates' minimum was 0.20773. The relatively high value of this rate has guaranteed those agents survival and dominance in the long run. Thus, examining profitability of agents' actions, I condition on the proposed optimal saving rate and the risk free interest rate of 12%.

Long-term traders with annual portfolio (saving) decisions use a sliding window reinvestment scheme, presented in Figure 2. Training/ validation/ testing (Tr/V/Ts) periods indicate that following a yearly investment (24.01.01-23.01.02), agents reinvest their wealth for another year (24.01.02-23.01.03) and then for one more year (24.01.03-23.01.04).

In terms of ANN setup, **Tr** and **V** periods represent in-sample data and **Ts** period corresponds to out-of-sample data. In-sample performance determines the effectiveness of the network learning, where as out-of-sample performance presents its generalization capacity. An ANN minimizing a "vanilla" loss function tend to overspecialize on the training data. The validation set is used during the training phase to prevent over-fitting.

Figure 2. Sliding window reinvestment scheme

26.07.98**Tr**25.07.00**V**24.01.01**Ts**23.01.02
26.07.99 **Tr** 25.07.01 **V** 24.01.02**Ts**23.01.03
26.07.00 **Tr** 25.07.02 **V** 24.01.03**Ts**23.01.04

Tr: training period; V: validation period; Tr: testing period

GENETIC TRAINING OPTIMIZATION

GA applications for ANN structure optimization are presented in Muhlenbein and Kindermann (1989) and Cliff, Harvey and Husbands (1992). In this chapter, GA optimization is used for network's topology, performance surface, learning rules, number of neurons, and memory taps. The GA tests the performance of the following ANN topologies: Multilayer Perceptron, Jordan and Elman Networks, Time-Lag Recurrent Network, Recurrent Network, and Modular Network. I examine the performance surface optimized with GA for directional accuracy, discounting the least recent values and minimizing the number of large errors. For learning rule optimization, I consider Steepest Descent, Conjugate Gradient, Quickprop, Delta Bar Delta, and Momentum.

With GA optimization, I test the integer interval [1, 20] for hidden layers' neurons, expecting that a higher number increases the network's learning ability, although at the expense of harder training and a tendency to overspecialization. GA optimization examines the range [1, 20] for the number of taps, affecting the memory of the net (the input layer, having access to the least modified data, has typically the highest number, decreasing in the hidden layers). GA optimization of the weight update for static networks considers whether the weights are updated following all data (batch) or after each piece of data (online) are presented. For dynamic networks GA determines a number of samples to be examined each time ANN updates weights during the training phase.

The step size, controlling the speed of weight adjustment, manages the trade-off between slow learning and a tendency to overreact. Usually the hidden layer has a larger step size than the output layer, and memory components generally have lower step size than other components of the same layer. GA optimizes the step size of the learning rates in the range [0, 1]. The momentum, using the recent weight update, speeds up the learning and helps to avoid local minima. GA searches in the range [0, 1] for the value by which the most recent weight update is multiplied.

In terms of GA parameters, I apply the tournament selection with size 4, {prob=fitness/$\sum$fitness}. Four types of mutation are considered in the experiment: uniform, nonuniform, boundary, and Gaussian. Three types of crossover are examined in the simulation: random, one-point, and two-point. Probability of mutation (PM) tested in the range [0, 0.05] and probability of uniform crossover is considered in the range [0.7, 0.95]. I test the effect of the increase in population size in the range [25, 200] on performance and computational time. The training optimization continues until a set of termination criteria is reached, given by maximum generations in the range [100, 500].

When a model lacks information, trading signals' predictions often stay near to the average. If ANN output remains too close to the mean to cross over the thresholds that differentiate entry/exit signals, postprocessing is found to be useful (establishing thresholds within the range). Postprocessing with GA optimization, examines a predicted signal with simulated trades after each training, searching for the thresholds against the values produced by ANN to generate maximum profit (see Appendix A3 for details).

The GA tests various settings from different initial conditions (in the absence of a priori knowledge and to avoid symmetry that can trap the search algorithm). Although, the GA optimization aims to minimize the IEP value, profitability is employed as a measure of overall success[18].

EMPIRICAL APPLICATION

I consider daily closing prices for the MTMS (Moscow Times) share index obtained from Yahoo Finance. The time period under investigation is 01/01/97 to 23/01/04. There were altogether 1,575 observations in row data sets. Examining the data graphically reveals that the stock prices exhibit a prominent upward, but non-linear trend, with pronounced and persistent fluctuations about it, which increase in variability as the level of the series increases. Asset prices look persistent and close to unit root or nonstationarity. Descriptive statistics confirm that the unit-root hypothesis cannot be rejected at any significance. The data also exhibits large and persistent price volatility, showing significant autocovarience even at high order lags.

Changes in prices increase in amplitude and exhibit clustering volatility. The daily return displays excess kurtosis and the null of no skewness is rejected at 1% critical level. The tests statistics lead to the rejection of the Gaussian hypothesis for the distribution of the series. It confirms that daily stock returns follow a distribution incompatible with normality, habitually assumed under the analytical approach.

Experimental Results

ANN with GA optimization is programmed with various topologies[19]. I have generated and considered 93 forecasting and 143 trading strategies settings. The effectiveness of search algorithm was examined with multiple trials for each setting. The model was capable of learning the key turning points of price movement with the classification of the ANN output as different types of trading signals. GA discovered the 'optimal' settings on the average in 90% of 10 individual runs.

Efficiency of the search, balancing costs and benefits, is assessed by the time needed to find good results in terms of the performance criteria adopted. For the optimized architectures, at least 10% of improvement over the unoptimized outcome to be weighted against the processor time was required. The search with unoptimized ANN took several minutes, whereas the search with GA optimization lasted on average 120 minutes using a Pentium 4 processor. These results demonstrate that EANN is a useful tool in financial data mining, although a more efficient GA needs to be developed for the real-time financial applications.

I have run experiment with three memory time horizons, [6; 5; 2.5] years. The results show that in terms of predictive accuracy[20], the best five strategies include those with 6 and 2.5 years of training. Conspicuously, the most accurate 20 strategies do not have a one with 5 years training, where the least accurate 20 strategies are not represented by a one with 2.5 years training. Regarding accuracy of the forecast all three memory length are well presented in the best and worst five results, with the most accurate forecast produced with 2.5 years and the least accurate with 5 years of training.

In terms of strategy profitability, the best five results were produced with training duration of 6, 5 and 2.5 years, respectively. Also, the worst five losing strategies are with 2.5 years training. At the same time, for the whole set of trading strategies investigated, there is no dominance by strategies with a particular training horizon. Therefore, my results do not support a claim that longer training generates more statistically accurate or profitable strategies.

To maximize ANN generalization, with dividing the data into training, cross validation, and testing sets, I have considered a number of distributions. With all three time horizons, improvement in results was found with some fine-tuning. Table 1 presents the results of the search for best-performing (in economic terms) distributions.

Splitting the data as presented in Table 1 in comparison to a 60%/20%/20% distribution (common in ANN modeling) results in improved economic performance on average 38% for a 7-year period; 34.9 % for a 6-year period, and 22.1% for 3.5-year time series. Thus, financial modeling and forecasting with CI tools benefit profitability when there is some fine-tuning of Tr/V/Ts distribution.

By simulating the traders' price forecasts and their trading strategy evolution, the agents' economic performance is found to be best with a 1-year forward time horizon, and it deteriorates significantly for tests with horizons exceeding 2 years, supporting the idea of frequent structural breaks. Over a 1-year testing period, 19 trading strategies are able to outperform the B/H benchmark in economic terms, with an investment of $10,000 and a TC of 0.2% of trade value. Average return improvement over B/H strategy is 20%, with the first five outperforming the benchmark by 50% and the last three by 2%. The primary strategy (in profitability terms) superiority over B/H strategy was 72%.

For the five best performing strategies, the break-even TC was estimated to be 2.75%; increasing to 3.5% for the first three and nearly 5% for the primary strategy. Thus, the break-even TC for at least the primary strategy appears to be high enough to exceed actual TC.

When the investment horizon exceeds 3 years, the inferior economic performance characterizes traders without regular annual investment decisions. Nevertheless, the profitability of agents, who save an optimal percentage of wealth at a risk-free interest rate is not conclusively superior to the performance of those reinvesting the entire capital. These results contradict claims that agents' long-term fitness is not a function of an accurate prediction, but depends only on an appropriate risk aversion through a stable saving rate. I explain my findings through the relationships between the maximum drawdown measure, riskless, and risky returns.

A risk-free interest rate of 12% seems to be high enough to make saving decisions attractive. Nevertheless, when a risky return is well above a riskless return, and a strategy is sufficiently prone to losses during open trades, situations leading to a significant decrease in wealth will not necessarily appear. (Note that this explanation does not challenge the fact that investments including savings at a risk-free rate are less risky than total funds reinvestments in stock indexes, as illustrated with Sharpe ratio.) Simulations with different investment periods produce similar results, up to 7 years of forward horizon. I conclude, therefore, that a profitable strategy development (in terms of risk-adjusted returns) is not less important than an optimal saving decision for reasonably long investment horizons. Running an experiment on stock indexes from a number of markets, Hayward (2005) found that optimal memory length is a function of specific

Table 1. Training, cross validation, and testing sets' distributions

Period	01.07.97 - 23.01.04	23.01.98 - 23.01.04	23.07.00 - 23.01.04
Years	5.0/1.06/1.0	2.5/2.5/1.0	2.5/0.5/1.0
Distribution (%)	71/15/14	42/41/17	57/14/29

Tr: training; V: validation; Ts: testing

market conditions. My simulation confirms that a memory length is negatively correlated with a daily trading volume.

My experiment demonstrates that normalization reduces the effect of nonstationarity in the time series. The effect of persistency in prices diminishes with the use of the percentage change in values. Table 2, presenting the average effect of GA postprocessing on performance, shows that it has generally improved (positive values) statistical characteristics. Although only accuracy exhibits sizable change, the effects on IEP and correlation[21] are significantly smaller and not always positive.

The experiment with different types of GA crossover and mutation did not identify the dominance by a particular type. I have run simulations with different PM to test how the frequency of novel concepts' arrival affects modeling of the environment with structural breaks. The results, presented in Table 3, show that newcomers generally benefit the system. Although I have expected this outcome, its consistency among all (including short time) horizons was not anticipated. In economic terms, runs with a high probability of mutation {PM = 0.05} have produced the highest returns. At the same time, this relationship is of nonlinear character (e.g., {PM = 0.001} consistently outperforms {PM = 0.02}).

Some moderate though consistent relationship between PM and strategies' risk exposure was found. Higher PM resulted in low riskness, given particularly by the Sharpe ratio. I have also noticed some positive correlation between PM and annual trades' quantity, although this relationship appears to be of moderate significance and robustness. Trading frequency in simulations without mutation seems to be set at the beginning and stay until the end either at low or high values. The experiments without mutation have produced strong path-dependent dynamics, though not necessarily with suboptimal outcome. It seems there exist some optimal PM (in my experiment 0.05 and 0.001) and tinkering with this parameter can improve overall profitability.

I have not found a robust relationship between the memory length and PM > 0. Although, the memory length in simulations without mutation was on average 2.5 times shorter than in experiments with mutation. The relationship between PM and common statistical measures was inconclusive at acceptable significance or robustness.

Table 2. GA postprocessing effect

Stats./Sets	2000-2004	1998-2004	1997-2004
IEP	0.059	-0.838	0.001
Accuracy (%)	1.3	6.58	0.95
Correlation	0.016	0.011	0.001

Table 3. Economic and statistical measures under different probabilities of mutation

Measures/PM	0	0.001	0.02	0.05	0	0.001	00.2	0.05	0	0.001	0.02	0.05
Return (%)	76.9	85.7	76.4	99.8	65.6	75.1	62.1	86.8	68.3	74.7	60.8	82
Trades (№)	1	3	3	5	9	1	5	10	7	1	4	3
IEP	1.116	1.126	1.169	1.135	0.949	0.95	0.958	0.936	0.942	1.076	1.077	0.979
DA (%)	51.5	32.9	37.66	54.98	41.2	45.92	40.77	42.06	32.38	32.9	32.9	32.4
Data Sets	2000-2004				1998-2004				1997-2004			

GA optimization did not identify higher memory depth as optimal for long training periods in comparison to shorter ones. At the same time, the optimal number of hidden-layer neurons is found to be proportional to the length of training. Thus, longer training produces increased complexity in the relationships, where older data is not necessarily useful for the current/future state modeling and forecasting.

Model discovery with GA reveals that MLP and TLRN with focus Laguarre memory (FLM), with neurons number in the hidden layer in the range [5, 12], Conjugate Gradient learning rule and the hyperbolic tangent transfer function generate the best performance in statistical and economic terms for forecasting and acting nets. The seven most profitable strategies are represented by those ANN. They also have good performances in statistical terms, although there was not such a clear dominance as in economic performance. Among the ten most accurate predictions nine are basic MLP and TLRN-FLM. At the same time, the best accuracy was achieved by Jordan ANN with the output feedback to the context units. In price forecasting, among the ten most accurate networks, eight are basic MLP and TLRN-FLM, also sharing the first three positions. Among the five most accurate forecasting ANN is also generalized feedforward MLP, producing the accuracy that follows immediately the first three networks. I relate satisfactory performances of MLP and TLRN in financial data mining to their established links with ARMA processes. MLP and TLRN are nonlinear generalizations of those processes.

Generally models discovered with GA have lower trading frequencies, but without reduction in riskness. Annualized returns of those models were improved moderately. The effect of GA discovery on models' statistical performance was not conclusive, with a weak tendency towards accuracy amelioration. An increase in population size for GA optimization didn't lead to improvement in results. I explain this by the non-multimodal nature of the problem. Evidently, a higher population size has resulted in longer computational time.

The relationship between statistical measures (accuracy, correlation, IEP) and trading strategies' profitability seems to be of a complicated nature. Among the 10 statistically sound price forecasts, there is only one that was used in a trading strategy superior to B/H benchmark. The best five in economic terms strategies are among the worst 50% according to their accuracy. Three of the most accurate strategies are among the worst 25% in terms of their annualized return. Correlation of desired and ANN output characterizes one of the first five strategies with highest return among its best performers, another one among its worst results and the remaining are in the middle. IEP shows some robust relationships with annualized return. All five strategies with highest return have IEP < 0.9. Furthermore, one of the first five profitable strategies has one of the three best IEP values. Thus, if profits are not observable, IEP could be used as an evaluation criterion for an economic prediction.

ANN minimizing L_6 function performed satisfactory and consistently for all memory horizons. For instance, the annualized return of MLP minimizing L_6 function for 1997-2004 data series outperformed L_2 counterpart by 12.91% and L_1 function by 6.65%; for 1998-2004 return with L_6 function minimization was superior to L_2 minimization by 1.32% and L_1 function by 20.63%. Return of TLRN minimizing L_6 function for 2000-2004 series outperformed L_2 minimization by 57.17% and L_1 function by 27.35%.

If returns of MLP with L_2 and L_1 functions minimizations were losing to B/H strategy (by 10.85% and 4.59% respectively), the performance of L_6 loss minimization has beaten B/H strategy by 2.06% for 7 years series. Returns of TLRN with L_2 and L_1 functions minimizations were inferior to B/H strategy by 50.67% and 20.87% respectively, where performance of L_6 loss minimization was superior to B/H by 6.48% for 3.5 years series.

For the same time horizons and ANN topologies, strategies developed with L_6 loss minimization were less risky than strategies created with L_2 and L_1 functions. For instance, Sharpe ratios of strategies with L_6 minimization were superior to their competitors in all cases, except one, where risk exposures were equal. Profitability of ANN trained with L_6 loss function seems to be stable for multiple independent runs with different random seeds. Table 4, comparing profitability of strategies developed with L_6, L_2 and L_1 loss minimization for three ANN and training periods, demonstrates that strategies with L_6 loss minimization generally perform better than those obtained with L_2 or L_1 functions.

Regarding statistical accuracy of trading strategies, the results were different depending on the ANN topology. MLP with 7 (6) years of data, minimizing L_6 function, produce results superior to L_2 function by 16.66% (0.43%) and to L_1 function by 14.76% (10.73%). Accuracy of TLRN with 3.5 years of data, minimizing L_6 function, was inferior to L_2 function by 22.51% and L_1 function by 22.95%.

Considering price forecasts, accuracy with minimizing L_6 function is on average among the best 5%. In fact, a forecast based on L_6 loss minimization was the only one that was used in a trading strategy superior to B/H benchmark. Forecasts with L_2 minimization slightly underperforms, but is still among the best performing 20%. At the same time L_1 function minimization produces top accuracy, as well as being one of the worst performers. If the accuracy of forecast of MSE loss minimization is on average superior to the accuracy of MAE loss minimization, annualized return of trading strategies, based on those forecasts are close to each other. Furthermore, performance surface based only on L_1 or L_2 loss minimization (without optimization / L_ω minimization) does not generate profitable strategies.

The results produced with the L_∞ loss minimization are close to the overall average. At the same time, the detailed examination of the performance surface demonstrates that L_∞ minimization might be particularly appropriate for multi-objective optimization. A natural path for future work is to apply multi-objective GA for this kind of problem.

Having identified valuable relationships between the value of risk aversion coefficient and the order of the loss function, the results presented support 'active learning', where the knowledge about the target is gained by some means rather than random sampling. ANN learning with preliminary/partial information about the performance surface has proven to be more productive than assuming an infinite pseudo-dimensional class structure, driving the loss function to zero.

Table 4. Profitability of strategies developed with l_6, l_2 and l_1 loss minimization

Measures/Settings	1997-2004 MLP			1998-2004 MLP			2000-2004 TLRN (FLM)		
Loss Functions	L_6	L_2	L_1	L_6	L_2	L_1	L_6	L_2	L_1
Annual Return (%)	76.75	63.84	70.10	62.09	60.77	41.46	81.17	24.02	53.82
Sharpe Ratio	0.16	0.12	0.15	0.12	0.12	0.10	0.14	0.06	0.12

Regarding the performance surface optimization, two out of the three best strategies included an adjustment to treat directional information as more important than the raw error. I found that training ANN with the performance surface genetically optimized for DA, discounting least recent values or minimizing number of large errors generally improves profitability. Among 25% of the weak (in economic terms) strategies' annualized returns, there is none with learning criteria optimized. The experiment has shown that among three optimizations of the performance surface considered, strategies trained on learning the sign of the desired output were generally superior to those trained to reduce the number of large errors or focusing learning on recent values. At the same time, the impact of optimization for DA on common statistical measures was insignificant, confirming that DA only weekly relates to conventional statistical criteria.

My simulation generally supports a claim that DA relates to forecast profits more than mean squared or mean absolute errors criteria. At the same time, the experiment rejects an assertion that all other summary statistics are not related to forecast profit, as was demonstrated by the IEP relationship with profitability. As the results show that DA (alone or always) does not guarantee profitability of trading strategies trained with this criterion, it might be ineffective to base empirical estimates of economic relationships only on that measure. If conventional least squares are to be considered inadequate, an alternative estimation technique for economic behavior might use a combination of measures, demonstrated to have certain relationships with profitability; IEP and DA have been identified so far.

The best strategy in economic terms (basic MLP optimized for DA with discounted least recent values; trained on 6 years of data) traded seven times for the last year with overall 85.7% of profitable trades. Four long trades generated 100% wins, where short trades produced 66.7% wins. Annualized return over testing period was 128.13%, significantly exceeding the comparable return of B/H strategy, 74.69%. In terms of risk exposure, the primary strategy is less risky than B/H benchmark. Regarding the predictive ability of the primary strategy, accuracy, correlation and IEP are marginally better than the overall average (all three statistics decrease in values in the testing set comparing to the training and cross validation sets). The bootstrap method used to test the significance of the profitability and predictive ability produced p-values, indicating statistically different performance from a random walk with drift.

CONCLUSION

The system considered in this chapter is self-organized, given economic agents' abilities to learn and adapt to changes. The models examined are robust due to agents' ability to determine their future actions (form their expectations) using memory of their previous experiences. The primary strategy generated reveals good economic performance on out of sample data.

To model the turmoil in an economic system with frequent shocks, short memory horizons are considered optimal, as older data is not necessarily informative for the current/future state modeling/forecasting.

The mapping of economic agents' risk preferences into their predictions reveals strong relationships between the value of risk aversion coefficient in loss function minimization and stock trading strategies' economic performances, as well as moderate relationships between a loss function's order and statistical characteristics. Unlike L_2 and L_1 loss functions minimization, models with L_6 error-criterion demonstrate robust relationships with profitability. Traders with CRRA preferences display superior fitness in the short term through their portfolio rules. A search for profitable strategies is considered to be at least as important as an optimal saving contract adoption.

Setting up the performance surface with appropriate loss function minimization is an essential factor in the development of a computational model. EANN has proven to be a useful tool in financial data mining, capable of learning key turning points of price movement with the classification of the network output as different types of trading signals. Learning the mapping of forecasts into strategies establishes the predictive density that determines agents' actions and utility of wealth associated.

Measures of trading strategies' predictive power might significantly differ from criteria leading to its profit maximization. The choice of evaluation criteria combining statistical qualities and economic profitability is viewed as essential for an adequate analysis of economic structures.

GA postprocessing has generally improved statistical characteristics. Models discovered with GA have moderately higher profitability, but the impact on their statistical characteristics was inconclusive. GA optimization of performance surface (particularly for DA) has a positive effect on strategies' profitability, though with little impact on their statistical characteristics.

When profits are not observable, IEP is proposed as an evaluation criterion for an economic prediction, due to its robust relationships with annualized returns. If conventional least squares are to be considered inadequate, an alternative estimation technique for economic behavior might use a combination of measures, demonstrated to have certain relationships with profitability; IEP and DA have been identified so far.

The presence of at least two objectives (statistical and economic) to be satisfied at the same time could be considered as a multi-objective optimization problem for future work. It seems, evolutionary algorithms, capable generating the Pareto optimal set in a single run, might be particularly appropriate for this task. A natural path for further research is to apply multi-objective GA and extend the model to multi-assets environment.

APPENDIXES[22]

A1. Learning Algorithms

Consider the vector, Ψ as the weight space, I am searching for. The gradient descent is given by $\nabla L = \frac{\partial L}{\partial \psi}$. Expanding the loss function L about the current point ψ_o gives:

$$L(\psi) = L_0 + (\psi - \psi_0) \cdot \nabla L(\psi_0) + \tfrac{1}{2}(\psi - \psi_0) \cdot H \cdot (\psi - \psi_0) + \dots \qquad (15)$$

where H is the second derivative Hessian matrix evaluated at ψ_o, $H_{ij} = \frac{\partial^2 L}{\partial \psi_i \partial \psi_j}$. The gradient is obtained by differentiating (15):

$$\nabla L(\psi) = \nabla L(\psi_0) + H \cdot (\psi - \psi_0) + ... \tag{16}$$

For the optimization task, the minimum $L(\psi)$, where $\nabla L(\psi) = 0$ need to be located. A common approach here is to set (16) to zero, disregarding the higher-order terms:

$$\nabla L(\psi) = \nabla L(\psi_0) + H \cdot (\psi - \psi_0) = 0. \tag{17}$$

Solving (17) for ψ gives:

$$\psi = \psi_0 - H^{-1} \nabla L(\psi_0). \tag{18}$$

A popular minimization technique is to use the first derivative information (only) with line searches along selected directions. If D is a direction, starting from ψ_o, staying on the line $\psi = \psi_o + \alpha D$, α is chosen to minimize $L(\psi)$.

In the Steepest Descent Method one chose $D = -\nabla L(\psi_o)$, repeating minimization along a line in the gradient direction and re-evaluating the gradient. Since all successive steps are perpendicular, the new gradient descent ∇L^{new} is also perpendicular to the old direction D^{old}, giving zigzagging path after the line minimization:

$$0 = \frac{\partial}{\partial \alpha} L(\psi_0 + \alpha D^{old}) = D^{old} \cdot \nabla L^{new}. \tag{19}$$

The step size, η determines how far the movement should go before obtaining another directional estimate. For one step $(\sum_{n=1}^{N})$ the weight update with a step size, η is given by:

$$\Delta \psi_i (n+1) = \eta_i \nabla \psi_i \tag{20}$$

With small steps it takes longer to reach the minimum, increasing the probability of getting caught in local minima. On the other hand, large steps may result in overshooting, causing the system to rattle/diverge. Starting with a large step size and decreasing it until the network becomes stable, one finds a value that solves the problem in fewer iterations.

The momentum provides the gradient descent with some inertia, so that it tends to move along the average estimate direction. The amount of inertia (the amount of the past to average over) is given by the parameter, μ. For a given momentum μ and the step size η, the weight update is defined as:

$$\Delta\psi_i(n+1) = \eta_i \nabla\psi_i + \mu\Delta\psi_i(n). \tag{21}$$

The higher the momentum, the more it smoothes the gradient estimate and the less effect a single change in the gradient has on the weight change. It also helps to escape local minima, although oscillations may occur at the extreme.

A second order method, the Conjugate Gradient uses the second derivatives of the performance surface to determine the weight update, unlike the steepest descent algorithm where only the local approximation of the slope of the performance surface is used to find the best direction for the weights' movement. At each step a new conjugate direction is determined and movement goes along this direction to the minimum error. The new search direction includes the gradient direction and the previous search direction:

$$D^{new} = -\nabla L^{new} + \beta D^{old}, \tag{22}$$

where β is the choice parameter, determining the amount of past direction to mix with the gradient to form a new direction.

The new search direction should not change (to first order) the component of the gradient along the old direction. If α is a line search parameter, then:

$$D^{old} \cdot \nabla L(\psi_0 + \alpha D^{new}) = 0. \tag{23}$$

Therefore, the vectors D^{new} and D^{old} are conjugate in the following expression:

$$D^{old} \cdot H \cdot D^{new} = 0. \tag{24}$$

β in (22) is chosen such that the new search direction maintains as best as possible the minimization that was achieved in the previous step, for example with the Polak-Ribiere rule:

$$\beta = \frac{(\nabla L^{new} - \nabla L^{old}) \cdot \nabla L^{new}}{(\nabla L^{old})^2}. \tag{25}$$

For the quadratic performance surface with information from the Hessian, one can determine the exact position of the minimum along each direction, but for nonquadratic surfaces, a line search is often used. In theory, there are only N conjugate directions in a space of N dimensions, thus the algorithm is reset each N iterations. The advantage of the conjugate gradient method is that there is no need to store, compute and invert the Hessian matrix. Updating the weights in a direction that is conjugate to all past movements in the gradient, the zigzagging of first order gradient descent methods could be avoided.

The Scaled Conjugate Gradient method without real parameters is based on computing the Hessian times a vector, $H*\Psi$. An offset is added to the Hessian, $H+\delta I$ to ensure that the Hessian is a positive definite, so that the denominator in the expression below is always positive. For the step size α it could be expressed in the following way:

$$\alpha = -\frac{C^T G}{C^T (H + \delta I)C + \delta |C|^2}, \tag{26}$$

where C is the direction vector and G the gradient vector. The parameter δ is set such that for low values the learning rate is large and it is small for high values. δ adjusted in a way that if the performance surface is far from quadratic, δ is increased, resulting in smaller step size. To determine the closeness to quadratic performance surface, Λ is used and is given by:

$$\Lambda = \frac{2(L(\psi) - L(\psi + \alpha C))}{\alpha C^T G}. \tag{27}$$

For example, for $\Lambda > 0.75$ (very quadratic) δ is multiplied by 5; for $\Lambda < 0.25$, δ is multiplied by 4; for $\Lambda < 0$, there is no change in weights. By a first order approximation:

$$(H + \delta I)C \approx \frac{L'(\psi + \sigma C) - L'(\psi)}{\sigma} + \delta C, \tag{28}$$

implying that the Hessian calculations could be replaced with additional estimation of the gradients.

Delta-Bar-Delta is an adaptive step-size procedure for searching a performance surface. The step size and momentum are adapted according to the previous values of the error. If the current and past weight updates arc both of the same sign, the learning rate increases linearly. Different signs for the updates indicate that the weight has been moved too far and the learning rate decreases geometrically to avoid divergence. Therefore, the step size update is given:

$$\Delta\eta_i(n) = \begin{cases} k & S_i(n-1)\nabla\psi_i(n) > O \\ -\beta\eta_i(n) & S_i(n-1)\nabla\psi_i(n) < O \\ 0 & otherwise \end{cases}, \tag{29}$$

with

$$S_i(n) = (1-\delta)\nabla\psi_i(n-1) + \delta S_i(n-1), \tag{30}$$

where k is additive constant; β is multiplicative constant and δ is smoothing factor.

Considering how the data is fired through the network, synchronization in Static, Trajectory and Fixed Point modes are examined. Static learning assumes that the output of a network is strictly a function of its present input (the network topology is static). The gradients and sensitivities are only dependent on the error and activations from the current time step. Training a network in Trajectory mode assumes that each exemplar has a temporal dimension and that there exists some desired response for the network's output over the period. The network is first run forward in time over the entire period, during which an error is determined between the network's output and the desired response. Following that the network is run backwards for a prescribed number of samples to compute the gradients and sensitivities, completing a single exemplar. Fixed Point mode assumes that each exemplar represents a static pattern; that is to be embedded as a fixed point of a recurrent network. Here the terms forward samples and backward samples can be thought of as the forward relaxation period and backward relaxation period, respectively. All inputs are held constant while the network is repeatedly fired during its forward relaxation period. There are no guarantees that the forward activity of the network will relax to a fixed point, or even relax at all. After the network has relaxed, an error is determined and held as constant input to the backpropagation layer. Similarly, the error is backpropagated for its backward relaxation period, completing a single exemplar.

A feedforward network, where the response is obtained in one time step (an instantaneous mapper), can only be trained by fixed point learning. On the other hand, recurrent networks can be trained either by fixed point learning or by trajectory learning. A static ANN makes decisions based on the present input only; it can not perform functions that involve knowledge about the history of the input signal. On the other hand, dynamic networks are able to process time varying signals. They posses an extended memory mechanism, which is capable of storing past values of the input signal. In the time delay neural network the memory is a tap delay line (i.e., a set of memory locations that store the past of the input).

It is possible to use self-recurrent connections as memory, as in Jordan/Elman Network context units. Considering, for example, the gamma memory as a structure with local feedback, it cascades self-recurrent connections and extends the context unit with more versatile storage. It accepts the tap delay line as a special case. A form of temporal learning must be used to adapt the gamma parameter (e.g., real time recurrent learning). The advantage of this structure in dynamic networks is that it provides a controllable memory with a predefined number of taps. Furthermore, as the network adapts the gamma parameter to minimize the output error, the best combination of depth and resolution can be achieved.

A2. ANN Topology

Multilayer Perceptron (MLP) is the most basic of the ANN topologies for nonlinearly separable problems. The data in a MLP follows a single path with no recursion or memory elements. It is viewed that for static pattern classification, the MLP with two hidden layers is a universal pattern classifier. The discriminate functions can take any shape, as required by the input data clusters. In terms of the mapping abilities, the MLP with a (nonpolynomial) Tauber-Wiener transfer function is believed to be a universal approximator.

For three layers MLP used in this chapter for prediction and strategy development a one-period price forecast takes the following form:

$$Fc(C_{t+1}) = h_2(\psi_0 + \sum_{j=1}^{J} \psi_j h_1(\psi_{0j} + \sum_{i=O}^{I} \psi_{i,j} C_{t-i})) + \varepsilon_t. \quad (31)$$

In (31) the input layer has I inputs, $\{c_{t-0}, \ldots, c_{t-I}\}$; the hidden layer has J hidden nodes and the output layer has one output, $Fc(C_{t+1})$. Layers are fully connected by weights, $\psi_{i,j}$; ψ_o and ψ_{oj} are biases. Transfer functions are represented by h_1 and h_2. Experiments in this chapter are run under two transfer functions, the hyperbolic tangent, $h_s(x) = \frac{2}{1+\varepsilon^{-2x}} - 1$, with $-1 < h_s(x) < +1$ and the sigmoid, $h_t(x) = \frac{1}{1+\varepsilon^{-x}}$, with $0 < h_t(x) < +1$.

Jordan and Elman Networks (J/E) networks based on the concept of context in their processing. A set of context units is a layer (or a part of a layer) that receives feedback signals. Unlike the forward propagation the feedback signal occurs with reference to time. A context for processing at time t comes from the network state at time $t-1$ through the context units. Therefore, the state of the network at any time depends on an aggregate of previous states and the current input. It has been claimed that this type of ANN capable not only to recognize sequences, but also generate them in some cases.

Jordan architecture (Jordan, 1986, 1989) differs from Elman architecture (Elman, 1990), primarily by having the context units fed from the output layer and from themselves instead of the hidden layer. For the source of the feedback to the context units, four options are considered: the input, the 1st hidden layer, the 2nd hidden layer and the output. In linear systems the use of the past of the input signal generates the moving average (MA) representations. They are particularly suited for signals that have a spectrum with sharp valleys and broad peaks. The use of the past of the output results in the autoregressive (AR) representations. They are supposed to model well signals with broad valleys and sharp spectral peaks. In the case of non-linear systems, these two topologies are considered as nonlinear MA and AR (NMA and NAR). The Jordan net is viewed as a restricted case of NAR, while the configuration with context units fed by the input layer considered as a restricted case of NMA. Elman's net does not have a counterpart in linear systems.

Different values of the context unit's time-constant are considered in the experiment. It is expected to find a trade-off between extending the memory further back into the past and loosing sensitivity to details. As a rule of thumb, the value of the time-constant should produce an exponential decay rate that matches the characteristic time scale of the input sequence. Since the time-constant is the only control (the exponential decay) the weighting over time is inflexible. Furthermore, a small change in the context unit's time-constant is reflected in a large change in the weighting (due to the exponential relationship between time-constant and amplitude).

Time-Lag Recurrent Network (TLRN) is viewed as MLP's extension with short term memory structures that have local recurrent connections. It has smaller network size required to learn temporal problems when compared to MLP that use extra inputs to represent the past samples. On the other hand the backpropagation through time adopted with TLRN requires a lot of memory. TLRN is characterized by low sensitivity to noise. The recurrence of the TLRN provides the advantage of an adaptive memory depth (it finds the best duration to represent the input signal's past). In the experiment the following memory structures are considered: Time Delay Neural Network Memory (TDNN); Gamma memory (GM) and Laguarre memory (LM). With Focused topology only the past of the input is remembered.

It is noted that using a TLRN with Focused TDNN memory has a similar effect to using multiple samples for the inputs to a basic MLP. The primary difference between the two methods is that, focused TDNN memory only allows for one memory depth to be used for all of the inputs, whereas the lag input settings allow me to specify various memory depths.

Recurrent Network (RN) delays one or more of the processing values in the network so that they will be used in the calculation of the next output, rather than the current output. These are often combined with the memory elements found in TLRN. Fully RN does not include a nonrecurrent feedforward processing path. All data flows through the recurrent processing. On the other hand partially RN includes a nonrecurrent feedforward processing path. RN contains multiple processing paths. Each processing path has potential of specializing on a different aspect of the incoming data, allowing me to consider multiple conditions.

The support vector machine (SVM) is considered as a classifier capable to transform complex decision surfaces into simpler ones to apply linear discriminate functions. It uses only inputs that are near the decision surface as they provide the most information about the classification[23].

A3. GA Postprocessing

Use of thresholds within the ranges against values produced by ANN ($\in$ [-1, 1]) allows to set different levels for predicted signals. For Enter Long outputs the range is {$\geq$ 0.5}, with scaling based on the distance between the Enter Long and Enter Short thresholds (Enter Long and zero if thresholds are equal). Exit Short range is [0.2, 0.5], with scaling based on the distance between the Exit Short and Enter Long thresholds. For Exit Long the range is [-0.2, -0.5], with scaling based on the distance between the Exit Long and Enter Short thresholds. Enter Short range is {$\leq$ -0.5}, with scaling based on the distance between the Enter Long and Enter Short thresholds (Enter Short and zero if thresholds are equal). For Hold outputs the range is [-0.2, 0.2], with scaling based on the distance between the Exit Short and Exit Long thresholds.

REFERENCES

Allen, F., & Karajalainen, R. (1999). Using genetic algorithms to find technical trading rules. *Journal of Financial Economics, 51*(2), 245-271.

Arthur, W. B., Holland, J. H., LeBaron, B., Palmer, R., & Taylor, P. (1997). Asset pricing under endogenous expectations in artificial stock market. In W. B. Arthur, S. N. Duralauf, & D. A. Lane (Eds.), *The economy as evolving complex system II* (pp. 15-44). MA: Perseus Books.

Beltratti, A., Margarita, S., & Terna, P. (1996). *Neural networks for economic and financial modelling.* London: International Thomson Computer Press.

Bhattacharyya, S., & Mehta, K. (2002). Evolutionary induction of trading models. In S.-H. Chen (Ed.), *Evolutionary computation in economics and finance* (pp. 311-331). New York; Heidelberg, Germany: Physica-Verlag.

Blume, L., & Easley, D. (1992). Evolution and market behavior. *Journal Economic Theory, 58,* 9-40.

Chen, S.-H., & Huang, Y.-C. (2003). Simulating the evolution of portfolio behavior in a multiple-asset agent-based artificial stock market. Paper presented at the *9th International Conference on Computing in Economics and Finance*, University of Washington, Seattle, July.

Chen, S.-H., & Yeh, C.-H. (2001a). Evolving traders and the faculty of the business school: A new architecture of the artificial stock market. *Journal of Economic Dynamics and Control, 25,* 363-393.

Chen, S.-H., & Yeh, C.-H. (2001b). Toward an integration of social learning and individual learning in agent-based computational stock markets: The approach based on population genetic programming. *Journal of Management and Economics, 5*(5).

Chen, T., & Chen, H. (1995). Universal approximation to nonlinear operators by neural networks with arbitrary activation functions and its application to dynamical systems. *IEEE Transactions on Neural Networks, 6,* 911-917.

Cliff, D., Harvey, I., & Husbands, P. (1992). *Incremental evolution of neural network architectures for adaptive behaviour* (No. CSRP256). University of Sussex Cognitive Science Research Paper, School of Cognitive and Computer Sciences, UK.

Elman, J. L. (1990). Finding structure in time. *Cognitive Science, 14,* 179-211.

Fischer, L. (1966). Some new stock market indexes. *Journal of Business, 39,* 191-225.

Friend, I., & Blume, M. E. (1975). The demand for risky assets. *American Economic Review, 65*(5), 900-922.

Gordon, M. J., Paradis, G. E., & Rorke, C. H. (1972, January). Experimental evidence on alternative portfolio decision rules. *Journal American Economic Review, 62*(1), 107-118.

Hakansson, N. (1971). Capital growth and mean-variance approach to portfolio selection. *Journal of Finance and Quantitative Analysis, 6,* 517-557.

Hayward, S. (2005). The role of heterogeneous agents past and forward time horizons in formulating computational models. *Computational Economics* (in press).

Hommes, C. H. (2001, May). Modeling the stylized facts in finance through simple nonlinear adaptive systems. In *Proceedings of the National Academy of Science,* (pp. 7221-7228).

Hornik, K., Stinchcombe, M., & White, H. (1989). Multilayer feed-forward networks are universal approximators. *Neural Networks, 2,* 359-366.

Jordan, M. I. (1986). Attractor dynamics and parallelism in a connectionist sequential machine. Paper presented at the *Proceedings of the 8th annual Conference of the Cognitive Science Society,* Hillsdale, NJ.

Jordan, M. I. (Ed.). (1989). *Serial order: A parallel, distributed processing approach.* Hillsdale, NJ: Erlbaum.

Kelly. (1956). A new interpretation of information rate. *Bell System Technical Journal, 35,* 917-926.

Latane, H. (1959). Criteria for choice among risky ventures. *Journal of Political Economy, 67,* 144-155.

LeBaron, B. (1991). *Technical trading rules and regime shifts in foreign exchange* (Working Paper No. 91-10-044). Santa Fe Institute, New Mexico.

LeBaron, B. (2001a). *Empirical regularities from interacting long and short memory investors in an agent-based financial market.* (No 52). IEEE.

LeBaron, B. (2001b). Evolution and time horizons in an agent based stock market. *Macroeconomic Dynamics, 5,* 225-254.

LeBaron, B. (2002). Short-memory traders and their impact on group learning in financial markets (No. 99). *Proceedings of the National Academy of Science* (pp. 7201-7206). No 99, suppl. 3.

Leitch, G., & Tanner, E. (2001). Economic forecast evaluation: profits versus the conventional error measure. *American Economic Review, 81,* 580-590.

Lettau, M. (1997). Explaining the facts with adaptive agents: The case of mutual fund flows. *Journal of Economic Dynamics and Control, 21,* 1117-1148.

Levy, M., Levy, H., & Solomon, S. (1994). A microscopic model of the stock market. *Economics Letters, 45,* 103-111.

Markowitz, H. M. (1976). Investment for the long run: new evidence for an old rule. *Journal of Finance, 31,* 1273-1286.

Merton, R. C., & Samuelson, P. A. (1974). Fallacy of the log-normal approximation to optimal portfolio decision-making over many periods. *Journal of Financial Economics, 1,* 67-94.

Muhlenbein, H., & Kindermann, J. (1989). The dynamics of evolution and learning: towards genetic neural networks. In R. Pfeifer, Z. Schreter, F. Fogelman-Soulié & L. Steels (Eds.), *Connectionism in perspective* (pp. 173-197). Elsevier, North-Holland.

Neely, C. J., & Weller, P. A. (1999). Technical trading rules in the European monetary system. *Journal of International Money and Finance, 18*(3), 429-458.

Pereira, R. (2002). Forecasting ability but no profitability: An empirical evaluation of genetic algorithm-optimised technical trading rules. In S.-H. Chen (Ed.), *Evolutionary computation in economics and finance* (pp. 287-310). Heidelberg, Germany: Physica-Verlag.

Pictet, O. V., Docorogna, M. M., Choparad, B., Shirru, M. O. R., & Tomassini, M. (1995). Using genetic algorithms for robust optimization in financial applications. Paper presented at the *Parallel Problem Solving from Nature-Applications in Statistics and Economics Workshop,* Germany.

Principe, J., Lefebvre, C., Lynn, G., Fancourt, C., & Wooten, D. (2003). *Help and manual.* Retrieved January 17, 2003, from http://www.neurosolutins/downloads/documentation

Scholes, M., & Willams, J. T. (1977). Estimating betas from nonsynchronous data. *Journal of Financial Economics, 5*(3), 309-327.

Sweeney, R. J. (1988). Some filter rule tests: Methods and results. *Journal of Financial and Quantitative Analysis, 23,* 285-301.

ENDNOTES

1 CI is a development paradigm of intelligent systems with data-driven methodologies to model intelligence observed from natural behavior. It includes such areas, as artificial neural networks, evolutionary computation, fuzzy logic, as well as machine learning, probabilistic belief networks, and so forth.

2 Investment decision is considered as a combination of portfolio or trading decision and saving decision.

3 The order of polynomial, to a certain extent, reflects agents' attitude towards kurtosis and skewness, which might be important considering financial data characteristics.

4 For example, a signal generated with stop/limit orders would have higher complexity and may be harder to model.

5 Consider a negative exponential utility function and the response function of the form, $w_{t+1} = w(\varepsilon_{t+1}) \equiv -\ln[b|\varepsilon_{t+1}| 1(\varepsilon_{t+1} \geq 0) + c|\varepsilon_{t+1}| 1(\varepsilon_{t+1} < 0)]$, then $\alpha \equiv b^{\rho}/(b^{\rho}+c^{\rho})$, where b and c are positive constants, determining the rate of decrease of w_{t+1} with respect to ε_{t+1}. This rate of decrease is considered to be equal to b for positive errors and to c for negative errors. Similarly, for a power utility function and the response function of the form, $w_{t+1} = w(\varepsilon_{t+1}) \equiv [b| \varepsilon_{t+1}| 1(\varepsilon_{t+1} \geq 0) + c| \varepsilon_{t+1}| 1(\varepsilon_{t+1} < 0)]^{-1}$, the degree of asymmetry is $\alpha \equiv b^{\rho}/(b^{\rho}+c^{\rho})$.

6 ANN learning is the ability of a net to adapt its behavior to the environment, by autonomously building a representation of the map from inputs to outputs, training itself on a set of examples.

7 Chen and Chen (1995) claimed that Multilayer Perceptron with any (nonpolynomial) Tauber-Wiener transfer function is a universal approximator.

8 ANN generalization capacity is the ability to produce a coherent response to imperfect inputs, particularly those not presented during learning.

9 The set of weights encodes the information into the net and determines ANN behavior. Values of the weights are selected in such a way as to realize the desired learning.

10 Assuming there exists a possibility to approximate the derivative of the cost function.

11 Assuming the objective to be a monotone function of unbounded stochastic factors, the worst case is given by a number of standard deviations from the mean.

12 A possible solution to the symmetry problem could be to use a penalties matrix, penalizing the false negative decisions more than the false positive ones.

13 Chen and Huang (2003) found correlation between the Kolmogorov-Smirnov statistics and the length of validation period. Assuming that traders' beliefs with longer validation periods get closer to the true process in simulations and agents' accuracy increases, they consider the time horizon that agents use for validation as a representation of the accuracy of prediction.

14 Note, market efficiency testing is not an objective of this study per se. However, learning a profitable forecast/strategy is, in a way, discovering market inefficiency.

15 If prices exhibit random walk behavior, equally likely to change up or down, the average forecast have a change of zero from the last value. This makes the last value a good benchmark to determine if the prediction can improve on a random chance.

16 The profit produced by winning trades divided by the losses made by losing trades.

17 Given by the average return divided by the standard deviation of that return.

18 Another possibility would be to use profit as the performance surface determinant. I leave this option out, since it wouldn't allow me to consider the questions proposed at the beginning. Setting the performance surface determined by the overall objective would not guarantee minimization of the underlying loss function used in forecasting and would not permit me to examine the relationship between statistical qualities and economic profitability.

19 The simulation code in Visual C++, v. 6.0 is available upon request. I have run tests on TradingSolutons, v. 2.0, NeuroSolutions v. 4.22 and Matlab v. 6.

20 Accuracy is given by the percentage of correct predictions.

21 Correlation of desired and ANN output.

22 More details of the technical points considered are in Principe, Lefebvre, Lynn, Fancourt, and Wooten (2003).

23 The support vector machine loss function is used to implement the large margin classifier segment of the SVM model and takes the following form: $L_{SVM} = I^{-1} \Sigma(Y_i - \tanh\Phi_I)^2$.

Chapter II

Pricing Basket Options with Optimum Wavelet Correlation Measures

Christopher Zapart
Advanced Financial Trading Solutions Ltd., UK

Satoshi Kishino
Musashi Institute of Technology, Japan

Tsutomu Mishina
Akita Prefectural University, Japan

ABSTRACT

This chapter describes a new procedure for designing optimum correlation measures for financial time series. The technique attempts to overcome some of the limitations in existing methods by looking at correlations among wavelet features extracted at different time scales from the underlying time series. New correlation coefficients are further optimised with help of artificial neural networks and genetic algorithms using a nonparametric adaptive wavelet thresholding scheme. The approach is applied to the problem of pricing basket options for which the pricing formula depends on accurate measurements of correlations between portfolio constituents. When compared with standard linear approaches (i.e., RiskMetrics™), an optimised predictive wavelet correlation measure offers potentially large reductions (over 50% in some cases) in static delta-hedging errors.

INTRODUCTION

The traditional linear correlation measure may not always be the most suitable measure of real or future correlations between returns from two financial assets (Zapart, 2003a). Although it may not be easy to quantify what the true correlation coefficient should be, it is worth trying to find a technique that would give practitioners a much better control over the process of measuring it. The choice of a particular correlation measure has important implications as the correlation coefficients are used during pricing of certain types of exotic options; for example, basket options in which the final pay-off depends on more than one underlying asset. The risk management industry also uses correlation coefficients to provide accurate Value-at-Risk (VaR) estimates to financial institutions. Correlations between share prices can also be used in conjunction with other factors when establishing long-short equity pair positions by the hedge fund industry.

Current linear approaches attempt to estimate correlations between financial assets directly from the time series (i.e., from the history of daily closing prices). The financial time series can be described as a nonstationary and nonlinear behaviour characterised by random shocks, jumps, potentially non-Gaussian noise, and lagging returns (Hazarika & Lowe, 1997; Zapart & Lowe, 1999). The presence of such artifacts is inconsistent with the basic assumptions made by linear methods that are used to estimate correlations, which may result in the financial institutions and the research community using suboptimum correlation coefficients. Moreover, existing approaches only use present instantaneous correlations (Hull, 1997, p. 480) instead of more correct *future* correlations that would be more appropriate when pricing basket derivatives. This issue has been addressed to some extent with the introduction of GARCH forecasts of linear correlations (Engle & Mezrich, 1996; Morgan, 1996).

Preliminary experiments reported in (Struzik & Siebes, 1999; Zapart, 2003a) have explored an alternative nonlinear approach, designed specifically to deal with the presence of nonstationarities and shocks in the time series and hence being capable of overcoming some of the limitations of current methods. The new algorithm works by looking at correlations between different wavelet features extracted from the underlying financial time series. This chapter builds upon an earlier work by Zapart (2003a) by further exploring the alternative approach and constructing appropriate feature spaces with help of techniques borrowed from such diverse fields as signal processing (discrete wavelet transform; Graps, 1995; Gençay, Selçuk, & Whitcher, 2001; Mallat, 1998), artificial neural networks (Haykin, 1994) and evolutionary programming (Holland, 1975). The approach differs from existing methods in that it tries to calculate correlations in appropriately selected feature spaces instead of operating in the time domain. By working in the feature space it is possible to separate the main signal components from random shocks or jumps and model the nonstationary and potentially nonlinear nature of financial time series, thus escaping the limitations of current methods (Aussem, Campbell, & Murtagh, 1998; Copabianco, 2002; Murtagh, Zheng, Campbell, & Starck, 1999; Zapart, 2002, 2003a, 2003b). Furthermore, by using neural networks coupled with genetic algorithms, the new approach can optimise the feature spaces by automatically discovering which features of the time series are more relevant to the calculation of the correlation coefficients. The work is strongly related to wavelet thresholding and noise reduction schemes (wavelet filtering). The crucial difference between it and existing wavelet thresholding literature is that our approach performs a nonparametric wavelet filtering without making any prior assumptions about the data (e.g., without assuming a Gaussian white noise, as in Percival & Walden, 2000). Instead, artificial neural networks, trained by genetic algorithms, are allowed to discover an appropriate data model from direct observations.

The approach is demonstrated on a real-life example: pricing equity basket options on portfolios containing two equities traded on the New York Stock Exchange (NYSE) over short- to medium-term time horizons. In basket options, the final payoff at expiry depends on the performance of more than one underlying asset. Standard numerical techniques for pricing options—such as binomial trees (Hull, 1997)—can deal with pricing an option dependent on two uncorrelated assets by constructing a three-dimensional tree that represents all possible movements of two assets. However, any degree of correlation between the underlying assets introduces an extra layer of complexity to the problem. In order to price basket options, the three-dimensional binomial tree is typically extended (or transformed) by taking into account the correlation coefficient ρ between the time series of daily returns for the two stocks. An accurate measurement of correlations between two assets (financial time series) becomes crucial as significant amounts of money can be made or lost by mispricing options. Apart from the equity markets, basket options are often used in the interest rate markets, which are closely linked to the transactions in the international currency markets.

THEORETICAL

Linear Correlation

The standard historical linear correlation between returns of daily closing prices r_i^A and r_i^B, $i = 0 \ldots N-1$ from two financial assets A and B at time t is defined by (1):

$$\rho_{linear}(t) = \frac{\sum_{i=0}^{N-1}\left(r_{t-i}^A - \bar{r}^A\right)\left(r_{t-i}^B - \bar{r}^B\right)}{\sqrt{\sum_{i=0}^{N-1}\left(r_{t-i}^A - \bar{r}^A\right)^2}\sqrt{\sum_{i=0}^{N-1}\left(r_{t-i}^B - \bar{r}^B\right)^2}} \tag{1}$$

where $\bar{r}^A$ and $\bar{r}^B$ are the means of the daily closing returns for stocks A and B, respectively. When applied to financial data, linear techniques need to be robust enough in order to deal with such issues as nonstationarity or a presence of non-Gaussian noise. Also, financial time series are often characterised by sudden, random jumps and potentially short-lived shocks. In (1) the equation has been enhanced by J. P. Morgan to make it better able to deal with such problems. Their industry benchmark RiskMetrics™ approach (Morgan, 1996, p. 83) is a form of an exponentially weighted moving average (EWMA) correlation given by (2):

$$\rho_{ewma}(t) = \frac{\sum_{i=0}^{N} \lambda^i r_{t-i}^A r_{t-i}^B}{\sqrt{\sum_{i=0}^{N} \lambda^i \left(r_{t-i}^A\right)^2} \sqrt{\sum_{i=0}^{N} \lambda^i \left(r_{t-i}^B\right)^2}} \tag{2}$$

where λ determines the attrition rate at which the influence of the past information decays to a negligible level. By exponentially weighting each data point the RiskMetrics™ correlations are less sensitive to sudden changes when the effect of random shocks falls out of the data range $\left[r_0^A, r_{N-1}^A\right]$, $\left[r_0^B, r_{N-1}^B\right]$. Its correlation forecasts can also react faster to the changes in the GARCH variances and covariances. The drawback of (2) is that it requires significantly longer (even 10 times) price histories than (1) in order to arrive at reliable correlation estimates.

Linear correlation measures make some very strict assumptions about the time series (i.e., Gaussian noise and stationarity). Similarly, the Black-Scholes options pricing formula assumes following a random walk (see endnote 1) with a normal distribution, which makes the underlying differential equations convenient to analyse and solve. Although in practice the assumptions may hold 95% of the time, it is the latter 5% that is most interesting. It accounts for the fat tails in the assumed distribution of returns and it encompasses the so-called extreme events, irregular features of the time series (sudden large jumps) and global or local trends (nonstationarities). Basket options pricing in particular relies heavily on the stationarity assumption. Linear returns correlation coefficients, reflecting correlations between stochastic processes, are based on the past estimates of returns distributions. These past estimates are extrapolated into the future and the assumption is made that future correlation levels can be approximated by their past values, which may not always be the case for nonstationary time series (Struzik & Siebes, 1999). The irregular behaviour and nonstationarity, characteristic of real-world financial time series, challenges the underlying assumptions that at present may be resulting in suboptimum correlation coefficients being used.

Wavelet Correlation Measure

There is a need for a flexible and robust technique capable of dealing with both normal and abnormal trading patterns. The wavelet-based time-series analysis is one such technique. It can deal with jumps and discontinuities present in the financial time series (Dempster & Eswaran, 2000). Performing a signal/noise decomposition of the underlying time series becomes a straightforward operation in the non linear wavelet domain (Aussem et al., 1998, Zapart, 2002). Struzik and Siebes (1999) introduced a so-called wavelet correlation measure in the context of data mining large financial databases. The new measure of similarity between financial time series was designed specifically to deal with nonstationarities, shocks, and lagging returns present in financial time series. Preliminary results of applying it to pricing basket options were presented in Zapart (2003a), where some suggestions for possible improvements were also made. An application to designing a long-short trading system utilising the techniques described in this chapter was presented in Zapart (2004).

Given a source signal $s(t)$ with a discrete measure of time t, (3) shows its wavelet decomposition (Copabianco, 2002):

$$s(t) = \sum_k c_{j0,k} \Phi_{j0,k}(t) + \sum_{j>j0} \sum_k d_{j,k} \Psi_{j,k}(t) \tag{3}$$

where $\Phi_{j0,k}(t)$ is a scaling function, $\Psi(t)$ is a so-called mother wavelet function satisfying the condition $\Psi_{j,k}(t) = 2^{j/2}\Psi(2^j t - k)$, and $c_{j0,k}$ and $d_{j,k}$ are the wavelet coarse and detail coefficients:

$$\begin{aligned} c_{j,k} &= \int s(t)\Phi_{j,k}(t)\,dt \\ d_{j,k} &= \int s(t)\Psi(t)\,dt \end{aligned} \tag{4}$$

In (3) and (4), j is the so-called level index and k is the translation index. One type of the wavelet transform—the Haar—has been particularly popular in applications dealing with analysing financial time series. The Haar transform uses a convolution of a simple block function with the derivative operator to yield a Haar wavelet function as defined by (5) (Chui, 1992):

$$\Psi_H(t) = \begin{cases} 1 & for \quad 0 < t < \frac{1}{2} \\ -1 & for \quad \frac{1}{2} < t < 1 \\ 0 & otherwise. \end{cases} \tag{5}$$

Other types of the wavelet transform (e.g., Daubechies) could also be used and have been tried, but they are computationally more expensive and more difficult to implement in software. Moreover, the Haar wavelet transform is well suited to analysing financial time series because it can cope well with the presence of sudden jumps, jagged transitions and other discontinuities in the financial data and also because of its detrending (differencing) effect.

For given discrete time-series x_i and y_i, where $i = 1 \ldots N$ and N is a power of 2, the discrete Haar wavelet transform used in this work will produce coarse wavelet coefficients c_x, c_y and $N-1$ detail wavelet coefficients d_k^x, d_k^y, where N is the total number of points in the time series and $k = 1 \ldots N-1$. In its most basic form the wavelet correlation can be defined by (6) (Struzik & Siebes, 1999):

$$\rho_{wavelet} = \frac{C(\mathbf{x},\mathbf{y})}{\sqrt{C(\mathbf{x},\mathbf{x})C(\mathbf{y},\mathbf{y})}} \tag{6}$$

where

$$C(\mathbf{x},\mathbf{y}) = \sum_{k=1}^{N-1} d_k^x d_k^y \tag{7}$$

The normalisation step ensures that the wavelet correlation values lie within $[-1,1]$. Instead of taking into account all $N-1$ detail wavelet coefficients, one could selectively use only the low- or high-order coefficients, corresponding to lower or higher signal frequencies, respectively, to tailor the wavelet correlation to a particular problem and make it more sensitive to selected signal features.

Static Wavelet Correlation

Note that (6) and (7) define a so-called *static* version of the wavelet correlation measure since at any given time a snapshot of the past N (e.g., 128) days is used to obtain and correlate the wavelet coefficients. In addition, if all $N-1$ detail wavelet coefficients were to be used in (7), then the corresponding $\rho_{wavelet}$ as given by (6) would be equivalent to calculating (1) with absolute price levels x_i and y_i in place of their daily returns r_i^A and r_i^B. To demonstrate this, a linear regression has been performed on 1,264 samples of static wavelet correlations with all $N-1$ detail coefficients and the corresponding absolute levels linear correlations for a sample financial time-series. A perfect $y = 1.0x$ fit was found with the $R^2 = 0.46$. However, major differences begin to emerge if, for example, only the last $N/2$ detail coefficients are used in (7); the obtained regression line is $y = 0.64x + 0.1$, with $R^2 = 0.46$.

To derive any potential benefits and improvements on linear techniques one would need to consider using only selected subsets of all $N-1$ detail wavelet coefficients. Figure 1 shows one such subset: a high-order wavelet correlation that uses only the last $N/2$ detail coefficients with a superimposed plot of the corresponding absolute levels linear correlation. It can be observed that for certain periods of time the high-order

Figure 1. A time-series with a high-order wavelet correlation measure (gray) superimposed onto an absolute levels linear correlation (dashed black).

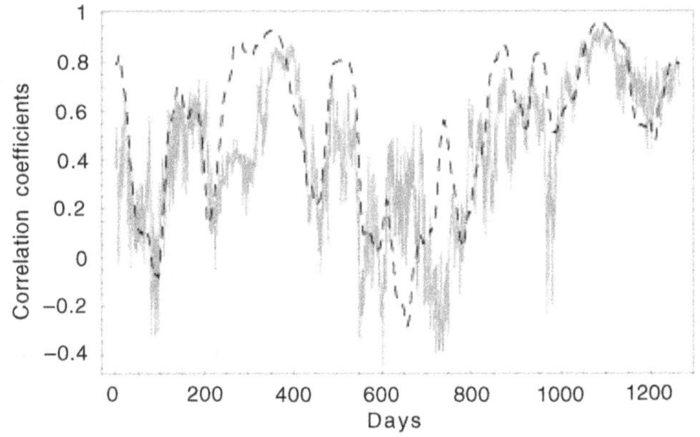

wavelet correlation coefficients exhibit a different sign than the corresponding linear correlation. Instead of arbitrarily deciding to use the last $N/2$ coefficients one could also assign a soft weight $w_k \in [0,1]$ to each pair of wavelet detail coefficients d_k^x, d_k^y. The equation (7) would need to be modified accordingly:

$$C_w(\mathbf{x},\mathbf{y}) = \sum_{k=1}^{N-1} w_k \, d_k^x \, d_k^y \,, \tag{8}$$

and (6) would become

$$\rho_{wavelet} = \frac{C_w(\mathbf{x},\mathbf{y})}{\sqrt{C(\mathbf{x},\mathbf{x})C(\mathbf{y},\mathbf{y})}} . \tag{9}$$

It is not clear at first which correlation measure is better: the linear measure or a weighted wavelet measure, as per (8) and (9). It may be reasonable to assume that different correlation measures may be more suitable for performing different tasks. This chapter attempts to examine the feasibility of designing wavelet-derived correlation measures that would outperform the industry-standard linear correlations on the task of pricing basket options.

Assigning soft weights to different wavelet coefficients as in (8) also enables a successful elimination of spurious correlations. Let us assume that two time-series X and Y are correlated with an average correlation coefficient close to zero over a medium to long term. For example, based on the past $N = 128$ days in the short-term (1) - (7) might give rise to significantly positive or negative correlations (e.g., over 0.5 or below -0.5) between X and Y. The inclusion of weights w_k that can be set to zero through an adaptive learning algorithm can effectively prevent wavelet correlation coefficients $\rho_{wavelet}$ from significantly deviating from zero for uncorrelated assets.

Dynamic Wavelet Correlation

In contrast to the *static* approach, which only looks at vectors of wavelet coefficients calculated for fixed windows with the past *N* days (e.g., $N = 128$), the *dynamic* version of the wavelet correlation measure examines the time evolutions of the wavelet coefficients over long time horizons (e.g., 500 or 1,000 days) on a rolling window basis. The windows with a fixed length of *N* days are moved forward along the time axis in steps of one day. At each step a wavelet transform is applied to the windows containing data points x_i and y_i, $i = 1 \ldots N$, $N = 128$ resulting in *N* wavelet coefficients d_k^x and d_k^y, $k = 1 \ldots N$. The coefficients d_k^x and d_k^y for subsequent time steps t form the time evolutions $d_k^x(t)$ and $d_k^y(t)$.

Figures 2 and 3 show the first five wavelet coefficients as a function of time for the share price of ALCOA corporation. The first coarse wavelet coefficient does not exhibit much variability over the sampled window and could be regarded as a trend line or a principal feature of the time series. However, the subsequent wavelet coefficients, corresponding to finer time scales, show some interesting dynamics.

Figure 2. A wavelet decomposition for the share price of ALCOA Inc. listed on the New York Stock Exchange. The first plot shows seventy four daily closing prices and the subsequent plots present the time evolutions of the first two most significant wavelet coefficients.

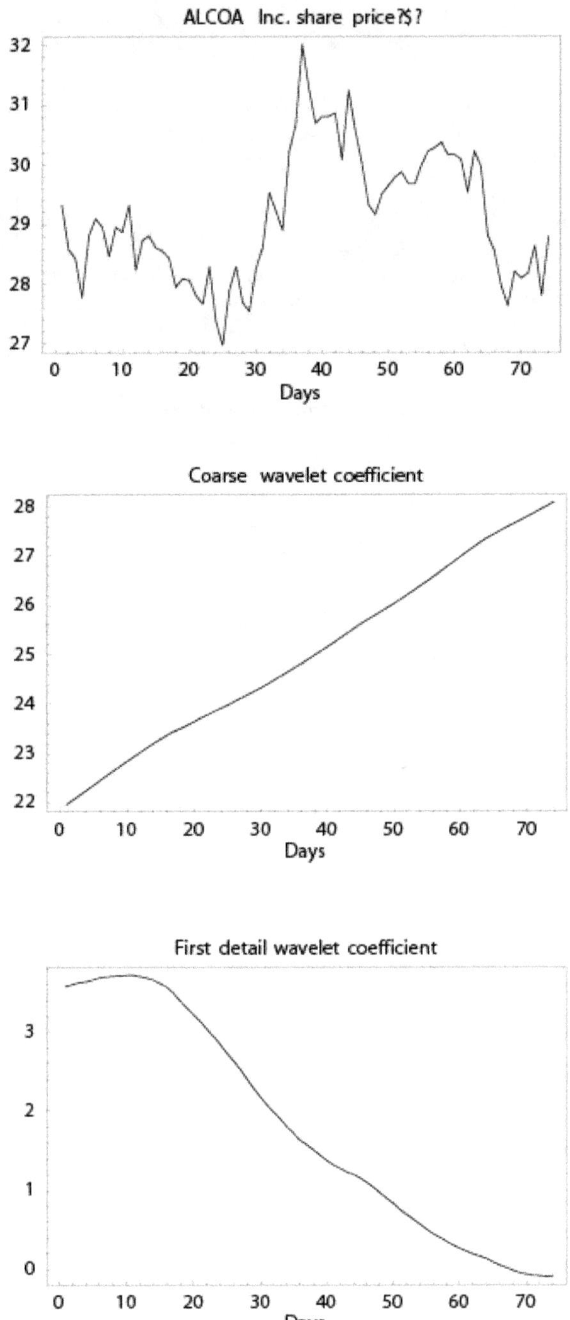

Figure 3. Time evolutions of the next three wavelet coefficients

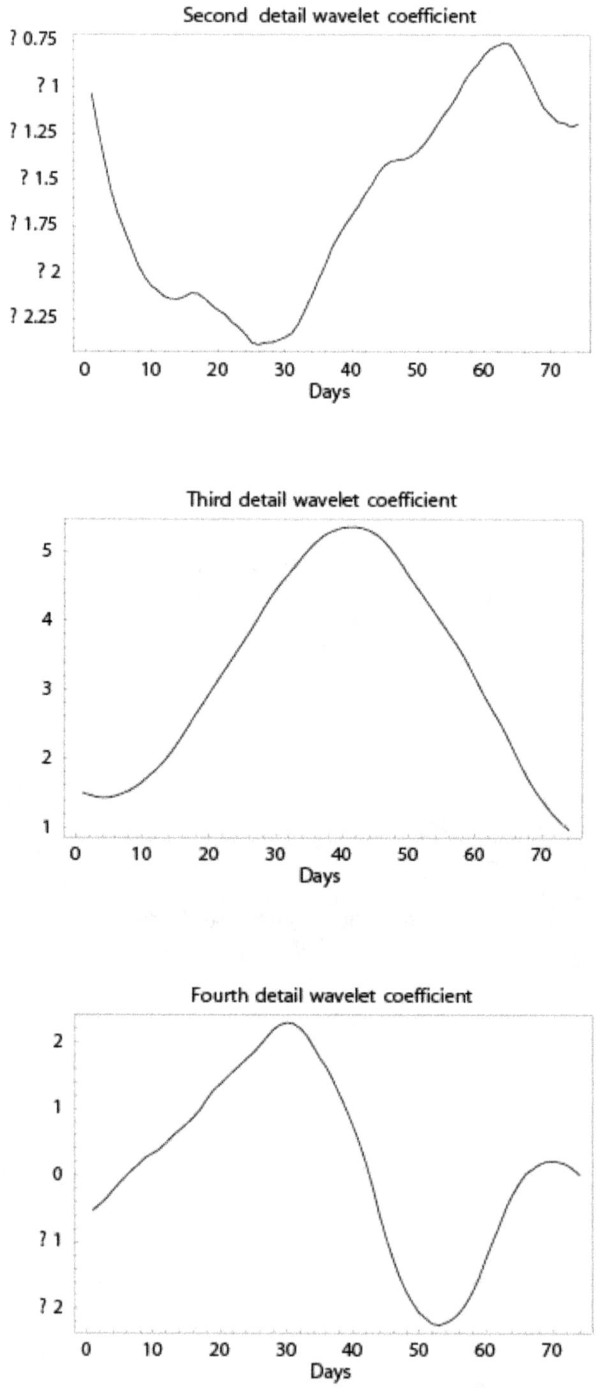

For any two time-series X and Y, the *dynamic* wavelet correlation measure would take into account correlations between these evolutions of wavelet coefficients $d_k^x(t)$ and $d_k^y(t)$, where *k* would index a selected subset of all *N* wavelet coefficients (e.g., $k = 1 \ldots M$, $M \leq N$). The dynamic correlation coefficients would be calculated as a weighted average of correlations between the first *M* pairs of wavelet coefficients $d_k^x(t)$ and $d_k^y(t)$:

$$\rho_{wavelet} = \left(1 \Big/ \sum_{k=1}^{M} w_k \right) \sum_{k=1}^{M} w_k \, \rho_{linear}\left(d_k^x(t), d_k^y(t)\right) \tag{10}$$

In its current form, (10) could still lead to significant correlations (values close to -1 or 1), even if all the weighting coefficients w_k were to approach zero. This would prevent the dynamic correlation from being able to filter out spurious correlations as described in the section on the static wavelet correlation. For this reason the dynamic correlation measure would be using an extra auxiliary weight w_{M+1} in the denominator of (10). For weakly correlated stocks it is anticipated that the weight w_{M+1} would dominate all the other weights w_k, which would lead to dynamic correlations $\rho_{wavelet}$ being close to zero irrespective of individual correlations between $d_k^x(t)$ and $d_k^y(t)$. The final formula for the dynamic correlation measure is given by (11):

$$\rho_{wavelet} = \left(1 \Big/ \sum_{k=1}^{M+1} w_k \right) \sum_{k=1}^{M} w_k \, \rho_{linear}\left(d_k^x(t), d_k^y(t)\right) \tag{11}$$

An Example

Figure 4 shows 128 closing prices for two stocks, A and B, taken from the same stock market sector. The straight gray line is a prevailing trend line for the stock B. In Figure 5, a single downward shock was introduced to the share price of the stock B which changed its trend from rising to falling. A closer inspection of the time-series B in Figure 4 reveals that it consists of two parts with slight downward biases: the first part between days 1 and 60 and the second part between days 80 and 128. Between days 60 and 80 it exhibits a strong rising trend. The introduction of a downward shock at day 50 cancels the effect of the subsequent rising trend between days 60 and 80, which is reflected in a falling trend line in Figure 5.

Correlations between the two stocks A and B have been measured using a standard linear returns correlation as defined by (1), and compared with the values obtained for different wavelet correlation measures. Table 1 shows their comparison. The length of the time series is too short for the EWMA (RiskMetrics™) approach. The static wavelet correlation measure used all 127 detail wavelet coefficients, the low-order wavelet measure used only the first four low-order coefficients and the high-order wavelet measure used the last 64 detail wavelet coefficients. All correlation measures indicated a positive correlation between the time-series A and B from Figure 4 (without a shock).

Figure 4. Daily closing prices (price series) for stocks A (solid black line) and B (dashed line) with a superimposed trend (straight gray line) for the stock B

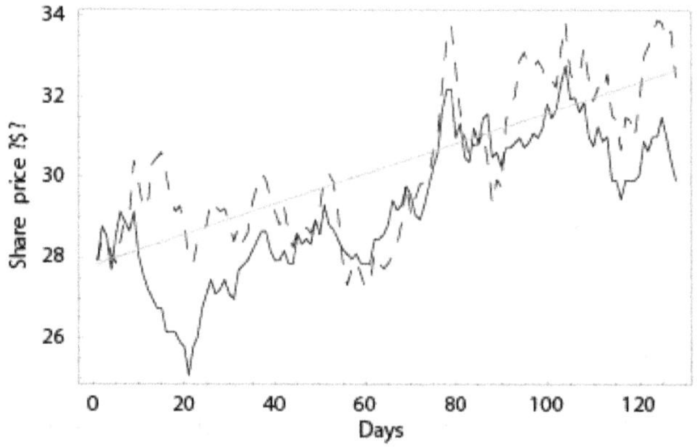

Figure 5. Daily closing prices (price series) for stocks A (solid black line) and B (dashed line) with a superimposed trend (straight gray line) for the stock B. At time t=50 days a sudden shock—a drop with a magnitude of 10%—was introduced to the share price B.

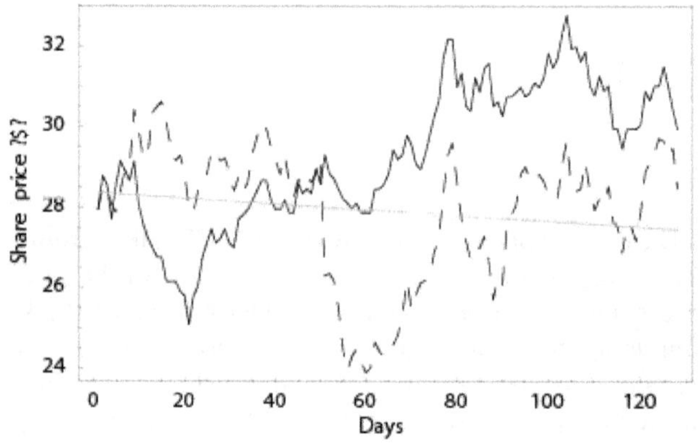

Table 1. Correlation coefficients $\rho_{A,B}$ between stocks A and B obtained using different correlation measures with and without an artificial shock

Correlation type	$\rho_{A,B}$, ***no shock***	$\rho_{A,B}$ ***with a shock***
Linear returns	0.61	0.48
Static wavelet	0.79	-0.02
Low-order wavelet	0.85	-0.25
High-order wavelet	0.70	0.37

After the introduction of a single shock as shown in Figure 5 the historical linear returns correlation decreased by 20% but maintained a positive sign, despite the trends for stocks A and B now being divergent (the trend for the stock A is still upward but the trend for the stock B is now clearly pointing down). Both the full static wavelet correlation as well as the low-order wavelet correlation seem to reflect the general trends in time series as they have reversed their signs. It is interesting to note that the high-order wavelet correlation behaved similarly to the linear returns correlation and maintained its positive sign despite a nearly 50% decrease in its value.

It is not clear which is the "correct" correlation coefficient in this example; it would depend on being able to see how well each correlation coefficient performs over time as part of a larger system (e.g., a basket option pricing application). The linear returns correlation seemed to be the least affected by the downward shock. Moreover, the basket option pricing formula, which is described in the next section, has been derived using linear returns correlations between stochastic processes governing stocks A and B. However, it is not clear intuitively whether it is indicating a correct correlation $\rho_{A,B}$ as the trends for stocks A and B in Figure 5 are clearly divergent, despite a positive correlation between daily returns that can be confirmed by a visual inspection of the time series. It is also not clear if, in a nonstationary environment, a linear returns correlation coefficient derived from past data can act as a reliable guide to future correlations needed to price basket options over a certain period of time in the future. Perhaps correlation coefficients should be made a function of the time horizon over which they serve their purpose (i.e., the option maturity time which in this study is a duration set between 5 days and 3 months). One could speculate that over short time horizons a "good" correlation measure should resemble linear returns coefficients, whereas over long time horizons it should assign more weight to long-term trends present in financial time series.

The previous example draws attention to the uncertainty surrounding accurate measurements of correlations between time series of financial assets. It also highlights a large degree of flexibility exhibited by wavelet correlation measures that can be designed either to be particularly sensitive to correlations between general price trends or to behave more like a linear returns correlation, depending on which signal features are needed for computing optimum correlation coefficients satisfying an external success criterion.

Basket Options

Portfolios containing two or more assets can be hedged by using a special type of exotic derivatives called a basket option. In basket options the final payoff that an option holder stands to receive depends on the performance of more than one underlying asset. For the purposes of this research only baskets containing two assets will be considered as this simplifies developing the supporting software without any adverse impact on the main thought process.

Let us assume that a given portfolio contains assets A and B with a strong negative correlation ρ. Any movements in the price of the stock A would effectively be offset by movements in the opposite direction in the price of the stock B. The overall value of a hypothetical portfolio would not change much, which would lead to a reduced risk of holding this portfolio and a relatively low price of a corresponding basket option. By analogy, if strongly positively correlated stocks were used, the hypothetical portfolio would experience large variations in value because both stocks would move in the same direction at the same time. This would increase the risk and, consequently, a corresponding basket option would be more expensive to purchase than one in the first case. In order to hedge the value of a hypothetical two-stock portfolio, one could use derivatives either purchased separately for stocks A and B or in a form of a single basket option. Using two separate options on A and B is equivalent to assuming a zero correlation between these two assets. However, in case of negatively correlated assets, the cost of purchasing a single basket option should be lower compared to hedging the portfolio with two separate options.

Single asset option pricing techniques, such as binomial trees (Hull, 1997), have been extended to cover cases of multiple assets. An alternative binomial tree technique (Hull, 1997) can be used in which the probabilities of up and down price moves at each node are set equally to 0.5. Such equal-probabilities binomial trees are constructed for each underlying asset. The binomial trees for two assets A and B are subsequently combined together at each node and their node probabilities are altered to reflect a certain degree of correlation between the two assets. Table 2 shows the new probabilities that depend on the correlation coefficient ρ.

An alternative binomial tree uses modified equations for estimating the up and down movements in stock prices during a time step Δt:

$$u = \exp\left(\left(r - \frac{\sigma^2}{2}\right)\Delta t + \sigma\sqrt{\Delta t}\right)$$

$$d = \exp\left(\left(r - \frac{\sigma^2}{2}\right)\Delta t - \sigma\sqrt{\Delta t}\right), \tag{12}$$

where r is a prevailing risk-free interest rate and standard deviations σ_A and σ_B for assets A and B should be used in place of σ. When the two alternative binomial trees for A and B are combined, the expected payoff f at each node of the tree can be expressed in terms of all the possible combinations of up and down movements of A and B. There are four such possible outcomes, and their probabilities p_i are shown in Table 2. The expected future payoff, given by (13), needs to be discounted at the risk-free rate r:

$$f = \exp(-r\Delta t)\sum_{i=1}^{4} p_i f_i , \tag{13}$$

where the payoffs f_i correspond to moves in prices of A and B as outlined in Table 2.

Table 2. Adjusted node probabilities that take into account a degree of correlation between assets A and B with a given correlation coefficient ρ.

	Stock A up	***Stock A down***
Stock B up	$p_1 = 0.25(1+\rho)$	$p_2 = 0.25(1-\rho)$
Stock B down	$p_3 = 0.25(1-\rho)$	$p_4 = 0.25(1+\rho)$

As the probabilities p_i contain the correlation coefficient ρ the final price of a basket option will be highly dependent on using reliable estimates of correlations between the two given assets. From a theoretical point of view, the basket option pricing scheme has been developed within the context of a linear correlation measure and the correct formal approach is to use linear correlation coefficients between assets A and B. In practice the presence of nonstationarities and other irregular features in financial time series introduces correlation estimation errors (a systematic risk), which may provide a justification for trying to use alternative correlation coefficients in experimental studies. If experimental evidence can be found to support the use of other correlation measures then the practitioners in the field of computational finance can derive tangible benefits in terms of reduced systematic risk and lower hedging costs.

This chapter proposes to replace a standard linear correlation measure with correlation coefficients $\rho_{wavelet}$ provided by specially optimised wavelet correlation measures. The advantages of such an approach may be provided by the flexibility of wavelets when dealing with shocks and nonstationarity present in financial time series and their ability to analyse data at different time scales within a wavelet feature space. The nonparametric approach with neural networks and genetic algorithms can explore a space of potential correlation measures to find the optimum ones within a framework of a given basket option pricing algorithm, but without the constraints of standard linear techniques. The wavelet-neural networks models can also approximate the standard linear correlation measure if it is found to be most optimum one for the assumed options pricing scheme.

The training algorithm, which will be described in the next section, can work with any basket options pricing technique. Other option pricing methods have been explored, for example the multivariate Monte Carlo simulation, in which ρ is the correlation coefficient among standarised normal distributions of daily stock returns for A and B. However, in practice, the binomial tree method has proven capable of providing good answers to a desired accuracy level in much shorter time frames than the probabilistic Monte Carlo method.

Training Algorithm

Defining *static* and *dynamic* correlation measures, (9) and (11), are functions of "soft" weighting coefficients $w_k \in [0,1]$. These coefficients would depend both on an overall level of correlation between the assets under consideration as well as a certain level of noise and shocks present in financial time series. Their role is to enhance or suppress signal features extracted at different time scales from the wavelet decomposition of the underlying time series. The values of the weights w_k, which are difficult to derive analytically, need to be inferred directly from the data sets, as they are likely to be different for different pairs of stocks. To solve the problem of finding the right values of w_k we propose to:

1. use nonlinear artificial neural networks (ANN) to model the weights w_k, and
2. employ genetic algorithms (GA) to train the neural networks used to map w_k.

Concise descriptions of neural networks and genetic algorithms can be found in the appendixes. Assigning variable weights to wavelet coefficients amounts to performing wavelet thresholding. Many different thresholding schemes have been proposed in the literature, ranging from a hard keep-or-kill approach, where all wavelet coefficients past a selected cut-off point are set to zero, a soft-shrinkage rule where coefficients smaller than a variable threshold are zeroed to adaptive soft-thresholding techniques such as BayesShrink (Chang, Yu, & Vetterli, 2000) and RiskShrink (Donoho & Johnstone, 1994) that may be better at separating the signal part from the noise than a simple hard rule (keep or kill). Deciding on correct cut-off points or good levels of thresholds is not a trivial task. Imposing an a priori noise model as in (Percival & Walden, 2000) is also too restrictive. Therefore, in this research, we follow a full nonparametric approach that does not make any prior assumptions about the nature of the signal or the noise parts. Instead it relies on artificial neural networks trained with genetic algorithms adapting themselves to the data sets and hence deriving optimum thresholding schemes directly from the observations. As artificial neural networks are proven universal approximators (Haykin, 1994), they are capable of performing any nonlinear mappings that may be needed by adaptive wavelet thresholding.

Most evolutionary programming methods such as genetic algorithms require a definition of a so-called fitness function. They do not require any prior knowledge of target output values, which is directly applicable to our problem as the optimum target values for w_k are unknown. During successive iterations of genetic algorithms a fitness function enables them to compare potential candidate solutions with each other. Only the best solutions are carried over to the next iteration and the worst candidates are removed. The goal of a genetic algorithm is to find optimum solutions that would maximise a given fitness function. Genetic algorithms belong to a class of optimisation techniques. They require that the problem to be solved should be posed as an optimisation task. In the search for optimum weighting coefficients w_k, genetic algorithms could be directed to minimise hedging errors from writing delta-hedged basket call options. They would perform an evolutionary search for free parameters of artificial neural networks for which the obtained values w_k would lead to correlation coefficients $\rho_{wavelet}$, such that the corresponding hedging error arising from writing basket options would be at its minimum (see Figure 6).

A concept that is underused in practical studies is that of using committees of experts in place of single models. Although computationally more expensive, the technique has the advantage of combining several forecasts made by independently trained models. This method is best applied when each expert model is trained on an

Figure 6. A complete training cycle. Feedback received in the form of hedging errors enables genetic algorithms to improve artificial neural networks.

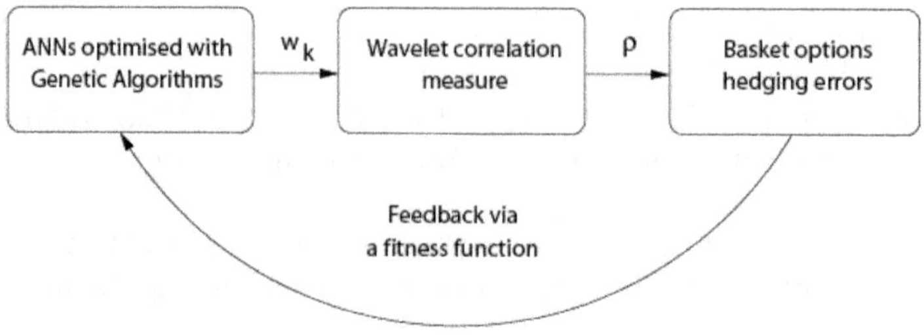

independent data set, which improves confidence intervals of the combined forecasts by pooling together different error distributions of each expert model (Lowe, 2002). This study uses committees of experts to model the weighting coefficients w_k. Instead of using a single artificial neural network for each w_k, between 5 and 10 networks are trained on different randomly selected training sets. The outputs from all models are subsequently combined together to give a final value for each weight w_k.

EXPERIMENTAL

To compare optimum wavelet correlation measures with standard linear methods as represented by the RiskMetrics™approach (see (2)), the training procedure described in the previous section has been applied to pricing two-stock basket options in the US equity markets. The experiments were carried out for both correlated and uncorrelated stocks. The inclusion of companies from different industry sectors will help determine whether or not a wavelet correlation measure is able to differentiate between real and spurious correlations.

Training Set

Stocks of IBM and Dell have been selected for inclusion in a correlated portfolio in which equal amounts of capital are invested in the two basket constituents. Both these companies belong to the same technology sector and as such a certain degree of an intrinsic correlation between their share prices can be expected. A second, uncorrelated portfolio contains share prices of IBM and Cardinal Health, Inc. (New York Stock Exchange ticker symbol CAH). Price histories containing the last 10 years of dividend and split-adjusted daily closing prices are divided into two parts: a training set 7 years long and a test set with the last 3 years of data. The training set is used to train artificial neural networks to provide the weighting coefficients w_k. The multilayer perceptron (MLP) neural networks take two inputs:

1. an index k of the wavelet coefficients d_k^x and d_k^y, and
2. the maturity T of a particular basket option.

The inputs are scaled so that they belong to an interval [0,1]. Each expert neural network has one output used to provide optimum values of $w_k \in [0,1]$.

The committees of experts use five neural networks trained on different training sets from within the initial 7-year period. For each training set, 50 random dates are selected on which two-stock American-style at-the-money (see endnote 2) basket call options are written. Their maturities are drawn at random from the range of between 5 and 90 days. Short positions in options are offset by delta-hedged long trades in the underlying basket of two stocks. The hedging errors on the expiry date of each basket option are summed up for all 50 samples and used subsequently to derive estimates of fitness functions. Each neural network is trained separately with a genetic algorithm. The estimates from five expert networks are combined together using a simple arithmetic mean during the evaluation phase on the test sets.

Fitness Function

During the optimisation process, genetic algorithms start with a large number (e.g., 100) of potential solutions to the problem. Each candidate solution—or a neural network encoded into a binary string of zeroes and ones—is ranked according to its measure of fitness. The best members of the initial population are selected as starting seeds for the next generation of solutions and the worst models are removed from the population. The process is repeated until a satisfactory solution is found. In the experiments two alternative fitness functions have been tried:

1. an average wavelet correlation hedging error

$$fitness_1 = \frac{1}{N}\sum_{i=1}^{N}\left|wavelet\ hedge_i\right|, \quad N = 50 \tag{14}$$

2. an average relative hedging error in comparison with standard linear correlation coefficients provided by (1) and (2)

$$fitness_2 = \frac{1}{N}\sum_{i=1}^{N}\exp\left(\frac{\left|wavelet\ hedge_i\right| - \left|linear\ hedge_i\right|}{\left|linear\ hedge_i\right|}\right), \quad N = 50 \tag{15}$$

In both cases, genetic algorithms are expected to find sets of free parameters of neural networks in order to minimise the respective fitness functions. In the second case, neural networks are specifically trained to outperform standard linear techniques while at the same time assigning an equal importance to both small and large hedging errors $wavelet\ hedge_i$.

Test Set

After training, the wavelet correlation measure models are tested on the last 3 years of price histories to see how well they perform in comparison with linear approaches given by (1) and (2). Basket options are typically traded in over-the-counter (OTC) transactions. Without access to detailed OTC transaction records it is not possible to test wavelet correlation coefficients on real transactions. Instead, the new models are tested on random sequences of two hundred generated basket options with maturities chosen randomly to be between 5 and 90 days. For each basket option, both wavelet correlation coefficients and standard linear correlation coefficients are used. Over the duration of the test set, the average linear and wavelet hedging errors as in (14) are measured together with the total net hedging error, which is a balance of a trading account at the end of the sequence of 200 basket option trades, as given by (16):

$$account\ balance = \left|\sum_{i=1}^{N} wavelet\ hedge_i\right| \tag{16}$$

Static Wavelet Correlation Models

Figures 7 and 8 show the mappings w_k learned by neural networks optimised by genetic algorithms with help of the second fitness function (15). Relatively small neural networks were used, with one hidden layer and two hidden neurons. Static models look at windows containing 128 end-of-day prices. As the exponentially weighted moving average correlation requires significantly longer price histories to produce reliable estimates, (15) uses a linear correlation as defined by (1). Compared with the first surface, the second mapping—obtained for a pair of IBM and CAH—exhibits lower levels of weighting coefficients w_k, which suggests that neural networks identified a lower overall level of correlation between IBM and CAH in comparison with IBM and DELL. Because IBM and CAH belong to different sectors, one would expect them to be less correlated than the IBM and DELL pair, which belong to the same sector. In the experiments, the coefficients w_k have been modeled as a function of two parameters: k and T. By visually inspecting Figures 7 and 8 one can observe a greater dependence of w_k on the wavelet coefficient index k than on the options maturity time T. This is illustrated in Figure 9, where two cross-sections of the surface $w_k = f(k,T)$ from Figure 7 have been plotted for $k = 1$ and $k = 128$. However, the shape of the functional relationship between $f(k,T)$ and T may look different for other pairs of stocks or different fitness functions used in the optimisation phase.

The models were tested on 10 randomly generated test sets in order to estimate the error reductions to be gained by using wavelet correlation models in place of linear techniques. Table 3 tabularises the reductions of the average hedging errors as in (14) and the total net hedging errors (see (16)) obtained by optimising the neural networks using two different fitness functions. The results have been averaged over 10 test sets. Models trained using the second fitness function offer a better overall reduction in the hedging errors compared with the first function. The second function has been specifically designed to minimise relative errors in comparison with linear models; it is insensitive to the magnitude of individual errors $|wavelet\ \ hedge_i|$. In the case of the first

Figure 7. A surface $w_k = f(k,T)$ reconstructed by neural networks for the stocks of IBM and DELL and used by static wavelet correlation models. T is the option maturity and k indexes wavelet coefficients d_k.

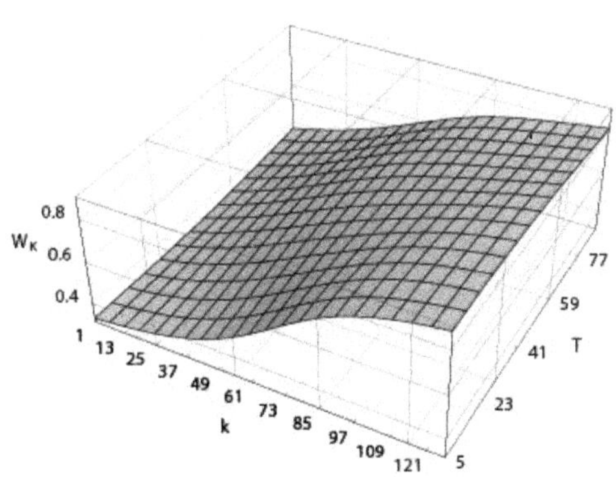

Figure 8. A surface $w_k = f(k,T)$ reconstructed by neural networks for the stocks of IBM and CAH and used by static wavelet correlation models. T is the option maturity and k indexes wavelet coefficients d_k.

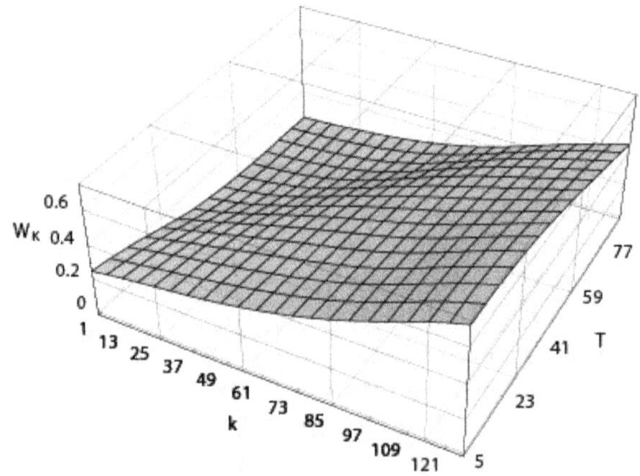

Figure 9. Plots of w_k for the first $k = 1$ (solid line) and the last $k = 128$ (dashed line) detail wavelet coefficient as a function of option maturity T for IBM and DELL

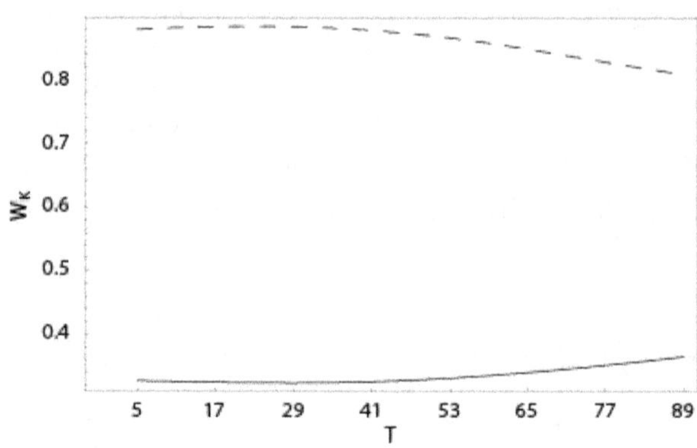

Table 3. Test set reductions of the total net hedging error (column 2) and the average hedging error (column 3) in comparison with a linear correlation measure

Stock pairs symbols (NYSE)	*Average reduction in closing account balances*	*Average reduction of hedging errors per contract*	*Fitness function*
IBM, DELL	20.00%	5.40%	$fitness_1$
IBM, CAH	51.00%	4.60%	$fitness_1$
IBM, DELL	56.00%	4.00%	$fitness_2$
IBM, CAH	58.00%	4.00%	$fitness_2$

fitness function the results may be skewed by unusually large hedging errors caused by static delta hedging. However, models trained with both fitness functions outperform standard linear techniques.

Dynamic Wavelet Correlation Models

The dynamic models examine correlations between wavelet features extracted from long price histories of the past 1,250 days. Initially they were trained using a full range of wavelet coefficients w_k, $k \in [1,M]$ for $M = 128$ with an additional auxiliary weight w_{M+1}. A visual inspection of the weights associated with each wavelet coefficient, as shown in Figure 10 for a pair of stocks of IBM and DELL, reveals that for most high-order wavelets (large k values) the corresponding weight w_k is an order of magnitude smaller than that of the first 5 or 10 low-order wavelet coefficients. The high-order coefficients could therefore be removed from (11) without losing too much of the information content, which will help reduce the computational complexity of the training process. Therefore, in the subsequent experiments with dynamic wavelet correlations, only the first five wavelet coefficients (one coarse and four detail coefficients) will be used together with an auxiliary weight w_{M+1}. Unlike the static wavelet models, the dynamic models process share price histories long enough to allow the use of the exponentially weighted moving average (RiskMetrics™) correlation coefficients for a comparison.

The surfaces $w_k = f(k, T)$ for pairs of companies IBM, CAH, and DELL, learned by neural networks optimised with the second fitness function (15), are shown in Figures 11 and 12. In both cases, $w_k(k,T)$ for $k = 6$ corresponds to the auxiliary weighting coefficient introduced in the equation (11) to help filter out spurious correlations. For shares of IBM and DELL, the last auxiliary weighting coefficient w_6 begins to rise for maturities T longer than 30 days as shown in Figure 13.

Its rise could be indicative of a gradual loss of predictive abilities of the wavelet coefficients used in the models for longer time horizons. It is interesting to note that for stocks of IBM and CAH the most dominant term in the surface $w_k(k,T)$, and therefore in the equation (11), is the last auxiliary term w_6. This would suggests that the training

Figure 10. A sample cross-section of $w_k(k,T)$ obtained for $T = 60$ for IBM and DELL.

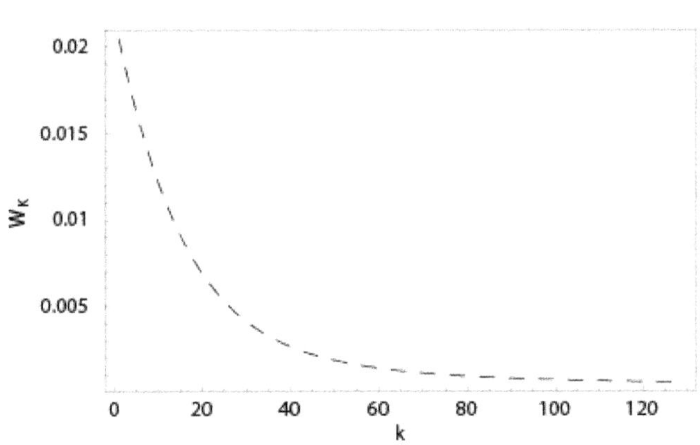

Figure 11. A surface $w_k = (k,T)$ reconstructed by neural networks for the stocks of IBM and DELL and used by dynamic wavelet correlation models. T is the option maturity and k indexes wavelet coefficients d_k.

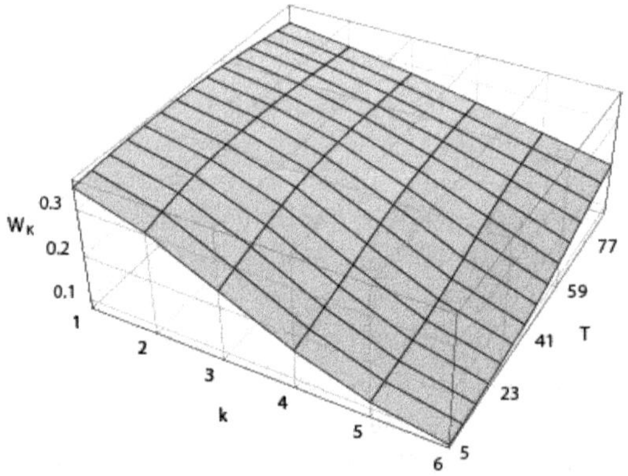

Figure 12. A surface $w_k = f(k,T)$ reconstructed by neural networks for the stocks of IBM and CAH and used by dynamic wavelet correlation models. T is the option maturity and k indexes wavelet coefficients d_k.

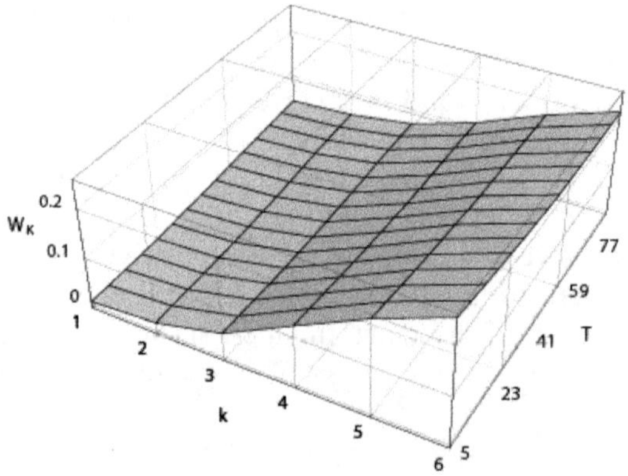

Figure 13. Plots of w_k for the first wavelet coefficient $k = 1$ (solid line) and the last auxiliary weight w_6 (dashed line) as a function of option maturity T for IBM and DELL.

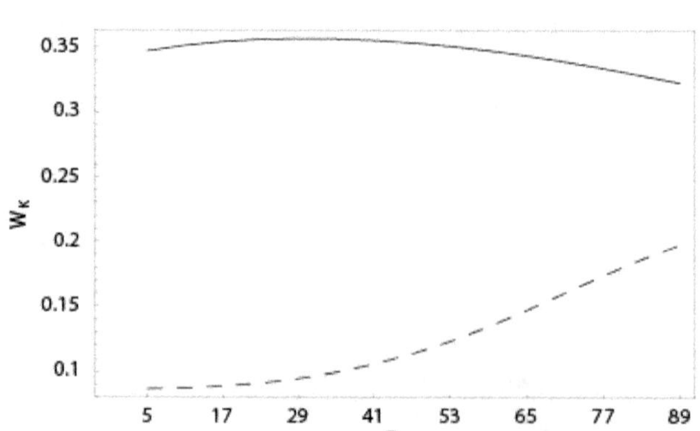

procedure has identified an overall weak underlying correlation between IBM and CAH, confirming the results obtained by the static wavelet correlation models. It is not surprising given the fact that IBM and CAH belong to two completely different sectors—technology and health care respectively.

The error reductions obtained by dynamic models are summarised in Table 4. The benchmark linear exponentially weighted moving average correlation (RiskMetrics™) given by (2) used the attrition rate $\lambda = 0.94$. When compared with static models, the dynamic ones offer bigger overall reductions in the net trading account closing balances although the average reductions in hedging errors per contract are somewhat smaller. The second fitness function offers a small improvement during the training process.

FURTHER RESEARCH

The wavelet models were so far demonstrated on two pairs of stocks: IBM vs. DELL and IBM vs. CAH. A wider study involving 11 other stocks was also carried out, with the results shown in Table 5. Although in most cases the net hedging errors were reduced, in once instance (NEM vs. PDG) the wavelet correlation models nearly doubled the risk. Further study of the failure modes of the models and of the confidence intervals on the outputs should be carried out. The models should also be evaluated within the context

Table 4. Test set reductions of the total net hedging error (column 2) and the average hedging error (column 3) in comparison with the RiskMetrics™ approach

Stock pairs symbols (NYSE)	***Average reduction in closing account balances***	***Average reduction of hedging errors per contract***	***Fitness function***
IBM, DELL	70.00%	6.40%	$fitness_1$
IBM, CAH	47.00%	2.60%	$fitness_1$
IBM, DELL	70.00%	3.70%	$fitness_2$
IBM, CAH	58.00%	2.40%	$fitness_2$

Table 5. Test set error reductions for six randomly selected pairs of stocks listed on the New York Stock Exchange belonging to the sector MATERIALS. Dynamic wavelet correlation models were trained with the second fitness function and compared with the RiskMetrics™ approach.

Stock pairs symbols (NYSE)	***Average reduction in closing account balances***	***Average reduction of hedging errors per contract***
DD, WY	59.00%	4.00%
DOW, PDG	12.00%	1.00%
NEM, PDG	-87.00%	-1.00%
HAN, VMC	10.00%	1.00%
PX, APD	62.00%	6.00%
GP, N	-2.00%	2.00%

of dynamic delta hedging. It would be interesting to see how much different the wavelet correlation coefficients would be under different options hedging regimes.

A completely different line of research could also be pursued based on a game theory. For example, correlation coefficients between two financial time series could be expressed in terms of temporal correlations between trading strategies arrived at by intelligent agents participating in minority games (Lamper, Howison, & Johnson, 2002).

CONCLUSION

On out-of-sample test sets static as well as dynamic wavelet correlation models have outperformed standard linear techniques used to estimate correlations between two financial assets. Of the two wavelet variants tried, the dynamic models offer bigger error reductions. They do so with fewer wavelets coefficients used in the computation but with significantly longer price histories required. In cases with only a limited amount of past data available, the static wavelet correlation models should be preferred. In all other cases the suggested approach would be to employ dynamic correlation models in place of traditional linear techniques. Operating in a wavelet feature space enables the models to separate the noise part from the signal components and learn which latent signal features should be used to estimate the underlying correlations between financial time series.

The added advantage of using predictive wavelet correlation models is their inherent ability to differentiate between the real underlying and accidental (spurious) correlations. The models do so through adapting the surface of weighting coefficients used to calculate correlation coefficients. This enables them to permanently suppress the signal features that give rise to unwanted correlations.

ACKNOWLEDGMENT

The authors would like to acknowledge the financial support received from Akita Prefectural University in Japan.

REFERENCES

Aussem, A., Campbell, J. G., & Murtagh, F. (1998). Wavelet-based feature extraction and decomposition strategies for financial forecasting. *Journal of Computational Intelligence in Finance, 6*(2), 5-12.

Capobianco, E. (2002). Multiresolution approximation for volatility processes. *Quantitative Finance, 2,* 91-110.

Chang, S. G., Yu, B., & Vetterli, M. (2000). Adaptive wavelet thresholding for image denoising and compression. *IEEE Transactions on Image Processing, 9,* 1532-1546.

Chui, C. K. (1992). *An Introduction to wavelets.* San Diego, CA: Academic Press.

Dempster, M. A. H., & Eswaran, A. (2000). Wavelets methods in PDE valuation of financial derivatives. *Proceedings of the 2nd International Conference of Intelligent Data Engineering and Automated Learning (IDEAL 2000, pp.* 215-238).

Donoho, D. L., & Johnstone, I. M. (1994). Ideal spatial adaptation by wavelet shrinkage. *Biometrika, 81,* 425-455.

Engle, R. & Mezrich, J. (1996). GARCH for groups. *Risk, 9*(8), 36-40.

Gençay, R., Selçuk, F., & Whitcher, B. (2001). *An introduction to wavelets and other filtering methods in finance and economics.* San Diego, CA: Academic Press.

Graps, A. (1995). An introduction to wavelets. *IEEE Computational Sciences and Engineering, 2*(2), 50-61.

Haykin, S. (1994). *Neural networks.* New York: Maxwell Macmillan.

Hazarika, N., & Lowe, D. (1997). Iterative time-series prediction and analysis by embedding and multiple time-scale decomposition networks. *Proceedings of SPIE, Applications and Science of Artificial Neural Networks,* (Vol. 3, pp. 94-104).

Holland, J. H. (1975). *Adaptation in natural and artificial systems.* Ann Arbor: University of Michigan Press.

Hull, J. C. (1997). *Options, futures and other derivatives* (3rd ed.). Englewood Cliffs, NJ: Prentice Hall International.

J. P. Morgan. (1996). *RiskMetrics™ technical document* (4th ed.). New York.

Lamper, D., Howison, S. & Johnson, N. F. (2002). Predictability of large future changes in a competitive evolving population. *Physical Review Letters, 88,* 017902.

Lowe, D. (2002). Information Fusion Applied to Selected Financial Problem Domains. *Multisensor Fusion (NATO Science Series), 70,* 749-764.

Mallat, S. (1998). *A wavelet tour of signal processing.* San Diego, CA: Academic Press.

McCulloch, W. S., & Pitts, W. (1943). A logical calculus of the ideas immanent in nervous activity. *Bulletin of Mathematical Biophysics, 5,* 115-133.

Murtagh, F., Zheng, G., Campbell, J. G., & Starck, J. L. (1999). Multiscale transforms for filtering financial data streams. *Journal of Computational Intelligence in Finance, 7,* 18-35.

Percival, D. B., & Walden, A. T. (2000). *Wavelet methods for time series analysis.* Cambridge University Press.

Rosenblatt, F. (1962). *Principles of neurodynamics.* New York: Spartan Books.

Rumelhart, D. E., Hinton, G. E., & Williams, R. J. (1986). Learning internal representations by error propagation. *Parallel distributed processing: Exploration in the microstructure of cognition, 1*(8). MIT Press.

Struzik, Z., & Siebes, A. (1999). The Haar wavelet transform in the time series similarity paradigm. *Proceedings of the 3rd European Conference on Principles and Practice of Knowledge Discovery in Databases* (pp. 12-22).

Werbos, P. J. (1974). *Beyond regression: New tools for prediction and analysis in the behavioral sciences.* Doctoral dissertation, Harvard University, Boston.

Widrow, B. (1962). Generalization and information storage in networks of adaline "neurons." *Self-organizing systems* (pp. 435-461). New York: Spartan Books.

Zapart, C. (2002). Stochastic volatility options pricing with wavelets and artificial neural networks. *Quantitative Finance, 2*(6), 487-495.

Zapart, C. (2003a). Application of the wavelet correlation measure in computational finance. *Proceedings of the 3rd International Workshop on Computational Intelligence in Economics and Finance* (CIEF'2003, pp. 1080-1083).

Zapart, C. (2003b). Beyond Black-Scholes: A neural networks-based approach to options pricing. *International Journal of Theoretical and Applied Finance, 6*(5), 469-489.

Zapart, C. (2004). Long-short trading with optimum wavelet correlation measures. *Proceedings of the 2nd IASTED International Conference on Financial Engineering and Applications (FEA 2004)* (pp. 239-248). Cambridge, MA: MIT.

Zapart, C., & Lowe, D. (1988). Non-linear iterated forecasting.

ENDNOTES

1 In recent years, advances in the field of econophysics have begun to challenge successfully the Random Walk Theory. The new Minority Game Theory can recreate many features of financial time series better than the standard approach and it has even been used to make predictions about future large changes in prices of financial assets (Lamper et al., 2002).

2 Options with an expiry price set close to the current price of the underlying instrument (a single stock or a portfolio).

APPENDIX A. ARTIFICIAL NEURAL NETWORKS

The concept of modeling data with artificial neural networks inspired by biological systems is not new (Haykin, 1994). A human brain is capable of large-scale information processing and computation to perform such complex tasks as pattern recognition (speech and vision) or mathematical model formulation (trying to catch a falling ball). Although early research into neural networks date back to the first part of the 20th century (McCulloch & Pitts, 1943), real breakthroughs in adapting biological systems to perform computer calculations were made in the 1960s: Rosenblatt's perceptrons (Rosenblatt, 1962) and Widrow's madalines (Widrow, 1962)). Their pioneering work on multilayer perceptrons was followed by the introduction of a new training algorithm—the error back-propagation—in 1974 (Werbos, 1974), which was rediscovered and popularised in the context of artificial neural networks by Rumelhart et al. in 1986 (Rumelhart, Hinton, & Williams, 1986).

In the late 1980s and throughout the 1990s, the field of neural networks underwent a renaissance, with a wide adoption of an efficient error back-propagation training algorithm. Artificial neural networks are an example of nonparametric models: they derive from training data sets not only the values for the free parameters but also the type and shape of the underlying (nonlinear) functional relationship between the inputs and outputs. In standard linear modeling the underlying model is imposed a priori by the use of a linear type of the input–output function. Only the free parameters of the linear function are obtained through the process of linear regression fitting. In contrast to linear models neural networks are universal approximators (Haykin, 1994). They can approximate arbitrary nonlinear mappings, which are discovered during the training process using, for example, the aforementioned error back-propagation algorithm. Artificial neural networks attempt to mimic the way human brains work, by employing a network of individual neurons, all working in parallel, and all making a partial contribution to the final solution to a given task, be it pattern recognition (speech and vision) or controlling the latest aircraft.

Illustration A shows one type of the neural network that has been often used in practical applications: the multilayer perceptron (MLP). In multilayer perceptron networks neurons are typically organised in at least three layers. The input layer does not perform any computation and simply passes its inputs to the subsequent hidden layers, which may contain any number of computational units (neurons).

Although multilayer perceptrons can employ more than one hidden layer, a single hidden layer is sufficient to satisfy the universal approximation theorem (Haykin, 1994). The output layer computes and returns the desired output values. Each neuron performs basic summation and transformation operations given by (A.1):

$$y = f\left(\sum_{i=1}^{N} w_i x_i + c\right) \tag{A.1}$$

where N is the number of inputs to a particular neuron, x_i is the value of the ith input, w_i is the weight (connection strength) to the ith input, c is an offset (a so-called bias), y is the neuron output and $f(x)$ is a so-called activation function. Neurons are independent of each other and have their own sets of weights and a bias. The information flows from the inputs through the hidden layers to the output layer. At each stage the neurons perform their calculations according to (A.1), with their inputs being taken either directly from the input layer (depicted as squares in the illustration A) or from the outputs of neurons in the preceding layers. Typically the hidden layers use a nonlinear sigmoid

Illustration A. The multilayer perceptron artificial neural network with an input layer, two hidden layers and an output layer. The squares denote the inputs and the circles represent individual neurons.

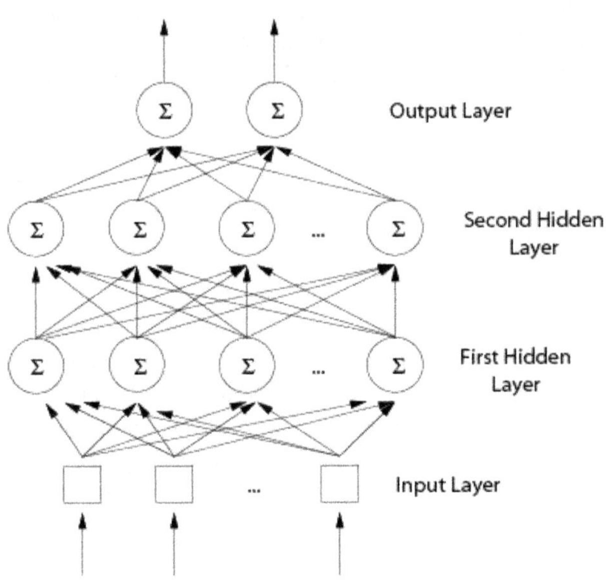

activation function, for example $f(x) = \tanh(x)$. The output layer may consist of either linear neurons $f(x)=x$ or the same nonlinear units with sigmoid activation functions. The choice of which output neurons should be used is application-specific. It depends on the type of outputs and a range of output values found in the data sets.

A neural network can be fully described by its free parameters (the weights w_i and biases c) and the type of the activation functions used. Training it to perform a given task can be reduced to finding an optimum set of the free parameters that is appropriate for a given task. Multilayer perceptrons are typically trained in a supervised learning mode: the target output values for any given input data set are known in advance. If a given training data set consists of M samples, with $t_{i,k}$ denoting the kth target output value for the ith input vector and $o_{i,k}$ the actual output from k^{th} neuron in the output layer, the supervised training process will attempt to minimise the following *sum-of-squared errors* measure:

$$E = \frac{1}{2}\sum_{i=1}^{M}\sum_{k=1}^{N}\left(t_{i,k} - o_{i,k}\right)^2 \qquad \text{(A.2)}$$

where N denotes the number of neurons in the output layer and the outputs $o_{i,k}$ are obtained by presenting the neural network with input vectors and propagating this information forward by applying (A.1) to the successive layers/neurons. Standard optimisation techniques like the Least Mean Squares (LMS) and their variants (for example conjugate gradients) can be applied to find a set of network coefficients (weights and biases) minimising the error surface given by (A.2). Alternatively, evolutionary programming methods such as genetic algorithms can also be applied to the search for optimum network parameters.

APPENDIX B. GENETIC ALGORITHMS

The early 1990s experienced a marked revival in research interest in genetic algorithms (GAs, evolutionary programming methods), which date back to Holland's pioneering computer experiments in the 1970s (Holland, 1975). Researchers discovered that they could apply the GAs with a reasonable success to a fast-growing field of artificial neural networks.

Given an appropriate cost function (a measure of fitness), through evolution and natural selection genetic algorithms perform a stochastic search in the space of parameters (DNA) to find a near-optimum string of chromosomes that optimises the search criteria. The free parameters of neural networks are specially encoded in binary strings consisting of zeroes and ones that represent genes on a chromosome. A large population of networks is initialised with random DNA strings (chromosomes). This artificial population is iterated a number of steps until the stopping criterion is satisfied (i.e., the best individuals are able to solve a given problem satisfactorily). At each step, chromosomes with the best fitness scores are given a chance to reproduce by exchanging genes with other, less successful individuals. Their offspring replace the weakest members of the population. Occasional random mutations ensure that enough diversity is maintained and the population as a whole is able to explore new areas in the parameters space. Although it is often a slow process, the advantage of GAs over conventional methods is their inherent ability to escape local minima in the error surface.

Chapter III

Influence Diagram for Investment Portfolio Selection

Chui-Che Tseng
Texas A&M University, USA

ABSTRACT

The goal of an artificial intelligence decision support system is to provide the human user with an optimized decision recommendation when operating under uncertainty in complex environments. The particular focus of our discussion is the investment domain—the goal of investment decision making is to select an optimal portfolio that satisfies the investor's objective or, in other words, to maximize the investment returns under the constraints given by investors. The investment domain contains numerous and diverse information sources, such as expert opinions, news releases, economic figures and so on. This presents the potential for better decision support but also poses the challenge of building a decision support agent for selecting, accessing, filtering, evaluating and incorporating information from different sources, and for making final investment recommendations. In this study we use an artificial intelligence system called influence diagram for portfolio selection. We found that the system outperform human portfolio managers and the market in the year of 1998 to 2002.

INTRODUCTION

Twenty years ago, most people had very little daily exposure to the investment world. Perhaps the only reminder was hearing a 10-second announcement on the radio about the fortunes of the Dow Jones Industrial Average that day. Today, radio, TV and the exponential growth of the Internet have created many sites specializing in business and investment coverage. An investment is simply any vehicle into which funds can be placed with the expectation that they will generate positive income or that their value will be preserved or increased. There are different types of investments; they can be categorized based on the following:

- **Securities or Property:** Investments that represent evidence of debt or ownership or the legal right to acquire or sell an ownership interest are called securities. The most common types are stocks, bonds, and options. Property, on the other hand, consists of investments in real property or tangible personal property.
- **Direct or Indirect:** Direct investment is one in which the investor purchases stocks, bonds, homes or precise metals. Indirect investment is when the investor purchases a mutual fund.
- **Debt, Equity or Derivative Securities:** Debt is like a bond in which you lend money to the issuer. Equity represents ongoing ownership in a specific business or property; the most popular type is common stock. Derivative securities are those in which the investments derive their value from an underlying security or asset. Options are an example of derivative securities.
- **Low or High Risk:** Investments can sometimes be differentiated based on risk.
- **Short or Long Term:** The life of an investment can be described as either short or long term. Short term typically matures within a year, whereas long terms are those with longer maturities.
- **Domestic or Foreign:** Investment can be made on either the domestic markets or the international markets.

The investment process is the mechanism for bringing together suppliers of extra funds with demanders who needs funds. The investment process adapted from Gitman and Joehnk (1998) is shown in Figure 1. In the diagram, financial institutions are organizations that channel the savings of governments, business, and individuals into loans or investments, and financial markets are forums in which suppliers and demanders of the funds make financial transactions. The ultimate goal of an investor is an efficient portfolio, one that provides the highest return for a given level of risk or that has the lowest risk for a given level of return. With today's market and investment environment, an investor has to consider a lot of internal and external factors as well as numerous financial information. The investment process has become a complex and computationally demanding task for a human to perform. Thus, it provided a motivation to develop a decision support system that will aid the investor in pursuit of their wealth.

The investment domain, like many other domains, is a dynamically changing, stochastic, and unpredictable environment. Take the stock market as an example; there are more than 2,000 stocks available for a portfolio manager or individual investor to select. This posts a problem of filtering all those available stocks to find the ones that

Figure 1. The investment process

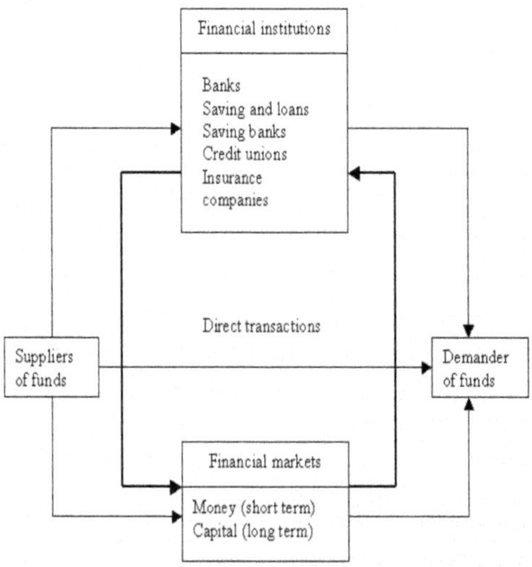

are worth investment. There are also vast amounts of information available that will affect the market to some degree.

These problems motivate us to investigate ways for equipping our system with decision support mechanisms to be applicable in complex situations. The decision support system is to provide the investor with the best decision support under time constraints. For this purpose, we propose a system that uses the Influence Diagram as the framework to create a system that will provide the user with decision recommendations.

RELATED WORK

We explored the way to reduce the complexity of the investment decision deliberation that might cause the investor to lose money under urgent situations, and, at the same time, to provide the highest quality investment recommendations possible.

For portfolio management, there is related work by Sycara and Decker (1997) that focused on using distributed agents to manage investment portfolios. Their system deployed a group of agents with different functionality and coordinated them under case-based situations. They modeled the user, task and situation as different cases, so their system activated the distributed agents for information gathering, filtering and processing based on the given case. Their approach mainly focused on portfolio monitoring issues and has no mechanism to deal with uncertainty. Our system, on the other hand, reacts to the real-time market situation and gathers the relevant information as needed. Other related research on portfolio selection problems has received considerable attention in both financial and statistics literature (Cover, 1991; Cover & Gluss, 1986).

In the field of model refinement, there are several approaches. The value of modeling was first addressed by Watson and Brown (1978) and Nickerson and Boyd (1980). Chang and Fung (1990) considered the problem of dynamically refining and coarsening the state variables in Bayesian networks. However, the value and cost of performing the operations were not addressed. Control of reasoning and rational decision making under resource constraints, using analyses of the expected value of computation and consideration of decisions on the use of alternative strategies and allocations of effort, has been explored by Horvitz and Barry (1995) and Russell and Wefald (1991). Poh and Horvitz (1993) explored the concept of expected value of refinement and applied it to structural, conceptual and quantitative refinements. Their work concentrated on providing a computational method for the criteria to perform the refinement. However, their work did not address the need of a guided algorithm to perform the node refinement throughout the network. In our work, we used a guided method to perform the conceptual refinement for our model. We see significant performance improvement of the model after applying the refinement algorithm.

BAYESIAN THEORY

The natural reaction for a decision maker to have when making a decision under uncertainty is to remove the uncertainty by finding the true state of the problem. In other words, the decision maker is to choose among actions (a_1, a_2,...a_n) when one of the uncertain events (e_1, e_2, ...,e_n) is found out for certain. If the uncertain event is found to be e_k; then the decision maker need only consider the consequences (c_{1k}, c_{2k}, ...,c_{nk}) and select the action/consequence pair with the highest value. This is certainly one way to solve the decision maker's problem, but unfortunately, it is rarely practical. In most domains, the uncertain event refers to the future and the decision has to be made now, so there is no means of ascertaining the correct event. It may not be possible to remove all the uncertainty for the problem domain but it may be feasible to reduce it by obtaining relevant information.

The decision maker has the initial probabilities $p(e_1)$, $p(e_2)$, ... $p(e_n)$, representing the uncertainty of the events. If the decision maker obtains complete information then one of the probabilities will go to one and the remainder will go to zero. Partial information will produce a less significant change. If X denotes the additional information, the revised values will be $p(e_1|X)$, $p(e_2|X)$, ... $p(e_n|X)$. To relate the probabilities $p(e_j)$, the prior probabilities, available before the additional information is obtained and the $p(e_j|X)$, the posterior probabilities, after the additional information is collected, we apply the Bayes theorem. Bayes theorem combines prior probabilities with the likelihood probabilities to obtain the posterior probabilities. The theorem says that, for any two events E and F, E not having probability zero,

$$p(F \mid E) = \frac{p(E \mid F)p(F)}{p(E)} \tag{3.1}$$

where

$$p(E) = p(E \mid F) \times p(F) + p(E \mid \neg F) \times p(\neg F). \tag{3.2}$$

In the decisio- making context replace the event F by e_j and E by the additional information X. Bayes theorem then reads

$$p(e_j \mid X) = \frac{p(X \mid e_j)p(e_j)}{p(X)}, \tag{3.3}$$

immediately relating the $p(e_j|X)$ and $p(e_j)$. The $p(X|e_j)$ in the formula is the likelihood of e_j, it represents the probability of additional information conditioned on the event. Using a stock investor example, an investor is trying to invest in a stock, and he feels it is worth while to obtain expert advice on the subject before reaching a decision. Given the investor has no information about the stock movement, we have $p(e_1) = 0.5$, where e_1 denotes the stock appreciation and $p(e_2) = 0.5$, where e_2 denotes the stock depreciation. Let X denote the stockbroker's opinion that the stock will appreciate. We want to find out the $p(e_1|X)$, the chance of appreciation given the expert advice. Let

$$p(X|e1) = 0.8$$

$$p(X|e2) = 0.4$$

be the likelihood, where $p(X|e1)$ is the probability that the expert predicts the stock will appreciate given that the stock appreciates and $p(X|e2)$ is the probability the expert predicts it will appreciate given the stock depreciates. These probabilities represent the predicting accuracy of the expert, which can be obtained from the historical data on expert's recommendations. Using Bayes theorem, we get

$$p(e1 \mid X) = \frac{p(X \mid e_1)p(e_1)}{p(X)} = \frac{p(X \mid e_1)p(e_1)}{p(X \mid e_1) \times p(e_1) + p(X \mid e_2) \times p(e_2)}$$

$$= \frac{0.8 \times 0.5}{(0.8 \times 0.5) + (0.4 \times 0.5)} = \frac{0.4}{0.6} = 0.67,$$

meaning that when the expert predicts that the stock will appreciate it has the probability of 0.67 that the stock will actually appreciate. It is better than the investor's current information of the probability of 0.5 that the stock will appreciate. Thus, it is worth consulting the expert and the investor can follow the expert's advice to purchase the stock.

Bayes theorem can be stated as follows: The posterior probability is proportional to the prior probability multiplied by the likelihood. It is inadvisable to attach probabilities of zero to uncertain events, for if the prior probability is zero so is the posterior, whatever the data are. In other words, if a decision maker thinks something cannot be true and interprets this to mean it has zero probability, then the decision maker will never be influenced by any new incoming information. A probability of one is equally dangerous because then the probability of the $\overline{E}$ will be zero. So a Bayesian never believes in anything absolutely and leaves some room for doubt. Here are four extreme cases on the priors and likelihood to avoid: (a) Uniform priors: This represents a no information model, then the posterior probabilities are proportional to the likelihood. (b) Extreme priors: These are the cases we previously mentioned. In these cases the likelihood does not matter and the posterior probabilities will equal the prior probabilities. (c) Uniform likelihood: If all the likelihoods are the same, then the posterior probabilities are equal to the prior probabilities. (d) Extreme likelihood: If the likelihood is zero or one, then the posterior probabilities are equal to the likelihood.

INFLUENCE DIAGRAM

An influence diagram is a special type of Bayesian network (see Figure 2), one that contains the decision node and the utility node to provide a decision recommendation from the model. Influence diagrams are directed acyclic graphs with three types of nodes—chance nodes, decision nodes, and utility nodes. Chance nodes, usually shown as ovals, represent random variables in the environment. Decision nodes, usually shown as squares, represent the choices available to the decision maker. Utility nodes, usually shown as a diamond or flattened hexagon shape, represent the usefulness of the consequences of the decisions measured on a numerical utility scale. The arcs in the graph have different meanings based on their destinations. Dependency arcs are the arcs that point to utility or chance nodes representing probability or functional dependence. Informational arcs are the arcs that point to the decision nodes implying that the pointing nodes will be known to the decision maker before the decision is made.

When using an influence diagram for decision-support problems, there are some fundamental characteristics of the influence diagram that one must take into consideration. These characteristics influence the data requirements and the choice of the appropriate influence method. The first characteristic is the granularity of the values for each node. This characteristic affects the memory requirement for storing the probabili-

Figure 2. A simple influence diagram

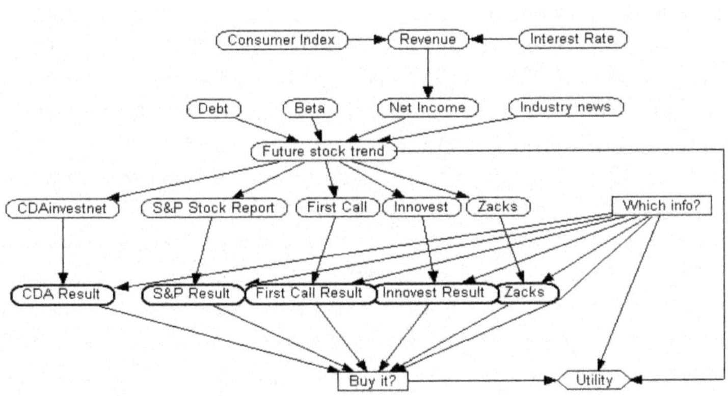

ties and the computational time required for updating the probabilities. The more values within each node, the larger the memory required and the longer it will take to propagate the probability update. The second characteristic is the integration of the user's preference into the utility node. This characteristic will affect the decision outcome of the model. Given different preferences among users, the model might return a different decision recommendation. Another issue of this characteristic is how to model the user's preference into a set of values for the utility node. Different fields of research have suggested different approaches for this problem. Some suggest learning from the user's behavior, others suggest obtaining data from a user survey, and still others simply query the expert and assign subjective values.

The third characteristic to consider is the availability of the knowledge about the structure, probabilistic knowledge for the prior and the conditional probabilities. There are many variables in a specific problem domain and there might exist several concepts in the problem domain that are observationally equivalent, which means they are not distinguishable even with infinite data. To find out which of those are relevant to the problem and the casual relationships among them presents a challenge to the knowledge engineer. There has been much research and many tools devoted to the learning of the model structure from the data. For the probability distribution for the node, there are two methods to obtain the probabilities. First, the probability distributions can be based on frequency by obtaining the data from gathered statistics. The second method is to obtain the probability distributions through knowledge acquisition sessions from the domain experts, who convey their subjective beliefs. In both cases, the probabilities can be refined through a feedback mechanism. Finally, the size, topology and connectivity of the model should also be considered. Applying good knowledge engineering techniques (Laskey & Mahoney, 1997) throughout the construction of the model will help keep the network manageable.

Inference Methods

Influence is the computation of results to queries with respect to a given network in the presence of given evidence. In general, Bayesian networks can be used to compute the probability distribution for any subset of network variables given the values or distributions for any subset of the remaining variables. However, exact inference of probabilities in general for an arbitrary Bayesian network is known to be NP-hard. Topology is the main cause for complexity in the exact inference. The approximate inference of probabilities is also NP-hard. The main sources of the complexity in this case are the low likelihood of evidence and functional relationships. Howard and Matheson (1984) suggested a method consisting of converting the influence diagram to a decision tree and solving for the optimal policy within the tree, using the exp-max labeling process. The disadvantage of this method is the enormous space required to store the tree. Pearl (1997) suggested a hybrid method using branch and bound techniques to prune the search space of the converted decision tree from the influence diagram. The disadvantage of this method is the trading off time for space, so it will require more time to obtain the optimal policy. There are several other major techniques for model influence, adapted from D'Ambrosio and Fung (1994), which are shown in Figure 3.

Our system uses the graphic reduction method for the inference process, which is implemented in the Netica package. Another popular Bayesian network package is

Figure 3. Influence algorithms for the Bayesian network

- **Exact Algorithms**
  - Joint Computation
  - Simple Bayes
  - Graphic Reduction
  - Polytree Algorithm
  - Clustering
  - Symbolic Probabilistic Inference
  - Cutset Conditioning
  - QuickScore
  - Recursive Decomposition
  - Potential ID
  - Vegas
- **Approximate Algorithms**
  - Forward Sampling
  - Stochastic Simulation
  - BNRAS
  - Top N
  - Term Computation
  - Poole
  - Backward Sampling

Hugin, which implements a variation of the clustering algorithm. We briefly examine these methods and an approximate method in the following sections.

Shachter and Poet (1989) show that any probabilistic or decision-theoretic query can be represented as a subnet of the network; by reducing the network to that subnet, we can find the answer to the query. This algorithm consists of eliminating nodes from the diagram through a series of value preserving transformations. Each transformation leaves the expected utility intact, and at every step, the modified graph is still an influence diagram. There are four operations for this algorithm, namely arc reversal, barren node removal, conditional expectation and maximization. Here are the descriptions of each operation:

1. **Arc Reversal:** If there is an arc (x,y) between chance node x and y, but no other direct path from x to y. Then this arc can be reversed to (y,x) to transform the diagram in order to compute the probabilities for x and y using Bayes rule.
2. **Barren Node Removal:** Barren nodes are the chance or decision nodes without successors. These can be removed from the diagram because their values do not affect other nodes.
3. **Conditional Expectation:** A chance node preceding the value node can be removed.
4. **Maximization:** Once all the barren nodes are removed, the decision node that directly precedes the value node can be removed by maximizing the expected utility. Shachter proved that the transformation does not affect the optimal decision policy and the expected value of the optimal policy. However, it still requires a large amount of space to support the transformation steps.

Learning Methods

It is assumed thus far that the structure and the conditional probabilities necessary for characterizing the network were provided externally by a domain expert or an intelligent agent capable of encoding real-world experience in such terms. This section deals with the problem of constructing a network automatically from observations, thus bypassing the human link in the knowledge acquisition process. The learning task of the Bayesian network is separated into two subtasks: learning the numeric parameters (conditional probabilities) for a given network topology and learning the structure of the network topology. Combining the two subtasks with complete and incomplete observation data, the learning task of the Bayesian network is divided into four categories.

Known Structure, Complete Data

This is the category when the structure of the network is known and the observation data is complete. Complete data means there is no missing data in the observation. The goal here is to learn the parameter by using statistical parameter estimation.

Known Structure, Incomplete Data

Observed data from the real-world applications are often incomplete. This scenario happens when there are missing values and hidden values in the observed data. An example of missing values is medical records for patients since not all patients undergo every possible test, therefore there are bound to be some missing values in the records. Hidden values are the ones that are never observed. One of the algorithms used for this type of learning is the gradient ascent algorithm proposed by Binder, Koller, Russell and Kanazawa (1997).

Unknown Structure, Complete Data

The goal of learning the structure of the Bayesian is to find a good network that is representative of the observed data. The operations include adding, reversing and deleting edges to search over the space of the network structures. For each candidate network, fill the parameters using the algorithm described in the above categories and evaluate the network using the scoring function. Cooper and Herskovits (1992) present a Bayesian scoring metric for choosing among alternative networks. They also present a heuristic search algorithm called K2 for learning network structure when the data is observable.

Unknown Structure, Incomplete Data

Given the complexity of the problem, this is the hardest learning case of all four categories and it is still under investigation by researchers. One of the algorithms proposed by Friedman (1998) is the Structural EM algorithm.

MODEL REFINEMENT

Any model is inevitably a simplification of what the expert knows, which is itself a simplification of the real-world problem. The essential issue is to decide which variables and relationships are important and which can be omitted or are redundant. The structure

Figure 4. The four categories of Bayesian learning

The four categories of learning
- Known structure, complete data.
- Known structure, incomplete data.
- Unknown structure, complete data.
- Unknown structure, incomplete data.

of the diagram was constructed by consulting with the domain expert. After several interviews with the domain expert, we came up with the portfolio selection model shown in Figure 3. We then applied the heuristic guided refinement algorithm (Tseng, Gmytrasiewicz & Ching, 2001) that we developed to the system. The algorithm uses mutual information as a guide to refine the model in order to increase the model's performance.

In our decision model, the probabilities are learned from historic financial data and the structure of our network is built by consulting with a financial expert on portfolio selection. In order to improve the influence model, there are three types of refinement that we can perform on it: (1) quantitative, (2) conceptual and (3) structural. Our system focuses on the method of conceptual refinement by using the mutual information and expected utility of refinement as our criteria to improve our model.

Mutual information (Shannon & Weaver, 1949) is one of the most commonly used measures for ranking information sources. Here we apply this to our nodes in the network in order to provide guidance for refinement. Mutual information is based on the assumption that the uncertainty regarding any variable X represented by a probability distribution P(x) can be represented by the entropy function.

$$H(X) = -\sum_{x} P(x) \log P(x) \tag{5.1}$$

Assume that the target hypothesis is H and we want to know the uncertainty of H given that X is instantiated to x, which can be written as

$$H(H|x) = -\sum_{h} P(h \mid x) \log P(h \mid x), \tag{5.2}$$

summing over all the possible outcomes of x, we get

$$H(H|X) = -\sum_{x} \sum_{h} P(h \mid x) \log P(h \mid x) \tag{5.3}$$

where x, h are the possible values of the variable X and hypothesis H.

Figure 5. Influence diagram structure for stock portfolio selection

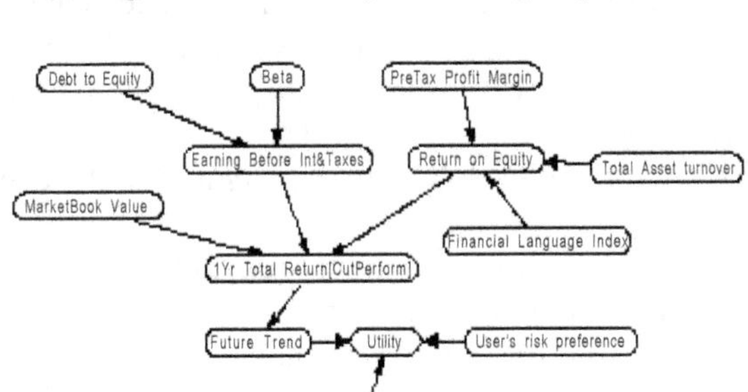

Then when we subtract H(H|X) from the original uncertainty in H prior to consulting X H(H), we can obtain the uncertainty reduction of H given X. This reduction is called Shannon's mutual information.

$$(H|X) = H(H) - H(H|X) = -\sum_{x}\sum_{h} P(h,x)\log\frac{P(h,x)}{P(h)P(x)} \tag{5.4}$$

The value of refinement is defined as the difference between the model performance before and after the refinement. The performance of the model is measured by the average expected utility of the model run on the test cases. The current model performance MP(C) is represented as:

$$MP(C) = avg_n \sum_{n} EU(a \mid x_n, C) \tag{5.5}$$

where x_n is the test case input to the model.

The performance of the model after the refinement MP(R) is represented as:

$$MP(R) = avg_n \sum_{n} EU(a \mid x_n, R) \tag{5.6}$$

Then the value of the refinement VR is:

$$VR = MP(R) - MP(C) \tag{5.7}$$

We applied the value of refinement to increase the values in the nodes and to increase the number of nodes in the decision model.

Once the initial diagram was constructed, the next stage was to define the number of values for each variable. Most of the variables are continuous, but all were modeled as discrete. For the first prototype, we modeled the diagram as simply as possible, and each value of each variable was carefully defined. For example, the beta value was defined as two values each representing two ranges of beta values. Such explicit definitions are necessary to avoid ambiguity when assessing conditional probabilities.

For model refinement purpose, our model uses the S&P 500 index companies as our target. We trained our network on the 1987 to 1996 financial data we obtained from the CompuStat and tested it on 1997 data. Our performance metric is the average expected utilities from the companies that our model selected. We applied the refinement algorithm to only the financial factor change nodes (beta, ROE, etc.), the risk tolerance remains unchanged for this experiment. The target node is the outperform node in our network. The actual refinement part of our network is shown in Figure 6 and the refinement results are shown in Figure 7.

After the model construction and refinement process finish the final network will contain all the information needed for the influence process. All the conditional probability tables are filled based on the historic data, here is one of the conditional probability tables (see Figure 8) showing the relationship among the "beta" node, the

Figure 6. The nodes that apply to the refinement algorithm

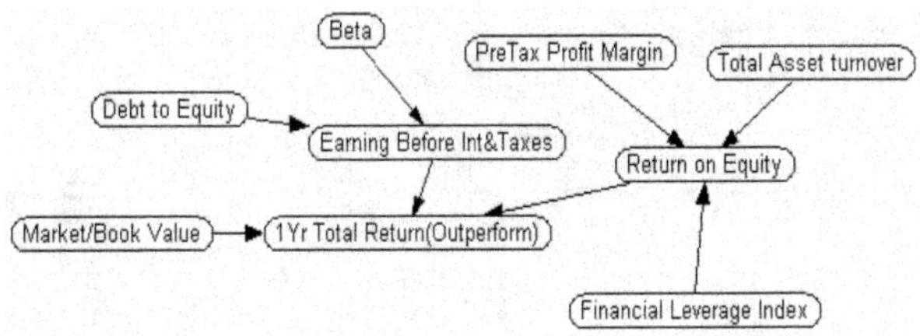

Figure 7. Model performance increases with the refinement steps

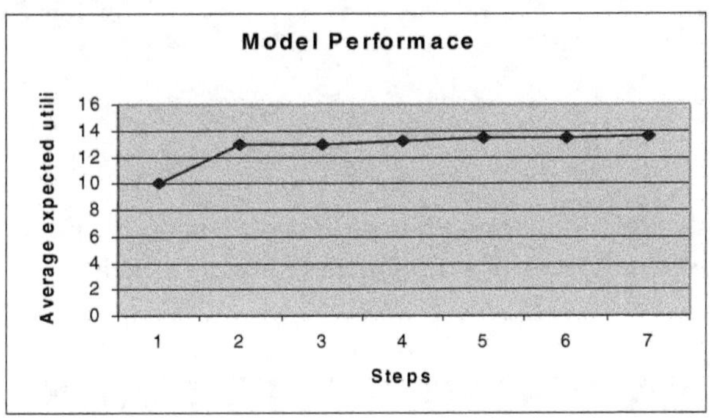

Figure 8. Conditional probability table for the node "earning before interest and taxes"

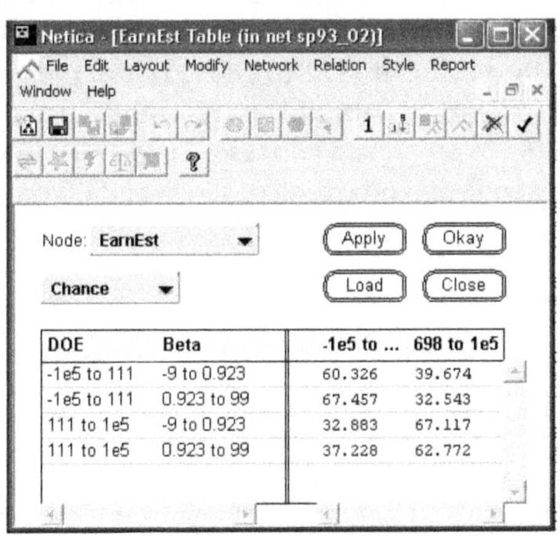

DOE	Beta	-1e5 to ...	698 to 1e5
-1e5 to 111	-9 to 0.923	60.326	39.674
-1e5 to 111	0.923 to 99	67.457	32.543
111 to 1e5	-9 to 0.923	32.883	67.117
111 to 1e5	0.923 to 99	37.228	62.772

Figure 9. Influence diagram shown with prior probabilities for each node

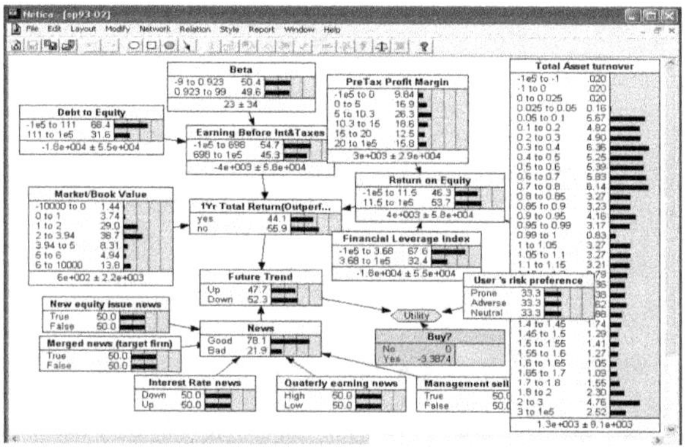

"debt to equity" node and the "earning before interest and taxes" node. And the network is shown in Figure 9 with the prior probabilities shown in each node.

EXPERIMENT SETTINGS

Our model of the investment domain consists of a number of stocks for the investor to construct an investment portfolio. The goal is to maximize the profit from the investment portfolio. The experiments are written in C++ and built on top of the Netica Belief network package, running on a LINUX platform.

In the experiments we ran, we selected eight financial ratio data from the S&P 500 companies as the input factors to the system. The training data is collected from the Compustat database from the period of 1988 to 2001. To test the performance, we trained the system with previous 10 years of data and test it for the current year, for example, we trained the system with 1988 to 1997 data and tested it with 1998 data and let the system made the decision recommendation on which of the S&P 500 companies to be included in the investment portfolio. We tested the system on 1998 to 2002 data.

Table 1. Performance comparison

	Our system	Market SP500	Vanguard Index 500	Fidelity Spartan 500
1998	40.59%	28.58%	28.62%	28.48%
1999	60.07%	21.04%	21.07%	20.65%
2000	22.03%	-9.10%	-9.06%	-9.13%
2001	4.61%	-11.89%	-12.02%	-12.05%
2002	-10.23%	-22.10%	-22.15%	-22.17%

RESULTS

We used the 1-year total returns as our criteria to evaluate the portfolio performance. Our system will select among S&P 500 companies and use the average 1-year total return as the performance metric of our portfolio. On the 1998 to 2002 testing data, our system outperforms major index funds and the market for each year (see the results summaries in Table 1).

The results in Table 1 show that our system has significant advantage over major index funds and the market itself.

CONCLUSION

We conducted some performance analysis with our systems. Our system outperforms the leading mutual fund by a significant margin in 1998 to 2002.

Our decision support system uses the influence diagram as the decision model; the structural information of the influence diagram plays an important role on the performance of our system. We obtained the structural information from the domain expert and the information represents what the expert's opinion on the causal relationships among the nodes.

Given our analysis, we could conclude that by using an artificial intelligence system for portfolio selection has performance edge over the human portfolio manager and the market. The systems we selected for this study are only one among numerous artificial intelligence systems available. We would like to conduct further study to better qualify and quantify various artificial intelligence systems for use in the portfolio selection domain.

FUTURE RESEARCH

Currently we are working on a system based on the work done in this chapter, which will provide real time decision support with external information gathering capabilities. The system is resided on an object-oriented Bayesian knowledge base framework, allowing the system to create influence diagram on the fly and with different levels of detail. This will allow the system to react to the time critical constraint environment and reducing the computational time as needed.

We are also working on external information gathering and filtering portion of the system that will enable the system to incorporate external information such as online expert opinions, news releases and so on, into the system to provide better decision support. The value of information has been use in the current system, there are several methods for determining the information value, and we will investigate those. For the model refinement issues on the influence diagram, we are investigating other methods in order to increase the system's performance.

REFERENCES

Binder, J., Koller, D., Russell, S., & Kanazawa. K. (1997). Adaptive probabilistic networks with hidden variables. *Machine Learning, 29,* 213-244.

Cooper, G., & Herskovits, E. (1992). A Bayesian method for the induction of probabilistic networks from data. *Machine Learning, 9,* 309-347.

Cover, T. M. (1991). Universal portfolios. *Mathematical Finance, 1,* 1-29.

Cover, T. M., & Gluss, D. H. (1986). Empirical Bayes stock market portfolios. *Advances in Applied Mathematics, 7,* 170-181.

Chang, K. C., & Fung, R. (1990). Refinement and coarsening of Bayesian networks. *Proceedings of the 6th Conference on Uncertainty in Artificial Intelligence* (pp. 475-482). Cambridge, MA.

D'Ambrosio, D., & Fung, R. (1994). *Inference in Bayes nets.* Summer Institute on Probability in AI. Corvallis, OR.

Friedman, N. (1998). The Bayesian structural EM algorithm. *Proceedings of the 15th International Conference on Machine Learning.* Madison, WI.

Gitman, L. J., & Joehnk, M. D. (1998). *Fundamentals of investing.* Addison-Wesley.

Horvitz, E. J., & Barry, M. (1995). Display of information for time-critical decision making. *Proceedings of the 11th conference on Uncertainty in Artificial Intelligence* (pp. 296-305). Montreal, Quebec, Canada.

Howard, R. A. (1990). Influence to relevance to knowledge. In R. M. Oliver & J. Q. Smith (Eds.), *Influence diagrams, belief nets and decision analysis* (pp. 3-23). John Wiley & Sons.

Howard, R. A., & Matheson, J. E. (1984). *Influence diagrams, the principles and applications of decision analysis* (Vol. II) . Menlo Park, CA: Strategic Decisions Group.

Laskey, K. B., & Mahoney, S. M. (1997). Network fragments: Representing knowledge for constructing probabilistic models. *Proceedings of the Conference on Uncertainty in Artificial Intelligence* (pp. 334-341). Providence, RI.

Nickerson, R. C., & Boyd, D. W. (1980). The use and value of models in decision analysis. *Operation Research, 28.*

Pearl, J. (1997). *Probabilistic reasoning in intelligent systems: Networks of plausible inference* (Rev. ed). San Francisco: Morgan Kaufmann.

Poh, K. L., & Horvitz, E. (1993). Reasoning about the value of decision model refinement: Methods and application. *Proceedings of 9th Conference on Uncertainty in Artificial Intelligence* (pp. 174-182). Washington, DC.

Russell, S. J., & Wefald, E. H. (1991). Principles of metareasoning. *Artificial Intelligence, 49,* 361-395.

Shachter, R. D., & Poet, M. A. (1989). Simulation approaches to general probabilistic inference on belief network. *Proceedings of the 5th Conference on Uncertainty in Artificial Intelligence.* North Holland.

Shannon, C. E., & Weaver, W. (1949). *The mathematical theory of communication.* University of Illinois Press, Urbana.

Sycara, K. P., & Decker, K. (1997). Intelligent agents in portfolio management. In N. R. Jennings & M. J. Wooldridge (Eds.), *Agent technology.* Germany: Springer-Verlag.

Tseng, C., Gmytrasiewicz, P. J., & Ching, C. (2001). Refining influence diagram for stock portfolio selection. *Proceeding of the 7th International Conference of the Society for Computational Economics,* New Haven, CT.

Watson, S. R., & Brown, R. V. (1978). The valuation of decision analysis. *Journal of the Royal Statistical Society, 141*(Pt. I), 69-78.

Section II

Market Making and Agent-Based Modeling of Markets

Chapter IV

Minimal Intelligence Agents in Double Auction Markets with Speculators

Senlin Wu
University of Illinois, USA

Siddhartha Bhattacharyya
University of Illinois, USA

ABSTRACT

This chapter explores the minimal intelligence conditions for traders in a general double auction market with speculation activities. Using an agent-based model, it is shown that when traders and speculators play together under general market curve settings, zero-intelligent plus (ZIP) is still a sufficient condition for market prices to converge to the equilibrium. At the same time, market efficiency is lowered as the number of speculators increase. The experiments demonstrate that the equilibrium of a double auction market is an interactive result of the intelligence of the traders and other factors such as the type of the players and market conditions. This research fills in an important gap in the literature, and strengthens Cliff and Bruten's (1997) declaration that zero is not enough for a double auction market.

INTRODUCTION

The double auction is a multilateral process in which the buyers and sellers can freely enter orders (bids or asks) and accept orders (asks or bids) entered by others. Many major stock markets, currency markets, commodity markets, and the derivative markets are organized as a form of double auctions; some over-the-counter (OTC) markets are also de facto double auction markets. In a double auction market, buyers can enter bids for an asset or raise existing bids. Sellers can enter offers or lower existing offers. A match or cross of bids and offers implements a transaction. Specifically, buyer i who is given a redemption value of λ_i for a certain asset shouts a bid price b_i, with a potential profit of $\lambda_i - b_i$; seller j who is given a cost of λ_j to obtain the asset shouts an offer price s_j, with a potential profit of $s_j - \lambda_j$. The redemption value λ_i and the cost λ_j of the asset are the private information for the buyer or the seller accordingly (Gibbons, 1992). The success of a trade depends on whether the trader's shout is accepted or not. Furthermore, if the current market has a bid b_i, a new bid shout will replace this market bid only when this new bid is higher than the old one; if the current market has one offer s_j, a new offer shout will replace this market offer only when this new offer is lower than the existing one. This is the basic structure of the double auction market.

Smith (1962) was one of the first to apply an experimental method to the double auction market. He studied the market equilibrium and convergence with a method of Walrasian competitive equilibrium. Note that for historical reasons, Smith's experiments were limited by the small sample size of traders, in relation to actual double auction markets. At the same time, the physical conditions of his experiments, such as the round time, and the traders' quantities, were also different from real world double auction markets, which further weakened the comparison power. In recent years, the development of the computational tools and especially agent-based models has stimulated extensive studies in many directions. Agent-based models help overcome some limitations of human experiments. For example, once a model is constructed, it is quite easy to adjust the parameters with little cost. Therefore, this modeling method is increasingly being used today for addressing a range of research questions in diverse fields from economics and finance to sociology and engineering (Chan, LeBaron, Lo & Poggio, 1999; LeBaron, 2000). A research stream pertaining to double auction markets studies strategies used by the traders in a game theoretic sense. For example, Chen (2000) studied variant "bargaining strategies" in the double auction market. Hsu and Soo (2001) compared the performance of traders with different trading strategies and that of traders with a Q-learning ability. Some studies have also extended to examine interactions between the software traders and the human traders. For example, Das, Hanson, Kephart and Tesauro (2001) compared the performance of software agents and human traders. Grossklags and Schmidt (2003) studied the influence of software agents to the market performance of the human traders in the market. Another research direction has been the study of the influence of the trader's intelligence on the market. For example, Chen and Tai (2003) studied the effect of the intelligence of the traders on the market efficiency by exerting limits on the spaces where the traders can shout their bid and ask offers.

This chapter addresses the minimal intelligence needed for traders in the context of double auction markets convergence to equilibrium. There have been a number of studies on this topic. Gode and Sunder (1993) were the first to examine this problem. Using their zero intelligent–unconstrained (ZI-U) and zero intelligent–constrained (ZI-C) agents, they studied the double auction mechanism for the single symmetric market without speculators. Bosch-Domènech and Sunder (2000) extended this research into the multiple symmetric markets with arbitrageurs or speculators. Using their ZIP agents, Cliff and Bruten (1997) studied the single generalized market, in which the market curves were not necessarily symmetric, with no speculators present. ZI-C and ZIP models have been popularly used as the benchmark to test research questions or construct other types of agents. However, although Cliff and Bruten (1997) pointed out that ZIP is the minimal intelligence necessary for a generalized double auction market, it is not clear whether this condition is still applies in a generalized market where speculation activities are permitted. This chapter tries to fill in this gap in the literature (see Figure 1). Additionally, we need to know whether the scale of the speculation activities affects the market characteristics. Therefore, we reconstruct ZIP traders and speculators and let them play under generalized market conditions to test their performance. Furthermore, we compare these results with the performance of ZI-C traders and speculators, so as to check whether ZIP is necessary to reach the market equilibrium.

LITERATURE REVIEW

In this section we briefly review the historical development of the variants of minimal intelligent traders originating from Smith's (1962) experimental economics work on the double auction market. By assigning different limit prices (the private information) to the traders in his experiments, the researchers were able to adjust the market demand and supply curves (see Figure 2). The left triangle represents the so-called social welfare, and its size can be easily calculated by the simple geometry.

Among many measurements, Smith (1962) monitored the following two outcomes:

- **Market Efficiency.** Defined as the percentage of total profit actually earned by all the traders of the maximum possible total profit. The former is the sum of the profit earned by each trader, and the latter is the social welfare.

Figure 1. The research gap

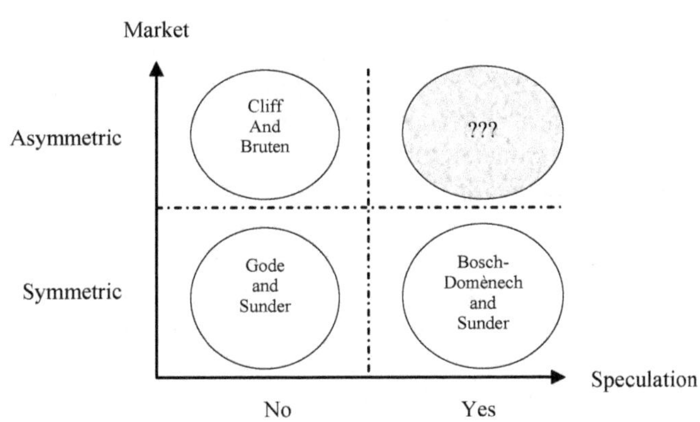

Figure 2. Social welfare in the market

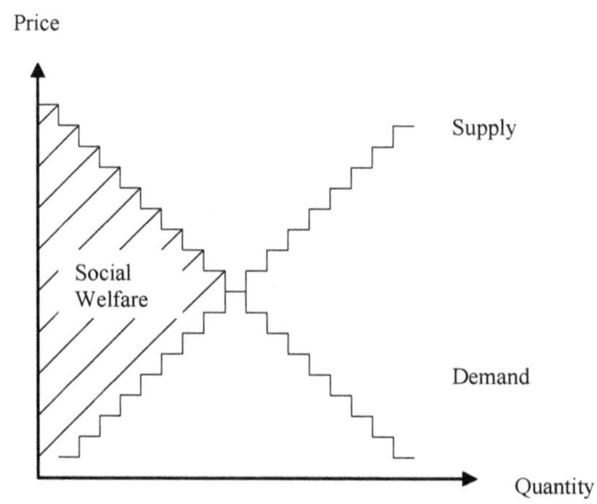

- **Price Convergence Rate.** α**:** for one period in which a total of K transactions occurred with prices p_j, $j = 1...K$. Here, $\alpha = \sigma_0 / P_0$, where P_0 was the theoretical equilibrium price given by the intersection of the supply and demand curves, and σ_0 was calculated as:

$$\sigma_0 = \sqrt{K^{-1}\sum_{j=1}^{K}(p_j - P_0)^2}.$$

Zero Intelligence Traders

Gode and Sunder (1993) used software traders to study the double auction market. They explored the performance of both the ZI-U traders and the ZI-C traders, and compared their performance with that of human traders operating under the (approximately) same experimental conditions. They used symmetric market curves, which meant the magnitudes of the demand and supply curves were approximately the same and the slopes were the opposite. Specifically, they set the bids and offers to be limited to the range 1 to 200 units of arbitrary currency. The forms of the market demand and supply curves could also be described as in Figure 2.

Although the ZI-U and ZI-C traders played in the similar market (curves), they were found to behave differently. ZI-U traders shouted the prices unconstrained across the range mentioned above—that is, the shout prices were uniformly distributed between 1 and 200, which was clearly not rational. If the shout was accepted by another trader, the trader who shouted the price would possibly incur a loss, since the trade price might be outside his or her limit price (lower than the cost or higher than the redemption value). In contrast, ZI-C traders were subject to a "budget constraint," that is, they shouted prices subject to their private information such that they would not engage in loss-making deals. The transaction also canceled the unaccepted bids and offers, and the traders dealt with a single unit of commodity at a time. Results showed that prices in the ZI-U markets exhibited "little systematic pattern and no tendency to converge toward any specific level" (Gode &

Sunders, p. 126). Price histories in the markets with human players were similar to those in Smith's experiments—the transaction prices soon settled to stable values close to the theoretical equilibrium price, after some initial learning and adjustment. For the ZI-C trader model, despite being more volatile than the human price series, prices were found to converge slowly to the equilibrium during each day's trading. Besides, ZI-C model also exhibited surprisingly high levels of the efficiency by Smith's (1962) measure.

Multimarket Speculators Under Specific Market Conditions

Bosch-Domènech and Sunder (2000) extended Gode and Sunder's (1993) single-market findings to multimarket economies. ZI-C traders played in every symmetric market, while arbitrageurs (who trade in different markets at the same time to take risk-free advantage of the price difference) played in each middle market located between two adjacent double auction markets. The constraints on the arbitrageurs were relaxed so that speculation activities – short selling and long buying—were permitted. Each speculator might engage in an unlimited number of purchase and sale transactions within her inventory constraint (say, short sell or buy long at most three products). This limit represented the extent to which speculators could borrow goods or money to fulfill their trading activities. In reality, when buying to increase their inventory, the speculators use borrowed funds that must be paid back through subsequent inventory liquidation. Similarly, when selling to expand their short position (negative inventory), the speculators use borrowed goods that must be returned through subsequent purchases to close the short position. In the experiment, the speculators initiated the trades and then used the opposite trades to offset their inventories. The researchers created a subsidiary market that served this function of settling the accounts among each set of speculators at the end of each period.

Under the multimarket condition, the prices were found to still converge to the equilibrium. When no speculators were permitted, the market efficiency was almost 100%. When speculators were permitted, efficiency dropped sharply as the inventory limit and the number of markets were increased.

Zero-Intelligent Plus Traders

Cliff and Bruten (1997) examined the theoretical characteristics of the market curves. They pointed out that the driving mechanisms to determine the average transaction price and the market equilibrium price differed with market curves. While the market equilibrium price was the intersection of the curves, if it existed, the average transaction prices observed in the market were determined by the intersection of the probability density functions (PDFs) for the buyers' random bids and the sellers' random offers. This may result in a triangular distribution. For the specific triangular distribution shown in Figure 3, P_0 is the theoretical equilibrium price, while the mean price—according to a triangular distribution—is the average of S_{min}, P_0, and D_{max}, which is not necessarily P_0.

In general, the mean transaction price of ZI-C traders differs from the theoretical equilibrium price. The main reasons were

- the different styles of the demand and supply curves, and
- the different PDFs of the bid or offer prices.

Figure 3. Left: the triangular area (ICH shows the intersection of the assumed PDFs for offer and bid prices (ABCD and EFGH); this area indicates the PDF for transaction prices, but requires normalization so that the area of the triangle is one. Right: corresponding normalized PDF for transaction prices (I'CH). P_{min} *and* P_{max} *define the possible price range;* S_{min} *and* S_{max}*,* D_{min} *and* D_{max} *define the supply and demand curves range.* P_0 *is the theoretical equilibrium price.*

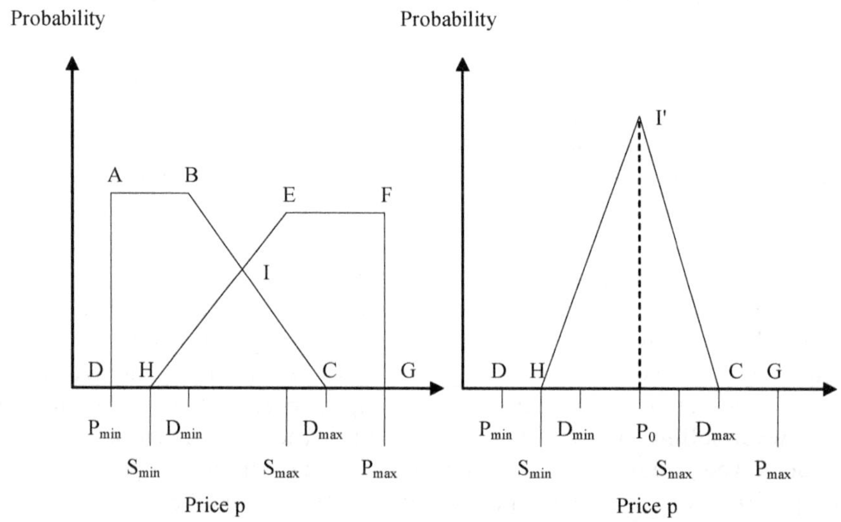

From Cliff and Bruten (1997)

Cliff and Bruten (1997) pointed out that the mean or expected value of the transaction price distribution was shown quantitatively to be close to the equilibrium price only in situations where the magnitude of the gradient of linear supply and demand curves was roughly equal. Therefore, the tendency of the ZI-C traders to achieve a price close to the theoretical equilibrium was a consequence of the underlying probability distributions of the traders, and could only be found in a symmetric market condition. Any similarity between ZI-C traders' transaction prices and the theoretical equilibrium price was more likely to be coincidental than causal. Thus, more than zero intelligence was necessary to account for convergence to equilibrium in general.

The ZIP traders they introduced was similar to ZI-C traders except that the former had some extra learning power—the traders could alter their profit margin (a measure of profit expectation)—based on the previous settlement price or shout price. Each ZIP trader altered its profit margin based on two factors: (a) the trader's status (active or inactive; i.e., an active trader could still make a transaction and was thus allowed to learn, whereas an inactive trader who had sold or bought its full entitlement of units and had "dropped out" of the market for the remainder of this trading period, did not have any learning power in the current trading period); and (b) the last (most recent) shout (i.e., the price level, whether it is a bid or an offer, whether it is accepted or rejected).

Increasing the profit margin would raise the shout price for a seller, and lower the shout price for a buyer. The learning ability enabled a trader to modify his or her profit margin according to the latest transaction price, or the latest market bid or offer price. When the last shout resulted in a transaction, for a buyer b_i, if his or her shout price p_i was higher than or equal to the last shout price q (it was a transaction price then), he or she would increase the profit margin. Similarly, for a seller s_j, she would raise her profit margin whenever p_j is lower than or equal to the shout price q. Active traders would sometimes also lower their profit margin under certain circumstances, say, when a new bid or a offer did not result in a transaction. Cliff and Bruten (1997) gave the detailed pseudo code.

After the change direction of the profit margin was decided, the traders updated their profit margin according to an adaptive procedure (Cliff & Bruten, 1997). Suppose there are N traders in the market. Trader i, $i = 1 \ldots N$, maintained a profit margin μ_i, which was a percentage of the limit price λ_i for a unit. Therefore, when he or she shouted a price, the shout price p_i was determined by

(1) $$p_i(t) = \lambda_i (1 + \mu_i(t)),$$
(2) $$\mu_i(t+1) = (p_i(t) + \Gamma_i(t)) / \lambda_i - 1,$$
(3) $$\Gamma_i(t+1) = \gamma_i \Gamma_i(t) + (1 - \gamma_i)\Delta_i(t),$$
(4) $$\Delta_i(t) = \beta_i(\tau_i(t) - p_i(t)),$$
(5) $$\tau_i(t) = R_i(t)q(t) + A(t).$$

where t determines the order by which the shouts occurred in the market. Trader i's potential shout price at t was determined by her limit price and the profit margin at t, which is shown in (1). The dynamical profit at $t + 1$ in (2) was decided by p_i and actual change of the shout price Γ_i at t. This actual change was created with a momentum-based update method as shown in (3), where the momentum coefficient was γ_i, and Δ_i in the second item showed her desired change at t. Therefore, the actual change of the potential shout price at $t + 1$ is the weighted average of the actual change and the desired change at t. Assuming the trader i had a target shout price τ_i at t and her individual fixed learning rate was β_i, her desired shout change $\Delta_i(t)$ is as shown in (4), which is a basic learning procedure. The target shout price t_i at t was determined based on the market shout price q at t, which is shown in (5). R_i sets the target price relative to the market shout price at t, and A is a small perturbation.

ZIP traders were found to demonstrate more humanlike market performance and achieved results that were impossible for ZI-C traders and which were closer to those expected from human participants or traditional rational-expectations theoretical predictions. These findings were obtained using the same ZIP parameter values under a variety of market conditions.

MODEL DESIGN

Let us consider a double auction market with some ZIP traders and speculators. This configuration differs from that of Cliff and Bruten's (1997) market with ZIP traders only, and Gode and Sunder's (1993) symmetric market with ZI-C traders and speculators. Only one kind of product is traded in the market. In a single period (day), one buyer can buy at most one unit; one seller has only one unit to sell. A speculator can hold at most one unit (borrow money from someplace), or sell at most one unit (borrow product from someplace). This means the possible inventory for a speculator is –1, 0 or +1 (short one product, no inventory, or long one product). This limitation helps simplify the model without losing generalizability, since the reality of greater inventories held by one speculator can be realized by one inventory held by more speculators. At the end of every day, the speculators who still have open positions (either long or short) must close their position with the last market shout price (bid or offer) in the market. At the next day, all the traders and speculators recover to their initial positions. We set 10 days as a "run."

We set the minimal price for the market as one unit of a certain currency, and maximal price as 100 units of a certain currency. The ZIP traders have different limit prices, which are used to define the market curves. They have different profit margins, which float according to the market condition. A bid or offer worse than the current market bid or offer is ignored by the market; a bid or offer better than the current market replaces the current one, until the bid and offer meet or cross such that a trade is completed. If no shouts (or trades) occur for a long time, one day's trading is closed, the positions of the speculators are cleared, and the next day follows at once. Everything restarts except for the traders' profit margins.

The speculators can open a position at any time. We define their behaviors after opening a position as a ZI-C trader instead of a ZIP trader. The argument is if they do not hinder the market converging to some point, neither will the speculators with the characteristics of ZIP. They open positions by accepting the market bid or offer randomly and passively. After that, they will be randomly selected to check their potential profits, as they all know their limit prices. They will close the position if there is any profit when they shout; otherwise, they will keep their positions. At the end of the day, those speculators that are forced to close their positions may incur a loss.

The market curves provide the environment in which the traders and the speculators operate. We define the following market curves (see Figure 4):

- **Symmetric market curves.** We define 100 buyers with limit prices 1 to 100 units of arbitrary currency and 100 sellers with limit prices from 100 to 1. Therefore, the market equilibrium price (the price for the intersection of the supply and demand lines) is 50.5, and the maximum possible profit is 2,500, which is the size of the social welfare.
- **Asymmetric market curves.** We define 100 buyers with limit prices from 100 to 51, with every two buyers having the same limit price, and 100 sellers having limit prices from 1 to 100. Based on simple geometric calculation, the market equilibrium price (the intersection of the market curves) is calculated as 66.7, and the size of the social welfare is 3,333.3.
- **Flat-supply curves.** 100 buyers are the same as in the above two scenarios, while the 100 sellers have the same limit price 50. The market equilibrium price is therefore 50, and the social welfare is 1,250.
- **Flat-demand curves.** This scenario is the opposite of the third one, and we expect the analogous result.

Within these market curves, we define the number of the speculators to be 10, 30 or 50. First, we construct ZI-C traders and ZIP traders to validate our model, and results

Figure 4. (a) Symmetric market; (b) asymmetric market; (c) flat-supply market; (d) flat demand market. The left triangle of the curves in each market is the social welfare.

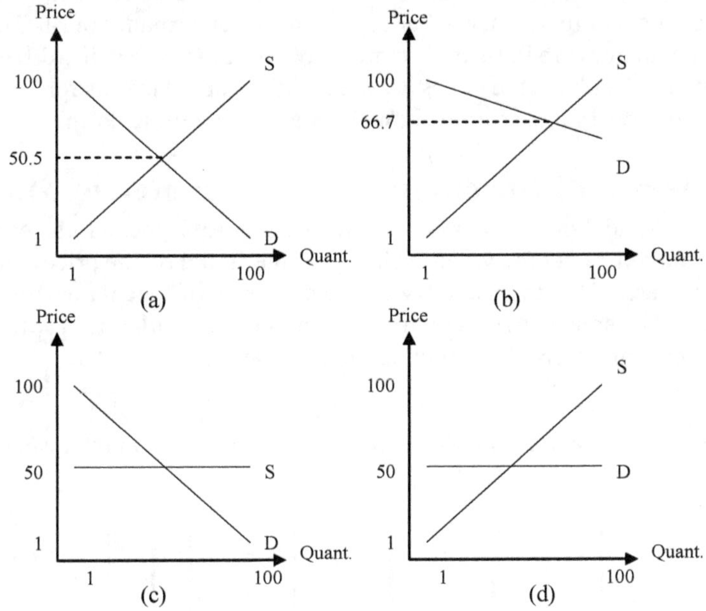

are found to match those in the literatures very well. Then, based on ZIP traders, we add the third type of agents—speculators—into our model. This allows a comparison of the effects of speculation activities.

The parameters we monitor include the following:

- **Average Price:** it is the average price for all the transaction prices in all the 10 runs.
- **Equilibrium Price:** this is simply the price at the cross point of two market curves.
- **Efficiency:** this is defined as the sum of all the agents' payoffs in the market divided by the total social welfare, which has the same meaning as in Smith's experiment, except that the agents here include the speculators.
- **Convergence Rate:** this is a measure to see how the market price converges to the equilibrium price, which has the same formula as in Smith's experiment. A smaller convergence rate means a tighter or earlier convergence to the equilibrium.
- **Loss:** it shows the percentage of the sum of the net loss originating from the forced buy-in or sell-out by the speculators at the end of each day, in the total social welfare.

The Swarm agent-based modeling platform (www.swarm.org) is used in our experiments. The agent design for the traders and the speculators is listed in the Appendix, and the activities within a day is also listed.

RESULT AND ANALYSIS

This section reports the simulation results. The first three subsections test the symmetric market curve, the asymmetric market curve and the flat-demand and supply market curves. For comparison, we then report on the performance of ZI-C traders in the presence of speculators in a flat-supply market. We start each run with a different random number seed. The results in the tables are the averages or the results for 10 independent runs, and the figures in this section show the market in a typical run.

ZIP Traders and Speculators in a Symmetric Market

Figures 5, 6 and 7 show ZIP traders with 10, 30 and 50 speculators, respectively, in a symmetric market. After the volatile change in the first day, the price settles down to the equilibrium area. However, because of the existence of speculators, there are many sudden spikes. The spikes increase with the number of speculators. Table 1 shows the average market characteristics excluding the first day.

Figure 5. 100 ZIP buyers and 100 ZIP sellers with 10 speculators in a symmetric market

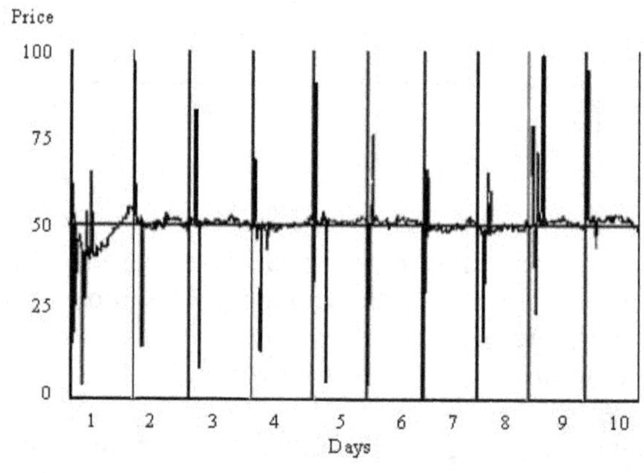

Figure 6. 100 ZIP buyers and 100 ZIP sellers with 30 speculators in a symmetric market

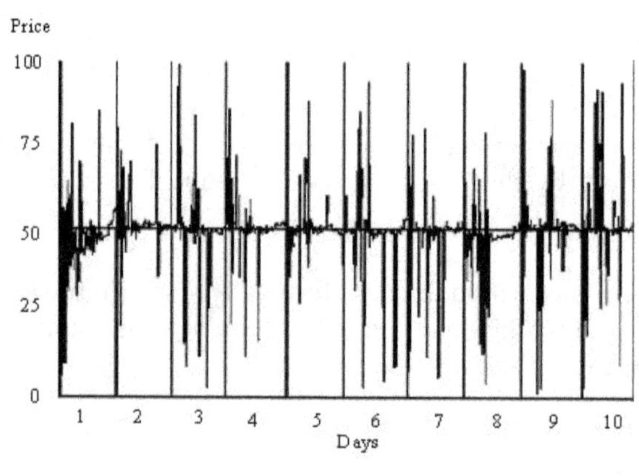

Figure 7. 100 ZIP buyers and 100 ZIP sellers with 50 speculators in a symmetric market

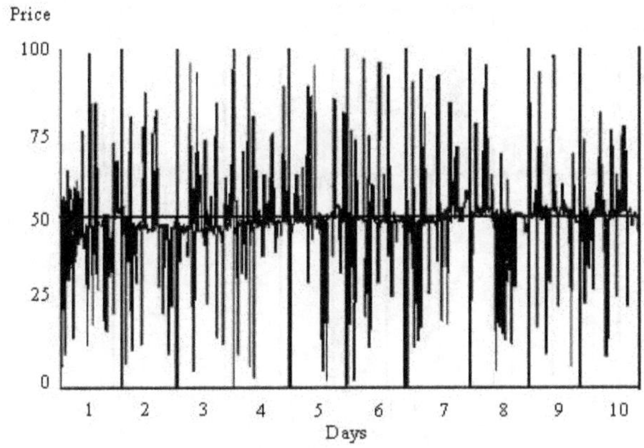

Table 1. Simulation results for the scenarios shown in Figures 5, 6 and 7

Speculator number	10	30	50
Average Price	50.9	49.6	49.4
Equilibrium Price	50.5	50.5	50.5
Efficiency	96%	83%	73%
Loss	4%	13%	27%
Convergence Rate	19%	26%	28%

The average price of all the trades is very close to the theoretical equilibrium price in all the three scenarios; the efficiency decreases with increasing number of speculators. In the 50-speculator scenario, the efficiency is lower than 75%. At the same time, the convergence ability also becomes worse. An interesting observation is that these two indicators deteriorate at different rates. In comparison, Cliff and Bruten's (1997) results showed a smaller convergence rate, since their market had no speculators; Bosch-Domènech and Sunder's (2000) market setting will be more volatile—considering a plot of a single market chart with the speculators—since their traders are ZI-C traders.

ZIP Traders and Speculators in an Asymmetric Market

Figure 8, 9 and 10 show ZIP traders with 10, 30 and 50 speculators in an asymmetric market. Table 2 shows the average market characteristics excluding the first day.

The average price here is also very close to the equilibrium price in all three scenarios. The efficiency decreases as the number of speculators increase, but not as significantly as in the symmetric market case of the previous section. The loss is much lower than in the symmetric market case; the convergence rate is much better and does not change much with the number of speculators. These results may be explained by the narrower price ranges under which the agents here have to operate. With the learning ability of ZIP agents, the price range in the market becomes narrower earlier than in the symmetric market case. The speculators' price range is also narrowed, and thus the spikes

Figure 8. 100 ZIP buyers and 100 ZIP sellers with 10 speculators in an asymmetric market

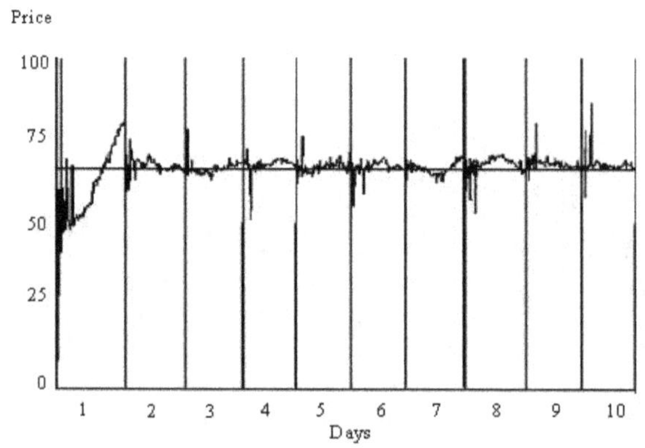

Figure 9. 100 ZIP buyers and 100 ZIP sellers with 30 speculators in an asymmetric market

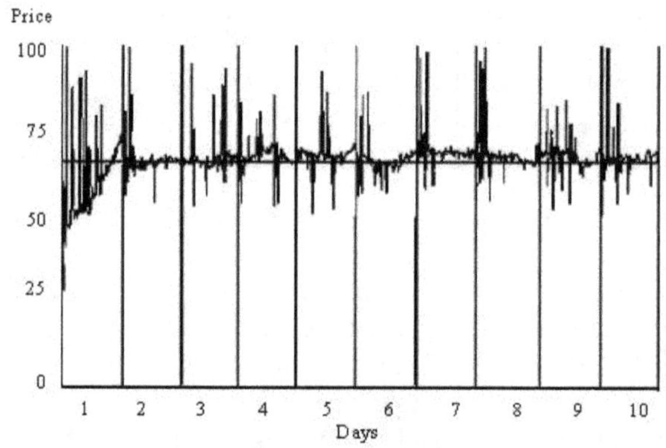

Figure 10. 100 ZIP buyers and 100 ZIP sellers with 50 speculators in an asymmetric market

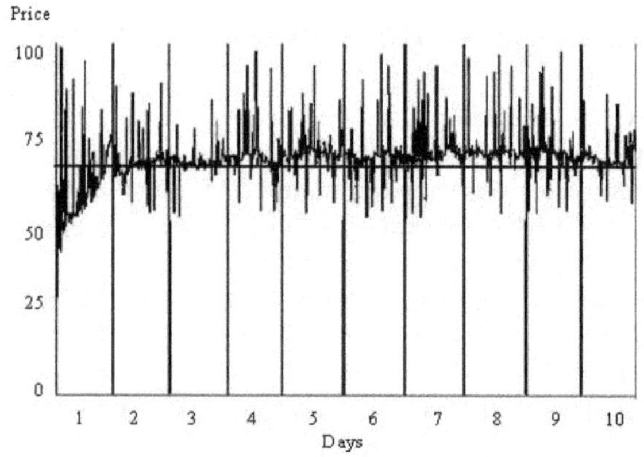

Table 2. Simulation results for the scenarios shown in Figures 8, 9 and 10

Speculator number	10	30	50
Average Price	67.2	67.3	68.4
Equilibrium Price	66.7	66.7	66.7
Efficiency	99%	95%	90%
Loss	1%	5%	10%
Convergence Rate	12%	13%	13%

are not as long as in the symmetric market. Similar results can be expected from other kinds of asymmetric markets where the market price range is narrowed.

ZIP Traders and Speculators in Other Special Markets

Figure 11, 12 and 13 show ZIP traders with 10, 30 and 50 speculators in a flat-supply market. Table 3 shows the average market characters excluding the first day.

The average price is very close to the equilibrium price in all three scenarios. The efficiency decreases as the number of speculators increases. The loss also becomes much higher with the presence of larger number of speculators, and is similar to the loss in a symmetric market. The convergence rate also worsens with more speculators in the market. The one-sided spikes in the figures arise from the fact that speculators accept the price passively and do not initiate trade in the other market area. The same situation happens for the flat-demand market curves.

Figure 14, 15 and 16 show ZIP traders with 10, 30 and 50 speculators in a flat-demand market. Table 4 shows the average market characters excluding the first day.

The average price is very close to the equilibrium price in all three scenarios. The efficiency decreases with increasing number of speculators. The loss is observed to be high, as in the flat-supply market. The convergence rate also worsens as more speculators enter the market.

Figure 11. 100 ZIP buyers and 100 ZIP sellers with 10 speculators in a flat-supply market

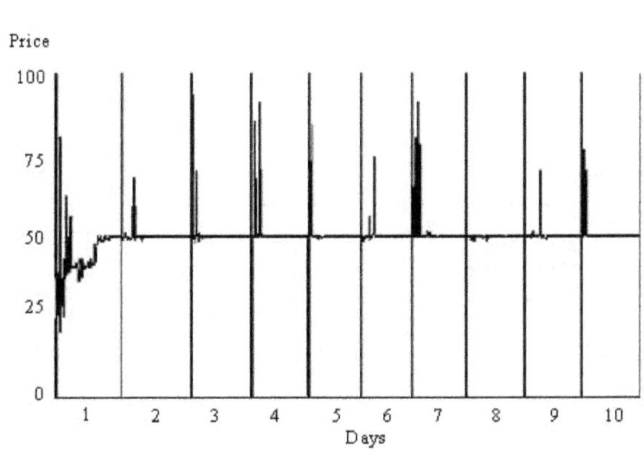

Figure 12. 100 ZIP buyers and 100 ZIP sellers with 30 speculators in a flat-supply market

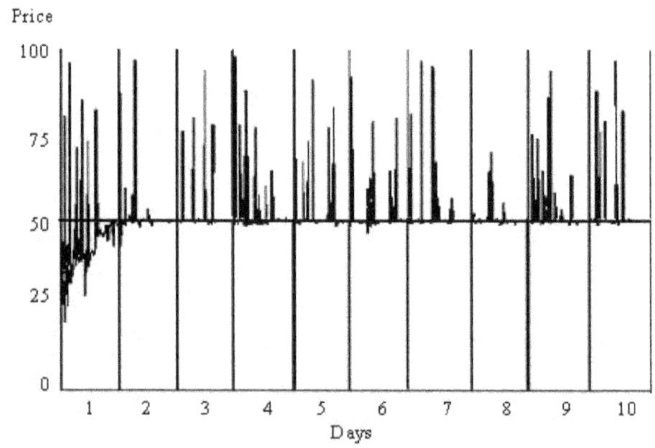

Figure 13. 100 ZIP buyers and 100 ZIP sellers with 50 speculators in a flat-supply market

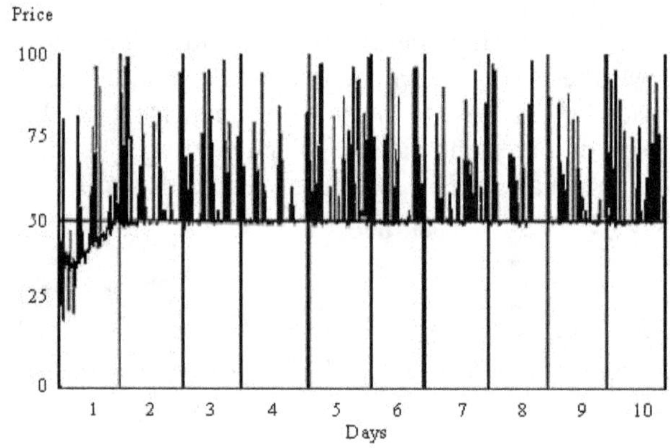

Table 3. Simulation results for the scenarios shown in Figures 11, 12 and 13

Speculator number	10	30	50
Average Price	51	52	53
Equilibrium Price	50	50	50
Efficiency	94%	84%	73%
Loss	4%	7%	27%
Convergence Rate	16%	19%	24%

Figure 14. 100 ZIP buyers and 100 ZIP sellers with 10 speculators in a flat-demand market

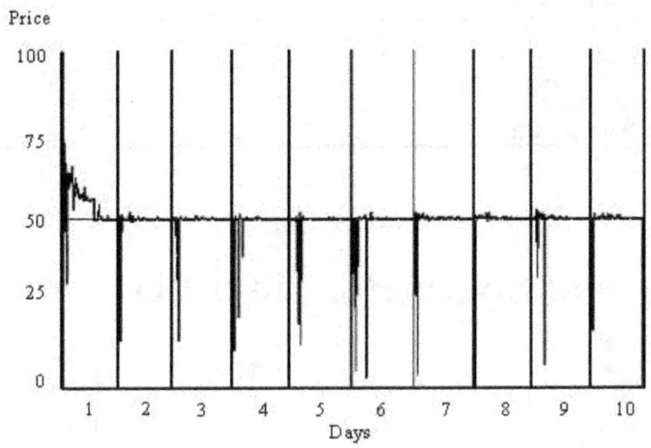

Figure 15. 100 ZIP buyers and 100 ZIP sellers with 30 speculators in a flat-demand market

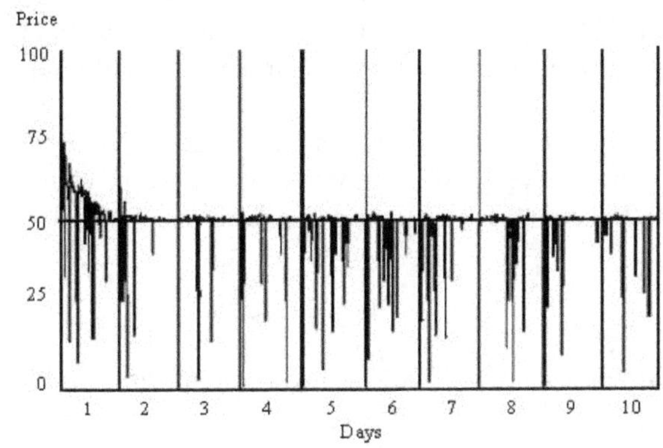

Figure 16. 100 ZIP buyers and 100 ZIP sellers with 50 speculators in a flat-demand market

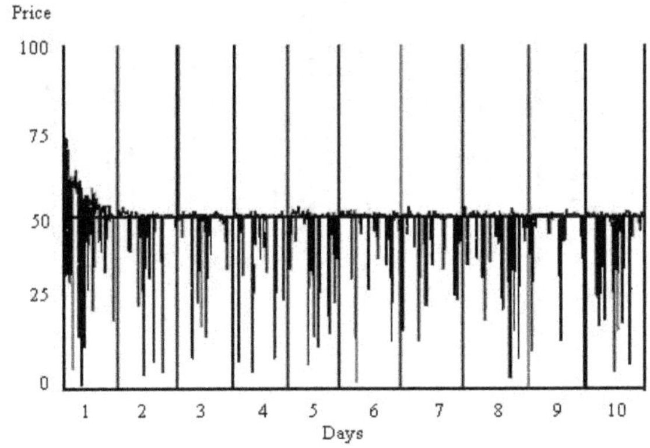

Table 4. Simulation results for the scenarios show in Figures 14, 15 and 16

Speculator number	10	30	50
Average Price	49	48	47
Equilibrium Price	50	50	50
Efficiency	97%	86%	78%
Loss	5%	17%	25%
Convergence Rate	17%	20%	21%

ZI-C Traders and Speculators in a Flat-Supply Double Auction Market

ZI-C traders are not expected to perform well in the presence of speculators. For a basic comparison with the results given here, we examine ZI-C traders with 30 speculators in a flat-supply market. Figure 17 shows the results for one run and Table 5 gives the average market characters excluding the first day.

It is clear that the average price is not as close to the equilibrium price as in the case of ZIP traders. It helps reiterate that ZI-C is not a sufficient condition to reach the market equilibrium. However, we also find that the difference is not as significant as described by Cliff and Bruten (1997). This arises from the nature of operation of the speculators, which leads to some trades in the area where no trades would happen if there were no speculators.

Note that although it is a flat-supply market, trades can happen on both sides of the equilibrium price, which is very different from the flat-supply market with ZIP traders. Here, the traders do not change their limit prices and the market price range is therefore not narrowed.

Figure 17. 100 ZI-C buyers and 100 ZI-C sellers with 30 speculators in a flat-supply market

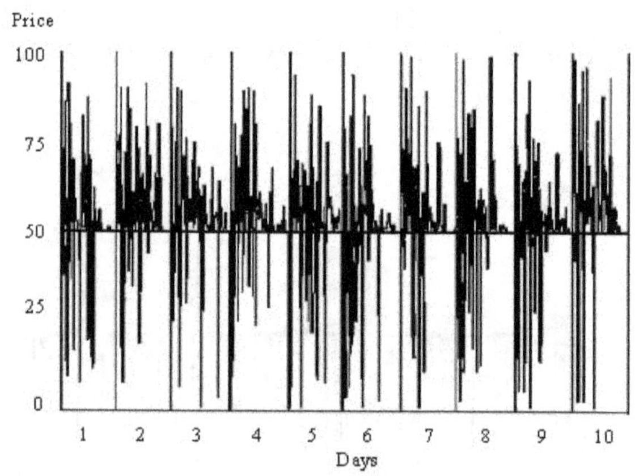

Table 5. Simulation results for the scenario show in Figure 17

Speculator number	30
Average Price	54
Equilibrium Price	50
Efficiency	89%
Convergence Rate	33%

CONCLUSION

In Gode and Sunder's (1993) experiments, ZI-C is shown to be a sufficient condition to reach the equilibrium in a symmetric market. Considering the ZI-C traders' minimal intelligence, this can lead one to conclude that the double-auction market can reach the equilibrium without considering the specific players in the market. Cliff and Bruten (1997) realized that the symmetric market condition in which the ZI-C traders were playing was too specific to allow such generalization; they showed that under a more generalized market condition, the market equilibrium could not be reached with ZI-C traders in the market. They constructed their ZIP traders, and found that the market equilibrium and efficiency could be reached under generalized market conditions with ZIP traders. Bosch-Domènech and Sunder (2000) extended Gode and Sunder's (1993) research into a multimarket perspective and added in arbitrageurs and speculators. They found that following an increase in the number of the speculators, the market equilibrium could still be reached with the assumption of ZI-C under the symmetric market condition, although the market efficiency was lowered.

This paper considered the double auction markets with speculators under varied market conditions, and fills an important gap in this body of work. Our results show that ZI-C is not a sufficient condition to reach the equilibrium price in a double-auction market with speculators. It is also observed that when there are not too many speculation activities in the market, ZIP is a sufficient condition for equilibrium. Therefore, the level of speculation activities in the market is also an important factor for the market to converge to the equilibrium price. Comparing to ZI-C, ZIP is also a necessary condition.

The factors that influence market convergence can be summarized as

- **Self Adjustment ability of the DA Markets:** Under symmetric supply and demand curves, the double auction mechanism itself will lead to convergence to the equilibrium price, as long as the traders follow basic budget constraints (ZI-C), with limited speculation activities.
- **Intelligence of the Agents:** Under general market conditions, ZIP presents a necessary and sufficient condition for double auction markets to achieve the equilibrium price, as long as speculation activities are limited.
- **Scale of Speculation Activities:** As speculation activities increase, the equilibrium can still be reached for general markets with ZIP traders, but with decreasing efficiency, arising from losses made through speculation. Convergence to the equilibrium is also worse as speculators increase. Note that the same holds true with ZI-C traders where the market curves are restricted to be symmetric.

The overall performance of the market depends on which of these factors dominate. When the number of speculators in the market is small compared to the number of traders, speculation is just a kind of singular activity (noise) which produces some unrelated spikes only. However, when the number of speculators is comparable to the number of traders, the market efficiency is seen to deteriorate. In some scenarios, the efficiency loses about one fourth of the total social welfare due to the speculators.

REFERENCES

Bosch-Domènech, A., & Sunder, S. (2000). Tracking the invisible hand: Convergence of double auctions to competitive equilibrium. *Computational Economics, 16*(3), 257-284.

Chan, N. T., LeBaron, B., Lo, A. W., & Poggio, T. (1999). *Agent-based models of financial markets: A comparison with experimental markets* (Working Paper). MIT.

Chen, S. H. (2000). Toward an agent-based computational modeling of bargaining strategies in double auction markets with genetic programming. *Intelligent data engineering and automated learning—IDEAL 2000: Data mining, financial engineering, and intelligent agents, lecture notes in computer sciences 1983* (pp. 517-531). Springer.

Chen, S. H., & Tai, C. C. (2003). Trading restrictions, price dynamics and allocative efficiency in double auction markets: Analysis based on agent-based modeling and simulations. *Advances in Complex Systems, 6*(3), 283-302.

Cliff, D., & Bruten, J. (1997). *Minimal-intelligence agents for bargaining behaviors in market-based environments* (Tech. Rep. No. HPL 97-91).

Das, R., Hanson, J., Kephart, J., & Tesauro, G. (2001). Agent-human interactions in the continuous double auction. *Proceedings of the International Joint Conferences on Artificial Intelligence (IJCAI),* Seattle, WA.

Gibbons, R. (1992). *Game theory for applied economists.* NJ: Princeton University Press.

Gode, D., & Sunder, S. (1993). Allocative efficiency of markets with zero-intelligence traders: Market as a partial substitute for individual rationality. *The Journal of Political Economy, 101*(1), 119-137.

Grossklags, J., & Schmidt, C. (2003). Artificial software agents on thin double auction markets—A human trader experiment. *Proceedings of the IEEE/WIC International Conference on Intelligent Agent Technology (IAT-2003),* Halifax, Canada.

Hsu, W. T., & Soo, V. W. (2001). Market performance of adaptive trading agents in synchronous double auction. *Proceedings of the 4th Pacific Rim International Workshop on Multi-Agents, Intelligent Agents: Specification, Modeling, and Applications (PRIMA-2001).*

LeBaron, B. (2000). Agent based computational finance: Suggested readings and early research. *Journal of Economic Dynamics and Control, 24,* 679-702.

Smith, V. L. (1962). An experimental study of competitive market behavior. *The American Economic Review, 70*(2), 111-137.

APPENDIX

Here we list the definition parts of the agents. There are two kinds of agents in the model: ZIP traders and speculators. The traders are differentiated by their limit price and the identification of buyer or seller. The trading procedure may change their status of active or inactive. They maintain (potential) shout prices, which are updated with their learning ability. To describe their learning abilities, some parameters including learning rate have to be set. Comparing with ZIP traders, the configuration of the speculators is much simpler. They have different costs by opening their positions rather randomly. By checking the market, they open long or short positions randomly. They behave like ZI-C traders, therefore they have no the learning modulo. We also list the pseudo code for the actions happening in one day. The difference between the ZIP traders and the speculators is mainly that the former may shout prices actively while the latter react market prices passively.

Trader

```
@interface Trader: SwarmObject
{
      int limitPrice;                    //Limit price
      int identification;                //BUYBER; SELLER
      int status;                        //ACTIVE; INACTIVE
      float shout;                       //Shout price

      float learnRate;                   //Learning rate
      float momRate;                     //Momentum Rate
      float Gamma;                       //Actual change of shout price in last time
}
- setLimitPrice: (int)limit;
- (int)getLimit;
- setIdentification: (int)identification;
- (int)getIdentification;

- setInitialLearningParameters;
- setShout: (float)newShout;
- (float)getGamma;
- (float)getLearnRate;
- (float)getMomRate;

- shouting;
- (float)getShout;
- goInactive;
- goActive;
- (int)getStatus;
@end
```

Speculator

```
@interface Speculator: SwarmObject
{
int position;                    //LONG; SHORT
float cost;                      //Price when opening a position
}
- (int)getPosition;
- setPosition: (int)position;
- (float)getCost;
- setCost: (float)cost;
@end
```

Actions within 1 Day (Pseudo Code)

```
Within 1 day
    Select a trader or a speculator
    If a trader is chosen
            This trader shouts
            If there is a trade
                    Update market information
                    Record trade information
            Traders update profit margins
    If a speculator is chosen
            If this speculator has no position, or can make money by closing current
            position
                    This speculator accepts the latest shout
                    Record trade information
                    Traders update profit margins
Close all the open positions of speculators in the market
Record trade information
```

Chapter V

Optimization of Individual and Regulatory Market Strategies with Genetic Algorithms

Lukáš Pichl
University of Aizu, Japan

Ayako Watanabe
Ochanomizu University, Japan

ABSTRACT

An optimal policy problem is formulated for evolutionary market settings and analyzed in two applications at the micro- and macrolevels. First, individual portfolio policy is studied in case of a fully computerized, multiagent market system. We clarify the conditions under which static approaches—such as constraint optimization with stochastic rates or stochastic programming—apply in coevolutionary markets with strictly maximal players under scaled genetic algorithms. Convergence to global optimum is discussed for (a) coevolution of buying and selling strategies and for (b) coevolution of portfolio strategies and asset distributions over market players. Because only a finite population size in our setting suffices for the asymptotic convergence, the design criteria for genetic algorithm given (explicit cooling scheme for mutation and crossover, exponentiation schedule for fitness-selection) are of practical importance.

Second, system optimization policy is studied for a model economy of Kareken and Wallace (1982) type. The income redistribution, monetary and market regulation policies are subjected to a supergenetic algorithm with various objective functions. In particular, the fitness function of a policy (i.e., a supercreature) is computed by means of a conventional genetic algorithm which is applied to the market players (creatures) in a fixed evaluation period. Here, the underlying genetic algorithm drives the infinite market dynamics and the supergenetic algorithm solves the optimal policy problem. Coevolution of consumption and foreign currency saving policies is discussed. Finally, a Java model of a stationary market was developed and made available for use and download.

INTRODUCTION

Evolutionary market models are a useful tool to investigate properties of real markets. This work deals with applications of the genetic algorithm (GA) in simulated agent-based artificial markets at micro- and macrolevels from methodological viewpoint. GA applications to agent's portfolio optimization problem (micro) and market/society optimization problem (macro) are discussed in the context of *coevolution*.

The microlevel problem of choosing optimal portfolio has been intensively studied since the pioneering works on portfolio optimization Markowitz (1952) and Tobin (1958) by financial investment companies and in academia (cf. Markowitz, 1991; Michaud, 1998). The first research direction is based on phenomenological studies, statistics and data mining applied to aggregate data from asset markets and their derivatives. The second line of investigation is based on computerized bottom-up techniques, starting with behavioral models at the microlevel, implementing market information models, and the price-making mechanism. This yields complete data time series both at the micro- and macrolevels. Although macroscale simulation results are a subject to comparison with real markets, microscale simulation output data offer insight into the market dynamics and its underlying mechanisms.

This work first deals with the portfolio optimization problem in closed simulated markets, in which total finance m and nominal amounts of all kinds of stock, $q_i, i = 1,...n$, are constant; price matching is a deterministic algorithm adjusted to imperfect information condition by using time series of closed auctions. In particular, we adopt the common market model by Yuuki, Moriya, Yoshida and Pichl (see Figure 1). In the YMYP model, the self-contained market is further coupled to the external world through stochastic time series of dividend yields per each stock simulating data from actual markets. In this framework, the time series of stock prices and traded volumes result from the actions taken by each agent: keep, buy, or sell. In addition, we consider an alternative non-correlated investment asset d with a fixed yield rate r. Hence the portfolio is a tuple of $\{m, d, q_i\}$ which is recursively evaluated in discrete steps (market sessions). The portfolio is to be optimized with respect to a certain utility function. If the market initial state is set and the agents behavioral rules are fixed, each agent/portfolio holder optimizes the function of n–1 variables, which is computed by fully deterministic algorithm A consisting of a set of agent behavioral rules and the price making mechanism.

Either A is ex ante known to each dealer (shared theory) or A is generally unknown (individual behavioral rules). In the latter case, A can be studied ex post by data mining

Figure 1. Simulation environment: YMYP model, selected price series

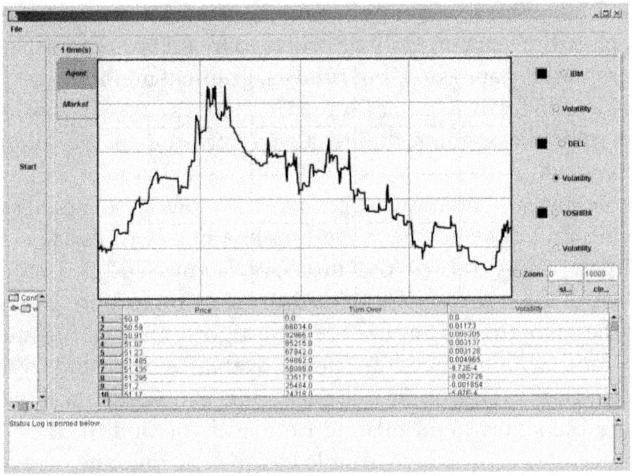

techniques applied to the market time series and stochastic dividend chains. Our model (and a real market) is more complex, because the market agents learn and adopt various behavioral rules. Therefore static theories do not apply, and genetic algorithms (GA), genetic programming (Chen & Yeh, 1995) and artificial intelligence methods should be used (Chen & Yeh, 2001) to determine realistic behavioral patterns of players. In this chapter, we develop an implementation scheme based on coevolutionary approaches for such purpose.

To provide more general guideline on the use and applicability of genetic algorithms and principles of their hierarchical nesting in market settings, we distinguish the GA as (a) a mathematical optimization tool and (b) a learning algorithm. GA can be used as an optimization tool in case there exists a certain optimum—for instance, a regulatory market policy that is best evaluated over a certain (real, artificial) market run (stochastic averages, minimax criteria, etc.). Here, the GA acts as an optimization tool on the macrolevel. Nevertheless, if the GA is used for determining optimal investment strategies of market players, for instance, then it also acts as one of the driving forces of the entire market dynamics. As a consequence, there exists no stable optimal strategy for a single agent, as the market instantaneously changes. In such a case, the GA is intrinsically coupled with the market microlevel as it represents the way in which individual market players attempt to learn or adapt to its overall dynamics. Hierarchical nesting of GAs presented in this chapter discusses a case in which the lower level GA represents agent learning (microlevel) and drives the entire market (also the entire society) with no optimum, while the upper level GA acts on the space of regulatory market strategies (macrolevel) as a policy optimization algorithm—for which an optimum exists. Ya-Chi Huang and Shu-Heng Chen employed another kind of GA nesting in the reverse order: their lower level GA is an optimization tool for finding optimal portfolio in a stochastic Markov process of investment opportunities whereas their upper level GA is a learning mechanism in which agents adapt their beliefs (probabilities in the Markov process of investment options they expect to have) over a longer time scale. Note that the reverse nesting of both GAs in this case is applied on the microlevel of market agents. GA as an optimization algorithm can certainly be replaced by other methods, such as brute force sampling of parameter space (slow but robust), gradient methods (fast but vulnerable at local extremes) and so forth. We opt for the GA here as a possible compromise between the speed and robustness goals, being also interested in the algorithmic structure previously described.

The macrolevel problem how to optimize the structure of agent society and system rules for a specific purpose has been studied in a number of case studies and general frameworks (Epstein & Axtel, 1996; Kurashi & Terano, 2002). Here we elaborate on a hierarchic nesting of GAs, (a) which evolve the society for infinitely long and (b) optimize its structure at the same time. The supergenetic algorithm used for such purpose acts on the space of societies which fitness function is evaluated by an underlying GA. To obtain a consistent definition, (a) the underlying GA must evolve the society through the entire space of its possible states in an infinite time horizon, and (b) the fitness function of society must be a certain objective variable *weighed* on the state–space trajectory in (a). For this purpose, we adopt a model economy of Kareken and Wallace (1982) type, which is driven by genetic algorithm (Arifovic 1996, 2000). This model is suitable from the viewpoint of the previous definition. It includes a financial market (a foreign exchange market between two countries) and it couples to the real economy (individual consumption and saving decisions). As Lux and Schornstein (2005) have shown, it reproduces the stylized stochastic features observed in complex systems (Kaizoji, 2000; Stanley, 1999), if the number of agents in the society is rather limited and a small mutation probability is used in the underlying GA.

The chapter is organized as follows. The next section concerns the microlevel of investment strategies among market players. We outline the basic portfolio determinants and introduce an original java simulation model of a financial market. This YMYP model serves as a testbed for coevolutionary GAs (CGAs). We note that as any other market simulation model, YMYP can also be used as a fitness evaluator for regulatory market policies. Next, we elaborate on CGAs, providing the conditions for their asymptotic convergence in a coevolutionary setting involving portfolio strategies vs. investment options among market players. Importantly, this yields market implementation guidelines for convergent CGAs, such as the minimal requirements on gene length or the rate of selection pressure. As an illustration, the duality underlying the fitness function for CGAs is computed by the results of YMYP simulation experiments for portfolio optimization (cf. Figures 1 and 2). Then, in the next section, we discuss the hierarchical nesting of GAs on the macrolevel of market regulation. The supergenetic algorithm (SGA) is defined and its particular implementation shown for a GA-driven Kareken and Wallace (1982) two-country economy. The level of abstraction in this model allows us to discuss the SGA structure in large detail for the sake of didactic clarity. We note that the SGA applies exactly in the same way to arbitrary market system model of any sophistication, in case such model uses the genetic learning in agent strategies. We conclude the chapter with final remarks.

MICROLEVEL

Portfolio Definition

The actual earning rate of a portfolio is the linear combination of earning rates r_i of n portfolio brands,

$$r_P(t)=\sum_{i=1}^{n} x_i r_i, r_i(t)=\frac{P_i^{(t)}}{P_i^{(0)}}-1, \text{ where} \tag{1}$$

$$x_i \equiv P_i^{(0)} q_i^{(\forall t)}/(m-d) \text{ and } (m-d) \equiv \sum_i P_i^{(0)} q_i^{(\forall t)}. \tag{2}$$

In the above equation, P_i denotes price of asset i and the rates x_i can be time dependent.

Portfolio Optimization

The application of data covariance to risk diversification should not restrict the portfolio to low-risk–low-return assets. Instead, higher growth–higher risk assets are combined in a way that cancels the negative fluctuations out. In other words, the combined standard deviations should be low compared to the individual asset volatility. Dynamic portfolio optimization for a time period T then means the best sequence $\{x_i(t)\}$ for $i=1,\ldots,n$ and $0 \le t \le T$ that realizes maximum profit. Static portfolio optimization, on the other hand, means the best values $x_i(t) \equiv x_i(0)$ for $i=1,\ldots,n$ and $0 \le t \le T$. The optimization criterion is the realization sum at a certain targeted time T, $\sum_i P_i(T) q_i(T)$. Note that the opportunity costs and discount factors should be included in general. Throughout the rest of this chapter, we do not explicitly consider the role of financial market, except for (a) fixed-term deposits and (b) inflation or deflation. In terms of the efficiency, GA is not superior for finding the sequence $x(t)$ compared to DP derivatives, but it is considered more robust with respect to local extremes.

Static Lagrange Multipliers

We implement the static portfolio optimization strategy for the asymptotically converged market. All input data are from online Java YMYP market simulation model, with three classes of portfolio pricing strategies and three kinds of stock. Series of discrete closed auctions clear the market and fix the prices. An example of typical price series in the model is shown in Figure 1.

The portfolio pricing in the conservative approach is $M(t)=m+d(1+r)^t+\sum_i p_i(t)q_i$, where m is the call-on funds and d a deposit at rate r. Fixing m and d at some particular values, one can generalize the term $\sum_{i=1}^{n} p_i(t)q_i$ for a stochastic market, where $p_i(t)$ are *apriori* unknown but follow a certain distribution observable in the market history. Then,

$$M = E[\sum_{i=1}^{n} x_i (1+r_i)]. \qquad (3)$$

Unless the investors are risk-neutral, M is not the only criterion to evaluate the portfolio. To account for the saturation effects, we replace M with a utility function, $M \to u(\{x_i\})$, which is a nondecreasing function of M. A particular case of utility function $u(M\{x_i\})$ is discussed below (returns on hedging costs), but other market settings can also be used with CGAs. We optimize the Lagrangian

$$L = E[u(M\{x_i\})] + \Lambda(1 - \sum_{i=1}^{n} x_i), \qquad (4)$$

where Λ is a multiplier and $\{x_i\}$, $i = 1,..,n$, the portfolio. Candidates for optimal x and Λ are found solving the transcendent equations $\{\partial L/\partial x_i = 0$, $i = 1,..,n$ and $\sum_{i=1}^{n} x_i = 1\}$. In practice, a brute force approach with iterative refinement is often advantageous, that is, to sample $x_i^{(j)} = j/N, j = 0,..,N$, where N is a large number, $i = 1,..,n-1$, and $x_n = 1 - \sum_{i=1}^{n-1} x_i^{(j_i)}$. Then any local maximum at $[j_0^*,..,j_{n-1}^*]$ can be further refined by reiterating the above procedure in the multidimensional cube between $[j_0^* - 1,.., j_{n-1}^* - 1]$ and $[j_0^* + 1,.., j_{n-1}^* + 1]$. We adapt this method for its simplicity and robustness in the YMYP model.

The amount of published work on portfolio optimization problem and investment strategies has been vast and excellent reviews exist in the literature (Luenberger 1998; Markowitz, 1991; Michaud 1998; Sutton & Barto, 1998). In case the investor portfolio is small compared to the market volume, investment strategies are not shared, and the market is relatively stable, it is possible to observe probability distributions over the market and discover the optimal investment strategy for with the dynamic programming (DP). DP proceeds recursively from easy optimization problems (few steps before the target maturity date in future) to more complex ones (extending thus to the entire optimization period). Note that the GAs discussed in this work do not necessarily require the Markov property of the market.

Figure 2. Market clearing algorithm (YMYP bid-ask array)

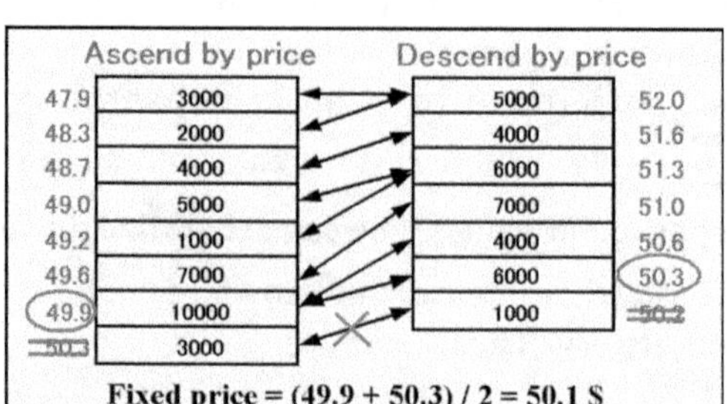

Certain features in genetic learning, for instance the not necessarily smooth change in strategy parameters during crossover and mutation, are of concern in high-detail simulations of complex markets with a predictive ambition. That is where the reinforcement learning (RL) are more appropriate, following the smoother anatomy of human learning process. RL algorithms (cf. e.g., Sutton & Barto, 1998), on the other hand, must be predesigned with great care to reflect the real system, unlike from the more exploratory—hence also more robust—GAs.

For short-term, high-liquidity, high-frequency trading, pattern recognition (e.g., with neural networks) and robotic trading proves a very appropriate strategy (Guppy, 2000). Time value of money and discounting factors can be of crucial importance when the monetary market comes into play (Scott & Moore, 1984). It was observed from the analysis of NYSE composite index, for instance, that most of the time the ex post optimal strategy for a minor investor appears binary (100% deposit or 100% stock; cf. Slanina, 1999). Perhaps the closest fellow of the group of genetic algorithms discussed in the following is the genetic programming (GP) method that acts on the space of parse trees (evolving grammatically correct programs that represent e.g., investment strategies; cf. Chen & Yeh, 1995). The GP is especially useful for analysis of emerging phenomena on the microlevel of market players and its survival ability. Since GP is not really advantageous in case of static optimization problems, we leave this technique with the note that a hybrid algorithm, HSGP, could also be defined as GA+GP.

Because of the discrete formulation with various constraints in agent-based simulations, gradient optimization methods cannot be applied in a straightforward manner. The brute-force approach with iterative refinement on the hypercube defined by parameter ranges is the most robust option whenever it is computationally tractable. Beyond these limits, only some sort of sampling searching algorithms can be used. The two major options are simulated annealing (SA) and the GA. Since the SA ties closely with a special case of GA (crossover operator neglected), we restrict to the case of GAs in what follows.

COEVOLUTIONARY GENETIC ALGORITHM

Here we develop a framework for a realistic, applicable scaled genetic algorithm that converges asymptotically to global optima in a coevolutionary setting involving one, two, or several species. In what follows, we discuss two special cases of dual populations (buying vs. selling strategies, portfolio strategies vs. asset distributions). The CGA acts on constant size populations that contain two types of creatures which are supposed to be in canonical duality defining a population-dependent fitness function. If a nonempty set C_{max} of creatures of one or both types exists that have strictly maximal fitness in every population they reside in, then the CGA described here converges asymptotically to a probability distribution over biuniform populations that contains only the elements of C_{max} wherever these exist. The algorithm employs multiple-spot mutation, various crossover operators and power-law scaled proportional fitness selection. In order to achieve asymptotic convergence to global optima (homogenous population that includes at least one of the maximal creatures, as in Schmitt, 2003), the mutation and crossover rates have to be annealed to zero in proper fashion, and power-law scaling is used with logarithmic growth in the exponent. A large population size allows for a particularly slow annealing schedule for standard crossover operators.

Creatures and Populations

The CGA model uses an inhomogeneous Markov chain over a finite set of pure states (populations) $\wp$ which are considered as strings of letters over the underlying alphabets. We shall consider (the genome of) the two types of creatures (candidate solutions) to which the CGA is applied as strings of length ℓ_j over disjoint alphabets A_j where usually $2 \leq \ell_j \in \mathbf{N}, j \in \{0,1\}$. Let $C^{(j)}$ denote the two disjoint sets of possible creatures and $C = C^{(0)} \cup C^{(1)}$ the set of all possible creatures. The set of populations $\wp$, to which the CGA is applied, is the set consisting of ordered tuples of s_0 creatures from $C^{(0)}$ followed by s_1 creatures from $C^{(1)}$. This division of the population shall be kept fixed to optimize stably coexisting, interacting species (cf. Schmitt, 2003).

Genetic Operators

The coevolutionary setting is based on the most commonly used and analyzed GA operators.

Multiple-Spot Mutation

We consider the most common mutation operators as, e.g., in Goldberg, 1989; Vose, 1999; and Schmitt, 1998, 2001, and further allow for a non-uniform, neighborhood-determined change on the alphabet level. Let $\mu \in [0,1]$ denote the mutation rate and L the length of population as word over the combined alphabet. The multiple-spot mutation algorithm is then: for $\hat{\lambda} = 1 \ldots L$ do ((STEP 1: Decide probabilistically whether or not to change the letter at spot $\hat{\lambda}$ in the current population with probability μ. STEP 2: If the decision is positive in step 1, then the letter at spot $\hat{\lambda}$ is altered in accordance with the transition probabilities set by a spot mutation matrix $\mathbf{m}_{\mu_o}^{(j)}$ acting on the alphabet level.))

Crossover

We allow for essentially all standard crossover operators, in particular, single-cutpoint regular crossover (cf. Schmitt, 1998; Vose, 1999), unrestricted crossover (cf. Schmitt, 1998), regular multiple-cutpoint, uniform crossover (cf. Vose, 1999), and gene-lottery crossover (cf. Schmitt, 2003).

The Fitness Function and Selection

We adopt scaled proportional fitness selection based upon a canonical duality $<\cdot,\cdot>: C^{(0)} \times C^{(1)} \rightarrow \mathbf{R}$. This canonical duality $<\cdot,\cdot>$ is associated with the action of two members of the two species on each other (see examples below). If $p = (c_1, c_2, \ldots, c_s)$ is a population, $c_\sigma \in C$, $1 \leq \sigma \leq s$, then we define their fitness function: $f(c,p) = \exp(\sum_{\sigma=s_0+1}^{s} < c, c_\sigma >)$, for $c \in C^{(0)} \cap p$; and $f(c,p) = \exp(\varphi \sum_{\sigma=1}^{s_0} < c_\sigma, c >)$, for $c \in C^{(1)} \cap p$, $\varphi \in \{\pm 1\}$. The duality can be understood as a scalar product while ϕ determines the sign of interaction. (1) For $\varphi = 1$ there are two interacting, coevolving species having essentially the same objective. For example, one could evaluate or simulate the performance $<c,d>$ of a market dealer where c stands for the "buying strategy" and d stands for "selling strategy." (2) For $\varphi=-1$ there are two species having opposite objectives. For example, $C^{(0)}$ can be a collection of finite length portfolio optimization algorithms, $C^{(1)}$ a collection of investment opportunities. The duality $<\cdot,\cdot>$ then means negative or inverse profit. In this situation, a *high* value $<c,d>$ means that the strategy c performs *well* on the investment opportunity set d. With opposing goal, d has better fitness value, if the associated profit is smaller, that is, d is more difficult for market players to cope with.

Strictly Maximal Elements

The duality introduced above has *globally strictly maximal elements*, if there exists a set $C_{max} \subset C$ such that $C_{max} \cap C^{(0)} \neq \varnothing$ and for every $\hat{c},\hat{c}' \in C_{max} \cap C^{(0)}$, $c \in C^{(0)} \backslash C_{max}$, $d \in C^{(1)}$ one has: $<c,d> << \hat{c},d> = <\hat{c}',d>$. If $C_{max} \cap C^{(1)} \neq \varnothing$, then we shall also suppose that elements in $C_{max} \cap C^{(1)}$ are strictly maximal with respect to $<\cdot,\cdot>$ satisfying similar, dual identities. A well-behaved duality requires that $C^{(0)}$contains at least one element strictly superior with respect to the aspects measured by $C^{(1)}$ via $<\cdot,\cdot>$.

Optimal Population

The optimization algorithm is supposed to *maximize* f in the sense of finding elements of the set C_{max}. Let for $j \in \{0,1\}$: $Q_j = \{f(\hat{c},p)/f(c,p) : p \in \wp, \hat{c} \in p \cap C_{max}, \neq \varnothing, c \in p \setminus C_{max}\} \neq \varnothing\}$ and $\rho_2(f) = \min(Q_0 \cup Q_1) > 1$. Here $\rho_2(f)$ measures "maximal strength" of second-to-best $c \in C$ in all $p \in \wp$ that contain $\hat{c} \in C_{max}$.

Power-Law Scaling

Scaling of the fitness function should be in accordance with Goldberg (1989) and Schmitt (2001) as follows: for $c \in p$, $B \in \mathbf{R}_*^+$ let $f_t(c,p) = (f(c,p))^{g(t)}$ with $g(t) = B \cdot \log(t+1)$. In addition, set $f_t(t,p) = 0$, if $c \notin p$. In the following, only *logarithmic scalings* $g(t)$ as listed above are considered. Let us note that faster scalings with, for example, linear growth $g(t) = a_1 t + a_0$ in the exponent are of limited value in regard to the use of a crossover operation (Pichl, Schmitt & Wtanabe, 2003; Schmitt, 2001). Such algorithms are asymptotically equivalent to a "take-the-best" algorithm (Schmitt, 2001), where one cycle of the algorithm consists of (a) mutation and (b) selecting creatures of maximal fitness in the current population.

Scaled Proportional Fitness Selection S_t

Suppose that $p = (c_1, c_2, ..., c_s) \in \wp$ is the current population with $c_\sigma \in C$, $1 \leq \sigma \leq s$. For $c \in C$ let $\#(c,p)$ denote the number of copies of c in p. Now, the new population $q = (d_1, d_2, ..., d_s)$ is assembled as follows: for $\sigma = 1, ..., s$ do: ((If $\sigma \leq s_0$ set $j = 0$, otherwise $j = 1$. Select creature $d_\sigma \in q$ probabilistically among the creatures in p such that a particular $c \in p \cap C^{(j)}$ has relative probability $(\sum_{\sigma'=1+js_0}^{s_0+js_1} f_t(c_{\sigma'}, p))^{-1} \cdot \#(c,p) f_t(c,p)$ for being selected as d_σ)). Here, $\#(c,p)$ is the number of copies of c in p.

Convergence to Global Optima

Schmitt (2003) proved that the scaled GA (including the well-behaved duality) converges to a probability distribution over biuniform populations containing only elements of the set of maximal creatures $C_{max} \neq \varnothing$ wherever they exist under the condition $m(l_0 + l_1) < \min(s_0, s_1, LB \log(\rho_2(f)))$, $m \in \mathbf{N}$ fixed. Let us note in this respect that an annealing procedure is indispensable to obtain convergence to global optima. The simple GA executed finitely often or its asymptotics does not yield convergence to global optima. This makes it necessary to scale the parameters mutation-rate μ, crossover-rate χ and the fitness function with time. In fact, one has to anneal the mutation rate to 0 to steer the "thermal noise" in the overall ensemble towards "freezing" and, simultaneously, to increase the selection pressure via unbounded exponentiation of the fitness function, in order to achieve "freezing" in the desired globally optimal states. If the selection pressure increases too fast, the algorithm asymptotically reduces to a trivial "mutate and take-the-best" procedure without crossover and based on trivial selection.

Implementation Issues

The complete model is represented by the regular GA operations mutation $M_{\mu_o(t),\mu(t)}$, crossover $C(\chi_t)$ and selection S_t as stochastic matrices that act on the population state space $S_\wp$ of probability distributions over populations $p \in \wp$. Mutation and selection are represented by the above definitions, and almost any previously described and analyzed crossover matrix in the literature (see, e.g., Schmitt, 1998; Schmitt, 2001) is allowed. The prescribed algorithm is realistic as it acts on a small population where the population size does not depend upon the problem instance itself but upon the lengths of the genome of creatures. The explicit annealing schedules (Schmitt, 2003) for mutation rate $\mu(t) = (t + 1)^{-1/L}$, crossover rate $\chi_t = \mu(t)^{1/m}$, and fitness scaling are easy to implement. No infinite population size limit is necessary to achieve asymptotic convergence to global optima.

Results and Discussions

Let us derive the duality of portfolio strategy and asset distribution for market players to be optimized with CGA. If the average earning rate of asset i is $r_i = E[R_i]$, the expected portfolio rate of return and dispersion are

$$R = E\left[\sum_{i=1}^{n} x_i R_i\right] = \sum_{i=1}^{n} x_i r_i, \tag{5}$$

$$s^2(\{x_k\}) = \sum_{i,j=1}^{n} x_j x_i cov(R_j, R_i). \tag{6}$$

We employ hedging adapted utility function $\sim R/s$,

$$u(\{x_k\}) = \sum_i r_i x_i / s(\{x_k\}), \tag{7}$$

as the rate of return on hedging costs. Earning rates and covariances are obtained from the ensemble of 300 simulation runs of the YMYP program (each representing a period of 3 months; cf. Figure 1) by ensemble averaging. For the three particular earning rates $\{0.015059, 0.15673, 0.00606\}$ and their 3-by-3 covariance coefficient matrix $\{\{0.10278, 0.90171, 0.06792\}\ \{0.90171, 10.87852, 1.21145\}\ \{0.06792, 1.21145, 0.36622\}\}\times 10^{-4}$, the optimum of $u^* = 4.91$ is reached at $x_1^* = 89.8\%$, $x_2^* = 10.2\%$. Here, the asset correlation increases with the size of the off-diagonal matrix elements of the covariance matrix. Diagonal terms show the variance of each asset. The portfolio risk has been dealt with by minimizing strong positive correlations. A dual transform by uncorrelated asset m based on (7) ($s_r^2 = 10^{-3}$ for rate r) is shown in Figure 3. The underlying duality $<\text{strategy}, \text{asset}>$ evaluates to overall profit in every particular simulation run.

MACROLEVEL

To optimize system structures, Kareken and Wallace (1982) model society is subjected to an SGA. Lux and Schornstein (2005) analyzed the universal properties of GA as an evolutionary engine for this model in great detail. First, we review their approach for an equal wealth distribution w as in previous works (Arifovic, 1996, 2000; Lux & Shornstein, 2005). The SGA then operates on the genome of $w_i(t)$ ($i = 1, ..., N$ denotes society members, t indexes life periods, and the total wealth is fixed, $\sum_{i=1}^{N} w_i(t) = W$).

Market Model

The model of two coupled economies adopted here was introduced by Kareken and Wallace in 1981. The society consists of N members, half of them young (index 1), the rest being old (index 2). As the time step advances by one unit from t to $t + 1$, the young (relative to t) enter the population of the old (relative to $t + 1$) and the old population passes away (step $t + 1$). The deceased are replaced by the same number of descendants

Figure 3. Noncorrelated asset transform of x_1^* and x_2^* vs. r

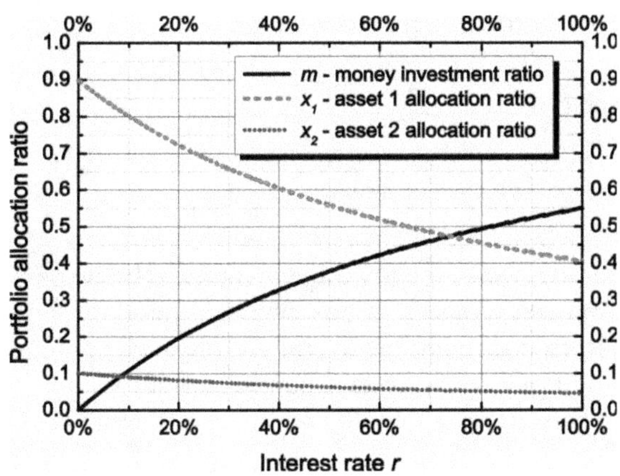

at $t + 1$. In the context of the underlying GA the children are called offspring and have somewhat different genes from the parents. Because a rigorous quantification of the difference depends on the actual implementation of GA operators (e.g., genome encoding, magnitude of mutation probability, or strength of the election operator), we summarize the properties of the underlying GA in detail.

Offspring do not inherit assets from their parents. They produce constant endowment (w_1, w_2) and equivalent earnings. Savings are defined in a twofold way, either as (a) a deferred consumption (physical units) or (b) a money deposit (currency units). Endowment is large at youth (w_1) and small in old age (w_2). The only way to redistribute the consumption level smoothly throughout the life is a deferred consumption and money holding of both domestic and foreign currency. The problem at question is to determine the optimal values of savings and the optimal ratio of domestic currency to hold at the time of youth. The agents are assumed to be rational and fully consume the old-age endowments and all savings.

Life of society members is evaluated by a utility function which depends on their consumption values,

$$U(c_i(t), c_i(t+1)). \tag{8}$$

Standard economics argues for over-proportional utility growth of the poor and a saturation effect at high consumption levels. Various functional dependencies are possible, in principle. Considering a two life period span of society members - the artificial agents, we set

$$U(c_i(t), c_i(t+1)) = c_i(t) * c_i(t+1). \tag{9}$$

Here $c_i(t)$ is agent i's consumption level at time t (when he is young), and $c_i(t+1)$ is agent i's consumption level at time $t+1$ (when he is old). A plausible feature of the above equation is that zero consumption in either period of life is suppressed and optimum exists in between. For realistic applications, inter-temporal valuation can be added (discount rates, etc.). The model can also be easily generalized to L periods of life, instead of just a two, and the utility function modified accordingly. The consumption values are subject to the following constraints:

$$c_i(t) = w_1 - s_i(t) \text{ and} \tag{10}$$

$$c_i(t+1) = w_2 + \alpha s_i(t). \tag{11}$$

Here $s_i(t)$ is the *physical* savings of i's agent at time t. In the next time period, $t+1$, the agent uses his monetary savings to buy physical goods in order to increase his consumption by the deferred amount. In general, the physical amount of savings and the physical amount of additional old-age consumption (with w_2 not included) differ by inflation or deflation. This effect is denoted by the coefficient α in (11). Precisely, the savings are

$$s_i(t) = \frac{m_{i,1}}{p_1(t)} + \frac{m_{i,2}}{p_2(t)}, \text{ and} \tag{12}$$

$$\alpha s_i(t) = \frac{m_{i,1}}{p_1(t+1)} + \frac{m_{i,2}}{p_2(t+1)}, \tag{13}$$

where $m_{i,1}$ and $m_{i,2}$ is the money holding of domestic and foreign currency for agent i, respectively. The price level in domestic currency at time t is denoted as $p_1(t)$ ($p_2(t)$ for foreign currency). There are no geographic restrictions and agents choose their portfolio purely by their preference encoded in their chromosome. Denoting the nominal money supply of domestic and foreign currency H_1 and H_2, the price level in standard economics equates the currency supply and demand for goods,

$$p_1(t) = \frac{H_1}{\sum_i f_i(t) \cdot s_i(t)}, \quad p_2(t) = \frac{H_2}{\sum_i (1 - f_i(t)) \cdot s_i(t)} \tag{14}$$

and f_i is the rate of savings in domestic currency,

$$f_i(t) = \frac{m_{i,1}(t)}{p_1(t) \cdot s_i(t)}. \tag{15}$$

Note that the previous definition of $f_i(t)$ in (15) theoretical. In practical implementation, the value of $f_i(t)$ is simply decoded from the chromosome yielding a value in [0,1], and therefore $m_{i,1,2}$ is already determined (s_i is also encoded in the chromosome; p_1 and p_2 result from the algebraic relation in (14)). A simple generalization of the nominal monetary supply in which $H_1(t)$ and $H_1(t)$ become time-dependent quantities allows for studying the effects of monetary policy, for instance. Taxation or disasters can be modelled by time-dependent endowments $w_1(t)$ and $w_2(t)$, social inequality may come into play by allowing for distributions $\{w_{1,2}^{(i)}\}$, $i = 1,..,N$ and so forth.

The equilibrium exchange rate between both currencies must be $e(t) = p_1(t)/p_2(t)$, otherwise arbitrage would be possible. The exchange rate can be constant over time as long as the consumption plans of all agents are stationary. There are extreme situations in which every agent chooses foreign currency only ($f_i = 0$, $e^* = \infty$) or vice versa ($f_i = 1$, $e^* = 0$). This can occur only if no restrictions on FX trading are present. Agents are completely passive to GA force and follow policies in their genes. The model is self-contained (i.e., no outer force drives any of its properties). Only the endogenous forces produced as a result of genetic operations are responsible for the model dynamics (cf. Lux & Shornstein, 2005).

Underlying Genetic Algorithm

The model implementation follows that of Arifovic and Gencay (2000). Each agent's lifetime consumption and currency portfolio plan (cf. Figure 4) is encoded in his chromosome (a binary string) of length 30. The first 20 bits encode the consumption c_i while the rest defines the currency portfolio f_i. These values can be decoded from the chromosomes as follows:

$$c_i = \sum_{k=1}^{20} a_i^k \cdot \frac{2^{k-1}}{K_1}, f_i = \sum_{k=21}^{30} a_i^k \cdot \frac{2^{k-21}}{K_2}, \tag{16}$$

where a_i^k denotes the k-th bit of chromosome i (each chromosome encodes one creature). K_1 and K_2 are normalization constants that restrict c_i within $[0,w_1]$ and f_i within $[0,1]$. From (16), one immediately finds $K_1 = (2^{20}-1)/10$ and $K_2 = 2^{20}-1$. The length of the chromosome binary string does not have an appreciable impact on the properties of the model unless the grid of possible values is too sparse.

To evaluate the utility function of each agent, the consumption in both life periods must be known. Here, $c_i(t)$ is encoded in agent i's chromosome

$$c_i(t+1) = w_2 + s_i(t) \cdot [f_i(t)\frac{p_1(t)}{p_1(t+1)} + (1-f_i(t))\frac{p_2(t)}{p_2(t+1)}], \tag{17}$$

and $s_i(t) \equiv w_1 - c_i(t)$. The fitness (the degree of "how much the creature fits its environment") reads

$$\mu_{i,t-1} = U(c_{i,t-1}(t-1), c_{i,t-1}(t)) = c_{i,t-1}(t-1) \cdot c_{i,t-1}(t), \tag{18}$$

and $\mu_{i,t-1}$ stands for "fitness of agent i who was born at time $t-1$ and evaluated at time t". After the calculation of fitness, new offspring are initialized by copying old agents as candidates for children. The frequency of chromosome copies depends on their fitness function, which is referred to as a "biased roulette wheel" (cf. Arifovic & Gencay, 2000). More precisely,

Figure 4. Binary-encoded and real-encoded agents

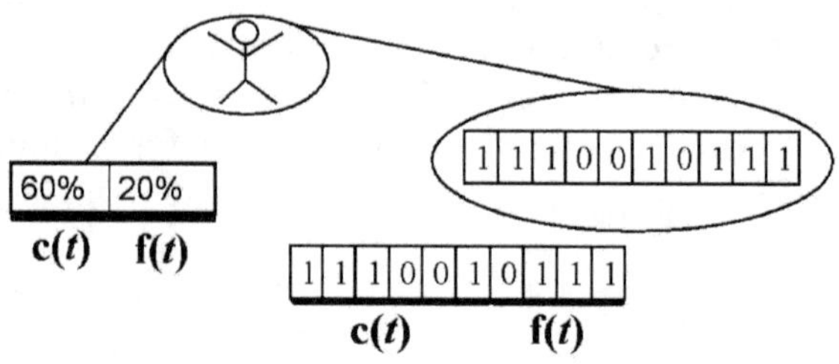

$$P(C_{i,t-1}) = \frac{\mu_{i,t-1}}{\sum_{i=1}^{N} \mu_{i,t-1}}, i \in [1, N], \tag{19}$$

which means a copy of i's agent chromosome C is chosen with the probability P in (19). Namely, agents that perform well agents provide their copies to the new generation more frequently. After N copies (the same number as that of the parents) are made, the newly produced agents in the *matingpool* are exposed to three operators: mutation, crossover, and election (cf. Lux & Shornstein, 2005).

Local Attractors

Omitting the time and agent indices in the notation of savings and currency portfolios, the utility function reads

$$U(s, f) = (w_1 - s)\cdot\left(w_2 + s\cdot\left[f\pi_1 + (1-f)\pi_2\right]\right), \tag{20}$$

with

$$\pi_i \equiv \frac{p_i(t)}{p_i(t+1)}, \quad i = 1, 2. \tag{21}$$

The first differential equation for the optimal condition $\partial U / \partial s = 0$ implies $s^* = (\kappa w_1 - w_2)/(2\kappa)$ with $\kappa \equiv f\pi_1 + (1-f)\pi_2$. In the stationary state $\kappa = 1$ and $s^* = (w_1 - w_2)/2$. The second stationary condition $\partial U / \partial f = 0$ implies $\pi_1 - \pi_2 = 0$ (i.e., the exchange rate $e(t)$ is constant). In such a case, all possible values of f are optimal. Otherwise, for $\pi_1 > \pi_2$ ($\pi_1 < \pi_2$), the maximum value is obtained at the boundaries of the constrained interval as $f^* = 1$ ($f^* = 0$). Here, $f^* = \{0,1\}$ are equivalent attractor points between which the market dynamics oscillate in evolutionary races. This is because for $\pi_1 = \pi_2$, a small fluctuation in either direction can ignite selection pressure towards $f^* = 1$ ($f^* = 0$). Since the s_i and f_i chromosomes only weakly couple through the market mechanism and not via agent's strategy, CGA discussed in section III can evolve separate f and s populations in a cooperative way although there exists no stable optimum.

Model Parameters

We have used the following parameter values to evaluate encoding method and effects of GA operators: $H_1 = 3000$, $H_2 = 3600$, $w_1 = 10$ and $w_2 = 4$. Probabilities of *crossover* and *mutation* varied in order to understand the effects of these GA operators. Because the definition of the utility function is $c_i(t) * c_i(t+1)$, the equilibrium consumption value $0.5(w_1 + w_2)$ equals 7.0 (cf. Lux & Shornstein, 2005).

The underlying GA model was first analyzed by using binary encoding. A plateau is found in the variance of the histogram of normalized returns on exchange rate for moderate values of mutation probability $p_m \in (0.01, 0.1)$, which is very suitable for numerical experiments (cf. Figure 5). The crossover operator stabilizes the market and increases the power law exponent at low p_m. Next, substantial impact on market dynamics was found according to the GA encoding method. In particular, the leading term mutations in binary-encoded GA are responsible for the large widths in returns histogram distribution compared to real-encoded GA. Large differences can appear in the power law exponent, depending on whether the election operator is included in the model or not. On the other hand, the crossover operator hardly affects simulation results in real-encoded GA. The creature genome in the real-encoded and binary-encoded cases is schematically shown in Figure 4. In order to develop system structure optimization models (e.g., for determining the wealth distribution w_1 and w_2 among agents), the above findings must be included in the SGA setting properly. This reference case has been settled previously (cf. Lux & Shornstein, 2005) and the corresponding histograms and sample data are given in Figsures 5a–c) for reference.

Supergenetic Algorithm The GA model discussed in the previous sections never stops. It reproduces the appropriate statistics of normalized returns within the simple economy by sampling the phase space of parameters in a reasonable way. It should be noted this is very different from causative predictions of $e(t+\Delta)$ from $e(t' < t)$ or society optimization in complex market simulators. The model (Lux & Shornstein, 2005) represents an ideal reference case for parameterless comparative studies. The problems of interest in policy making here is optimizing the endowment distribution in the society, $w_1^{(i)}$ and $w_2^{(i)}$ $(i = 1, ..., N)$, for the active (1) and retirement (2) periods by means of fiscal and tax policy, or determining monetary policies in the two countries, $H(0 \leq t \leq T) \equiv H_1(t)/H_2(t)$. Both cases represent an SGA genome. The fitness function for SGA creatures (endowment distributions or periodic $H(t)$ patterns) is evaluated by the underlying GA model based on the selected objectives,

Figure 5. Histogram of normalized log returns: (a) using binary-encoded GA, p_m = 2, 4, 6, 8%, (b) daily, weekly, and monthly log returns (USD/JPY), (c) without the crossover operator for p_m = 2, 4, 6, 8%, (d) change of the histogram width during the SGA evolution

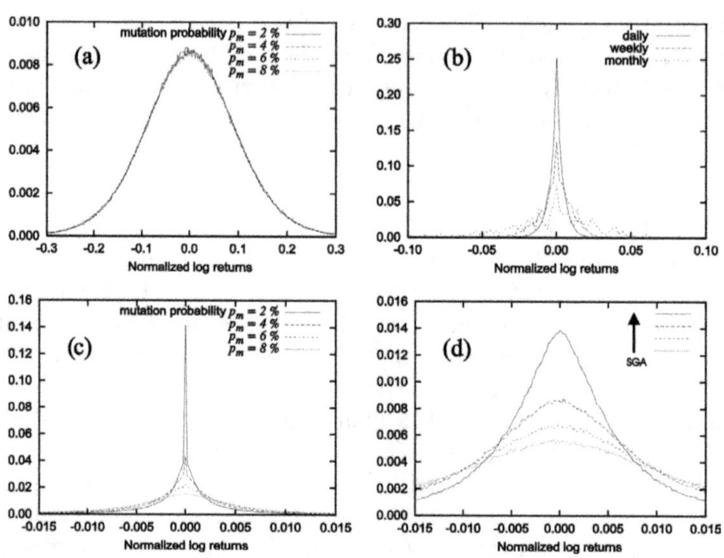

1. Social issues, $\left\langle \sum_{i=1}^{N} (U(c_i(t), c_i(t+1)) \geq U_0?0:1) \right\rangle_t$,
2. Volatility, $\left\langle \sigma_{p_{1,2},e}(t) \right\rangle_t$,
3. Consumption, $\left\langle \sum_{i=1}^{N} c_i(t) \right\rangle_t$,

where $< ... >_t$ means weighing by the underlying GA and the symbol "?" evaluates the left-hand-side expression to 1 (inequality satisfied) or 0 (inequality not satisfied). With respect to the statistical properties of the underlying market with 100 agents, 1 mil. iterations provides at least 3 significant digit weighing accuracy (with corresponding CPU time in the order of minutes). Various social criteria (e.g., social welfare of entire society $\Sigma_i U_i$) are possible in principle. Other policies (e.g., fiscal, taxation) can be studied only if the structure of the underlying society is allowed more complex. Because it requires introduction of new parameters and discarding the reference case, we do not consider this here. Figure 5d shows the stepwise narrowing of the histogram of normalized returns when being minimized with SGA. The plot displays the underlying market histogram for the best supercreature. Here $w_i(t)$ is parameterized by a polynomial of 3rd order and the best supercreature is always kept in SGA population.

The macrolevel model above appears to be limited by involving only two countries. This drawback can be removed easily, since the country of residence is, in fact, unspecified. In a straightforward manner, the model can be reformulated for two different saving assets, for instance. Also the age discrimination may be softened by adding more periods of life or restating the age period as a learning interval instead. The original terminology of the Kareken, Wallace, Arifovic and Lux model has been maintained here especially for the sake of clarity and easy comparison.

Having accomplished the SGA and CGA formulations above, one can explore a variety of interesting problems, for instance to study how the microbehavior of market players may resist against or coordinate with social planner's optimization. In the SGA framework, because of the clear distinction between immediate agent behavior and the macroregulation imposed (and evaluated) on the space of all market states, such analysis is possible only at the homogenous aggregate level of converged populations. Using the SGA, on the other hand, in principle allows for the study of response dynamics of the system to its regulator.

CONCLUSION

We have formulated a policy optimization problem for an evolutionary (GA) market setting. On the microlevel, portfolio optimization policy has been analyzed in the context of coevolutionary genetic algorithm (CGA). On the macrolevel, social and regulatory policies have been stated in the context of supergenetic algorithm (SGA).

For the microlevel investment portfolio optimization, (a) an online, agent-based market simulation model was developed, (b) the portfolio optimization problem was studied in this simulated environment, and (c) conditions for asymptotic convergence of scaled CGA used in optimization were clarified (cf. Pichl et al., 2003) The setting for the CGA involves a specific duality such as profit realization for interacting portfolio strategies and asset distributions provided that there exist strictly maximal creatures in the population. Otherwise, the analytical discussion presented here sets guidelines and boundary conditions for likely successful applications of CGA regardless of the condition on globally strictly maximal creatures. It is also noteworthy that larger population size favors crossover for optimal convergence.

On the macrolevel of system policies, the SGA appears as a promising tool for *qualitative* analysis of various market and social policies. The hierarchical nesting of the genetic algorithms as (a) an evolutionary engine and a (b) policy optimization tool is methodologically interesting. Since the underlying market simulation is very fast (CPU time in the order of minutes), qualitative effect of market policies can be thoroughly explored. The model case of Kareken and Wallace (1982) economy allowed for analytical insight into this approach, suitable for calibrations of SGAs.

The formalism of SGA developed and discussed in this chapter can be of significant practical interest to regulatory economic policies, resolving controversial issues and assessing stability of market trends. While the underlying GA drives the market to pass through the phase space of possible states (not necessarily even observed before in real markets), the upper level GA optimizes the economic policy to account for all such possibilities. Therefore various macroeconomic policies can be *tested* and *assessed* in this algorithmic framework.

ACKNOWLEDGMENT

L. P. acknowledges partial support by JSPS Grant-in-Aid for young scientists. We would like to thank the anonymous reviewers for very helpful comments.

REFERENCES

Arifovic, J. (1996). The behavior of the exchange rate in the genetic algorithm and experimental economies. *Journal of Political Economy, 104*(3), 510-541.

Arifovic, J., & Gencay, R. (2000). Statistical properties of genetic learning in a model of exchange rate. *Journal of Economic Dynamics and Control, 24,* 981-1006.

Chen, S.-H., & Huang, Y.-C. (2005). On the role of risk preference in survivability. *IICNC, 3,* 612-621.

Chen, S.-H., & Yeh, C.-H. (1995). Predicting stock returns with genetic programming: Do the short-term nonlinear regularities exist? In D. Fisher (Ed.), *Proceedings of the 5th International Workshop on Artificial Intelligence and Statistics* (pp. 95-101). Ft. Lauderdale, FL: Society for Artificial Intelligence and Statistics.

Chen, S.-H., & Yeh, C.-H. (2001). Evolving traders and the business school with genetic programming. *Journal of Economic Dynamics and Control, 25*(3-4), 363-393.

Epstein, J., & Axtel, R. (1996). *Growing artificial societies.* Washington, DC: Brookings Institution Press.

Goldberg, D. E. (1989). *Genetic algorithms in search, optimization and machine learning.* Boston: Addison-Wesley.

Guppy, D. (2000). *Market trading tactics: Beating the odds through technical analysis and money management.* Singapore: Wiley Asia.

Kaizoji, T. (2000). Speculative bubbles and crashes in stock markets: An interacting-agent model of speculative activity. *Physica A, 287,* 493-506.

Kareken, J., & Wallace, N. (1982). On the indeterminacy of equilibrium exchange rates. *Quarterly Journal of Economics, 96,* 207-222.

Kurahashi, S., & Terano, T. (2002). Emergence, maintenance and collapse of norms on information communal sharing: Analysis via agent-based simulation, in agent-based approaches in economic and social complex systems. *Frontiers in Artificial Intelligence and Applications* (pp. 25-34). Tokyo: IOS Press.

Luenberger, D. G. (1998). *Investment science.* New York: Oxford University Press.

Lux, T., & Schornstein, S. (2005). Genetic learning as an explanation of stylized facts of foreign exchange markets. *Journal of Mathematical Economics, 41*(1-2), 169-196.

Markowitz, H. M. (1952). Portfolio selection. *Journal of Finance, 7*(1), 77-91.

Markowitz, H. M. (1991). *Portfolio selection: Efficient diversification of investments.* Cambridge, MA: Blackwell.

Michaud, R. O. (1998). *Efficient asset management.* Boston: Harvard Business School Press.

Pichl, L., Schmitt, L. M., & Watanabe, A. (2003, September 26-30). Portfolio optimization with hedging in strictly convergent coevolutionary markets. In *Proceedings of Joint Conference on Information Sciences* (pp. 1251-1254). Cary, NC: AIM.

Schmitt, L. M. et al. (1998). Linear analysis of genetic algorithms. *Theoretical Computer Science, 200,* 101–134.

Schmitt, L. M. (2001). Theory of genetic algorithms. *Theoretical Computer Science, 259,* 1-61.

Schmitt, L. M. (2003). Theory of coevolutionary genetic algorithms. *Lecture Notes in Computer Science, 2745,* 285-293.

Scott, D. L., & Moore, W. K. (1984). *Fundamentals of the time value of money.* New York: Praeger.

Slanina, F. (1999). On the possibility of optimal investment. *Physica A,* 269, 554-563.

Stanley, H. E., Amaral, L. A. N., Canning, D. Gopikrishnan, P., Lee, Y., & Liu, Y. (1999). Econophysics: What can physicists contribute to economics? *Physica A, 269,* 156-169.

Sutton, R. S., & Barto, A. G. (1998). *Reinforcement learning: An introduction.* Cambridge, MA: MIT Press.

Tobin, J. (1958). Liquidity preference as behavior towards risk. *The Review of Economic Studies, 26,* 65-86.

Vose, M. D. (1999). *The simple genetic algorithm: Foundations and theory.* Cambridge, MA: MIT Press.

Chapter VI

Fundamental Issues in Automated Market Making

Yuriy Nevmyvaka
Carnegie Mellon University, USA

Katia Sycara
Carnegie Mellon University, USA

Duane J. Seppi
Carnegie Mellon University, USA

ABSTRACT

The goal of this chapter is to establish an analytical foundation for electronic market making. We use two classes of models to reason about this domain: structured and relaxed. In our structured model, we will formalize the decision process of a dealer and then use a simple class of trading strategies to highlight several fundamental issues in market making. In our relaxed model, we treat the dealer's quotes and transaction prices as a simple time series. We apply statistical techniques to discern possible structure in the data and then make conclusions about the dealer's optimal behavior. Our main interest is a normative automation of the securities dealer's activities, as opposed to explanatory modeling of human traders, which is the primary concern of earlier studies in this area.

INTRODUCTION

What is market making? In modern financial markets, the market makers (or dealers) are agents who stand ready to buy and sell securities. The rest of market participants are therefore guaranteed to always have a counterparty for their transactions. This renders markets more efficient, orderly, and less volatile. The market maker is remunerated for his or her services by being able to "buy low and sell high." Instead of a single price at which any trade can occur, the dealer quotes two prices—bid (dealer's purchase, customer's sale) and ask (dealer's sale, customer's purchase). The ask is higher than the bid, and the difference between the two is called the spread, which is the market maker's source of revenue. Although market maker's job description sounds fairly straightforward, his or her impact on the market's functioning is manifold. A market maker can be seen as a simple auctioneer—someone who intermediates trading and clears the market. In other cases, he or she may be the one responsible for "demand smoothing"—absorbing short-term shocks and preventing price jumps and crashes. A dealer can also be perceived as an "information aggregator" of sorts, since he or she observes the entire order flow and sets quotes accordingly. Finally, and in our opinion most important, a market maker is a source of liquidity in the market—he or she makes trading cheaper for other agents by being always ready to take the opposite side of any trade.

Now that the significance of the market maker's role has been established, the next question to ask is why it is necessary or desirable to automate this activity. This is an important task from both academic and practical points of view. First of all, we face a formidable intellectual problem: How can a machine automatically update the bid–ask spread, anticipate or react to the changes in supply and demand for a security, manage risk, adjust to market conditions, and so on? Second, this is a great test bed for machine learning and statistical techniques. Finally, creation of an electronic market maker is an attempt to replicate the human decision process, which is widely recognized as being notoriously difficult to model or imitate. The task of making a computer behave like a human has been one of the main goals of AI for decades.

From a more pragmatic point of view, electronic market makers could eventually replace highly paid human professionals, or, more realistically, give these professionals a tool to boost their productivity and their contribution to the markets. Automated dealers, if designed properly, will not engage in market manipulation and other securities laws violations that recently resulted in a number of dealer-centered scandals on both the NASDAQ (Christie & Schultz, 1994) and NYSE (Ip & Craig, 2003) markets. Also, a more in-depth knowledge and understanding of the dealer's behavior will give us a better guidance in extreme situations (such as market crashes) and will facilitate the regulatory oversight. In recent years, financial markets saw a surge in automated trading strategies to the point that markets populated by electronic traders are becoming a possibility. Many questions arise from this reality, such as "will the markets become extremely volatile and prone to crashes, or will the removal of 'the human factor' make them more rational and stable?" We hope our research can shed some light on what financial evolution holds in store for us.

Last, we expect automated market making to contribute to areas other than finance and artificial intelligence: It can make an impact in disciplines that employ various market mechanisms to solve distributed problems. In robotics, wherein large groups of autonomous robots "buy" and "sell" tasks that have to be accomplished for the grater common good (as described in Zlot, Stentz & Thayer, 2002), a presence of a centralized "task dealer" will replace the current system of one-on-one negotiations that can be costly or even impossible due to technical constraints. In the intelligent agent's domain (see e.g., Klusch & Sycara, 2001), so-called middle agents already play an important role in putting different parties in touch. These infrastructure entities can be further augmented with the information aggregation capabilities of electronic market makers. Implications for electronic commerce (Huang, Scheller-Wolf & Sycara, 2002) should be clear—automated intermediation can greatly facilitate negotiations among agents. The list of disciplines that stand to benefit from our research goes on: distributed computing, experimental economics and so forth.

In this chapter, we showcase two approaches to implementing an automated market maker. Most of the chapter will be devoted to a structured model of market making, where we use the insights from the market microstructure branch of finance (balanced inventory, for example) as fundamental building blocks for creating an electronic dealer. We concentrate on applying these principles in the real-world environment, however, making as few assumptions and simplifications as possible about the price-formation process. To achieve this, we employ a trading simulator, which merges the data feed from the Island ECN with the artificial orders created by trading agents. We propose a very simple market making strategy aimed at highlighting the important issue in this domain and serving as a benchmark for more sophisticated methods.

Our second task is to step away from modeling a dealer as a rational agent and to simply analyze available data. We demonstrate the usefulness of time series analysis, which can help find some underlying structure in historical prices and quotes. Armed with this structure, we can then make conclusions about the dealer's optimal behavior.

The overall goal of this chapter is to establish an analytical framework of the electronic market making, using a simple class of strategies to highlight some central issues and challenges in this domain. The chapter is organized as follows. The next section explains where our effort is situated relative to research in related areas, emphasizing the normative and interdisciplinary nature of our approach. Then we describe the simulator used in our experiments and present a separation between market making as an institution vs. market making as a trading strategy to explain the pertinence of our approach. In the following section we outline major ideas from the field of market microstructure that help us think formally about the dealer's decision problem and present a general taxonomy of possible strategies. The next section makes a case for so-called nonpredictive market-making strategies and then presents the relevant experimental results followed by their analysis. The final section introduces a concept of relaxed models that are based largely on time series analysis and describes some preliminary results. We conclude with a recap of important issues and the description of future work.

RELATED WORK COMPARISON

In this section, we present an overview of relevant research from both finance and computer science fields and outline how our efforts differ from previous work.

Although automated market making is of a significant practical importance, and a lot of work in this area has been done in the brokerage industry over the past 2 decades, published results are few and far between for fairly obvious reasons. To the best of our knowledge, there are no comprehensive books on the subject, not even on the human dealers' activities. There are no written guidelines or "how-to" rule books on what is the optimal action for a dealer in a given situation. In the spirit of this chapter's goal—to establish an analytical foundation for electronic market making—our approach will be based on general economic principles applied to financial markets: supply and demand for a security, strategic decisions based on available information, expectations maximization and so forth. The branch of economics that aims to quantify these aspects is called *econometrics,* and Campbell, Lo, and MacKinlay (1997) serve an excellent, even if rather broad, primer on this subject. We are primarily interested in market mechanisms on the lowest levels—individual transactions and not end-of-the-day prices—that fall within the domain of market microstructure. O'Hara (1995) provided a comprehensive overview of leading theories in this area.

The number of individual academic papers on financial modeling and market organization is very large, so we will mention only a handful of the more pertinent ones. Securities prices are generally modeled as variations of a random walk process, which is a consequence of the efficient market hypothesis. For an overview of related mathematical models, see Hull (1993). For a recent attempt to reconcile efficient markets and technical analysis (predictable patterns in prices) see Kavajecz and Odders-White (2002) and Kakade and Kearns (2004). In more specific settings, Madhavan (1992) and H. Stoll and Whaley (1990) developed theoretical frameworks for the process of price formation under different market mechanisms. Black (1971) produced a visionary paper describing the advantages of automated securities exchanges, which are becoming more and more of a standard. The evolution of this trend of automated trading and the related challenges are documented in Becker, Lopez, Berberi-Doumer, Cohn and Adkins (1992). And, finally, Domowitz (2001) looks ahead at potential future developments in electronic exchanges, concentrating on liquidity provision and the role of financial intermediaries.

We emphasize our reliance on market microstructure theory in our work, and thus we find surveys on this topic very helpful. The earliest progress in the area is documented in Cohen, Maier, Schwartz and Whitcomb (1979). H. R. Stoll (2001) is probably the most accessible and comprehensive review, which includes the discussion of the trading process, bid-ask spread, market organization, and implications for other areas of finance. Madhavan (2000), although similar in its nature and structure, provides a complimentary reading to the previous work, because the author manages to present every topic from a slightly different perspective. Madhavan (2002) provides a guide tailored specifically for market professionals and, thus, is the most accessible, if slightly simplified. All the market microstructure theories that are particularly relevant to market makers are rehashed in H. Stoll (1999), where the author presents a number of ways that the dealer's role can be interpreted: auctioneer, price stabilizer, information aggregator, and liquidity provider. In reality, it is likely the mixture of all of the above. Another interesting take on the same problem is presented in H. Stoll (2000), where all the microstructure effects (discrete prices, bid-ask spread, transparency, reporting, etc.) are called "frictions"—as in "in the frictionless markets none of this would have mattered and prices would have been a perfect reflection of available information." The underlying theories are essentially the same, but this chapter helps one to better understand the nature of the issues we are dealing with.

Because the bid-ask spread is the central aspect in the study of dealers' activities, it is necessary to mention Cohen, Maier, Shwartz and Whitcomb (1981), which proves that the existence of the spread is inevitable in all but perfect markets. Amihud and Mendelson (1980) and Ho and Stoll (1981) are the two founding papers in the bid-ask spread literature. They essentially postulate that the market maker's quotes are primarily functions of his or her inventory holding, and that the dealer adjusts them to balance his or her inventory (i.e., to prevent the accumulation of large positive or negative position in the underlying security). In other words, using his or her quotes, the dealer induces such transactions from the rest of market participants that move his or her inventory toward some desired levels. A more recent work, which also adopts inventory as the central explanatory variable is Madhavan and Smidt (1993). Its main finding is that inventory effects are indeed important, at least in the middle to long term. Another empirical study, which attempts to establish the importance of inventory effects is Hasbrouck and Sofianos (1993), which confirms that inventory adjustments in response to trades can be delayed significantly—up to 1 or 2 months.

The other, perhaps alternative, approach to explaining the presence and behavior of the bid-ask spread is presented in Glosten and Milgrom (1985). Because the market maker is a committed counterparty to any trade, he or she is bound to loose out on transactions with traders who know more than he or she. The bid-ask spread exists to compensate the dealer for these loses, because it is being charged indiscriminately to both informed and uninformed traders. This same idea is expanded and cast in a more complex framework in Easley and O'Hara (1987, 1992), where more periods and more choices (higher branching factor) are introduced into the model.

The truth is that both effects—inventory and information—influence the dealer's decision making, and therefore must both be incorporated into market making models. O'Hara and Oldfield (1986) is one of the first publications to recognize this and to develop a joint model. A number of empirical studies sprung out of this "debate" trying to determine which effect is responsible for what portion of the bid-ask spread. Hasbrouck (1988) and (H. Stoll, 1989) are two prominent examples of such efforts. (Huang & Stoll, 1994, 1997) go even further by introducing other explanatory variables (e.g., a futures index and quotes covariance) to model the bid-ask spread evolution. Chau (2002) offers one of the more recent publication on this subject, which challenges some of the established concepts.

This brings us to a somewhat different class of models, which do not try to explain the underlying processes that affect price formation, but simply look at time series of variables and try to determine how these variables influence each other, without making many assumptions. Roll (1984), for example, suggested that the spread is simply a square root function of a covariance of stock price changes. This line of reasoning is extended in Glosten (1987); Choi, Salandro and Shastri (1988) and Hasbrouck (1991), all of the authors developing more complex "relaxed" (as opposed to "structured") models, which do not explicitly account for specific actions of market participants.

In our work, we strive to pull together past findings and useful tools from both finance and computer science to combine and leverage the strengths of these two disciplines. However, up to this point, the overwhelming majority of literature reviewed came from the finance side. This does reflect the reality that computer science publications on in this area are scarce, perhaps because this particular domain is considered "too applied." Indeed, many of the CS papers use the market-making domain as a setting to test some algorithm rather than a problem that requires a solution (the way it is treated in finance). We would like to reconcile the two approaches.

The first publication on automated market making (i.e., Hakansson, Beja & Kale, 1985) is a testimony that the interest in creating an electronic dealer has been around for 2 decades. The authors created a simple agent with a single goal of "demand smoothing"—acting as a counterparty when misbalances arise on either buy or sell side. They tried an array of "rules" that a market maker should follow, and some of their experiments are fairly insightful. The bottom line of this work is perhaps not very surprising—any "hard-coded" (nonadaptive) set of rules is bound to fail sooner or later on a set of new data to which it has not been specifically tailored.

A number of interesting recent publications on electronic market making came out of the MIT AI Lab—particularly Chan and Shelton (2001), Kim and Shelton (2002) and Das (2003). Although all three papers describe an implementation of an electronic dealer, there are significant differences between their approaches and ours. These authors employ simulated markets, as opposed to using a real-world price feed, and they only use market orders, without looking at limit order books. They rely mostly on the information-based models, similar to those in Glosten and Milgrom (1985). These studies implement both the analytical solutions of the financial theories and reinforcement learning algorithms that can be trained on past data.

Simulated markets are probably the strongest contribution of the CS community to date. Pitting trading agents in a controlled competition has always been an exciting event and a great motivation for research advancement. One of the first steps was taken by the Santa Fe Institute Double Auction Tournament (Rust, Miller & Palmer, 1994). Trading Agent Competition (TAC) (Wellman, Greenwald, Stone & Wurman, 2003) is a more recent and still extremely popular event. While these markets are highly stylized and based on a variety of auction mechanisms, the simulation of financial markets has also been attempted (see Kearns & Ortiz, 2003; Poggio, Lo, LeBaron & Chan, 1999). We have adopted the later simulated environment as a testing platform for our research. For a comprehensive survey of the recent efforts in artificial markets and agents-based financial simulations refer to CIEF (2003).

The field of econophysics probably deserves a special mention here. This discipline that attempts to reconcile physics' rigorous analytics with the real-world concerns of economics is particularly useful in microstructure studies like ours. For a general presentation see Montegna and Stanley (1999). Specifically useful in the market-making domain, Bouchaud, Mezard and Potters (2002) postulated that limit orders arrive under the power-law distribution. This knowledge can be used by an electronic dealer to efficiently anticipate and adjust to the order flow.

Finally, we should mention a significant overlap between the computer science and statistical work. For example, Papageorgiou's (1997) study is very similar to statistical time series studies discussed earlier, even though it is a product of MIT AI Lab. Another example is Thomas (2003), where the author combines technical analysis with the news-based trading. Although we are not explicitly looking for price patterns in our work, there may be a link between the technical analysis and market microstructure (as described in Kavajecz & Odders-White, 2002), plus the effect of unexpected news on stock prices is undeniable.

Although the research effort in the finance community is undeniably vast, there are certain shortcomings that we hope to address. First, when authors try to come up with a closed-form analytical solution, they necessarily have to make a number of assumptions and simplifications, which often times makes their formula not applicable when the real-world complexities get reintroduced into the picture. On the other end of the spectrum, empirical studies tend to concentrate on some specific data covering a limited number of securities over specified time. Models that emerge from such setups are explanatory in nature, and it is not evident that they can be applied to the new data. As mentioned, on the computer science side, market making is used more as an algorithmic test bed instead of a problem of its own. We will try to address these shortcomings by adapting a more normative approach to the problem. We hope to operationalize the knowledge from market microstructure theories, while being concerned with the system's future performance and identifying and quantifying main macrostructure factors that affect this performance.

EXPERIMENTAL SETUP

In our experiments, we used the Penn Exchange Simulator (PXS)—software developed at the University of Pennsylvania, which merges actual orders from the Island electronic market with artificial orders generated by electronic trading agents (Kearns, 2003). Island electronic marketplace is what is called an electronic crossing network (ECN). ECNs are somewhat different from traditional stock exchanges such as NYSE or the NASDAQ OTC market. NYSE and NASDAQ employ securities dealers to provide liquidity and maintain orderly markets, and use both market and limit orders. A market order is an instruction from a client to the dealer to buy or sell a certain quantity of stock at the *best available* price (i.e., "buy 100 shares of MSFT at the best price available right now"), whereas a limit order is an instruction to buy or sell a specified quantity of stock at a *specified or more advantageous* price (i.e., "sell 100 shares of MSFT at $25.53 or higher"). Therefore, market orders guarantee the execution of customer's transaction, but not the price at which such transaction will occur, whereas limit orders guarantee a certain price, but transaction may never happen. Island ECN is a purely electronic market, which only uses limit orders and employs no designated middlemen. All liquidity comes from customers' limit orders that are arranged in order books (essentially two priority queues ordered by price) as shown in Figure 1a (limit price—number of shares).

If a new limit order arrives, and there are no orders on the opposite side of the market that can satisfy the limit price, then such order is being entered into the appropriate order

Figure 1. Limit order trading

(a)		(b)	(c)
...		...	...
25.56 – 300	Sell Orders	25.56 – 300	25.56 – 300
25.55 – 1000	Sell Orders	25.55 – 1000	25.55 – 1000
25.35 – 200	Sell Orders	25.35 – 200	25.35 – 100
25.30 – 150	Sell Orders	25.30 – 150	
25.21 – 200	Buy Orders	25.21 – 200	25.21 – 200
25.19 – 300	Buy Orders	25.20 – 1000	25.20 – 1000
25.15 – 785	Buy Orders	25.19 – 300	25.19 – 300
25.10 – 170	Buy Orders	25.15 – 785	25.15 – 785
...		25.10 – 170	25.10 – 170
		...	...

book. For example, in Figure 1b, a new buy order for 1000 shares at $25.20 or less has arrived, but the best sell order is for $25.30 or more; thus no transaction is possible at the moment, and the new order gets entered into the buy queue according to its price. Say, another buy order arrives for 250 shares at $25.40 or less. This order gets transacted (or crossed) with the outstanding orders in the sell queue: 150 shares are bought at $25.30 and another 100 shares are bought at $25.35. The resulting order book is shown in Figure 1c. This shows that even though there are no designated market orders in pure electronic markets, immediate and guaranteed execution is still possible by specifying a limit price that falls inside the opposite order book. All crossing in ECNs is performed electronically by a computer respecting the price and time priority, without the intervention of any intermediaries. That is how a general electronic market functions.

What the simulator does is very simple: At each iteration, it retrieves a snapshot of the Island's order book, gathers all the outstanding limit orders from trading agents that participate in the simulation, and then merges all the orders (real and artificial) according to the ECN rules described previously: Some orders transact and some get entered into the appropriate queue. When transactions happen, agents get notified about the changes in their stock inventory and cash balances, and the new merged order book becomes available to all the agents to study and make decisions for the next iteration. This new order book is the state representation of the simulator's market, which can be different from the Island market because of the orders from electronic traders that are present in the simulator only. The inherent problem with such setup is that the Island (real-world) traders will not react to the actions of the traders in the simulator, which can lead to a disconnect between the two markets—the real and the simulated. This implies that in order for the experiment to remain meaningful, the simulator traders have to remain "low impact" (i.e., their actions should not move the simulated price significantly away from the Island price). We enforce this property by prohibiting the participating agents from accumulating a position in excess of 100,000 shares, either short or long. Such a simple rule gets the job done surprisingly well. To put thing in perspective, daily volume in the simulator reaches many million shares, and the number of participating agents is kept under 10 per simulation. Another approach is to force agents to close out their positions at the end of the day, which would naturally discourage them from accumulating significant one-sided holdings. (Note: deviation from the real-world price is guaranteed to be accompanied by a significant position held by at least one trader; thus inventory is indeed an effective variable to influence in order to prevent prices from deviating).

As stated before, the ECNs (and therefore our simulator) do not have market orders that have to flow through the dealer, or any designated dealers at all, for that matter, which can lead to a conclusion that such setup is ill-suited for studying the behavior of a market maker. It is necessary at this point to draw a distinction between the market making as an institution (as seen on the NYSE floor, for example) vs. the market making as a strategy (used on proprietary trading desks and certain OTC dealing operations). The former can be interpreted as a form of public service, where the market maker ensures a stable and orderly market. He or she is supposed to be compensated by the bid-ask spread, but because of heavy regulations aimed at the customer protection, the dealer often finds himself being restricted in trading opportunities, which heavily cuts into his or her profits (Ip & Craig, 2003). The latter can simply be interpreted as a strategy where the trader tries to keep his or her inventory around zero (being "market neutral") and to profit from short-term price fluctuations. And as far as low profile trading goes, the market maker is not supposed to "move" markets. As a matter of fact, the NYSE dealers are explicitly prohibited from doing so by the "negative obligation" principle. Therefore, our setup is perfectly well suited for studying market making as a strategy, which also happens to be the main part of market making as an institution.

MARKET MAKING: A MODEL

In this section, we decompose into two components the problem that the electronic market maker is facing: establishing the bid-ask spread and updating it. We further suggest a coarse subdivision of the update methods. The first step to creating an electronic market maker is the understanding of the responsibilities of a securities dealer. As mentioned before, the primary objective of a market maker is to continuously update the bid-ask spread. Doing this correctly is the key to making a profit: the spread has to be positioned in such a way that trades occur at the bid as often as at the ask, thus allowing the dealer to buy low and sell high. We will examine the mechanics of this process in great detail in the next section. The bid and the ask quotes are supposed to straddle the "true price" of a security (Ho & Stoll, 1981), and the difference between the two is the dealer's revenue. However, the true price is difficult to determine or model, plus it is not even clear if there is such a measure in the first place. Therefore, the first potential problem for a market maker (either human or artificial) is to decide where to establish the initial spread.

There are, essentially, two ways to approach this dilemma. The first, hard way is to perform the actual valuation of a security that is being traded: if it is a stock, try to determine the value of the company using corporate finance methods (cash flows, ratios, etc.); if it is a bond, determine the present value of the promised payments, and so on. An entirely new set of issues not discussed here arises if the market maker's valuation differs from the consensus among the rest of market participants. If there is no established market, or the market is very illiquid, then doing the valuation may be the only approach. Fortunately, the majority of the modern securities markets employ limit orders in some capacity. As discussed in the previous section, these orders are aggregated into an order book with two priority queues: one for buy and one for sell orders. These two queues should be a fairly accurate representation of the current supply (sell queue) and demand (buy queue) for the traded security. Presented with such supply–demand schedule, the market maker can determine the consensual value of a security. In the simplest case, the market maker can observe the top of each book—the best (highest) buy and the best (lowest) sell—also known as the "inside market". He or she can safely assume that the market's consensus of the true value of the security lies somewhere between these two numbers. For example, in Figure 2 the best bid is \$25.21, and the best ask is \$25.30; thus the inside market is referred to as "\$25.21-30", and the consensual price of the stock is somewhere in this interval. Now, the market maker can use the top of each book as a reference point for positioning his or her initial quotes—i.e., establish his or her own spread at \$25.23-28—and then start updating the bid-ask spread as the books evolve with new order arrivals, transactions and cancellations.

Updating the spread with a goal to maintain profitability is the essence of the market making. We classify market-making strategies into predictive and nonpredictive. The former try to foresee the upcoming market movements (either from the order book

Figure 2. Inside market

...
25.56 – 300
25.55 – 1000
25.35 – 200
25.30 – 150 □ Top sell

Inside Market

25.21 – 200 □ Top buy
25.19 – 300
25.15 – 785
25.10 – 170
...

misbalances, or from some established patterns) over a very short horizon, and adjust the spread according to these expectations, while the latter do not attempt to look forward, but are based solely on the information about the current inside market (top of each book). The nonpredictive strategies are inherently simpler, and, therefore, are better suited to serve as a base case for our introductory examination of electronic market making.

Here is a brief overview of predictive strategies. Generally, these strategies can be separated into two classes: structured and relaxed. Structured approaches try to explain and explicitly model all underlying forces that affect trading. In these models, we often deal with agents' preferences, think of traders as being informed or uninformed, patient or impatient, we model order arrival, and so on. In other words, we try to understand and take into account the actions of concrete real-world actors and processes that affect price formation. The simplest dealer models are probably inventory models, where the market maker's main risk stems from holding an unbalanced portfolio, and his or her actions are directed toward maintaining his or her securities holdings around some desired allocation. Information models, on the other hand, state that the dealer's main risk comes from loosing to better-informed traders, and that he or she has to be reimbursed for these losses through the bid–ask spread. Since both approaches are likely correct, we will need a comprehensive strategy, which accounts for the right mix of both sources of risk. These strategies can be further refined with optimal quoting—what prices to quote exactly, given all the outstanding orders in the market (essentially a representation for the supply and demand for a security). The question of optimal quantity to trade should also be answered.

Relaxed models, on the other hand, choose to ignore the presence of actors that influence prices and other market variables, but simply treat the time series of these variables as some abstract stochastic processes. The goal is to find relationships among various processes (variables). For example, some questions that we will ask are: Do past prices help forecast future prices? Do prices help forecast spreads? Can spreads help forecast arrival of certain order types? And Are volume misbalances meaningful? What we hope to find in this approach is some short-term predictive power, which can be either exploited by zero-cost traders (i.e., dealers), or integrated with the structural models to enhance them. In either case, if the time series analysis yields interesting results, we have to design and implement an appropriate strategy and test it on the real-world data. These models are discussed in depth later in this chapter.

Although predictive strategies are outside this chapter's scope, it is useful to have an idea about what they are to better understand the results and implication of the nonpredictive strategies. Furthermore, although nonpredictive strategies do not model some of the microstructure factors explicitly, they still have to address those factors, as we will see later in this chapter. The main thing to keep in mind about the nonpredictive approach is that it can serve as an excellent benchmark for more sophisticated techniques. As another building block toward a comprehensive market making strategy, we will demonstrate the application of time series analysis to the market microstructure domain.

NONPREDICTIVE STRATEGIES

First of all, in order to make a case for the nonpredictive strategies being even worth considering, let's re-examine in further detail how the market maker earns profit. The entire operation can be reduced to "buy low, sell high." Normally, examining the movement of the price of some stock over several hours or days, it is easy to discern some clear patterns: "The stock went up for a while, then went down a little, then got back up …" and so on. But if we reexamine the behavior of the stock over a very short time period (seconds or fractions of a second), then it becomes apparent that the stock constantly moves up and down, while going in the general (longer term) direction. To give an example, if the price of a stock is going up consistently for an hour, it does not mean that everyone is buying (or that all arriving orders are buy orders); selling is going on as well, and the price (along with the inside market in the order books) moves down as well as up. Why is this happening? It is not quite clear, and it is outside the scope of the present research. Having a lot of empirical evidence, we can accept this behavior as a fact exogenous to the system, at the very least for the liquid stocks. Figure 3 illustrates this scenario: While there is a general upward trend (the dotted line), we can see the simultaneous evolution of the order book, and transactions happening at the top of buy queue (market sale, dealer's purchase), then the sell queue (market purchase, dealer's sale), then buy, then sell again. While price is generally going up, the stock is being sold as well as bought. So, how does the market maker fit into all this? By maintaining his or

Figure 3. Bid–ask "bounce"

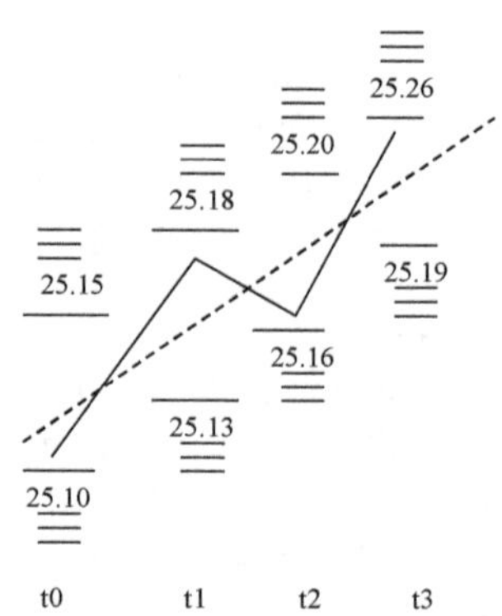

her quotes (the bid and the ask) on both sides of the market, at or close to the top of each order book, the market maker expects to get "hit" or transact at his or her bid roughly as often as at his or her ask because of these fluctuations. This way, after buying at the bid (low) and selling at the ask (high), the dealer receives the profit equal to the bid–ask spread for the two trades, or half the spread per trade. That is the fundamental source of the market maker's revenue. In the context of Figure 3, suppose that the top order in each queue is the dealer's; in this case, the dealer buys at $25.10, then sells at $25.18 (8 cents per share profit), then buys at $25.16 and sells for $25.26 (10 cents per share profit). If each transaction involves 1,000 shares, and all this happens over several seconds, it becomes clear that market making can be quite profitable.

Now, having understood the nature of the dealer's income, we can reformulate his or her task: adjust the bid-ask spread in such a way that the orders generated by other market participants will transact with the dealer's bid quote and the dealer's ask quote with the same frequency. In our example, we are looking for an algorithm to maintain the dealer's quotes on top of each queue to capture all incoming transactions. To facilitate thinking about the spread update, we can say that at any given point in time, the dealer has two possible actions: move the spread up or down relatively to its midpoint, and resize the spread—make it wider or narrower—again relatively to its midpoint. He or she may also want to change the "depth" of his or her quote—a number of shares he or she is committed to buy or sell. Let us put resizing and depth aside for the time being and assume that the size of the spread (and the inside market) is constant, and that the only thing the market maker does is moving the spread up and down as the price changes (state of the order book evolves). In our example, the stock price is steadily going up overall, while actually fluctuating around this general climb. If the market maker wants to capture the buy low, sell high opportunity, then his or her spread should also continuously move up straddling the stock price.

But how can the dealer tell at any given time looking forward that it is time to move the spread up and by how much? The nonpredictive family of electronic trading strategies would argue that he or she cannot and need not do so. Nonpredictive strategies postulate that while there are some patterns (streaks where the stock is either rising or falling) globally, the local evolution of the stock price is a random walk. If this random walk hits the bid roughly as often as it hits the ask, then the market maker makes a profit. If one subscribes to the theory that the short-term evolution of supply and demand for a security is random, then it is understood that an uptick in the stock price is as likely to be followed by a downtick as by another uptick. This implies the futility of trying to incorporate expectations of the future supply/demand shifts into the model governing the bid-ask spread updates. If this assumption holds, and if the market maker is actually able to operate quickly enough, then the trading strategy can be very simple. All the market maker needs to do is to maintain his or her bid and ask quotes symmetrically distant from the top of each book. As the orders arrive, transact, or get cancelled, the market maker has to revise his or her quotes as fast as possible, reacting to changes in such a way that his or her profitability is maintained.

In principle, the dealer should be market neutral (i.e., he or she does not care what direction the market is headed—he or she is only interested in booking the spread). On the other hand, the dealer is interested in knowing how the inside market will change over the next iteration in order to update his or her quotes correctly. The way the nonpredictive strategies address this is by assuming that the inside market after one time step will remain roughly at the same level as the current inside market (that is the best guess we can make, in other words). Therefore, being one step behind the market is good enough if one is able to react quickly to the changes. Such is the theory behind this class of strategies, but in practice this turns out to be more complicated.

PARAMETERIZING THE STRATEGY

Here is a general outline of an algorithm that implements the nonpredictive strategy; at each iteration:

1. retrieve the updated order book;
2. locate an inside market;
3. submit new quotes (buy and sell limit orders), positioned relatively to the inside market; and
4. cancel previous quote.

From this description and the theoretical discussion it is clear that there are three main factors, or parameters, that determine a nonpredictive strategy: position of the quote relative to the inside market, depth of the quote (number of shares in the limit order that represents the quote), and the time between quote updates.

Timing

Timing is, perhaps, the simplest out of the three parameters to address. In the spirit of the theoretical nonpredictive model presented in the previous section, the market maker wants to respond to changes in the market as soon as possible, and therefore, the time between the updates should be as close to zero as the system allows. Despite this property, it is still useful to think of the update timing as a parameter that should be minimized (i.e., the computational cycle should be performed as fast as possible), and the communication between the dealer and the market (how long does it take for an updated quote to show up in the limit order book) should also be minimized. In our experiment, the computational cycle is extremely short—less than 1 second—because of the inherent simplicity of the algorithm, but the communication delay can be rather significant because of the way the simulator is designed. It takes about 3-5 seconds for the order to get inserted into the book, and about the same amount of time for the order to get cancelled (if not transacted) after it appears in the book. This is one of the "frictions" of the simulator, which should not be overlooked. While these delays are not unreasonable by the real world's standards, they are not negligible. The dealer wants to access the market as quickly as possible, but such delays can prevent him from operating on a scale small enough to capture the small fluctuations. Therefore, other systems where these delays can be decreased can potentially be more effective and produce better results than our simulated setup.

Penny Jumping

Positioning the quote relative to the rest of the order book is the most important aspect. We use a simple distance metric—number of cents by which the dealer's quote

Figure 4. Improving each quote by 1 cent

...
25.56 – 300
25.55 – 1000
25.35 – 200
25.30 – 150 □ Top sell
25.29 – 500 □ Dealer's ask

Bid-Ask Spread

25.22 – 500 □ Dealer's bid
25.21 – 200 □ Top buy
25.19 – 300
25.15 – 785
25.10 – 170
...

differs from the top (nondealer) order in the appropriate book. We decided to start our strategy implementation from a fairly well-know, albeit somewhat controversial practice of "penny jumping."

In general, penny jumping occurs when a dealer, after entering his or her customer's order into the order book, submits his or her own order, which improves the customer's limit price by a very small amount. The dealer effectively "steps in front" of the customer: The customer's potential counterparty will now transact with the dealer instead; thus the dealer, arguably, profits from the customer's information, and, in some sense, trades ahead of the customer, although at a price improvement over the customer's limit order. Such practice is not exactly illegal (because the client's potential counterparty does get a better price by transacting with the dealer instead of the customer), but is considered unethical, and became the center of the recent NYSE investigation/review (Ip & Craig, 2003). In our case, we are simply undercutting the current inside market (or the de facto bid-ask spread) by 1 cent on both sides. The dealer's bid improves the current best bid by a penny, and the dealer's ask does the same on the sell side—Figure 4 shows that if the inside market is 25.21-30, our electronic market maker's orders will make it 20.22-29 (the size of the bid-ask spread goes from 9 to 7 cents). This way, the market maker is guaranteed to participate in any incoming transaction up to the size specified in the depth of his or her quote. We expect the following behavior from this strategy: The revenue (P&L) should rise slowly over time (because profit per share is tiny), while the inventory ought to fluctuate around zero (see Figure 5). We observed, however, that a typical run looks more like Figure 6: Although the inventory fluctuates around zero, the strategy gradually loses money over the course of a trading day.

The most fundamental problem is presented in Figure 7: Although we base our decision on the state of the book at time t_0, the outcome of our decision gets placed in a book at time t_1, which may or may not be different from the original t_0 book. We have already touched this problem in the update time discussion. Essentially, the nonpredictive market-making strategy places an implicit bet that the book at t_1 will be fairly close to the book at t_0, or at least close enough to preserve the profitable property of dealing. What actually happens in our experience with penny jumping, is that the inside market is tight

Figure 5. Expected pattern

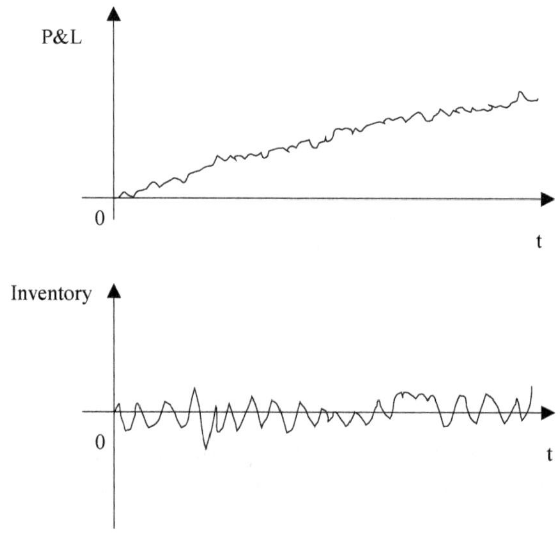

Figure 6. Observed pattern

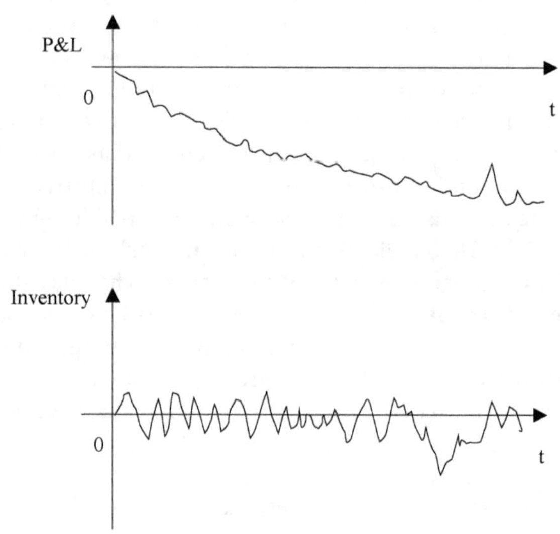

already, plus the book changes somewhat over in 3 seconds, and so, often times, both the bid and the ask quotes (limit orders) issued at t_0 end up on the same side of the market at t_1 (Figure 7). Then one of the orders transacts, and the other ends up buried deep in the order book.

Figure 7. Making decisions in one book, acting in another

…	…
25.56 – 300	25.56 – 300
25.55 – 1000	25.55 – 1000
25.35 – 200	25.35 – 200
25.30 – 150	25.30 – 150
25.29 – 500	**25.29 – 500**
	25.25 – 100
25.27 – 500	25.24 – 300
25.26 – 200	
25.22– 1000	25.22 – 750
25.19 – 300	25.19 – 300
25.15 – 785	25.15 – 785
25.10 – 170	25.10 – 170
…	…
t0	t1

If we find ourselves in this situation on a more or less regular basis throughout the day, we end up paying the spread instead of profiting from it. This explains why our actual P&L pattern mirrors the expected pattern. We discern three main reasons for the penny jumping fiasco: (1) making decisions in one book, acting in another; this is further aggravated by (2) the frictions of the simulator; and, finally, (3) spreads are extremely tight leaving little or no profit margin. Tight spreads (inside markets) deserve further notice. The way we have defined our penny jumping strategy implies that the spread has to be at least 3 cents, but because the stock used in the simulator is a very liquid Microsoft (MSFT), oftentimes during the day the spread becomes smaller than 3 cents. This forces our strategy to "sit out" for extended periods of time, which does not improve its profitability. The size of the spread is closely related to the decimalization of the US equity markets, which was implemented in 2001 and is still under scrutiny. Now stocks trade in increments of 1 cent, as opposed to 1/16 of a dollar, on both NYSE and NASDAQ. From the perspective of a nonpredictive market-making strategy, this can also have positive effects: When stepping in front of someone else's order, one wants to be as close as possible to the original price. Decimalization actually helps here, Because undercutting by 1/16 of a dollar is much riskier than undercutting by 1/100 of a dollar. But it also makes the spread a lot tighter, cutting into the dealers' profits (Barclay, Christie, Harris, Kandel & Schultz, 1999).

Does this mean that the nonpredictive strategies inherently lose money? Not at all; one small change can bring the profitability back. We do not really have to undercut the inside market, instead we can put our quotes at the inside market or even deeper in their respective books. This makes the dealer's spread larger (more profits per trade), but can reduce fairly drastically the overall volume flowing through the dealer. Essentially, one has to find a balance between the potential profitability and volume. In practice, by putting the quotes 1-3 cents away from the inside market works well, or, at least, alleviates the concerns that make penny jumping unprofitable. The dealer's spread is much wider now, so even when the quotes get put into a different book with a significant delay, more often than not they still manage to straddle the inside market and therefore preserve the buy low, sell high property. Figure 8 shows the exact same scenario as Figure 7, but with

Figure 8. Wider quotes

...	...
25.56 – 300	25.56 – 300
25.55 – 1000	25.55 – 1000
25.35 – 200	25.35 – 200
25.33 – 500	**25.33 – 500**
25.30 – 150	25.30 – 150
	25.25 – 100
	25.24 – 300
25.26 – 200	
25.23 – 500	**25.23 – 250**
25.22– 1000	25.22 – 1000
25.19 – 300	25.19 – 300
25.15 – 785	25.15 – 785
25.10 – 170	25.10 – 170
...	...
t0	t1

wider dealer quotes. Although this is certainly good news, there are still several issues that expose the vulnerability of the nonpredictive strategies to certain market conditions. For example, inventory management becomes an important issue.

Inventory Management

In theory, the market maker should buy roughly as frequently as he or she sells, which implies that his or her stock inventory should fluctuate around zero. The dealer makes money on going back and forth from long to short position. Because he or she gets a fraction of a penny for each stock traded, the dealer naturally wants to move as many stocks as possible to compensate in volume for thin margins. Therefore, the dealer would prefer to set the depth of his or her quote—the third fundamental parameter—as high as possible. Potentially, all trading in a stock could flow through the market maker. In practice, however, this does not always work out. If a stock price is going up consistently for some period of time, what ends up happening is that the dealer's ask gets hit more often than his or her bid. The dealer winds up with a (potentially large) short position in a rising stock—he or she is taking a loss. Again, the same issues that were discussed earlier in this section are in play. Plus, at times the main assumption behind the nonpredictive strategies just does not hold: for example, when a stock "crashes" there are actually no buyers in the marketplace, and the entire market-making model is simply not valid any more. Exchanges halt trading in the stock when this happens, but the dealer will have probably taken a considerable loss by then. Also, if a dealer accumulates a large position in a stock, he or she becomes vulnerable to abrupt changes in supply and demand (price fluctuations) (i.e., if a market maker has a significant long position) and the stock price suddenly falls, then he or she is taking a loss. And finally, there are some real-world operational issues, like certain predetermined limits on exposure. Securities firms, for example, can prohibit their traders from holding an inventory of more than 100,000 shares, long or short. The bottom line is that there is a trade-off for the market maker. On one hand, he or she wants to post deep quotes and have a large inventory to move back and forth from one side of the market to the other, but then he or she does not want to become exposed by having a large position that cannot be easily liquidated or reversed.

To reconcile these conflicting goals, some rules have to be implemented to manage the dealer's inventory. We have implemented and tested a number of such approaches. The most straightforward one is to impose some global limit (i.e., no position in excess of 20,000 shares, long or short). When the market maker reaches the said limit, he or she stops posting a quote on the side of the market that will make him or her go over the limit. The problem with this approach is that when the limit is reached, the market-making revenue model no longer holds. The dealer is only active on one side of the market, and is exposed to market movements by holding a large inventory, which makes this approach not very practical. One can also manage inventory by simply varying the depth of the dealer's quote: If the depth is 300 shares, the market maker is less likely to accumulate excess inventory than if the depth were 5,000 shares. This can certainly be effective—by setting the depth low enough, the dealer does not have to worry about the inventory side effects. However, as shown earlier, shallow quote translates into less volume and less revenue. Therefore, by getting rid of the inventory risk, the market maker gives up the necessary revenue to continue its operation. The compromise can be reached by establishing some schedule of quote depth as a function of inventory (e.g., see Table 1).

One can also establish an actual functional dependence between the dealer's inventory and the depth of his or her quote. For example: Depth = 5,000 – max(0, (Inventory – 20,000)/Inventory*1,000) means that the quote starts at 5,000 shares and decreases gradually when the inventory exceeds 20,000 shares. One may also be tempted to decrease the quote on the side of the market where the excess inventory is being accumulated while leaving the other side unchanged, but this will go against the definition of market making. This will induce the reduction of the position, but the lack of symmetry will cut into profits on future trades. Theoretically, this general approach of balancing the inventory through the depth of quote should work; in practice, however, it is very difficult to calibrate. The schedule and the formula given above are entirely ad-hoc; while they generally make sense, how can we tell that various levels, decreases, coefficients and so forth, are the optimal numbers for this case? The usual statistical/ML optimization techniques are not very effective here, since there is no straightforward relationship between the profitability (the outcome) and the depth of the quote because many other factors, such as the size of the spread, are in play. Therefore, while this approach is sound, it is difficult to implement effectively.

The one method that we believe to be practical is mitigating the inventory effects through repositioning the spread. If there is too much buying (the dealer's ask is being hit too often, and he or she accumulates a short position), then moving the ask deeper into the sell book should compensate for this. Also, if the stock is going in one direction

Table 1. Inventory control via depth of quote

Inventory (Absolute)	Depth of Quote
0 to 20,000 shares	5,000 shares
20,000 to 50,000 shares	1,000 shares
More than 50,000 shares	500 shares

Figure 9. Quote repositioning

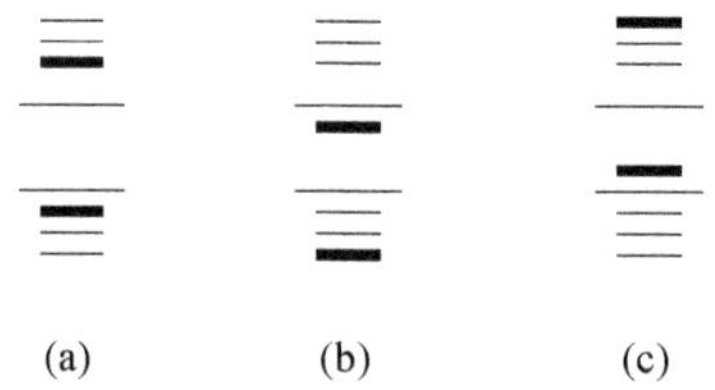

continuously, this approach will force the spread to also be continuously revised upward, using the inventory misbalance as a signal. Figure 9 shows one example: In case (a) dealer's inventory is balanced (close to some target holding, like zero); in case (b), dealer accumulated too much inventory, which forces him or her to quote more aggressively on the sell side to induce public buying; in (c), his or her inventory is less than his or her desired level, resulting in an aggressive buy quote. Together with moving the spread up or down, we can also resize it. We can set a wide spread, which will increase the profit margin, decrease the risk of inventory accumulation, but will also decrease the overall volume; or we can make it narrow, which will increase trading frequency, but decrease per-trade profits (Figure 10).

We found it effective to establish a functional dependence between how deep inside the book should the quote be and the stock inventory. Similar ideas were proposed before. Ho and Stoll (1981) suggest an analytical solution to a similar spread update problem, which involved solving a differential equation. We use a formula similar to the one in the depth of quote discussion: Distance from the inside market = MinimumDistance + alpha* max(0, Inventory–InitialLimit)/Inventory*MinimumDistance. The two main parameters to determine here are alpha and InitialLimit. (Minimum Distance is fixed

Figure 10. Narrow vs. wide spread: More trading vs. higher margins

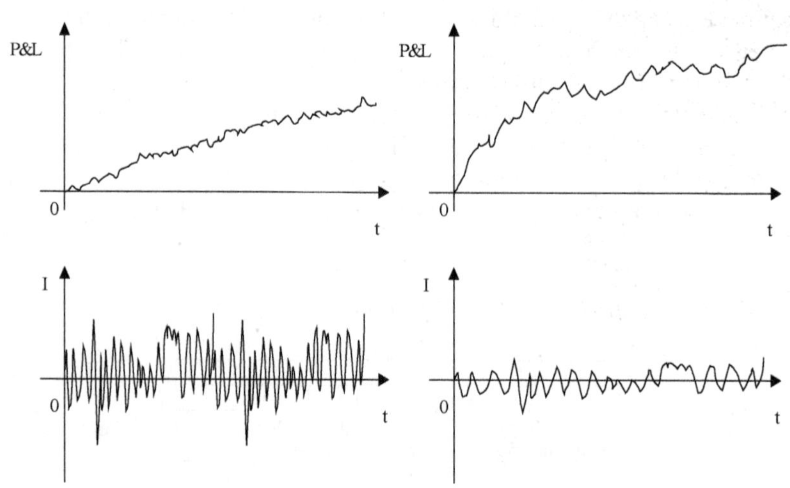

separately, guided by the volume vs. profit margins trade-off). When the position is within the InitialLimit, the quote is always set MinimumDistance away from the market, but if the inventory gets outside the limit, we start putting pressure on it to move in the opposite direction (see Figure 11).

The "rubber band" analogy is appropriate here: when the inventory gets too large, it is being pushed back by a rubber band—the band can be expanded more, but it becomes harder to do the further you go. Parameter alpha regulates the "stiffness" of the band—the higher you set it, the less expandable the band becomes. Experimentally, we have determined that it is beneficial to make both the InitialLimit and alpha relatively low. Figure 11 shows a fairly typical performance of this strategy: Inventory swings often from a large positive to a large negative position, generating solid profits.

SAMPLE STRATEGY ANALYSIS

Implementing and testing the nonpredictive market-making strategies, we arrived at a number of conclusions: faster updates allow to follow the market more closely and increase profitability; to combat narrow spread and time delays, we can put the quote deeper into the book, although at the expense of the trading volume; trading volume can be increased with deeper quotes; inventory can be managed effectively by resizing the spread. We have also found out, however, that the nonpredictive strategies do not solve the market-making problem completely. The performance of a market-making strategy with complete functionality over 10 trading days from April 28 to May 9, 2003, is summarized in Table 2.

As you can see, the outcome is not exactly stellar. So, what is the problem, if all the issues from Section 6 are taken into account? What happened early in the morning on May 9th (see Figure 12) exemplifies the general shortcoming of nonpredictive strategies:

Figure 11. "Rubber band" approach

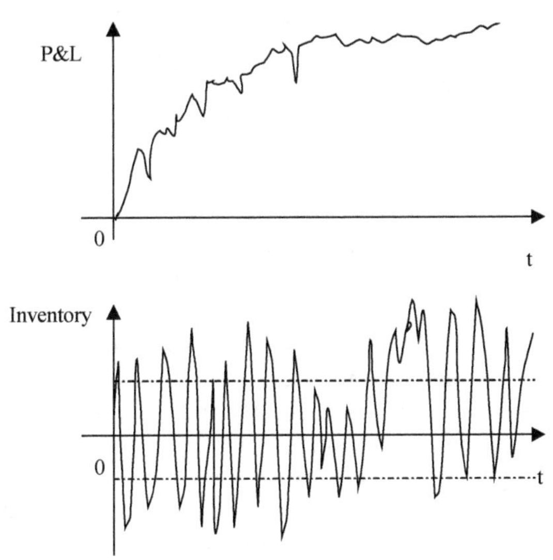

Table 2. End-of-the-day valuation

Day	P&L
April	-3,781
April	-4,334
April	4,841
May 1	-15,141
May 2	-3,036
May 5	6,405
May 6	33,387
May 7	24,021
May 8	1,380
May 9	-7,252
Total	36,490

Figure 12. Fundamental problem: extreme move

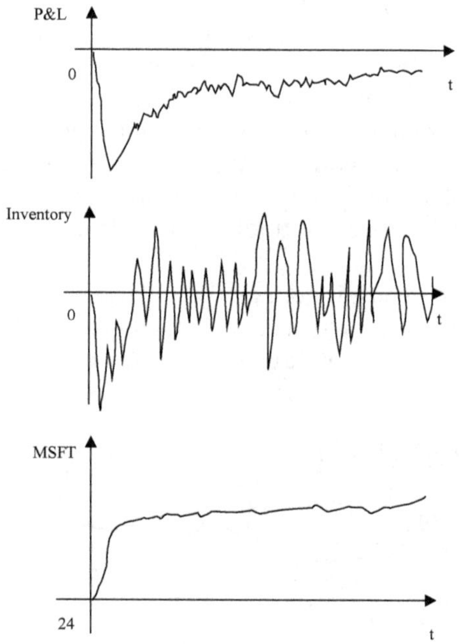

The price keeps going up, the market maker cannot get his or her quotes out of the way fast enough, accumulates a large short position, and loses a lot of money. All this happens in 10 minutes. The same scenarios can be observed on other money-losing days. This has been mentioned before, but we are back to the two fundamental problems. First, even an electronic market maker fails to operate on a small enough time scale to take advantage of the short-term fluctuations in supply and demand; second, there are times when such fluctuations just do not exist, and the entire premise behind the nonpredictive market making just no longer holds. These are the realities that have to be accounted for. We will have to use some predictive instruments—order book misbalances, past patterns, or both—in order to solve these problems.

Does this mean that the nonpredictive strategies are not suited for electronic market making and should be abandoned? Certainly not. They have many positive features that can be exploited. First, they are simple and computationally cheap, but, at the same time, a human trader can never replicate them. Their performance can be improved significantly by speeding up the access to the market, or by applying them to less liquid stocks. Because they use the inside market as pretty much the only decision anchor, they are immune to a large degree to the composition of the "trading crowd" (i.e., what are the other dominant strategies in the market should matter little to a nonpredictive market maker). And, finally, the problematic situations, such as morning of May 9 can be handled by special cases to boost the overall performance. Some further exploration of these strategies may also be necessary: a more rigid search for optimal parameters in various practical implementations and a more sophisticated distance metric for the quote placement (number of stocks weighted by their price, for example) amongst others.

TIME SERIES ANALYSIS

The bulk of this chapter is devoted to a family of models where we replicate the dealer's decision-making process (in a simplified form, admittedly). In this section, we will not analyze actions of specific economic actors, but instead just look at the data, searching for some underlying structure. We can think of this as a first step towards more complex predictive strategies, since we are essentially searching for short-term predictability in various microstructure variables, such as prices, quotes, spreads, volumes and so forth. This knowledge can be used to react to extreme events pointed out in the previous section. Also note that whereas the structured models discussion was largely conceptual, this section will rely heavily on numerical results.

Since our data is naturally indexed by time, time series techniques are particularly helpful in this case. The purpose of this analysis is to investigate whether some useful information can be extracted from the historical data of stock transactions and limit order books without explicitly building a market making strategy around this information yet. There are essentially two things that can be done: first, we can take a time series of a single variable and try to find some underlying structure there (i.e., the series tends to revert to its historical mean with a certain lag); second, we can take several variables and look for dependencies among them (i.e., midspread leads transaction prices by a certain number of time steps). If any useful information is discovered through this type of statistical studies, it can then be profitably incorporated into a market making strategy to compensate for the shortcomings discussed earlier. Below we outline the necessary steps—data collection, preprocessing, filtering, and model fitting, which can later be extended to more complex examples.

We tested the following hypotheses: (1) can past transaction prices help predict future transaction prices, (2) can spread size (together with past transaction prices) help predict future transaction prices, and (3) can the midspread help predict transaction prices. To run these experiments, we used frequently sampled MSFT (Microsoft Corp. stock) transaction data and order book evolution history during different time periods of one day. Essentially, we looked at three time series: transaction price, size of bid-ask spread, and midpoint of the bid-ask spread. We first fit the univariate autoregressive moving average (ARMA) model into each series searching for some underlying structure, and then used the spread size and the midspread to see if they can help model the transaction price.

All this analysis has been performed within SAS statistics software package—use (Delwiche & Slaughter, 2001) as a reference. For the detailed description of time series models see (Yafee & McGee, 2000). Very briefly we introduce two basic stochastic processes. First, we make an assumption that adjacent entries in a time series are related to one another via some sort of a process, which can be described mathematically. There are many ways this can be done, but we are mostly interested in two types of time series models: moving average MA(q) and autoregressive process AR(p).

Under the one-step moving average process MA(1), the current output Y_t is influenced by a random innovation e_t plus the innovation from the previous time step:

$$Y_t = e_t - \theta_1 e_{t-1}.$$

The lag between t and t-1 needs not be one step, but can be any lag q or multiple lags. Another process can be such that the current output is determined by previous value plus some innovation:

$$Y_t = \phi_1 Y_{t-1} + e_t.$$

We call this an autoregressive process, which again can have an arbitrary lag p. (θ and ϕ are parameters for MA and AR processes respectively.) These two processes put together form our main tool—process ARMA(p, q), which is simply a sum of the autoregressive and moving average components. Once again, notice that no microstructure variables enter this notation—in relaxed models, we deal only with numbers, regardless of where they came from.

We evaluate goodness-of-fit using three standard criteria: loglikelihood, Akaike information criterion (AIC), and Schwartz Bayesian criterion (SBC). The first one is essentially a logarithm of the mean square error. AIC and SBC penalize mean square error with the number of features in the model. AIC = exp(2k/T)MSE and SBC = T^kMSE, where k is the number of features, T is the number of observations, and MSE is the mean square error.

Our experimental findings mostly confirm accepted principles from Finance Theory:

1. Markets do appear efficient (at least in a very liquid stock such as MSFT) showing little or no structure beyond white noise;
2. Size of bid–ask spread exhibits a fairly prominent AR(1) behavior in most cases;
3. spread size does not help in transaction price forecasting;
4. Midspread is, in fact, useful for transaction price modeling, but only over extremely short time periods (3-15 seconds, if that).

Although none of this is revolutionary, these experiments highlight the power of multivariate ARMA models in the market microstructure analysis. The exact same approach can help investigate more complex relationships: Does volume misbalance signal upcoming price movement, does higher volatility lead to larger spreads and so forth.

Dataset Description

The first dataset we use includes MSFT transaction prices collected from Island Electronic Communications Network on April 28, 2003, from 9:30 a.m. to 4:00 p.m. The price was sampled every 3 seconds, resulting in the total of 7,653 data points. We then created a time variable starting at 9:30 a.m. for the first observation, and incrementing it by 3 seconds for every subsequent observation. This main dataset (MSFT.DAY) serves as a base for the smaller time-of-the-day dependent datasets (see Table 3).

In order to concentrate on the short-term behavior of the transaction price, we selected three 1-hour time periods during the day: beginning (10:30 a.m.-11:30 a.m.), middle (12:30 p.m.-1:30 p.m.), and end (2:30 p.m.-3:30 p.m.). Note that we avoided using the opening and closing hour because, presumably, price behavior during these periods will be significantly different from "normal" rest-of-the-day behavior. The first 3 datasets created (MSFT.MORNING, MSFT.NOON, and MSFT.EVENING) are just the subsets of the master dataset in the indicated time periods. Since the price is sampled every 3 seconds, each of them contains 1,200 observations. In case if such sampling is too frequent, we also created 3 more datasets for the same time periods, but with the price sampled every 15 seconds. These datasets are called MSFT.MSHORT, MSFT.NSHORT, and MSFT.ESHORT and contain 240 observations each.

The second collection of data that we examined was a list of top bids and asks from the order book sampled at the same time as the transaction price. We used this data to create two more time series: the size of the bid ask spread, calculated as (Ask-Bid), and the midpoint of the spread: (Ask+Bid)/2. The later is often used in market microstructure theory as a proxy for the "true price" of a security. Then we went through the same steps as for the transaction price and ended up with 12 smaller time series: For both the size and the midspread we had MORNING, NOON, and EVENING periods sampled at 3 and 15 seconds each.

Basic Statistics and Stationarity

Tables 3 and 4 summarize basic statistics for transaction prices and bid–ask spread, respectively. The midspread dataset's statistics are essentially the same as those for transaction prices (Table 3), and thus are not reproduced here.

We can clearly observe from Table 4 the U-shaped pattern of the bid–ask spread, which is mentioned on many occasions: average spread is the largest in the middle of the day and is tighter in the morning and afternoon. The same holds for the maximum spread as well.

Table 3. Basic statistics: prices

Name	Time	N	Mean	Min	Max
DAY	9:30-16:00	7653	25.7281	25.328	25.940
MORNING	10:30-11:30	1200	25.6798	25.551	25.770
MSHORT	10:30-11:30	240	25.6797	25.560	25.770
NOON	12:30-13:30	1200	25.8167	25.740	25.853
NSHORT	12:30-13:30	240	25.8169	25.740	25.853
EVENING	14:30-15:30	1200	25.8488	25.761	25.940
ESHORT	14:30-15:30	240	25.8489	25.761	25.936

Table 4. Basic statistics: spread

Name	Rate (sec)	N	Mean	STDev	Min	Max
DAY	3	7653	0.013639	0.0072	0.01	0.054
MORNING	3	1200	0.013039	0.00605	0.01	0.033
MSHORT	15	240	0.012846	0.0059	0.01	0.033
NOON	3	1200	0.01401	0.007384	0.01	0.054
EVENING	3	1200	0.013276	0.006776	0.01	0.043

In order for the ARMA model to be applicable, the time series have to be stationary—in simpler terms, we had to remove the trend and render the volatility homoskedastic (roughly constant). All the series that involve prices (transaction or midspread) have unit root in them and must be first differenced. Dickey-Fuller tests in SAS ARIMA procedure prove that this is sufficient. It is much less clear, however, if taking logs of prices is in order to stabilize the series volatility. Results for several significance tests—log likelihood, AIC, and SBC—are presented in Table 5 for both regular prices and their logs.

It appears that taking logs is not necessary for prices (transactions and midspread), but the difference is marginal.

Another issue is whether it is appropriate to work with actual prices, or should returns be used instead. The later approach is customary in financial literature, but may not matter for the kind of data we are using. To test which method is more appropriate, we initially fit all the ARMA models (see the following section) to transactions data using actual prices, and then replaced prices with log returns, but left all the models parameters unchanged. Both approaches yielded the same results, so we chose to work with actual prices for other experiments.

We also determined that we needed to take logs (but not first difference) of the spread size for all time series. Spread size models had a significant intersection term, while prices did not. This can be attributed to first differencing of prices.

Table 5. Stationarity tests

Series	Log Likelihood	AIC	SBC
DAY	30621.56	-61231.12	-61189.46
Log	30608.10	-61204.19	-61162.54
MORNING	4660.74	-9309.48	-9278.94
Log	4660.77	-9309.54	-9279.01
MSHORT	752.908	-1493.82	-1472.96
Log	752.843	-1493.69	-1472.83
NOON	5288.68	-10565.36	-10534.82
Log	5288.57	-10565.14	-10534.60
NSHORT	870.565	-1729.13	-1708.27
Log	870.532	-1729.06	-1708.20
EVENING	4841.19	-9670.39	-9639.85
Log	4841.06	-9670.11	-9639.58
ESHORT	794.220	-1576.44	-1555.58
Log	794.137	-1576.27	-1555.42

Table 6. ARMA parameters: prices

Model	P	Q
MORNING	1,3,4	1,3,4
MSHORT	23,37	0
NOON	23,257,258	0
NSHORT	1,42,43	0
EVENING	6,117,118,230	0
ESHORT	1,46	0

ARMA Models: Transaction Prices

We found it very challenging to fit an ARMA model to a time series of transaction prices, since they look very much as white noise. Surprisingly, however, when we extended the number of time periods to be examined by our model from 20 to 250 for 3 second series and to 50 for 15 seconds series, we found significant autoregressive terms that lag from 6 to 13 minutes:

We are very much inclined to discard these results as nonsensical from the market microstructure point of view (a price at the next period depends on a price 10 minutes ago but on nothing in between—sounds unlikely.), but these results have strong statistical support. Every one of the parameters is statistically significant (t-value is greater than 2), and both SBC and AIC are lower for the models than for the base p=0, q=0 model; and, finally, the residuals are generally improving in most cases compared to the white noise model. Overall, if there is any underlying structure for transaction prices, it is almost certainly an autoregressive (as opposed to a moving average) relationship.

ARMA Models: Spread Size

Unlike transaction prices, spread size showed much more structure in correlograms: most of them look very similar to AR(1) model. AR(1) turns out first- or second-best model in AIC/SBC scoring, but some low-level (1 or 2) MA process seems to be present as well. Here are the parameters that we estimated:

This autoregressive behavior has a coherent explanation from the market microstructure point of view: As the spread narrows, it becomes cheaper for traders to step over the spread and transact immediately with outstanding limit orders; by definition, this will remove orders from the book and thus widen the spread. As the spread get wider, submitting market orders becomes more expensive, and traders resorts to posting limit orders inside the wide spread, which, in turn, shrinks the spread.

Table 7. ARMA parameters: spread

Model	P	Q
MORNING	1	0
MSHORT	0	1
NOON	1	2
NSHORT	1	0
EVENING	1	1
ESHORT	0	1

Multivariate ARMA Models

We next attempted to use the spread size and midspread as exogenous variables that help predict the transaction price. Whereas we did manage to find lags that make the spread size significant for the transaction price estimation, the new models' SBC and AIC were always higher than the ones from the univariate model. Therefore, we reject our hypothesis that the spread size can be helpful for transaction price forecasting.

The midspread turns out to be a much more helpful variable especially when sampled every 3 seconds, which certainly is not surprising. We had to fit an ARMA model to the midspread series as well, again resulting in mostly AR models. After adding the midspread to the transaction price forecasting, we can conclude that in general, knowing the midspread at time t is useful for forecasting the transaction price at time t+1. SBCs and AICs are lower than without the exogenous variable, and lags are significant, but the residuals still leave a lot to desire in both cases. Does this finding have any practical significance? Not very likely, since one variable is leading the other one by an extremely short time period (plus lots of structure remains unexplained).

In all our experiments we obtained a vast amount of information describing significance of various coefficients, goodness of fit, behavior that still remains unexplained, some predictions and so forth; most of this data can also be plotted. But we are not reproducing all this numbers here because of the shear volume, and also because our primary goal is to demonstrate the process of finding out if there is some kind of relationship between various microstructure variables and not trying to forecast stock prices or other variables.

Relaxed Models' Significance

We have described the basic idea behind the relaxed models and shown a simple application of time series techniques to automated market making. In our opinion, the main contribution of these experiments is the proof of applicability of multivariate ARMA models to the market microstructure research where we are dealing with discretely sampled data. We were also pleasantly surprised to find some structure in the spread size, which can mean that this variable is actually forecastable, which can be used in creating an automated dealer. And finally, while our efforts have confirmed that prices are hard (read impossible) to forecast, the same needs not be true for other microstructure variables.

CONCLUSION

In this chapter we attempted to present a structured framework for reasoning about automated market making, analyzed a number of fundamental issues in this domain using a simple class of strategies, and showed how time series techniques (relaxed models) can be adapted to the market microstructure domain.

More specifically, we have first presented an overview of the relevant work done up to this day from both the finance and computer science standpoints and outlined the major microstructure factors that an autonomous market maker has to account for. Then we described both a simple strategy that works within our simulated environment and a statistical approach that can be applied to the same data. In their nature, our experiences—both a simple market making agent and a statistical model of quotes and prices—are demonstrations or proofs of concept rather than definitive solutions to specific problems. As opposed to the closed-form mathematical solutions, our approach is more normative—aimed at practical implementation of an electronic market maker rather than a theoretical analysis of human dealers' activities. We have shown that we have an appropriate experimental environment and all the necessary tools—both technical and analytical—to create, test, and improve market-making models of any level of complexity. Therefore, we can now move on to the next step—implementation of advanced models, structured quantification of relevant factors, and, ultimately, building a robust automated dealer.

While we have not provided all the answers, our main goal was to frame electronic market making as a coherent problem and to highlight the points that must be addressed in order for this problem to be solved. We believe that this is an interesting and promising area, and that advances in the electronic market making will be useful in disciplines beyond finance.

REFERENCES

Amihud, Y.,& Mendelson, H. (1980) Dealership market: Market making with inventory. *Journal of Finance, 42,* 533-553.

Barclay, M., Christie W., Harris, J., Kandel, E., & Schultz, P. (1999). The Effects of market reform on the trading costs and depth of NASDAQ Stocks. *Journal of Finance, 54.*

Becker, B., Lopez, E., Berberi-Doumer, V., Cohn, R., & Adkins, A. (1992). Automated securities trading. *Journal of Financial Services Research, 6,* 327-341.

Black, F. (1971, November–December). Toward a fully automated exchange. *Financial Analysts Journal.*

Bouchaud, J., Mezard, M.,& Potters, M. (2002). Statistical properties of stock order books: Empirical results and models. *Quantitative Finance.*

Campbel, J. Y., Lo, A. W., & MacKinlay, A. C. (1997). *The econometrics of financial markets.* Princeton, NJ: Princeton University Press.

Chan, N.,& Shelton, C. (2001). An electronic market-maker. AI Memo 2001, MIT.

Chau, M. (2002). *Dynamic trading and market-making with inventory costs and private information* (Working paper). ESSEC.

Choi, J. Y., Salandro, D., & Shastri, K. (1988). On the estimation of bid–ask spreads: Theory and evidence. *Journal of Financial and Quantitative Analysis, 23,* 219-230.

Christie, W. G., & Schultz, P. H. (1994). Why do NASDAQ market makers avoid odd-eighth quotes? *Journal of Finance, 49,* 1813-1840.

CIEF. (2003). Third international workshop on computational intelligence in economics and finance. In the *Proceedings of the 7th Joint Conference on Information Sciences, (JCIS).*

Cohen, K., Maier, S., Schwartz, D., & Whitcomb, D. (1979). Market makers and the market spread: A review of recent literature. *Journal of Financial and Quantitative Analysis, 14,* 813-835.

Cohen, K., Maier, S., Schwartz, D., & Whitcomb, D. (1981). Transaction costs, order placement strategy, and existence of the bid-ask spread. *Journal of Political Economy, 89,* 287-305.

Das, S. (2003). *Intelligent market-making in artificial financial markets* (AI Tech. Rep. 2003-005). MIT.

Delwiche, L., & Slaughter, S. (2003). *The little SAS book: A primer.* SAS.

Domowitz, I. (2001). Liquidity, transaction costs, and reintermediation in electronic markets. *Journal of Financial Services Research, 22.*

Easley, D., & O'Hara, M. (1987). Price, trade size, and information in securities markets. *Journal of Financial Economics, 19,* 69-90.

Easley, D., & O'Hara, M. (1992). Time and the process of security price adjustment. *Journal of Finance, 47,* 577-605.

Glosten, L. (1987). Components of the bid-ask spread and the statistical properties of transaction prices. *Journal of Finance, 42,* 1293-1307.

Glosten, L. R., & Milgrom, P. R. (1985). Bid, ask and transaction prices in a specialist market with heterogeneously informed traders. *Journal of Financial Economics, 14.*

Hakansson, N. H., Beja, A., & Kale, J. (1985). On the feasibility of automated market making by a programmed specialist. *The Journal of Finance, 40.*

Hasbrouck, J. (1988). Trades, quotes, inventories, and information. *Journal of Financial Economics, 22,* 229-252.

Hasbrouck, J. (1991). Measuring the information content of stock trades. *The Journal of Finance, 46,* 179-207.

Hasbrouck, J., & Sofianos, G. (1993). The trades of market makers: An empirical analysis of nyse specialists. *Journal of Finance, 48,* 1565-1593.

Ho, T., & Stoll, H. R. (1981). Optimal dealer pricing under transactions and return uncertainty. *Journal of Financial Economics, 9.*

Huang, R., & Stoll, H. (1994). Market microstructure and stock return predictions. *Review of Financial Studies, 7,* 179-213.

Huang, R., & Stoll, H. (1997). The components of the bid-ask spread: A general approach. *Review of Financial Studies, 10,* 995-1034.

Huang, P., Scheller-Wolf, A., & Sycara, K. (2002). Design of a multi-unit double auction e-market. *Computational Intelligence, 18*(4).

Huang, R. D., Stoll, & H. R. (1997). The components of the bid-ask spread: a general approach. *The Review of Financial Studies, 10.*

Hull, J. (2000). *Options, futures, and other derivatives.* NJ: Prentice Hall.

Ip, G., & Craig, S. (2003, April 18). NYSE's 'specialist' probe puts precious asset at risk: Trust. *The Wall Street Journal.*

Kakade, S., & Kearns, M. (2004). *Trading in Markovian price models* (Working paper). University of Pennsylvania.

Kavajecz, K., & Odders-White, E. (Forthcoming). Technical analysis and liquidity provision. *Review of Financial Studies.*

Kearns, M. (2003). The Penn-Lehman Automated Trading Project. Retrieved from http://www.cis.upenn.edu/~mkearns/

Kearns, M., & Ortiz, L. (2003). *The Penn-Lehman automated trading project.* IEEE Intelligent Systems.

Kim, A. J., & Shelton, C. R. (2002). *Modeling stock order flows and learning market-making from data (Tech. Rep. CBCL Paper #217/AI Memo #2002-009).* Cambridge, MA: MIT.

Klusch, M., & Sycara, K. (2001). Brokering and matchmaking for coordination of agent societies: A survey. In A. Omicini et al. (Eds.), *Coordination of Internet agents.* Springer.

Madhavan, A. (1992). Trading mechanisms in securities markets. *Journal of Finance, 47,* 607-641.

Madhavan, A. (2000). Market microstructure: A survey. *Journal of Financial Markets,* 205-258.

Madhavan, A. (2002). Market microstructure: A practitioner's guide. *Financial Analysts Journal, 58*(5), 28-42.

Madhavan, A., & Smidt, S. (1993, December). An analysis of changes in specialist inventories and quotations. *The Journal of Finance, 48.*

Mantegna, R., & Stanley, E. (1999). *An introduction to econophysics: Correlations and complexity in finance.* Cambridge University Press.

O'Hara, M. (1995). *Market microstructure theory.* Blackwell.

O'Hara, M., & Oldfield, G. (1986). The microeconomics of market making. *Journal of Financial and Quantitative Analysis, 21,* 361-376.

Papageorgiou, C. (1997). High frequency time series analysis and prediction using Markov models. CIFEr.

Poggio, T., Lo, A., LeBaron, B., & Chan, N. (1999). *Agent-based models of financial markets: A comparison with experimental markets* (MIT Artificial Markets Projects, Paper No. 124).

Roll, R. (1984). A simple implicit measure of the effective bid–ask spread in an efficient market. *Journal of Finance, 39,* 1127-1139.

Rust, J., Miller, J., & Palmer, R. (1994). Characterizing effective trading strategies: Insights from a computerized double auction tournament. *Journal of Economic Dynamics and Control, 18,* 61-96.

Seppi, D. J. (1997). Liquidity provision with limit orders and strategic specialist. *The Review of Financial Studies, 10*(1).

Stoll, H. (1989). Inferring the components of the bid–ask spread: Theory and empirical tests. *Journal of Finance, 44,* 115-134.

Stoll, H. (1999). Alternative views of market making. In J. Amihud, T. Ho, & R. Schwartz (Eds.), *Market making and changing structure of securities industries.*

Stoll, H. (2000). Friction. *Journal of Finance, 55,* 1479-1514.

Stoll, H. R. (2001). *Market microstructure* (Financial Markets Research Center, Working paper Nr. 01-16, First draft).

Stoll, H., & Whaley, R. (1990). Stock market structure and volatility. *Review of Financial Studies, 3,* 37-71.

Thomas, J. D. (2003). *News and trading rules.* (Doctoral dissertation, Carnegie Mellon University).

Wellman, M., Greenwald, A., Stone, P., & Wurman, P. (2003). The 2001 trading agent competition. *Electronic markets, 13.*

Yafee, R., & McGee, M. (2000). *Introduction to time series analysis and forecasting.* Academic Press.

Zlot, R. M., Stentz, A., Dias, M. B., & Thayer, S. (2002, May). Multi-robot exploration controlled by a market economy. In *Proceedings from the IEEE International Conference on Robotics and Automation.*

Section III

Games

Chapter VII

Slow Learning in the Market for Lemons:
A Note on Reinforcement Learning and the Winner's Circle

N. Feltovich
University of Houston, USA

ABSTRACT

Human-participants experiments using markets with asymmetric information typically exhibit a "winner's curse," wherein bidders systematically bid more than their optimal amount. The winner's curse is very persistent; even when participants are able to make decisions repeatedly in the same situation, they repeatedly overbid. Why do people keep making the same mistakes over and over again? In this chapter, we consider a class of one-player decision problems, which generalize Akerlof's (1970) market-for-lemons model. We show that if decision makers learn via reinforcement, *specifically by the reference point model of Erev and Roth (1996), their behavior typically changes very slowly, and persistent mistakes are likely. We also develop testable predictions regarding when individuals ought to be able to learn more quickly.*

INTRODUCTION

In a seminal theoretical paper, Akerlof (1970) argued that when asymmetric information is present in market settings, potential buyers rationally lower their willingness to pay (their bids, in auctions and related settings), resulting in a suboptimal number of exchanges: market failure. But a robust result in human-participant experiments, using environments such as Akerlof's "market for lemons," is that market failure generally does not result. Rather, participants in the role of potential buyers persistently overbid relative to the rational bidding strategy. Although overbidding increases the likelihood of transactions occurring, resulting in less market failure (and hence higher efficiency) than predicted, the participants/bidders often earn much less money than they would have by never bidding at all—even losing money in some cases. Even when they have the opportunity to learn—by making decisions repeatedly in the same situation, and receiving feedback after each decision—they continue to overbid, moving only slightly toward the prediction of rational play. Examples of this "winner's curse" in asymmetric-information market experiments include Ball (1991), Ball, Bazerman and Carroll (1991), Cifuentes and Sunder (1991) and Holt and Sherman (1994).[1]

Why do participants take so long to figure out this problem? It seems difficult, or perhaps even impossible, to reconcile the results of these experiments with the assumption of rational behavior normally made by economists. Holt and Sherman (1994) argued that "naive" behavior by bidders (which they defined precisely, and which we discuss in the next section) causes their choices to diverge substantially from optimal play. (See also Archibald & Wilcox, 2001, and Charness & Levin, in preparation, who look more closely at when naive behavior should be expected to be seen.) Although naive behavior might explain the initial divergence of bids from optimal play, it does not explain why this divergence persists. Surely, one might think, experience in this situation should lead bidders to learn how to play optimally. One possible explanation for the slowness of learning in these situations is that participants are learning via reinforcement. According to models of reinforcement learning, agents learn over time to play successful actions more often relative to unsuccessful actions.[2] However, reinforcement learning in these situations can be slow; according to such models, behavior changes very little, or even not at all, when an agent's bid is rejected. Also, learning is noisy; it sometimes happens that a bad action (one yielding a low expected payoff) yields a high, realized payoff, so that the bad action becomes more likely to happen in the future rather than less.

In this chapter, we will consider a class of one-player decision problems that are a generalization of Akerlof's market-for-lemons model. We report the results of a simulated experiment in which decision makers take part repeatedly in this market, and learn via reinforcement. The specific reinforcement-based learning model we use is a version of the "reference-point" model of Erev and Roth (1996), which they showed to characterize behavior well in several different experiments. We find that behavior changes very slowly in this decision-making situation, and repeated mistakes are likely. We also develop testable predictions regarding which decision problems in this class have optima that can be learned relatively quickly.

THE DECISION PROBLEM

The decision problems we consider are based on a class of two-player asymmetric-information market games, similar to those studied by Akerlof (1970). The players are a bidder and a seller. The seller has possession of a single unit of an indivisible good. This good has value $v>0$ to the seller and value λv to the bidder, where $1<\lambda<2$. The good is therefore worth more to the bidder than to the seller, regardless of what v actually is, and both bidder and seller know this. (Thus, efficiency requires the players to trade the good.) Only the seller knows the true value of v, however; the bidder knows only that v is distributed uniformly over the set $V=\{x_0, x_0+1, x_0+2, x_0+3, ..., x_0+9\}$, where x_0 is some nonnegative number. The bidder makes a bid $b \in V$ to the seller, which the seller may accept or reject. If the seller accepts the bidder's bid, the bidder pays the seller b in exchange for the good. If the seller rejects the bidder's bid, the seller keeps the good and no money changes hands. In either case, the game ends at this point.

In order to concentrate on bidder behavior, we reduce this game to a one-person decision problem by modeling the seller as an automaton which accepts the bidder's bid if and only if the bid is at least as large as the seller's valuation ($b \geq v$). This is how a rational seller would behave (i.e., such behavior constitutes a weakly dominant strategy for the seller), so optimal bidder behavior in this reduced decision problem corresponds to sequential equilibrium (the standard game-theoretic solution concept for situations of this type) in the original game.[3]

Optimal Bidder Behavior

From the bidder's point of view, the expected value of v, given b and *conditional on the bidder's bid being accepted* (which happens if $b \geq v$), is $(x_0+b)/2$. In this case, the expectation of the bidder's valuation of the good is $\lambda(x_0+b)/2$ and her expected profit is $\lambda(x_0+b)/2 - b$. The probability of b being accepted is $(b-x_0+1)/10$, and she receives zero profit if her bid is rejected, so her unconditional expected profit (given b) is

$$\Pi(b) = [\lambda(x_0+b)/2 - b]\,(b-x_0+1)/10.$$

The optimal choice of b depends on the values of the parameters x_0 and λ. The best-known version has $x_0=0$ (along with $\lambda \in (1, 2)$, as mentioned above). This gives rise to a "winner's-curse" situation, as studied by, for example, Ball (1991) and Ball et al. (1991). The optimal bid in this version is $b=x_0=0$, the lowest possible bid. Two other versions of interest use $\lambda=1.5$ and x_0 = either 10 or 5. When $x_0=10$, the unique optimal bid is $b=19$, the highest possible bid. When $x_0=5$, there are two optimal bids: $b=9$ or $b=10$; these are in the middle of the range of bids. Following Holt and Sherman (1994), we will refer to these games as a "loser's-curse" and a "no-curse" decision problem, in contrast to the winner's-curse problem with $x_0=0$.

As mentioned in the introduction, there have been several experimental studies of decision problems and games of this type. When all of these studies are considered, the main result is that optimal behavior has very little descriptive power. In winner's-curse experiments, the overwhelming majority of participants overbid, and the average bid tends to lie near the unconditional expected seller value. This tendency is unaffected by replacing "realistic" instructions (in which participants are told, for example, that they represent an acquiring firm, considering taking over a target firm) with context-free instructions (Ball, 1991; Cifuentes & Sunder, 1991). Overbidding decreases only slightly when participants are allowed to play repeatedly (Ball et al., 1991; Cifuentes & Sunder, 1991).

One explanation for overbidding in winner's-curse decision problems that has been put forth starts by pointing out that the above prediction of rational play takes "rational" to mean expected-payoff-maximizing, without regard to riskiness of those payoffs (i.e., it assumes that participants exhibit "risk-neutral" preferences). It may be, rather, that these participants are rational, but "risk seeking," preferring—in some cases—a risky gamble with a lower expected payoff rather than a safe, higher expected payoff. If so, they might choose a high bid (which is risky and leads to a negative expected payoff) over a low bid (which is safe and leads to a zero payoff); that is, they would overbid relative to the prediction previously discussed.

However, Holt and Sherman (1994) found evidence against the hypothesis of risk seeking as the cause of overbidding. As was mentioned, their experiment consisted of not only a winner's-curse decision problem, but also a loser's-curse problem in which the expected payoff-maximizing bid was the highest possible bid. They found, in contrast, that participants in the experiment repeatedly underbid in the loser's-curse problem. Rational, risk-seeking individuals would not underbid in this situation.[4] (In the loser's-curse treatment, as in the winner's-curse treatment, high bids are riskier than low bids.)

To explain their results, Holt and Sherman (1994) proposed a "naive model" of decision making. Rational bidders, when assessing the expected payoff to each of their possible bids, must calculate the probability of the bid being accepted and the expected payoff contingent on the bid being accepted (the expected payoff contingent on the bid being rejected is zero). The latter is a difficult cognitive task for most nonmathematicians; bidders must understand how this depends on the bid, and that the distribution of possible sellers' values *given that the bid is accepted* is truncated from above by the bid itself. Failure to take this truncation into account may result in overbidding in a winner's-curse situation or underbidding in a loser's-curse situation. Holt and Sherman considered naive behavior to be behavior where bidders mistakenly ignore this truncation; specifically, they consider the ex post distribution of sellers' values to be the same as the unconditional distribution—uniform over V. They found that the naive model, which predicts higher-than-optimal bids in their winner's-curse condition, lower-than-optimal bids in their loser's-curse condition, and approximately optimal bids in their no-curse condition, describes participant behavior substantially better than rational bidding does.

The Learning Model

Holt and Sherman's (1994) naive model accurately predicts the divergence between optimal and actual behavior in their experiment; however, they did not examine how behavior might change as participants became more experienced. As mentioned above, some learning typically occurs, but the tendency toward optimal behavior is very slight. One reason for the failure of participants in these experiments to play optimally, even after acquiring experience, might be that they are learning via reinforcement. As mentioned in the previous section, the optimal choice for bidders in our "winner's-curse" game is a bid of zero, the lowest bid possible. However, this bid is guaranteed to earn zero, regardless of whether it is accepted or rejected, so that it may not be substantially reinforced. Higher bids perform worse in expected value terms, but sometimes earn positive payoffs. A bid of 9 can possibly result in a payoff of $9(\lambda-1)$, the highest possible payoff, if the seller's value turns out to be 9 also. If there happen to be a few high seller values early in an experiment, participants may incorrectly "learn" to choose high bids rather than higher expected-payoff low bids; such learning may disappear only slowly.

The learning model is based on the adjustable-reference-point reinforcement-learning model of Erev and Roth (1996).[5] This model has two features that make it useful for modeling participant behavior in individual decision-making problems, such as lemons experiments. First, because it is a model of bounded rationality, rather than perfect rationality, it allows for the possibility that individuals make suboptimal decisions, possibly for long lengths of time. Second, reinforcement models allow learning (in the sense of changes in the likelihood of different actions) to occur in an individual decision problem. Choices that have led to better outcomes in the past become more likely to be chosen in the future. (This is the Law of Effect, which dates back at least to Thorndike, 1898.)

Not all learning models have these advantages. Besides reinforcement models, the main class of learning model is *beliefs-based* models. Beliefs-based models assume that individuals form beliefs about aspects of their situation (typically, the behavior of other decision makers), which are updated in response to new information about the situation, and actions are chosen based on their expected payoff given these beliefs. In an individual decision-making problem such as ours, the perceived expected payoff to any action will not depend upon beliefs about others' behavior; rather, it should simply be equal to the true expected payoff of that action. Fictitious play (Robinson, 1951), probably the best-known beliefs-based model, requires individuals in decision problems to choose, with probability one, the strategy yielding the highest expected payoff (given beliefs). Therefore, in our setup, it will require bidders to choose the optimal bid with probability one, so there will be no suboptimal play and no learning. Stochastic beliefs-based models, such as Fudenberg and Levine's (1998) "cautious fictitious play," allow for suboptimal play in individual decision-making problems. However, they do not allow the frequency of such play to change over time, so again, no learning can occur.[6]

The learning model we use is next described; we attempt to conform as closely as possible to Erev and Roth's (1996) parameterization, as they have shown it to characterize participant behavior well in experiments involving many different decision-making situations.[7] In round $t^{3}0$ and for $k \in \{0, 1, 2, ..., 9\}$, the n-th simulated player has a nonnegative *propensity* $q_n^t(k)$ to choose the k-th pure strategy (which corresponds to a bid of x_0+k). The sum of these propensities is her *strength of propensities* in round t:

$$Q_n^t = \sum_{j=0}^{9} q_n^t(j).$$

Her mixed strategy in round t is such that the *probability* of her choosing strategy k is proportional to the propensity:

Prob(Player n chooses the k-th pure strategy in round t)=$\frac{q_n^t(k)}{Q_n^t}$.

The payoff she receives in round t depends on the pure strategy she actually chooses, which determines her bid, and on the seller's realized value:

$$\Pi_n^t(k,v) = \begin{cases} \lambda v - (x_0 + k), & x_0 + k \geq v \\ 0, & x_0 + k < v. \end{cases}$$

The payoff is used to update the bidder's propensities. First, her payoff is compared to her *reference point* ρ_n^t (which can be thought of as an "aspiration level" for payoffs); then, her propensities are reinforced (augmented) by the difference between them. Most of the reinforcement is of the action that was played, but a small portion is added to actions adjacent to the one that was played, reflecting a tendency to experiment with strategies that are similar to successful strategies:

$$q_n^{t+1}(k)=(1-\delta)q_n^t(k)+(1-\varepsilon)[\Pi_n^t(k,v)-\rho_n^t],$$

$$q_n^{t+1}(j)=(1-\delta)q_n^t(j)+\frac{\varepsilon}{M}[\Pi_n^t(k,v)-\rho_n^t] \text{ for } |j-k|=1, \text{ and}$$

$$q_n^{t+1}(j)=(1-\delta)q_n^t(j) \text{ for } |j-k|>1,$$

where M is the number of strategies adjacent to k. (In the decision problems we consider, M is equal to 1 for k=0 and k=9, and 2 for all other k.) The value of $\varepsilon \in [0, 1)$ quantifies the amount of experimentation; it is meant to be nonnegative but close to zero. The parameter $\delta \in [0, 1)$ reflects "gradual forgetting" (or "recency") by the individual. Over time, strategies that have recently performed well become more likely relative to those that performed well long ago. Finally, in order to prevent propensities from becoming negative following repeated negative reinforcements—which would result in negative probabilities—any propensity below a lower bound μ is reset to μ.[8]

The reference point ρ_n^t can change over time. Following Erev and Roth, we set its initial value to $(\lambda-1)x_0-9$, the minimum possible payoff.[9] At the end of each round, it moves a small bit in the direction of the payoff earned in the just-completed round:

$$\rho_n^{t+1} = \begin{cases} (1-w^+)\rho_n^t+(w^+)\Pi_n^t(k,v), & \Pi_n^t(k,v) \geq \rho_n^t \\ (1-w^-)\rho_n^t+(w^-)\Pi_n^t(k,v), & \Pi_n^t(k,v) < \rho_n^t. \end{cases}$$

where the parameters w^+ and w^- represent the weights assigned to reinforcements following better-than-expected and worse-than-expected outcomes, respectively.

The learning model therefore has the following free parameters: ε, δ, μ, w^+, w^-, and the initial propensities for each strategy.

SIMULATION DESIGN AND RESULTS

In order to see the implications of the learning model, we simulated experiments based on our "winner's-curse," "loser's-curse," and "no-curse" games. As mentioned previously, sellers were programmed to always accept bids greater than or equal to their valuations. Bidders were programmed to act according to the learning model described in the previous section. The learning model parameter values were permitted to vary across bidders. At the beginning of a simulation, each bidder was assigned parameter values generated from a uniform distribution over those shown in Table 1; these ranges were chosen so that the expected value of each parameter conformed as closely as possible to those used by Erev and Roth. (As mentioned in the previous section, they used these values to successfully characterize participant behavior in several experiments.) The strength of initial propensities was set to $(\lambda-1)x_0$ (roughly the average magnitude of payoffs) in some simulations and to $3(\lambda-1)x_0$ in others. Because higher strengths of propensities mean that probabilities change less in response to a given reinforcement, learning is expected to be faster in the former case, slower in the latter. The strength of initial propensities was divided equally among the initial propensities for the 10 strategies, so that participants began the simulation choosing each strategy with equal likelihood. (This leads to initial behavior roughly similar on average to that predicted by Holt and Sherman's, 1994, naive model.) Note that the ranges of values for w^+ and w^- imply that w^- will usually be larger than w^+. This reflects a form of loss aversion, the phenomenon where an outcome viewed as a loss affects behavior more than a same-sized gain would have (Kahneman & Tversky, 1979).

Four sets of simulations were run, with varying values of x_0 and λ. A simulation consisted of 5,000 bidders, each playing one version of the game for 500 rounds. In two sets of simulations, the value of x_0 was fixed at zero, and the value of λ was allowed to vary between 1 and 2. These are winner's-curse environments, in which the unique optimal bid is zero; however, the penalty for suboptimal bids is lower for higher values of λ. (For higher values of λ, therefore, learning is expected to be slower.) In the other two sets of simulations, the value of λ was fixed at 1.5, and x_0 was allowed to take values of 0, 5, and 10. These values lead to winner's-curse, loser's-curse, and no-curse environments, respectively. Within each environment, we ran sets of simulations with Q_n^1 set to both $(\lambda-1)x_0$ (faster learning) and $3(\lambda-1)x_0$ (slower learning). As mentioned, learning model parameters varied across bidders even within a simulation, but they remained the same for a given bidder over all rounds. Sellers' values were independently and identically distributed over all bidders and rounds.

Figures 1 and 2 summarize the simulation results for the slower learning and faster learning simulations, respectively. In both figures, the left panel shows the results of simulations with fixed x_0 and varying λ, and the right panel shows the results of

Table 1. Learning model parameters and ranges

Parameter	Q_n^1	ε	δ	μ	w^+	w^-
Value (faster learning)	$(\lambda-1)x_0$	[0,0.2]	[0,0.002]	[0,0.2]	[0,0.02]	[0,0.04]
Value (slower learning)	$3(\lambda-1)x_0$	[0,0.2]	[0,0.002]	[0,0.2]	[0,0.02]	[0,0.04]

simulations with fixed λ and varying x_0. The horizontal axis shows the round, and the vertical axis shows the excess of average bids over the minimum value x_0 (so that simulation results with different values of x_0 can be compared). Recall that the optimal bid is the lowest possible bid in the winner's-curse environment, the highest possible bid in the loser's-curse environment, and one of the two midrange bids in the no-curse environment.

Comparing either panel of Figure 1 to the corresponding panel of Figure 2, we see that tripling the strength of initial propensities does indeed slow learning, but the effect is almost negligible; simulation trajectories are qualitatively the same in both figures. The figures show that changing the value of either λ or x_0 affects the results more substantially. Increasing λ in the winner's-curse environment (left panel) slows convergence to equilibrium, as expected. However, convergence is slow for all values of λ, even the lowest (λ =1.01). In both slow-learning and fast-learning simulations, even after 500 rounds, average bids remain above \$3.50 (compared to zero in equilibrium). When λ=1.50, average bids take almost 500 rounds to fall from \$4.50 to \$4.00, and when λ=1.99, expected bids stay essentially constant over the 500 rounds, except for a small decrease over the first 20 rounds. Indeed, for all levels of λ, we see that average bids decline by less than 50 cents over the first 20 rounds—a typical length for a human-participants experiment—and changes are even slower afterwards.

Figure 1. Average bids—slower learning (large strength of initial propensities)

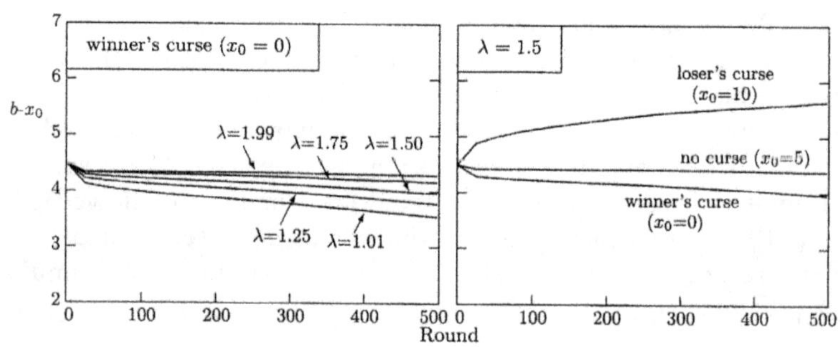

Figure 2. Average bids—faster learning (small strength of initial propensities)

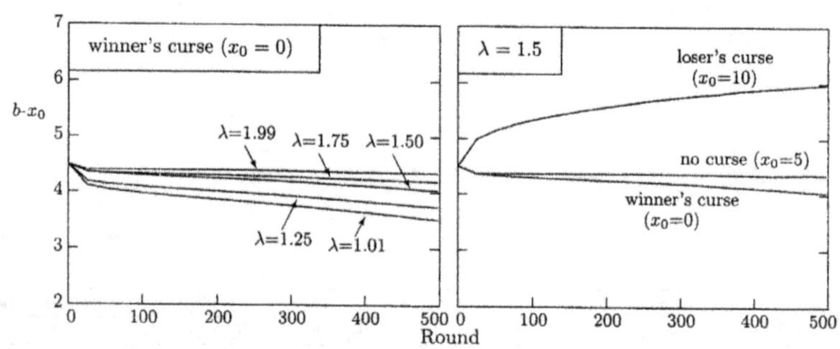

Changing x_0—that is, going from winner's curse to no curse to loser's curse (right panel)—changes the simulation trajectories qualitatively. Average bids in the winner's-curse (x_0=0) treatment move slowly downward, while they increase in the loser's-curse (x_0=10) treatment; in both cases, the movement is in the direction of optimal play, though play is still far from optimal after 500 rounds. The speed with which average bids change is substantially higher in the loser's-curse treatment than in the winner's-curse treatment, which is notable because they used the same value of λ. That is, raising x_0 from 5 to 10 seems to have more effect on learning speed than an equal lowering of x_0, from 5 to 0.

DISCUSSION

Experiments involving lemons markets have produced two main results: (a) bids typically start far away from optimal choices, and (b) even when individuals have the opportunity to make repeated decisions in this situation, any tendency to move in the direction of optimal choices is very slight. It is difficult to reconcile these results with the assumptions of optimizing behavior commonly made in economic models. However, models of bounded rationality may be able to characterize such behavior. In this paper, we consider one particular model of bounded rationality—the reinforcement learning model of Erev and Roth (1996). We find that simulated experiments in which decision makers are programmed to learn according to this model produce qualitative results that conform to the typical experimental results, in the sense that average bids do tend to move over time in the direction of optimal choices, but quite slowly.

Two caveats are in order, as we attempt to draw conclusions from our results. First, we hasten to mention that the objectives of this paper are limited. Our results are not meant to imply that Erev and Roth's (1996) model is the correct model of individual learning in these situations (let alone more generally). Indeed, many learning models have characteristics similar to this model (suboptimal decisions and changes over time in response to experience), such as other reinforcement models (e.g., Kirman & Vriend, 2001; Roth & Erev, 1995, 1998; Sarin & Vahid, 2001), as well as models that combine reinforcement with more sophisticated types of learning (e.g., Camerer & Ho, 1999; Grosskopf, 2003). We have deliberately avoided conducting a "horse race" involving any or all of these models. We conjecture that any of them would produce qualitative results similar to the results we found. We consider this to be a strength, not a weakness of our approach. Explaining the major features of the experimental results should not require strong assumptions about which reinforcement learning model to use; it should be sufficient to assume merely that agents do learn via reinforcement. (Recall that in the learning-model section, we pointed out that not all learning models could explain these results; in particular, models based purely on beliefs could not work.)

Second, we acknowledge that the decision problem studied here is highly abstract, and has only a tenuous connection to real-life markets. In particular, we have assumed that market interactions take place between one bidder and one seller; a more realistic treatment would have multiple bidders for each object, and probably multiple objects to be sold (perhaps with multiple sellers). This does not invalidate our results; in fact, allowing multiple bidders may exacerbate the slowness of learning. With more bidders (or even with more of both bidders and objects for sale, as long as bidders outnumbered objects, as seems reasonable), an even larger proportion of bids would be unsuccessful—leading to zero payoffs rather than negative payoffs in those cases, so that propensities would change even more slowly over time. Therefore, it is very possible that even in more realistic markets, the results we found could be expected to continue to hold.

We believe that more work needs to be done in this area. The implications of the model we use need to be further tested—either alone or in comparison to those of other learning models. As a first step toward this end, we have looked at some of the predictions that come from varying the parameters of Erev and Roth's (1996) model. The results of simulations with varying values of λ imply that lowering λ leads to faster movement toward optimal play. The results of simulations with varying values of x_0 imply that loser's-curse experiments might show faster movement toward optimal play than winner's-curse experiments. These implications suggest future treatments for market-for-lemons experiments; such experiments would not only further test the ability of this model (and perhaps others) to describe individual behavior, but perhaps also shed some more light on the reasons for persistent irrational behavior in these settings and others.

ACKNOWLEDGMENT

I thank participants at the Third International Workshop on Computational Intelligence in Economics and Finance (Cary, NC), and two referees, for helpful suggestions and comments. Any remaining errors had been rewarded in the past.

REFERENCES

Akerlof, G. A. (1970). The market for 'lemons': Quality uncertainty and the market mechanism. *Quarterly Journal of Economics, 89*(3), 488-500.

Archibald, G. (1998). *Coasian bargaining under incomplete information: Theories and experiments* (Doctoral dissertation, University of Houston, TX).

Archibald, G., & Wilcox, N. (1998). *How general are explanations of the winner's curse.* Mimeo, University of Houston.

Archibald, G., & Wilcox, N. (2001). *Two causes of 'naïve' behavior in takeover games.* Mimeo, University of Houston.

Ball, S. B. (1991). *Experimental evidence on the winner's curse in negotiations* (Doctoral dissertation, Northwestern University).

Ball, S. B., Bazerman, M. H., & Carroll, J. S. (1991). An evaluation of learning in the bilateral winner's curse. *Organizational Behavior and Human Decision Processes, 48*(1), 1-22.

Blackburn, J. M. (1936). *Acquisition of skill: An analysis of learning curves* (IHRB Report No. 73).

Camerer, C., & Ho, T. H. (1999). Experience-weighted attraction learning in normal form games. *Econometrica, 67*(4), 827-874.

Charness, G., & Levin, D. (2004). *The winner's curse: No seller and complexity.* Manuscript in preparation.

Cifuentes, L. A., & Sunder, S. (1991). *Some further evidence of the winner's curse.* Mimeo, Carnegie Mellon University.

Erev, I., & Roth, A. E. (1996). *On the need for low rationality, cognitive game theory: Reinforcement learning in experimental games with unique mixed strategy equilibria.* Mimeo, University of Pittsburgh.

Erev, I., & Roth, A. E. (1998). Predicting how people play games: Reinforcement learning in experimental games with unique, mixed strategy equilibria. *American Economic Review, 88*(4), 848-881.

Feltovich, N. (2000). Reinforcement-based vs. belief-based learning models in experimental asymmetric-information games. *Econometrica, 68*(3), 605-641.

Fudenberg, D., & Levine, D. K. (1998). *The theory of learning in games (economic learning and social evolution).* Cambridge: MIT Press.

Grosskopf, B. (2003). Reinforcement and directional learning in the ultimatum game with responder competition. *Experimental Economics, 6*(2), 141-158.

Holt, C. A., Jr., & Sherman, R. (1994). The loser's curse and bidder's bias. *American Economic Review, 84*(3), 642-652.

Kagel, J. (1995). Auctions: A survey of experimental research. In J. Kagel & A. E. Roth (Eds.), *Handbook of experimental economics* (pp. 501-586). Princeton, NJ: Princeton University Press.

Kahneman, D., & Tversky, A. (1979). Prospect theory: An analysis of decision under risk. *Econometrica, 47*(2), 263-291.

Kirman, A. P., & Vriend, N. J. (2001). Evolving market structure: An ACE model of price dispersion and loyalty. *Journal of Economic Dynamics and Control, 25*(3-4), 459-502.

Robinson, J. (1951). An iterative method of solving a game. *Annals of Mathematics, 54*(2), 296-301.

Roth, A. E., & Erev, I. (1995). Learning in extensive-form games: Experimental data and simple dynamic models in the intermediate term. *Games and Economic Behavior, 8*(1), 164-212.

Sarin, R., & Vahid, F. (2001). Predicting how people play games: A simple dynamic model of choice. *Games and Economic Behavior, 34*(1), 104-122.

Thorndike, E. L. (1898). Animal intelligence: An experimental study of the associative processes in animals. *Psychological Review, Monograph Supplements, No. 8.* New York: Macmillan.

ENDNOTES

1 Kagel (1995) discussed the winner's curse in the related setting of common-value auctions, where it was first discovered.

2 Roth and Erev's (1995) model was the first reinforcement model used to describe behavior in economic experiments. Later in this chapter, we will consider a more complicated reinforcement model, which they introduced in a follow-up paper (Erev & Roth, 1996).

3 This assumption about seller behavior also implies that limiting bidder's bids to elements of V is not a severe restriction. Given this seller behavior, any bid $b>x_0+9$ is dominated by a bid of exactly x_0+9, as both are always accepted, but the latter pays more. Any bid $b\in(x_0+k, x_0+k+1)$, for $k=0, 2, ..., 8$, is dominated by a bid of exactly x_0+k, as one is accepted if and only if the other is, and the latter pays more. Any

bid $b<x_0$ is never accepted, thus paying zero with certainty, and is therefore dominated by a bid of exactly x_0, which pays zero unless it is accepted (with probability 0.1), in which case it gives a positive payoff. Therefore, any bid outside *V* is dominated by some bid in *V*.

4 Holt and Sherman's (1994) loser's-curse results also deal with another explanation for overbidding in winner's-curse problems: a preference for bidding successfully per se (irrespective of monetary payoffs). Such a preference (which is often justified by appealing to the boredom that would result from round after round of unsuccessful bids following from rational play) would lead participants to overbid because higher bids are more likely to be successful than lower bids. Again, however, this would imply participants do not underbid in the loser's-curse treatment, while in fact they do.

5 See their paper for a more detailed description of the model and the rationale behind it.

6 Camerer and Ho's (1999) "experience-weighted attraction" combines elements of reinforcement and beliefs-based learning. Like the reinforcement model we use, it allows suboptimal play and satisfies the Law of Effect, as well as the Power Law of Practice (Blackburn, 1936), according to which learning slows as more experience is accumulated.

7 This model is relatively robust to small changes in parameter values (Erev & Roth, 1998; Feltovich, 2000; Roth & Erev, 1995).

8 Roth and Erev (1995) consider an alternative way of dealing with extremely low propensities: by "extinction." According to extinction, any propensity below ¼ is reset to zero. If there is no experimentation, the corresponding strategy then becomes extinct, never to be chosen again.

9 Erev and Roth (1996) also consider a "fixed reference point" model, in which the reference point simply stays at this value.

Chapter VIII

Multi-Agent Evolutionary Game Dynamics and Reinforcement Learning Applied to Online Optimization for the Traffic Policy

Yuya Sasaki
Utah State University, USA

Nicholas S. Flann
Utah State University, USA

Paul W. Box
Commonwealth Scientific and Industrial Research Organization, Australia

ABSTRACT

This chapter demonstrates an application of agent-based selection dynamics to the traffic assignment problem. We introduce an evolutionary dynamic approach that acquires payoff data from multi-agent reinforcement learning to enable an adaptive optimization of traffic assignment, provided that classical theories of traffic user equilibrium pose the problem as one of global optimization. We then show how these data can be employed to define the conditions for evolutionary stability and Nash equilibria. The validity of this method is demonstrated by studies in traffic network modeling, including an integrated application using geographic information systems applied to a complex road network in the San Francisco Bay area.

INTRODUCTION

When we think about alternative driving routes from an origin to a destination, there are several factors of travel time to consider, such as the distance, speed limit, and possible congestion. Although people appear to have an incentive to use the shortest distance routes, this does not happen in reality, because the supply function of traffic roads exhibits an increasing cost nature. In other words, we have monotonically increasing travel time with respect to increasing traffic flow volume.

Assume a simple example, where two agents travel from an origin to a destination, with only two paths available, a short path and a long path. Also assume that the long path has greater capacity, with more lanes than the shorter path. The supply function of the longer path has a flatter slope and a higher intercept (free-flow travel time) than the short path. Suppose that the two agents (denoted by A and B) make decisions simultaneously. Then the outcome cost matrix for the four possible pure-strategy combinations will look like Table 1. If both choose the greedy strategy (the short path), the tragic consequence is that both get trapped in severe congestion. The noncooperative equilibria in this pure strategy setting are thus the symmetric pair of (A:1 B: 2) and (A: 2 B: 1) in Table 1. Whenever some agents choose the shortest paths, others have to compromise by making inferior choices. The characteristics of traffic behaviors illustrated by this example will be analyzed more generally in the succeeding sections.

Notations and Definitions of Traffic Networks

A traffic network consists of nodes and arcs, where an arc is always closed by a pair of nodes. We use the term "O-D pair" to refer to a pair of origin and destination nodes in an agent's trip. A path is an ordered sequence of arcs that connects two nodes that are not necessarily adjacent to each other. Thus, an O-D path refers to an ordered sequence of arcs that connects the origin and destination nodes. Let I, J, and R denote sets of arcs, nodes, and paths in a network, respectively. R must be defined for each O-D pair, and I and J can be global for all the O-D pairs. Since we will focus first on the case of one O-D pair (later in this chapter we will consider multiple origins and one destination), we will not use any subscript or superscript to R. Let $I_j \subseteq I$ denote the set of arcs radiating from node $j \in J$, where I_j also represents the set of available strategies for agents being at node j. An arc is a component of the network in the entire system, although it can also be perceived as a "strategy," "next move," or "action" from decision-makers' viewpoint. We will exclusively use the term *arc* when the network structure is discussed, and the

Table 1. Example payoff matrix of four combinations of choices. (Note. The values are travel time in any time unit).

Time Matrix (larger values are worse)		B's Action: *short path*	B's Action: *long path*
A's Action	*short path*	A: 5 B: 5	A: 1 B: 2
	long path	A: 2 B: 1	A: 3 B: 3

term *strategy* interchangeably with *arc* will be used when we discuss agents' decision making.

Classical Theory of Traffic User Equilibrium

Before discussing the main idea, let us review classic theory of equilibrium states in traffic networks. Let **v** denote the vector of arc flow volumes for all elements in I, and let **w** denote the vector of path flow volumes for all elements in R. Correspondingly, let $\mathbf{t}(\mathbf{v})$ denote the vector of arc travel times as a function of arc flow volumes, and let $\mathbf{u}(\mathbf{w})$ denote the path travel times. Additionally, we use flag variable $\delta_{i,r}$, which is 1 if path r includes arc i, and 0 otherwise. Beckmann, McGuire and Winston (1956) introduced the following optimization problem, the solution to which yields deterministic user equilibrium for a fixed travel demand, d.

$$\min f(\mathbf{w}), \text{ where } f(\mathbf{w}) = \sum_{i \in I} \int_0^{v_i} t_i(x)dx .$$

Although f may seem unrelated to **w**, $\sum_{r \in R} w_r \delta_{i,r}$ can be substituted for v_i for all i. This problem is subject to the constraint of flow volume conservation

$$g(\mathbf{v}) = 0, \quad \text{where } g(\mathbf{v}) = d - \sum_{r \in R} w_r .$$

Thus, by setting up Lagrangean $L(\mathbf{w}, \lambda) = f(\mathbf{w}) - \lambda g(\mathbf{w})$, we obtain the following Kuhn-Tucker first-order conditions (the second-order conditions follows the monotonicity assumption on $t_i(v)$).

$$w_r \frac{\partial L(\mathbf{w}, \lambda)}{\partial w_r} = w_r (u_r(\mathbf{w}) - \lambda) = 0 \quad \forall r \in R,$$

$$\frac{\partial L(\mathbf{w}, \lambda)}{\partial w_r} = (u_r(\mathbf{w}) - \lambda) \geq 0 \quad \forall r \in R, \text{ and}$$

$$\frac{\partial L(\mathbf{w}, \lambda)}{\partial \lambda} = d - \sum_{r \in R} w_r = 0 \quad \forall i \in I .$$

The second condition implies that Lagrangean multiplier λ equals the minimum path travel time among all the paths in R. With this and the first condition, the path flow amount of r can be positive only if its path travel time equals the minimum path travel time. Intuitively, only those paths that bring about the minimum travel time in the network can attract vehicles. This basically extends the engineering principle proposed by Wardrop (1952), which will be further extended by multi-agent evolutionary dynamics, as discussed in the next section.

MULTI-AGENT GAME WITH REINFORCEMENT LEARNING

Model Description

Define a payoff matrix $\mathbf{A}_j$ for each node $j \in J$, where $\mathbf{A}_j$ is square and the number of columns and rows corresponds to the number of elements in I_j. Each element $a_{ii'}$ of $\mathbf{A}_j$ is a marginal payoff of flow on arc i' for those on arc i. Assume that agents being at node j have perfect information of the traffic volumes of all the arcs in I_j. Let $\mathbf{x}_j$ denote the vector representation of those volumes for node j. Provided that we only deal with one destination case, the value of $\mathbf{e}_i\mathbf{A}_j\mathbf{x}_j$ represents an estimated travel time to be spent from node j to the destination node provided that the agent chooses arc $I \in I_j$ as an available option at node j. Hence, agents should take strategy i such that $i = \arg\min_{\bar{i} \in I_j} \mathbf{e}_{\bar{i}}\mathbf{A}_j\mathbf{x}_j$ to minimize the total travel time from node j to the destination. Recalling the Bellman (1957) equation, we can find the relationship between this game approach and the conclusion of the classical theory discussed in the previous section. If agents are rational,

$$\mathbf{e}_{\bar{i}}\mathbf{A}_j\mathbf{x}_j = t_{\bar{i}} + \min_{\tilde{i} \in I_{\bar{j}(\bar{i})}} \mathbf{e}_{\tilde{i}}\mathbf{A}_{\bar{j}(\bar{i})}\mathbf{x}_{\bar{j}(\bar{i})} \tag{1}$$

holds from the Bellman equation, where $\bar{j}(\bar{i})$ is the succeeding node's index as a result of taking strategy $\bar{i}$ at node j. Thus

$$\lambda = \min_{i \in I_{Origin}} \mathbf{e}_i\mathbf{A}_{Origin}\mathbf{x}_{Origin}$$

$$= \min_{i \in I_{Origin}} (t_i + \min_{\bar{i} \in I_{j(i)}} \mathbf{e}_{\bar{i}}\mathbf{A}_{j(i)}\mathbf{x}_{j(i)})$$

$$= \min_{i \in I_{Origin}} (t_i + \min_{\bar{i} \in I_{j(i)}} (t_{\bar{i}} + \min_{\tilde{i} \in I_{\bar{j}(\bar{i})}} \mathbf{e}_{\tilde{i}}\mathbf{A}_{\bar{j}(\bar{i})}\mathbf{x}_{\bar{j}(\bar{i})}))$$

$$\vdots$$

where node $\bar{j}(\bar{i})$ succeeds node $j(i)$ through arc $\bar{i}$, which succeeds the origin node through arc i. An important implication is that the problem of $\min_{\bar{i} \in I_j} \mathbf{e}_{\bar{i}}\mathbf{A}_j\mathbf{x}_j$ at each node is equivalent to agents choosing only those paths with the least travel time, an obvious conclusion from backward recursion. Of course, a restriction arises that all of these formulations hold only if $\mathbf{A}_j$ is accurately defined for all j. When this is not true, agents will still have the incentive and ability to modify $\mathbf{A}_j$ to make it more accurate based on their experiences.

We formulate this process of modification of $\mathbf{A}_j$ through experience using reinforcement learning (Sutton, 1988; Sutton & Barto, 1998), an artificial intelligence approach. Although we have treated traffic volumes as elements of state space, let us now assume that the total volume departing from node j is constant in a unit time interval and that state $\mathbf{x}_j$ is contained by a simplex so that the model will be compatible with multiagent evolutionary games. Given these assumptions, let $\Theta_j = \{\mathbf{x}_j \in R^n_+ \mid \sum_{\bar{i} \in I_j} x_{j,\bar{i}} = 1, \mathbf{x}_j \geq 0\}$ be the simplex for node j, where n denotes the number of elements in I_j. Then, set I_j defined earlier in this chapter can be considered as a pure strategy set because $I_j = \{\bar{i} \in N^1 \mid e_{\bar{i}} \in \Theta_j\}$. Let $\Omega = \{(\bar{i}, \mathbf{x}_j) \mid \bar{i} \in I_j, \mathbf{x}_j \in \Theta_j\}$ be the set of (n+1)-tupple parameters of strategy-state pairs, and $\Lambda_j = \{(Q_j(\bar{i}))_{n \times 1} \mid \bar{i} \in I_j\}$ be the set such that $Q_j(\bar{i})$ is the agent's estimate of travel time, $\mathbf{e}_{\bar{i}}\mathbf{A}_j\mathbf{x}_j$. Note that set Λ_j specializes in node j for one destination. An agent performs decision making by using the modifiable function $F_j : \Omega_j \to \Lambda_j$. Though there exist many ways to realize this function, let us adopt a discretized state model or tabular state space. Suppose that Θ_j is partitioned into mutually disjoint subsets such that $\bigcup_l \Theta^l_j = \Theta_j$ and $\Theta^l_j \cap \Theta^m_j = \varnothing$ for all $m \neq l$. If the model employs **v** rather than **x**, a similar discretization on the set of **v** must be carried out instead. Define the new set $\overline{\Omega} = \{(\bar{i}, l) \mid \bar{i} \in I_j, \Theta^l_j \subset \Theta_j\}$, and with a discrete indexing by l, the former function can be rewritten as

$$\overline{F}_j : \overline{\Omega}_j \to \Lambda_j. \tag{2}$$

This simplification by discretization is employed for the sake of computational simplicity. From computational viewpoint, this is a simple tile coding technique with no overlapping cells. We employed the resolution of 10 tiles for each variable. For example, this allows the function ($\overline{F}_j$) to be represented by such simple forms as arrays or linked lists whose elements are easily modified by reinforcement learning. The function (F_j) could be defined continuously, but this would require more complex learning methods which employ neural networks as function approximators described in Tesauro (1995). As previously described, the decision process employing (2) is defined as $i^* = \arg\max_{\bar{i}} \overline{F}_j(\bar{i}, l)$.

Because the states are discretely defined, let $Q_j(i, l)$ denote the estimated value returned by the function $\overline{F}_j(i,l)$, thus we have the identity $\mathbf{e}_i\mathbf{A}_j\mathbf{x}_j \equiv Q_j(i, l)$ as a result of the completion of learning. Especially for the equilibrium state $\mathbf{x}^*_j$, this identity

$$\mathbf{e}_i\mathbf{A}_j\mathbf{x}^*_j \equiv Q_j(i, l^*) \quad \text{where } l^* = l' \, s.t. \, \mathbf{x}^*_j \in \Theta^{l'}_j \tag{3}$$

becomes an important resource in our analysis, as shown later. Note again that this variable specializes in node j for one destination. Suppose an agent having departed node j reaches the destination node, with his actually experienced travel time between these two nodes given by R_j. Then, the error of $Q_j(i,l)$ given by $R_j - Q_j(i, l)$ can be used by Monte Carlo learning to update $Q_j(i,l)$ is defined as

$$Q_j(i,l) := \frac{1}{t}\left[R_j - Q_j(i,l)\right] + Q_j(i,l), \tag{4}$$

where t is the number of times this update has occurred including the current time. This equation defines $Q_j(i,l)$ as the equally weighted average from all the past experiences. This function can be approximated by substituting a constant $0 \leq \alpha \leq$ for $1/t$ in (4), thereby obtaining a learning method where the value of $Q_j(i,l)$ is a weighted average, where more recent errors are weighted higher:

$$Q_j(i,l) := \alpha\lfloor R_j - Q_j(i,l) \rfloor + Q_j(i,l), \tag{5}$$

that is more effective for stochastic environment than (4). This parameter, α, may be considered analogously with what Roth and Erev (1995) referred to as the degree of forgetting.

Recall that our original purpose was to find the accurate representation of $\mathbf{A}_j$ for better estimates of $\mathbf{e}_i\mathbf{A}_j\mathbf{x}_j$. Finding the closed form unique solution to this is feasible only if exactly n unique values of R_j are obtained for each row of $\mathbf{A}_j$, thus making a system of n linear equations for n unknowns for each row. But it is very unlikely that this condition holds for real or simulated environments. Hence we replace this closed form approach by (5), and later (6) and (7).

As an extension to (5), Sarsa and Q-learning are the instances of temporal difference learning, which uses an incremental backup method in updating Q values. In temporal difference learning, the estimated travel time, R_j, at node j succeeded by node $\bar{j}$ is computed as $R_j := t_{\bar{i}} + Q_{\bar{j}}(\cdot)$, where $t_{\bar{i}}$ denotes the travel time that the agent actually spent on arc $\bar{i}$ between node j and $\bar{j}$, a temporal difference. The Sarsa algorithm, an online version of this, is formulated as follows.

$$Q_j(i,l) \Leftarrow Q_j(i,l) + \alpha[t_i + Q_{\bar{j}}(\bar{i},\bar{l}) - Q_j(i,l)], \tag{6}$$

where $\bar{l}$ is the index used to identify the state $\mathbf{x}_{\bar{j}}$. This updates $\overline{F}_j$ for the element of (i,l) in $\overline{\Omega}_j$. If node $\bar{j}$ succeeding node j is the destination node, then Monte Carlo update rule (5) is substituted for (6). Likewise, the offline version called Q-learning (Watkins, 1989) is formulated as follows.

$$Q_j(i,l) \Leftarrow Q_j(i,l) + \alpha[t_i + \max_{\bar{i}} Q_{\bar{j}}(\bar{i},\bar{l}) - Q_j(i,l)], \tag{7}$$

which resembles equation (1), implying that (7) improves learning by using Bellman optimality equation. Again, if node $\bar{j}$ succeeding node j is the destination node, then Monte Carlo update rule (5) is substituted for (7).

From replicator equation (Taylor & Jonker, 1978), $(\log x_{j,i}\dot{)} = \mathbf{e}_i\mathbf{A}_j\mathbf{x}_j - \mathbf{x}_j\mathbf{A}_j\mathbf{x}_j$, we derive $(\log x_{j,i}\dot{)} - (\log x_{j,\bar{i}}\dot{)} = \mathbf{e}_i\mathbf{A}_j\mathbf{x}_j - \mathbf{e}_{\bar{i}}\mathbf{A}_j\mathbf{x}_j$ which implies the equilibrium condition

$$\mathbf{e}_i\mathbf{A}_j\mathbf{x}_j^* - \mathbf{e}_{\bar{i}}\mathbf{A}_j\mathbf{x}_j^* = 0 \quad \forall i,\bar{i} \in I_j.$$

Provided that estimates $\mathbf{e}_i\mathbf{A}_j\mathbf{x}_j \equiv Q_j(i, l)$ are sufficiently accurate, then we may translate the previous equilibrium condition to the following definition.

Definition 1. *The interior equilibrium condition for multiagent reinforcement learning is defined as*

$$Q_j(i,l^*) = Q_j(\bar{i},l^*) \tag{8}$$

$\forall i,\bar{i} \in I_j$ *where* i *and* $\bar{i}$ *have strictly positive flow volumes.*

Additionally, we apply the Nash equilibrium condition, $\mathbf{x}_j^*\mathbf{A}_j\mathbf{x}_j^* \leq \mathbf{x}_j\mathbf{A}_j\mathbf{x}_j^*\ \forall \mathbf{x}_j \in \Theta_j$, to argue the following claim. (Notice that the Nash equilibrium condition usually has the reverse inequality sign as $\mathbf{x}_j^*\mathbf{A}_j\mathbf{x}_j^* \geq \mathbf{x}_j\mathbf{A}_j\mathbf{x}_j^*\ \forall \mathbf{x}_j \in \Theta_j$. But we have $\leq$ instead because we are *minimizing* travel time for optimality in our model, rather than *maximizing* it.)

Claim 1. *Nash equilibrium condition for multi-agent reinforcement learning is equivalent to*

$$\sum_{i\in I_j}(x_{j,i}^* - x_{j,i})Q_j(i,l^*) \leq 0 \quad \forall \mathbf{x}_j \in \Theta_j. \tag{9}$$

(And for usual setting, inequality $\geq$ *replaces* $\leq$ *in (9).)*

Proof. Nash equilibrium condition, $\mathbf{x}_j^*\mathbf{A}_j\mathbf{x}_j^* \leq \mathbf{x}_j\mathbf{A}_j\mathbf{x}_j^*\ \forall \mathbf{x}_j \in \Theta_j$, can be written as $\sum_{i\in I_j} x_{j,i}^* \cdot \mathbf{e}_i\mathbf{A}_j\mathbf{x}_j^* \leq \sum_{i\in I_j} x_{j,i} \cdot \mathbf{e}_i\mathbf{A}_j\mathbf{x}_j^*\ \forall \mathbf{x}_j \in \Theta$, which by identity $\mathbf{e}_i\mathbf{A}_j\mathbf{x}_j^* \equiv Q_j(i,l^*)$ of (3) turns out to be equivalent with what we desire to find. *QED*

We may define the condition for evolutionarily stable state (ESS) for multiagent reinforcement learning in a similar way. ESS condition in our setting, where smaller cost is better, is defined such that $\mathbf{x}_j^*\mathbf{A}_j\mathbf{x}_j < \mathbf{x}_j\mathbf{A}_j\mathbf{x}_j$ holds for all $\mathbf{x}_j \neq \mathbf{x}_j^*$ in the neighborhood of $\mathbf{x}_j^*$ in Θ_j.

Claim 2. *ESS condition for multi-agent reinforcement learning is for*

$$\sum_{i\in I_j}(x_{j,i}^* - x_{j,i})Q_j(i,l) < 0. \tag{10}$$

to hold for all $\mathbf{x}_j \neq \mathbf{x}_j^*$ *in the neighborhood of* $\mathbf{x}_j^*$. *(And for usual setting, inequality > replaces < in (9).)*

Proof. The proof is the same as that of Claim 1, except that $Q_j(i, l)$ replaces $Q_j(i, l^*)$ and that the strong inequality sign replaces weak inequality. *QED*

These definitions and claims are helpful in analyzing the dynamic behavioral properties of games based on simulation results of agent-based computational models, as shown in the next section.

A Note About Social Learning

The model described includes a social learning (Bandura, 1977) mechanism, as the shared policy $\{Q_j\}$ is used and updated by arbitrary agents at each time step. This is the form of shared knowledge with heterogeneous learning, as opposed to heterogeneous knowledge, which must be distinct in properties. This social learning approach is beneficial especially if the knowledge space is too broad for an individual to cover alone, and sharing of knowledge by a group will mitigate the burdens of learning about the world, which would be laborious otherwise. As the network is complicated, this feature will become not only useful, but almost necessary. However, we must note its drawbacks. As we will see later, shared knowledge can mislead the others' behaviors once atypical reinforcements wrongly influence the public knowledge.

EXAMPLE OF BEHAVIORAL ANALYSIS BY SIMULATION

Environment Description

We have developed a simple agent-based computational model to simulate and analyze the game behaviors of traffic policy. In this simplified environment, there is only one O-D pair, consisting of two paths connecting the O-D, and each path includes only one arc. Hence, there are no more than two options available in the network. This kind of state abstraction is common, for example, in analyses of commutation between urban center and suburban zonal center. The equation for arc travel time is given by a linear monotonic function of arc flow volume as $t_i = t_i^0 + (lsmt_i / leng_i) \cdot v_i$, where $leng_i$ is the arc length, $lsmt_i$ is the length-scaled marginal travel time, and t^0 is zero-flow travel time. The concrete values of parameters are given in Table 2. Arc 1 is longer but has a larger capacity. In other words, arc 2 is faster if the traffic volume is small and arc 1 will become faster as traffic volume increases. One or more artificial agents, in which Monte Carlo learning (5) is embedded, are instantiated at each discrete time step at the origin node. Agents travel on arc i at the speed of $leng_i/t_i$. One instance of $\overline{F}$ (and thus one set of $Q(i, l)$) is shared by all the agents in order to realize faster social learning.

In fact, this simple model is capable of being examined by analytics, by identifying mixed-strategy equilibria in a population context for varying levels of travel demand. One can indeed see that a unique interior equilibrium exists for a fixed demand. A purpose of our employment of computational model here is to confirm that the policy function built by the artificial agents with learning ability does not contradict with this analytic inference. Besides, the extensions to be discussed in the next section suggest that analytical approaches which would involve game behaviors with bootstrapped value functions would be difficult.

Table 2. Parameters used for behavioral analysis simulation

Arc ID	*lsmt*	t^0	*leng*
1	200	90	202
2	400	45	190

Results

After a run of 20,000 time steps, we obtained a set of $Q(i, l)$ and thus $\overline{F}(i,l)$ for each i and l. A policy graph of $Q(2, l) - Q(1, l)$ plotted over (v_1, v_2) state space is given in Figure 1. Because we varied the number of agents departing the origin node, we need to deal with $\mathbf{v}$ rather than $\mathbf{x}$. (Note that we do not have subscript j to $\mathbf{x}$, because we have only one decision node in this model. So, just as in usual vector notation, let subscript k of x_k represent the index of the component of vector $\mathbf{x}$, rather than node index.) However, a general normalization of $\mathbf{v}$ in a subspace $\{\mathbf{v} \mid |\mathbf{v}| = c\}$ for a constant c translates to $\mathbf{x}$. Hence, we will not lose generality. In Figure 1, there exists a subset of state space expressed as $\{\mathbf{v} \mid Q(2,l) - Q(1,l) = 0\}$, which by definition (8) represents the set of equilibria. Path 1 has greater travel time to the left of this equilibrium set, and Path 2 has greater travel time to the right of it. It is only along the equilibrium set where agents are indifferent between choosing Path 1 and Path 2.

In order to make a game approach, let us take an example of $c = 150$. The same policy graph plotted over this subset of the state space is given in Figure 2. Geometrically, this graph is a cross-sectional image of Figure 1 in the diagonal direction. Because we know $|\mathbf{v}| = 150$, we can normalize $\mathbf{v}$ to $\mathbf{x}$. It has a point at $\mathbf{x}^* \approx (0.65, 0.35)$ where policy geometry is crossing the horizontal line of $Q(2, l) - Q(1, l) = 0$. This is the equilibrium in this subspace, as defined in (8). For this equilibrium to be Nash equilibrium, $(0.65 - x_1)Q(1,l^*) + (0.35 - x_2)Q(2,l^*) \leq 0$ must hold for all $\mathbf{x} \in \Theta$ from (9). Since $n = 2$ or $x_2 = 1.0 - x_1$, this condition can be simplified to $(0.35 - x_2)Q(2,l^*) - Q(1,l^*) \leq 0$, which is obviously satisfied because of $Q(2,l^*) - Q(1,l^*) = 0$. Hence we conclude that $\mathbf{x}^* \approx (0.65, 0.35)$ is also Nash equilibrium. Additionally, (10) is requiring that $(0.65 - x_1)Q(1,l^*) + (0.35 - x_2)Q(2,l)$ < 0 must hold for all $\mathbf{x} \neq \mathbf{x}^*$ in a ball around $\mathbf{x}^*$ for this equilibrium to be an ESS. Again, by the same logic as what we used for Nash equilibrium identification, this condition can

Figure 1. Policy graph of Q(2, l) – Q(1, l) for two-path network.

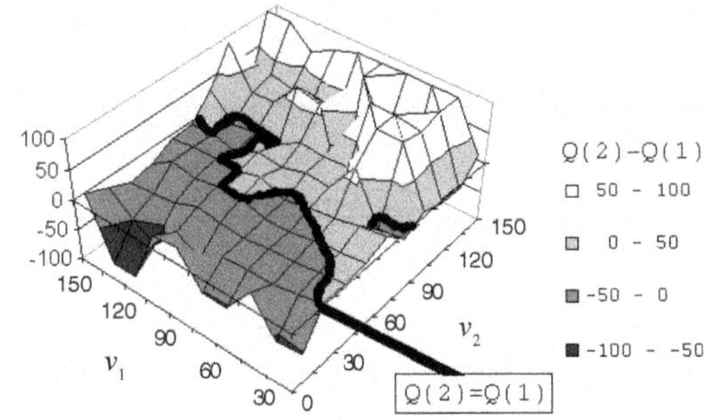

be simplified to $(0.35-x_2)Q(2,l)-Q(1,l)<0$, with which we can easily conclude from Figure 2 that $\mathbf{x}^* \approx (0.65, 0.35)$ is also an ESS. Actually, because the geometry of Figure 1 is formed such that $Q(2,l^*)-Q(1,l^*)>0$ to the left of equilibrium line and $Q(2,l^*)-Q(1,l^*)<0$ almost everywhere (and completely everywhere in the ball around $\mathbf{x}^*$) to the right of the equilibrium implies that all the elements in the set of equilibria are also in a set of ESS. This result shows that the dynamics has a continuous asymptotically stable set bounded by the border of Θ for this particular example, provided that the Q geometry (see Figure 1) generated by agents through learning is sufficiently accurate.

In this section, we showed a role that agent-based computational models play in helping our theoretical analyses for a relatively complicated dynamic system such as traffic network, based on the definition and claims discussed in the previous section. Simulation results of multiagent reinforcement learning showed that the model is capable of generating some resources from which we may derive equilibria, NE, and ESS.

DEMONSTRATIONS

A Simple Traffic Network

In this section, we use a simple network (see Figure 3) to examine the effectiveness of the three reinforcement learning algorithms (5)-(7) in the traffic policy optimization problem. The network is a directed graph connecting one pair of origin and destination by nine arcs and three intermediate nodes. There are seven paths in total in this network. Arc 4 is designed as a congested road, for three paths out of all the seven paths use this arc. In contrast, arc 8 and arc 9 are designed with flatter sloped supply functions common in high capacity roads. Agents leave the origin for the destination. At every time step, one agent is instantiated and put on origin node. There are three nodes at which agents make decisions. These nodes are marked with ellipsoidal symbols including the notation $Q_j(i, l)$, representing the value of the function $\overline{F}_j$ (Note that node 2 is not a decision node, since the solely available strategy there is $i = 4$). This value stores the estimated travel time to be spent from node j to destination given state l and strategy i. We expect that intelligent agents learn to avoid arc 1 and arc 5 as well as arc 4, because these deterministically lead to the congested arc in the directed graph. On the other hand, they may learn to choose arc 3 since it leads to arc 8 and arc 9.

Figure 2. Policy graph of Q(2, l) – Q(1, l) plotted over 1-dimensional subspace $\{\mathbf{v} \mid |\mathbf{v}|=150\}$

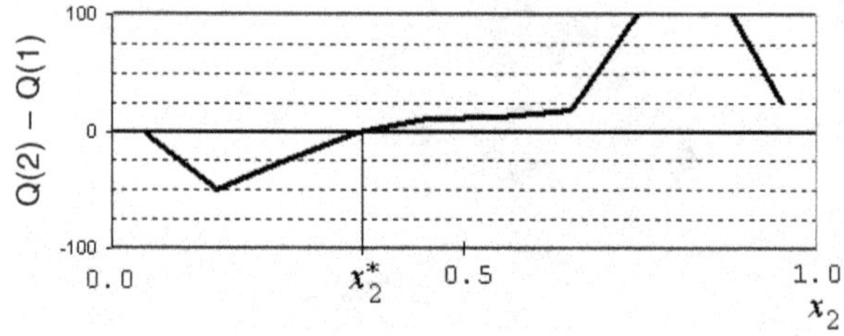

Figure 3. Graphical representation of simple traffic network and the attribute data of arcs

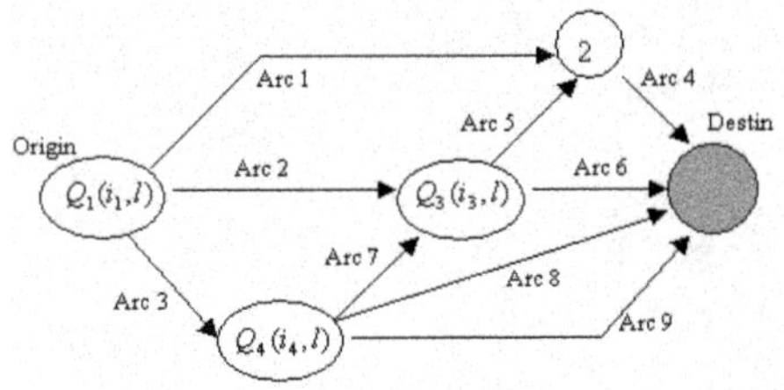

Arc	Intercept t_i^0	Slope of t_i (v_i)	Length len_i
1	40	0.625	160.2
2	15	2.105	95.0
3	15	1.329	60.2
4	20	1.661	60.2
5	10	2.500	64.0
6	10	2.105	95.0
7	10	1.875	64.0
8	20	0.731	150.4
9	30	0.750	160.2

The deterministic traffic user equilibrium discussed earlier implies zero variance of travel times among all the used paths at the optimum. The top row of Figure 4 shows the variances acquired from the simulation of 20,000 iterations with Monte Carlo learning (5) for $\alpha = 0.1$. Additionally, we define the exploration probability $\varepsilon = 0.3$ at which agents take nonoptimal action $i' \neq i$. (The need for exploration comes from the need to define A_j accurately *for each row* in our original problem.) In the initial phase, the variances are high, reflecting the inefficient traffic flows. This occurs because agents do not have sufficient knowledge at first, and have to go through explorations of the undiscovered world. Once the exploration period is over, the state continues to approach the equilibrium until the end of simulation. The learning rate of $\alpha = 0.1$ was chosen because of its relative superiority. When the learning rate is set too high Q_j values change too much based on each learning iteration and the resulting Q_j values mislead the agents. On the other hand, when the learning rate is too low the learning cannot "catch up" with the dynamics of the environment, and thus the modified Q_j values are likely to be obsolete. Hence, moderate values of α such as 0.1 work best. This is true not only for Monte Carlo control, but also for Sarsa and Q-learning.

The second and the third rows of Figure 4 show the variances generated by Sarsa and Q-learning, respectively. The results that use temporal difference seem inferior to Monte Carlo control for this special case of simple network, both in the closeness to equilibrium and stability. This sort of experimental result is rare since temporal difference learning usually improve the updates of Q values in many tasks (Sutton & Barto, 1998). This unusual result may be attributed to the unique property of multiagent model sharing one set of Q. For example, agents having traveled on arc 2 updates $Q_1(2, l)$ value based on $Q_3(i', l')$ using (6) or (7), but this update depends on what strategy i' these agents have chosen and the state l' they have perceived. If some agents chose to explore a nongreedy action such as $i' = 5$, where arc 4 proceeded by arc 5 is very congested, then the update to $Q_1(2, l)$ based on $Q_3(5, l')$ will be biased toward an overestimated value. While some agents update such a biased values of $Q_{j'}$, other agents simultaneously use this biased $Q_{j'}$ to backup other Q_j values, and this spiral of misdirected backups severely harms social knowledge. One way to lessen this disadvantage is to set the exploration probability ε as a diminishing variable instead of a constant. We tested this with a simple rule defined by the difference equation $\Delta\varepsilon/\Delta time = -0.001\varepsilon$. The variance generated with decreasing ε is shown in right side of Figure 4. This method gradually decreases the magnitude of oscillations for Sarsa and Q-learning.

Figure 4. Variances of travel times among seven paths for each of three reinforcement learning algorithms

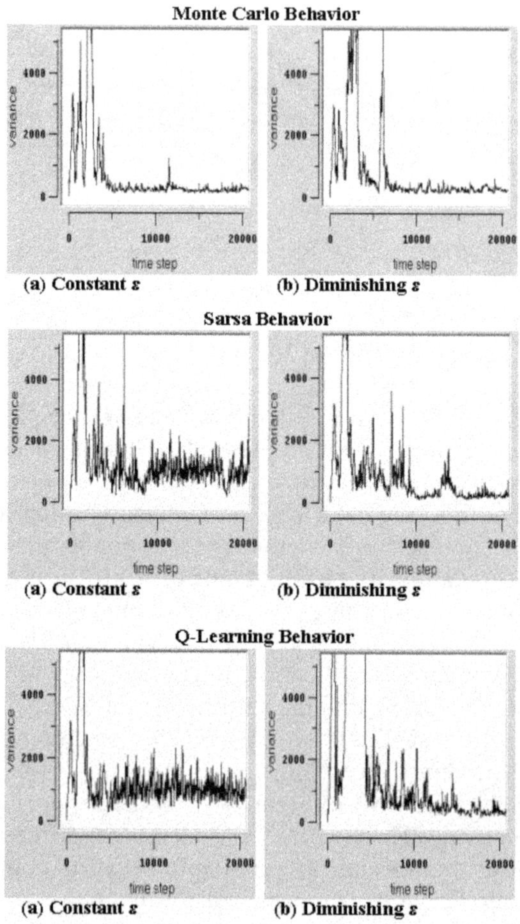

We also tested the same agent-based simulation, in which the agents make random choices instead of using reinforcement learning, which only resulted in variances remaining hundred thousands throughout simulation. In contrast, reinforcement learning brought about emergent traffic equilibrium, with variances around or even below 1,000. The variance of 300 by Monte Carlo control, for example, means that the standard deviation of path travel times are only 17 time steps, where 120 is the average path travel time. We see that the paths have close travel times with reinforcement learning. Specifically, simulation results with variances close to zero characterize rough convergences to equilibria; the equilibrium condition as given by Definition 1 requires the equality of the travel times for all the used path entailing a variance of zero.

Demonstration with a GIS Network Data

In this section, a demonstration of the algorithm in a little more sophisticated network than the previous section is examined. Some special-purpose tools, such as geographic information systems (GIS), become necessary when a data of actual traffic network is concerned. One idea is to load GIS data, instantiate each geographic object, and then put artificial agents in the modeled geographic space. Though most GIS data are given in tabular (database) format, employment of object-oriented graph algorithms allows the conversion of data into modeled objects. We skip the description of this process because it is beyond the scope of this paper. Refer to Gimblett (2002) for an integration of GIS and agent-based models.

We used data obtained from the San Francisco Bay area shown in Figure 5, which includes 207 nodes and 338 arcs. In this example, the traffic network is represented by a bidirectional graph, unlike the example of the previous section. We defined only one destination node at the center of San Francisco city, as indicated in Figure 5. A set of $Q_j(i, l)$ representing $\overline{F}_j$ is assigned to each node j in {1,2,…,207} including the destination node itself. Note that every element in the family of such sets specializes in the sole destination. Arcs are categorized into one of "limited access highways," "highways," and "others," and we defined travel time functions to each of them as $t_i = len_i / (3.0 - 0.1v_i)$, $t_i = len_i / (2.0 - 0.2v_i)$, and $t_i = len_i / (31.0 - 0.3v_i)$, respectively, where lengths are given by pixel unit. With the assumption that travel demand to this destination is uniformly distributed among all the nodes, two agents are instantiated at each time step at randomly chosen nodes except for the destination. This means that there are 207 O-D pairs with 207 origins. Though there are more than one origin, the number of destination node is one, implying that we only need to allocate one set of $Q_j(i, l)$ to each node j in J. It is assumed that tolls will not affect agents' decisions, thus only the estimated travel times to destination stored in each node as $Q_j(i, l)$ act as factors to drive agents. Initially, zero is assigned to $Q_j(i, l)$ for every i, j, and l in order to attract exploration of all the nodes for all possible states and strategies. Additionally, in order to tempt agents to head for the destination node, the value of $-10{,}000+R_j$, rather than mere R_j, is used upon the arrival at destination to update $Q_j(i, l)$ that the agent referred in the previous node.

Figure 5. Traffic network of San Francisco Bay area

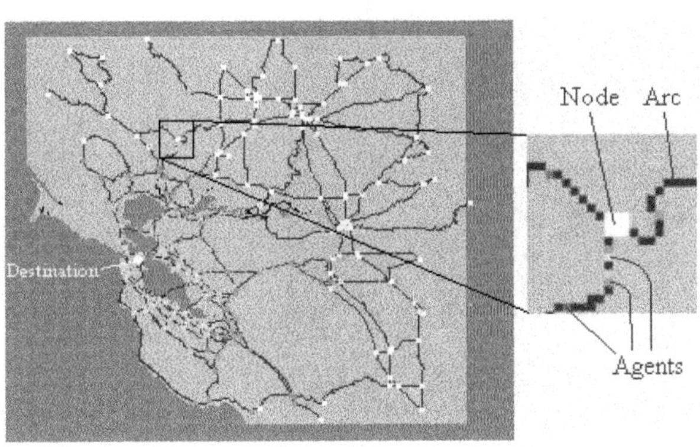

During the first 500 time steps, agents' movements appear random rather than rational. We call this exploration period. We may employ the A* algorithm, for example, to shrink the duration of this period. Once the exploration period is over, agents acquire some habits of using particular paths that they have found to be optimal. For example, many of them rush onto Bridge 2 (San Francisco-Oakland Bay), shown in right side of Figure 6, but this causes congestion, turning all the paths that include this bridge to be less optimal. As a consequence, divergence occurs so that some agents currently using Bridge 2 are reallocated to Bridge 1 (Golden Gate) and Bridge 3 (San Mateo-Hayward). We call this the adjustment period. The state converges to traffic equilibrium after the adjustment period, as noted previously. At this time, most, if not all, nodes store the sufficiently accurate estimated time, $Q_j(i, l)$, in equilibrium. We draw a convex hull of the nodes with $Q_j(i, l) \leq 100$ and another of nodes with $Q_j(i, l) \leq 200$, as shown in left side of Figure 6. Notice that the convex hull of $Q_j(i, l) \leq 100$ is longer to the south of destination than to the east and north. It can be inferred that the cause of this is the availability of more choices on land to the south than on the water body with fewer arcs (bridges). Additionally, we can observe the convex hull of $Q_j(i, l) \leq 200$ being strongly convex to the east. This is attributed to the existence of limited access highways leading to that region.

SUMMARY AND FURTHER APPLICATIONS

We have seen a strong relationship among the classical theory of traffic equilibrium, game theoretic approaches, and multiagent reinforcement learning, particularly through the use of the Bellman equation. For the complex features and the dynamic nature of traffic network problems, game theoretic approach would be difficult with a standard static method. With the reinforcement method discussed in this chapter, however, equilibria can be identified (if any exists) by empirical or simulated data. We also verified that computational simulation of multiagent reinforcement learning generate emergent equilibrium that agrees with the classical theory, in the sense that the travel times of all the used paths are equal to each other and to the minimum travel time, characterized by

Figure 6. Convex hulls of nodes within 100 and 200 time steps of travel time to destination (left); and three main bridges leading to the destination (right)

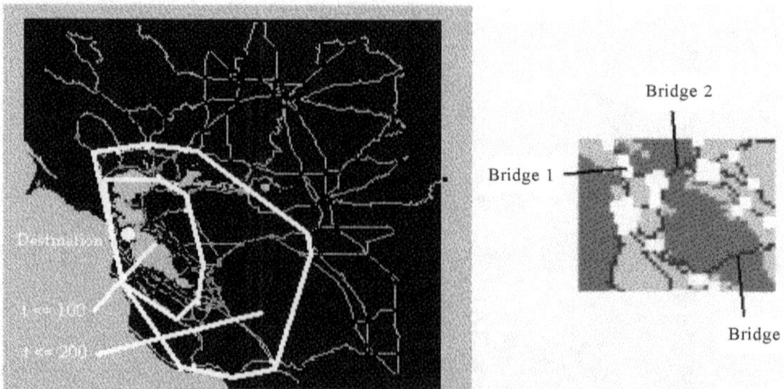

simulation results of very low variance among them. With these relationships, we find that these three paradigms are substitutable as well as complementary.

The attempt of our demonstration on GIS data is aimed at a real application. Though we need more precise and detailed data to apply it to the real traffic network, the basic principle we employed seems applicable. One possible application is to forecast the effects of governmental decisions, such as addition of lanes (capacity improvement), closure of road segments, and temporary constructions. Because it takes some positive time for agents to adapt to the new equilibrium with the delayed response to the road supply functions, the approach presented in this paper reflects the reality better than the standard static approaches. Another possible application is the extension of intelligent transportation systems (ITS) based on $Q(i, l)$, where client systems on agents' vehicles and a central server communicate. Suppose client systems can exchange or share $Q(i, l)$ values through a server-side database, and the flow amounts v_i on each arc i can be monitored by server-side system. Then it is expected to be able to efficiently navigate agents with online optimization of decisions. As an instance of concrete technological example, Choy, Srinivasan and Cheu (2002) showed a method that uses fuzzy-neuro evolutionary hybrid techniques with online reinforcement learning to enable real-time traffic control systems. This adds a technological application as well as sociopolitical applications of the model we have discussed.

ACKNOWLEDGMENT

We are grateful to the anonymous peer reviewers for their generous, to-the-point, and helpful comments. We also appreciate the comments given by the audience in the Third International Workshop of Computational Intelligence in Economics and Finance, 2003, Cary, NC, USA.

REFERENCES

Bandura, A. (1977). *Social learning theory*. Englewood Cliffs, NJ: Prentice Hall.

Beckman, M. J., McGuire, C. B., & Winston, C. B. (1956). *Studies in the economics of transportation*. New Haven, CN: Yale University Press.

Bellman, R. E. (1957). *Dynamic programming*. Princeton, NJ: Princeton University Press.

Choy, M. C., Srinivasan, D., & Cheu, R. L. (2002). Hybrid cooperative agents with online reinforcement learning for traffic control. *The Proceedings of IEEE FUZZ 2002, 2.* (pp. 1015-1020).

Gimblett, R. H. (2002). *Integrating geographic information systems and agent-based modeling techniques: For simulating social and ecological processes.* Oxford, UK: Oxford University Press.

Roth, A. E., & Erev, I. (1995). Learning in extensive-form games: Experimental data and simple dynamic models in the intermediate term. *Games and Economic Behavior [Special issue], Nobel Symposium, 8,* 164-212.

Sutton, R. S. (1988). Learning to predict by the methods of temporal differences. *Machine Learning, 3,* 9-44.

Sutton, R. S., & Barto, A. G. (1998). *Reinforcement learning: An introduction.* Cambridge, MA: MIT Press.

Taylor, P. D., & Jonker, L. (1978). Evolutionarily stable strategies and game dynamics. *Mathematical Bioscience, 40,* 145-156.

Tesauro, G. (1995). Temporal difference learning and TD-Gammon. *Communications of the ACM, 38*(3), 58-68.

Wardrop, J. G. (1952). Some theoretical aspects of road traffic research. *Proceedings of the Institution of Civil Engineers, Part II*(1), 325-378.

Watkins, C. J. C. H. (1989). *Learning from delayed rewards.* Doctoral dissertation, Cambridge University, UK.

Section IV

Cost Estimation and Decision-Support Systems

Chapter IX

Fuzzy-Neural Cost Estimation for Engine Tests

Edit J. Kaminsky
University of New Orleans, USA

Holly Danker-McDermot
New Orleans, USA

Freddie Douglas, III
NASA, Stennis Space Center, USA

ABSTRACT

This chapter discusses artificial computational intelligence methods as applied to cost prediction. We present the development of a suite of hybrid fuzzy-neural systems for predicting the cost of performing engine tests at NASA's Stennis Space Center testing facilities. The system is composed of several adaptive network-based fuzzy inference systems (ANFIS), with or without neural subsystems. The output produced by each system in the suite is a rough order of magnitude (ROM) cost estimate for performing the engine test. Basic systems predict cost based solely on raw test data, whereas others use preprocessing of these data, such as principal components and locally linear embedding (LLE), before entering the fuzzy engines. Backpropagation neural networks and radial basis functions networks (RBFNs) are also used to aid in the cost prediction by merging the costs estimated by several ANFIS into a final cost estimate.

INTRODUCTION

John C. Stennis Space Center (SSC) is NASA's primary center for testing and flight certification of rocket propulsion systems for the space shuttle and future generations of space vehicles. Because of its important role in engine testing for more than 3 decades, SSC has been designated NASA's Center of Excellence for Rocket Propulsion Testing. SSC tests all space shuttle main engines (SSME). These high-performance, liquid-fueled engines provide most of the total impulse needed during the shuttle's 8 1/2-minute flight into orbit. All SSME must pass a series of test firings at SSC prior to being installed in the back of the orbiter. Moreover, commercial engine and component tests are also performed at the SSC NASA facilities.

A few operations management software systems, including cost estimating algorithms, have been developed in the past (Lockheed Martin Space Operations, 2001; Lockheed Martin Space Operations, 2000; Rocket Propulsion Testing Lead Center, 1997, 1998; Sundar, 2001) to aid in scheduling and managing tests as well as to predict the cost of performing component and engine tests at NASA's John C. Stennis Space Center testing facilities: The cost estimating model (CEM), which includes cost estimating relationships (CER), the operations impact assessor (OIA), bottoms-up cost estimator (BUCE), and risk constrained optimized strategic planning (RCOSP). The results, however, have not been very encouraging and are not available in the open literature. OIA and RCOSP are very complex systems and require input data that are rarely, if ever, available before tests are performed. BUCE is a bottoms-up estimator and requires a level of detail for the input data (e.g., a complete list of parts and number of labor hours) that bans this tool from being used to generate a rough order of magnitude estimate. CEM is the simplest system and it prompts the user to input the same type of preliminary data as the systems presented in this Chapter. Results from CEM will be compared to the new computational intelligence systems which perform considerably better. CEM uses cost estimating relationships, parametric estimation, and statistics.

In this chapter, we present a system for this same purpose (cost prediction), based on adaptive network-based fuzzy inference systems (ANFIS) and neural networks (NN). The hybrid software suite was developed in Matlab[1] and combines the adaptive capabilities of neural networks and the ease of development and additional benefits of fuzzy logic based systems, detailed by the current authors in (Danker-McDermot, 2004; Kaminsky, 2002; Kaminsky & Douglas, 2003). The software-based system consists of several user-selectable subsystems ranging from simple fuzzy estimators, to medium complexity ANFIS systems that use normalized and transformed input data as well as more complex multistage fuzzy-neural or neural systems. We will discuss each here, and present comparative results indicating that these artificial intelligence procedures produce good cost estimates even when they are developed using very small sets of data. The accuracy of the predicted cost increases as the complexity of the system (as measured by number of processing routines, number of stages, and number of input variables) increases.

The goal of the project[2] was to develop a hybrid fuzzy-neural cost estimating system to obtain rough order of magnitude (ROM) estimates of the cost for both component and engine tests. A very small set of data, mainly from NASA's Project Requirement Documents (PRD) (NASA, 2001; University of New Orleans, 2000), were available for component and engine tests performed at NASA's John C. Stennis Space Center (SSC).

In this chapter, however, we detail only the hardest problem: predicting cost for engine tests. The available PRD data set for engine tests was much smaller and more incomplete than the component test sets. Results presented here are, therefore, easy to improve upon for component tests. For results of component tests, the reader may refer to Kaminsky (2002) and Kaminsky and Douglas (2003). A subset of the already small group of PRD data for engine tests was used to train the computational intelligence fuzzy-neural systems in the suite. The trained systems are then used to predict cost for unseen engine articles (the testing set).

Several prototypes were developed and are described in the rest of this chapter: Simple ANFIS cost estimators (ANFIS), principal component analysis (PCA) ANFIS cost estimators (PCA-ANFIS), parallel/cascaded ANFIS systems (Parallel-ANFIS), locally linear embedding (LLE) ANFIS estimators (LLE-ANFIS), fuzzy-neural estimators (Parallel-ANFIS-NN), and radial basis function network estimators (RBFN). These differ in complexity and amount of preprocessing needed. Accuracy of predicted cost, although similar in order of magnitude, varies depending on the complexity of the system.

Principal components and LLE are used as preprocessing stages to reduce the dimensionality of the data because we have many more variables (descriptors) than we have exemplars (articles in the training set). PCA yields a linear decomposition whereas LLE is a nonlinear reduction method.

The rest of this chapter is organized as follows: In the next section, the engine test data, data analysis, and the preprocessing routines used are presented. We then briefly summarize ANFIS theory and present the various prototypes, followed by results for each of these prototypes and comparative results among the various systems. A summary and suggestions for further work are given along with conclusions.

DATA DESCRIPTION AND PREPROCESSING

This section discusses the data, collected and provided by NASA at Stennis Space Center, used to develop and test the fuzzy-neuro systems. We first describe the raw data and their limitations, and later analyze these data. We also discuss preprocessing of the raw data.

Data Description

The systems developed are supervised (i.e., they are developed using training data to produce the mapping sought). The nonlinear mapping is from raw input data to output cost. The raw data, then, are of extreme importance, both in quality and in quantity. As many project requirements descriptions (PRDs; NASA, 2001) as possible were collected. These PRDs characterize the engines tested at SSC. Unfortunately, the total number of articles is very small, generating small sets of training and testing data. A total of only 11 articles are complete enough to be used. These data have been used in two ways: to develop the models using a training subset and to test the newly developed models with a testing set previously unseen by the trained systems. The cost of performing the tests for these articles ranged from a few hundred thousand dollars to about 12 million dollars.

PRDs contained 18 variables that had data for at least one article. Many of these variables, however, had no data for most of the articles, and had to be discarded or filled by methods discussed later in this Chapter. The PRD input data variables left are given in Table 1. All variables in this table were at least considered for use, but some were sometimes discarded after analysis of the predictive value of the variable indicated that they were of little use in predicting the cost of performing tests for the particular system under consideration. Not all variables were used in all prototyped systems.

A particular engine article has the data given in the last column of Table 1. Notice that variables 4-6 are codes (integer numbers) indicating the type of fuel, pressurant, and oxidizer. Codes 4, 6 and 8 are used, respectively, for GHe (gaseous helium), H_20_2 (hydrogen peroxide), and JP8 (jet propulsion fuel type 8). Test stand code 3 indicates NASA's stand E3 at Stennis Space Center. Data is not available for this article for variables 13-15. The cost to perform this test was slightly over $700,000.

The already extremely small collection of 11 sets of engine article data was randomly separated into training and testing sets. For some of our systems we used 6 articles for training and 5 for testing, while for others we increased the training set to 7 and reduced the testing set to 4 articles. The articles in the testing sets are only used to test the generalization ability of the cost prediction systems and were not used at all in the development of the ANFIS or the NNs.

Data Analysis

The number of data variables available (18) was larger than the total number of articles (11). When dealing with fuzzy systems or neural networks, it is always preferable to have more vectors in the set than the number of elements in those vectors. This was a large problem for the NASA engine test data because there were only 11 viable data exemplars, each with a maximum dimensionality of 19 when cost is included as the last variable. We need to somehow reduce the dimensionality of the set but must ensure that we do not discard any of the most important (most predictive) variables. In order to determine which data variables to discard, the information within and predictive value of the various variables had to be analyzed. Exhaustive and sequential searches were performed to determine the input attributes that have the most prediction power for ANFIS modeling. The exhaustive search, by its nature, yields the best results; however, it is extremely time consuming and computationally expensive.

In summary, variables 1, 2, 4, 7, 13 and 17 in Table 1 were the only ones that repeatedly showed to have predictive power for engine tests using the exhaustive search. When we used the sequential search mechanism, similar conclusions were reached,

Table 1. Input variables for engine tests (from PRDs)

No.	*Name*	*Description*	*Example Data*
1	DuratDd	Duration of test in days	45 days
2	NoTest	Number of tests	25 tests
3	TestDurMax	Maximum duration of test	200 sec
4	Fuel	Fuel code (integer)	8
5	Pressurant	Pressurant code (integer)	4
6	Oxidizer	Oxidizer code (integer)	6
7	Thrust	Thrust	5 450 lbs
12	ThrustMeas	Thrust Measurement (Boolean)	0
13	FuelFlow	Rate of fuel flow	N/A
14	PressuraPr	Pressure of pressurant	N/A
15	OxidizerFl	Rate of oxidizer flow	N/A
17	TestStand	Test stand code (integer)	3
19	TotalCost	Total cost of performing test	$702 000

except that variables 3, 5 and 6 also showed to be important in a few cases. The output variable in all cases is the total cost of the test (variable 19).

As an example, we summarize the relative importance of the three most important variables as a function of the number of fuzzy membership functions (from 2 to 4) in Table 2. Clearly the predictive power of a given variable depends on the number of membership functions allowed for that particular variable. Thrust rarely appeared as the most predictive variable, but it appeared as a variable to be included in almost all runs.

Missing Data

Another problem with the engine test data at our disposal is that frequently there is information missing for an article, but which piece of information was missing changed with each article. Ideally, if the information cannot be found for all articles, it would be best to eliminate these variables entirely. This is not a viable option in our situation, however, because almost all of the data variables have their value missing for at least one article. There does not seem to be a large body of published research dealing with small and incomplete data sets. The work we did find dealt mainly with incomplete data sets in neural classification systems. Ishibuchi, Miyazaki and Tanaka (1994) proposed a method for dealing with incomplete data by using an interval representation of incomplete data with missing inputs. After a network is trained using learning algorithms for interval training data, a new sample consisting of the missing inputs is presented along with an interval vector. The output from the neural network is also an interval vector. This output is then classified using four definitions of inequality between intervals.

Granger, Rubin, Gorssberg and Lavoie (2000) proposed using a fuzzy ARTMAP neural network to deal with incomplete data for a classification problem. This approach presented the fuzzy ARTMAP with an indicator vector that described whether a data component was present or not. Unlike replacement methods, the weight vector is modified as well as the input vector in response to missing components.

Another method to deal with incomplete data is to use the normal information diffusion model, which divides an observation into many parts according to a normal function (Chongfu, 1998). This technique attempts to find a suitable membership function to represent a fuzzy group that represents the incomplete data. This fuzzy group is then used to derive more data samples. Unfortunately, this method can be computationally intensive.

Finally, some other methods viable for the engine data test sets are the much simpler mean and multiple imputation. Mean imputation simply replaces the missing data with the mean value of the samples. This method can cause misleading results because the changed data cannot reflect the uncertainty caused by the missing data. Multiple imputation is similar to mean imputation, but the missing data are replaced by a set of

Table 2. Relative importance of the most important variables for engine tests with the number of ANFIS membership functions as a parameter

No. of MF	*Variables in order of importance* 1st	2nd	3rd
4	DuratDd	Fuel	Thrust
3	NoTests	Oxidizer	Thrust
2	DuratDd	Fuel	Thrust

possible values from their predictive distribution. This set reflects the uncertainty of the values predicted from the observed ones (Zhou, 2000). This method yields much better results than mean imputation, but it can also become computationally intensive.

In the work described here we use mean imputation, mode imputation, and median imputation. Mode imputation, where the most common value is used to fill in missing data, was used when codes (such as for fuel, pressurant, oxidizer, or test stand) were unknown. Mean imputation was used for FuelFlow, and median imputation (i.e., filling missing data with the median value of that variable over all training articles) was used to replace unknown values of the pressure of the pressurant, PressuraPr.

Dimensionality Reduction

Neural and fuzzy system training is performed more efficiently after certain processing routines are applied to the raw input data. Some of these processing routines, such as principal component analysis (PCA), not only expedite training, but also reduce the dimensionality of the data set and provide information about the data which is not obvious in their original state. Raw data were used in many cases, whereas in other cases preprocessing techniques were applied to the raw data for normalization, data transformation, and dimensionality reduction. We use the following preprocessing algorithms:

- Normalization to standard deviation of one and mean of zero
- Normalization to range of [-1,1]
- Principal components analysis (PCA)
- Locally linear embedding (LLE)
- Normalization of cost to [0, 1]

A common method used to ensure that a fuzzy or neural system quickly attains more accuracy is to somehow reduce the data set so that only the most important information is given to the network, while all other data are eliminated so as not to confuse the system. Unfortunately, there does not seem to be a large amount of research in the field of nonlinear dimensionality reduction for sparse data sets. Most of the research found on this topic was related to image processing, which does not suffer from the problem of small data sets as is the case of NASA's article test data. We use only PCA and locally linear embedding (LLE), discussed in the next subsections, but other methods are available.

The Isomap (isometric feature mapping) method, developed by Tenenbaum, Silva and Langford (2000), is a nonlinear dimensionality reduction method that has been applied to image processing. This algorithm attempts to use classical multidimensional scaling (MDS) to map data points from a high-dimensional input space into low-dimensional coordinates of a nonlinear manifold (Gering, 2003) by working within neighborhoods. The Isomap method, as well as the LLE, relies heavily on the nearest neighbor algorithm. Most nonlinear dimensionality reduction methods (Brand, 2003; Demartines & Herault, 1997; Friedrich, 2003; Gering, 2002; Roweis & Saul, 2000) require some sort of nearest neighbor processing. Once again, this is not viable for use in extremely small data sets. We simply do not have enough data to make a good neighborhood grouping. However, in order to exemplify the problem, we do present the LLE algorithm and the results obtained using LLE prior to ANFIS processing.

An overall processing block diagram with LLE preprocessing is shown in Figure 1. The LLE processing block should be replaced by a PCA block when principal components decomposition is used. The first normalizing procedure is applied before the transformation is computed. The raw data are normalized to have a mean of zero and a standard deviation of one. The second normalization procedure is applied to the transformed (either by PCA or by LLE) data before they are fed to the fuzzy-neuro system. This normalization step ensures that the input data's range is in the range [-1, 1]. Often we also normalized the cost to the range [0, 1].

We try both the locally linear embedding (LLE) algorithm (Roweis & Saul, 2000; Saul & Roweis, 2003) and principal components analysis (PCA; Cohen, 1998) to reduce the dimensionality of the data set, which is then used to train an ANFIS to predict the cost of engine tests. PCA is a linear operation, however, and this system is highly nonlinear. LLE is a nonlinear method of reducing the dimensionality of the data set and we therefore expected it to produce better results than PCA; this was not proven to be the case during testing. Nonetheless, we believe that the LLE method would yield good results if a large data set were available, so that better neighborhoods could be defined.

Locally Linear Embedding (LLE)

Locally linear embedding, developed by Roweis and Saul (Roweis & Saul, 2000; Saul & Roweis, 2003), is a nonlinear dimensionality reduction method originally applied to image processing. Liou and Kuo (2002) applied LLE to visualization of economic statistics data. We implemented the LLE method for nonlinear dimensionality reduction of input data for engine test cost estimation. A fuzzy system was then developed which predicts the engine test cost based solely on the reduced data, as shown in Figure 1. LLE attempts to map the input data to a lower dimensional global coordinate system that preserves the relationships between neighboring points (Gering, 2003). Locally, linear neighborhoods of the input data are then mapped into a lower dimensional coordinate system. Unfortunately, it is very difficult to work with neighborhoods when the size of the data set is as small as ours. However, one of the purposes of this chapter is to present ways of performing accurate cost estimates for general applications, and this method might prove useful to readers who have sets of data composed of many exemplars.

The LLE algorithm is divided into three steps: selection of neighbors; computation of weights that best reconstruct each data point by its neighbors; and mapping to embedded coordinates (Friedrich, 2002; Roweis & Saul, 2000). The first step simply involves finding K nearest neighbors. We accomplish this by finding Euclidean distances or finding all neighbors within a fixed radius. The reconstruction weights are determined by minimization of a cost function. The data consist of real-valued vectors, each of dimensionality sampled from an underlying manifold. As long as there are enough sample points, it is expected that each data point lies on or close to a locally linear section

Figure 1. Block diagram of complete ANFIS system, including pre-processing

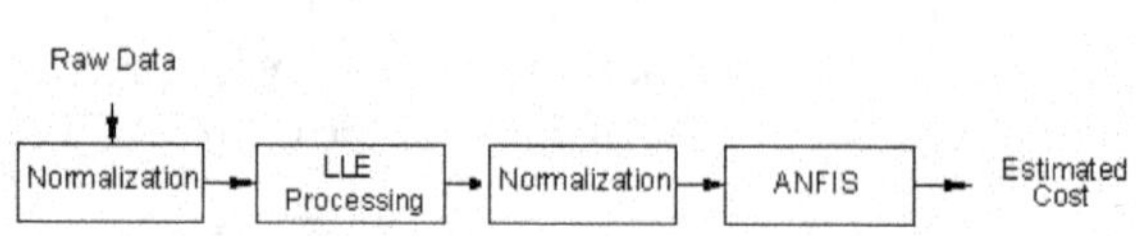

on the manifold. The local area is then characterized by linear coefficients that reconstruct each data point from its neighbors. The reconstructed errors are measured by

$$\varepsilon(W) = \sum_i \left| X_i - \sum_j W_{ij} X_j \right|^2 \tag{1}$$

This cost function adds up the squared distances between all of the data points, X_i and their reconstructions $W_{ij}X_j$. The weights represent the contribution of the jth data point to the reconstruction of the ith data point. The weights are computed by minimizing the cost function on two conditions: (a) each data point is reconstructed only from its neighbors, and (b) the cost function is minimized so that the rows of W sum to one. For any particular data point, these weights are invariant to rotations, rescalings, and translations of that data point from its neighbors, meaning that these weights reflect intrinsic geometric properties of each neighborhood (Saul & Roweis, 2003).

The final step in the LLE algorithm is mapping the high-dimensional data, X, to the new lower dimensional space coordinates, Y. Each high dimensional data point is mapped to the lower dimensional vector representing the embedding coordinates. The embedding coordinates, Y, are obtained by, once again, minimizing an embedding cost function

$$\Phi(Y) = \sum_i \left| Y_i - \sum_j W_{ij} Y_j \right|^2 \tag{2}$$

As with the previous function, (2) is based on locally linear reconstruction errors, but the weights are now fixed while Φ is optimized. This cost function can be manipulated into a quadratic form and minimized by solving a sparse N×N eigenvalue problem whose largest d nonzero eigenvectors provide the set of orthogonal coordinates centered on the origin, where d is the desired reduced dimension size. Pseudocode for implementing the LLE algorithm is given in Saul and Roweis (2003) and will not be repeated here.

The LLE-reduced data are fed to the LLE-ANFIS system and are not used for the other systems in our suite.

Principal Component Analysis (PCA)

We also applied principal component analysis to reduce the dimensionality of the data set (Kaminsky, 2000). The only disadvantage of using PCA in this situation is that PCA is a linear transformation and the data has a highly nonlinear relationship between individual data components. This is why using a nonlinear dimensionality reduction method, such as LLE, was thought to be a favorable alternative to using PCA. The nonlinearities, however, are addressed by the nonlinear ANFIS and neural systems to which the PCAs are fed. Principal component transformation proved to be a powerful preprocessing technique when applied to the normalized input data. There are two reasons why we are performing a PCA: to reduce data dimensionality (because we have an extremely small number of test articles) and to gain a further understanding of the relative importance and information content of the input data collected. This might yield insight into the data collection process itself, indicating redundant variables and, possibly, a need for other types of data input.

The main idea behind PCA is to (linearly) transform the original input data set into a different set which contains uncorrelated data. Principal component analysis uses singular value decomposition to compute the principal components of a set of data. The transformed vectors' components are uncorrelated and ordered according to the magnitude of their variance (Kaminsky, Rana & Miller, 1993). The new set, then, is ordered such that the first column contains the most informative data (as measured by variance), and the last column contains the least important data. This allows us to remove the last few columns of data, therefore reducing the dimensionality, while discarding as little information as possible (Cohen, 1988; Kaminsky, 2000). So by choosing only the first few principal components that influence the variance the most, we orthogonalize the input data, while eliminating vector components that contribute little to variations in the data set.

The principal components, or a normalized version of these, are the inputs to the fuzzy system PCA-ANFIS. Figure 2 shows a block diagram of the PCA-ANFIS system, with the main processing routines indicated in the rectangular blocks by the appropriate Matlab commands. Most of the figure shows processing routines; the "postreg" block

Figure 2. Block diagram of the process used in developing the PCA-ANFIS systems. Routines are shown by their Matlab commands.

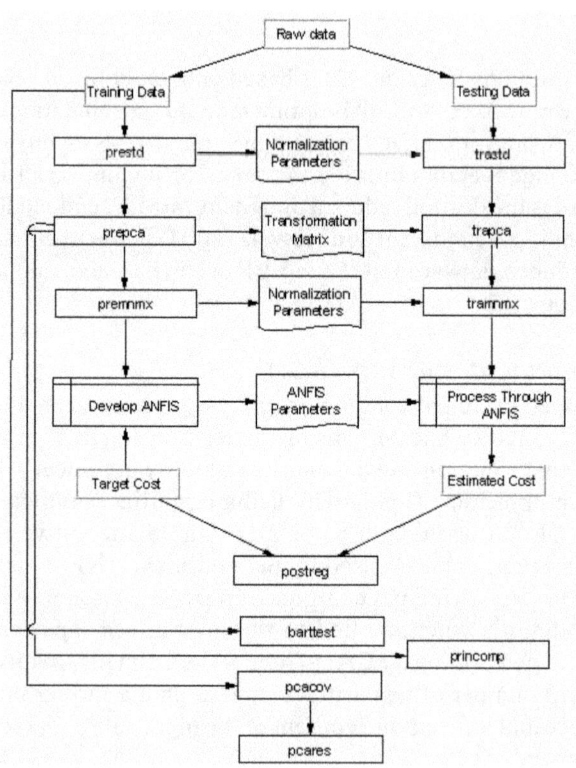

on down, shows analyses routines that are not used during regular processing. The block labeled ANFIS is discussed in detail elsewhere in this chapter.

Let us denote the original data, in our case the engine test data, by x. First, we compute the mean vector of the measurements, μ_x, and the covariance matrix, S_x. The eigenvalues, λ, of S_x are then computed. An orthonormal matrix U is made from the eigenvectors of S_x so that

$$L = U^T S_x U \tag{3}$$

where L is a diagonal matrix with the vector λ in the diagonal. The original vector, x, is transformed into its principal components, y, by:

$$y = U^T (x - \mu_x) \tag{4}$$

The most important (top rows) of the resulting principal components, y, are the inputs to the ANFIS system. The complete training data set (using all the variables listed in Table 1) was transformed using principal component analysis (PCA). This PCA indicates that the top six principal components (i.e., the six that contribute most to the overall variance in the cost estimate) provide a total of about three quarters of the information for engine tests, as indicated in Table 3. We see that even the most informative component of engine data only really contains between one fifth and one fourth of the total information available in the complete data set. Also, the second component of engine data is almost as "principal" as the first PC, and the third and fourth are, again, similar in information content to each other. Components 5 through 18 are much less important, although that set still contains a cumulative 33% of the total information for engine tests. Components 7 though 18 contain 27% of the information, slightly more than the first component alone, but were always discarded to reduce the dimensionality of the system.

We also obtained the eigenvalues of the covariance matrix of the normalized data, the Z-scores, and Hotelling's T-squared statistic for each data point. Hotelling's T^2 is a measure of the multivariate distance of each observation from the center of the data set. The eigenvalues and T^2 values are listed in Table 4.

The data shown in the column labeled Eigenvalues shows the value of the eigenvalue of the covariance matrix of the data and should be associated with each principal component. This, again, indicates that the first six principal components are important. For example, the largest eigenvalue is 4.5, followed by 2.4, which gives an idea of the relative importance of the principal components. The second data set, shown in

Table 3. Principal component analysis results for engine tests

PC No.	*Information (%)*	*Cumulative Information (%)*
1	22	22
2	21	43
3	13	56
4	11	67
5	4	71
6	2	73

Table 4. Covariance eigenvalues and T-square statistics of engine test data

PC No.	*Eigenvalues*	*Article No.*	*T^2 statistic*
1	4.5079	1	55.4088
2	2.4056	2	114.2291
3	1.7834	3	20.8178
4	1.4666	4	11.0769
5	0.6118	5	13.8477
6	0.5810	6	12.6355
7	0.3711	7	18.3934
8	0.1950	8	24.8131
9	0.1271	9	21.4780
10	0.0291	10	11.0796
11	0.0013	11	137.3189

the column labeled T^2 Statistic, is related to the data set itself (the engine articles), and gives an indication of the position of the data point within the set. The largest T-squared value, 137.32, indicates that this data point is very far from the mean or the center of the cluster of test data; this last article, as well as article 2, might be considered "outliers" and clearly have no close neighbors.

ADAPTIVE NETWORK-BASED FUZZY INFERENCE SYSTEMS

Adaptive network-based fuzzy inference systems (ANFIS) were first presented in Jang (1993) and Jang and Sun (1995). These systems combine the advantages of neural networks and fuzzy systems, generating fuzzy inference systems whose membership functions are trained using neural networks to produce the best results. Input–output mapping is therefore based on expert knowledge and training data. Highly nonlinear systems may be created using ANFIS theory.

Standard fuzzy inference systems (FIS) employ "if-then" rules in a noncrisp form (i.e., without using precise quantitative analyses), through the use of membership functions (Zadeh, 1965, 1968, 1978). ANFIS further tune the membership functions to maximize the system's performance. All our ANFIS used Gaussian-type curves for the membership functions; these include the two-sided Gaussian curve membership function (gauss2mf), the Gaussian curve membership function (gaussmf), and the generalized bell curve (gbellmf) membership function.

Our networks are of the type derived by Takagi and Sugeno (1983, 1985), with fuzzy sets only in the premise part (i.e., in the "if" part, not the "then" part). The membership function characterizes the linguistic label in the premise, while a nonfuzzy variable is used in the consequent.

The adaptive network within ANFIS is a multilayer feedforward network that adapts its weights to minimize an error criterion using a gradient search method such as the least mean squares (LMS) algorithm. Adaptation is performed for as many epochs as needed to reach the error criterion. Convergence was always achieved in fewer than 50 epochs.

In a sense, database mining applications such as this one, involve semiautomatic data analysis methods that help users discover some nontrivial knowledge. This knowledge is, in this case, the nonlinear relationship between several input parameters that describe the engines being tested (raw data from PRDs), and the actual cost[3] of performing the test of the article.

In its Matlab implementation, ANFIS is a training routine for Sugeno-type FIS based on adaptive generalized neural networks. ANFIS uses a hybrid-learning algorithm to identify parameters. It applies a combination of the least-squares (LS) method and the backpropagation gradient descent algorithm for training FIS membership function parameters to emulate a given training data set.

ANFIS SYSTEMS FOR COST PREDICTION OF ENGINE TESTS

Most of the ANFIS systems were developed using grid partition for the generation of the single-output Sugeno-type fuzzy inference system (FIS). We found, when working with the engine tests, that the results from grid partitioning were far superior to those from clustering. This is reasonable because the number of points is so small, that clustering is nearly impossible. When we tried using clustering with the component tests, for which we have somewhat larger (though still very small) training sets, results were more encouraging (Kaminsky & Douglas, 2003).

Membership functions were developed for each input variable. Fuzzification of all crisp quantities was performed. Initial values of the intervals for continuous linguistic variables were determined by the analysis of histograms and clustering methods. Statistical methods were suitable to select relevant features and provide initial intervals defining linguistic variables. Optimization of these initial rules (i.e., optimal intervals and other adaptive parameters) was done by maximizing the predictive (modeling) power of the system using neural networks.

We have also developed "parallel/cascaded" ANFIS: systems consisting of between 2 and 5 ANFIS in the first stage, each of which will concentrate on a subset of inputs and produce their best estimate of cost. A final "merging" of the results of the first stage parallel ANFIS is performed by a second stage (cascaded) ANFIS, or by a feed-forward neural network, which produces the final estimate of the cost. A graphical depiction of the general concept of a Parallel-ANFIS system is shown in Figure 3.

The Parallel-ANFIS system that we selected as prototype consists of two subsystems in the first stage, each with four inputs and one output. The diagram of this Parallel-ANFIS system is shown in Figure 4. We see that the first of the two parallel ANFIS (HEgrid42) uses two membership functions for all inputs, while the second uses 2, 2, 3, and 4 for the number of membership functions. The membership functions are of the gaussmf or gbellmf types. The final ANFIS, which takes the outputs of the first-stage ANFIS as it inputs, uses 3 membership functions of the Gauss2mf type to produce the final estimate of the cost.

We have developed and tested a large number of ANFIS systems. These various fuzzy systems use different number of inputs, different types of inputs, and various number and types of membership functions. The preprocessing applied, and the second stage, if used, also varied. Only a few of the systems developed, those selected to be delivered due to their performance, are discussed here.

Figure 3. Block diagram of the parallel/cascaded ANFIS system

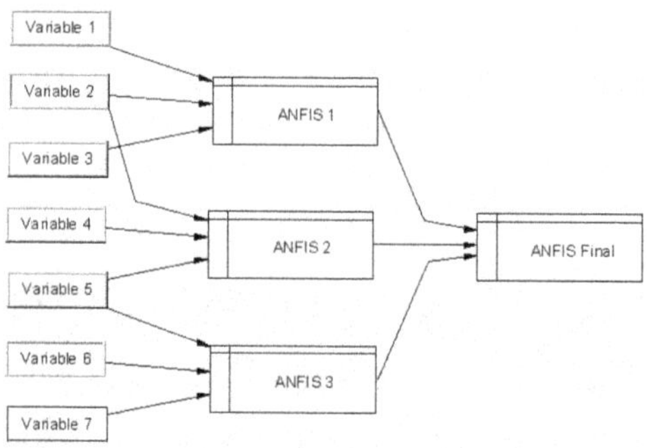

Figure 4. Block diagram of Parallel-ANFIS system showing the two parallel ANFIS systems and the final ANFIS stage

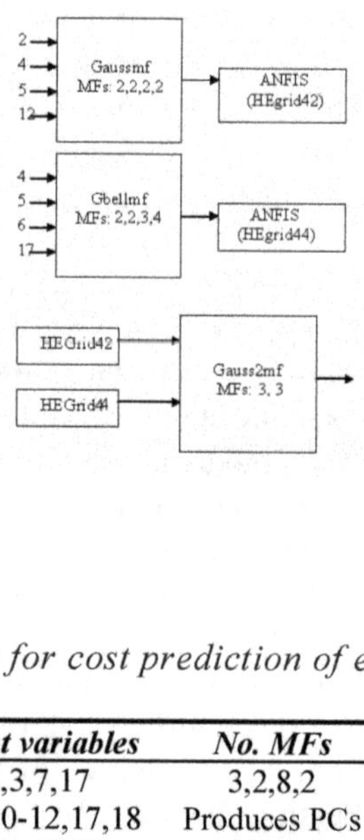

Table 5. Fuzzy/neuro systems for cost prediction of engine tests

ANFIS System	*Input variables*	*No. MFs*	*Comments*
ANFIS	1,3,7,17	3,2,8,2	Hybrid optimization
PCA	1-8,10-12,17,18	Produces PCs	For PCA-ANFIS
PCA-ANFIS	PC1-PC4	4,3,2,4	Gaussmf
Parallel-ANFIS	See Fig. 4	3,3	Gauss2mf & Gbellmf
Parallel-ANFIS-NN1	5,7,13-15,17	2-4	Imputation; 2 input, gaussmf, logsig
Parallel-ANFIS-NN2	1,3-5,7,13-15,17	2-4	Imputation; 3 input, gaussmf/gbell, logsig
LLE-ANFIS	1,3,5,7,13-15,17	4,3,3	Imputation, k=3, d=3
RBFN	All	6	k=6, p=4

In order to present our results in an orderly manner and discuss each of the prototypes, we first tabulate all the systems in Table 5. The simplest system in the suite, a single one-stage ANFIS system, is labeled ANFIS. PCA systems are not actual FIS, but they are systems that produce the transformed inputs to the PCA-ANFIS system. Variables 9, and 13 through16 were not used in computing the PCs. After PCA transformation we discarded all PCs except the first four. The principal components, or a normalized version of these, are the inputs to the fuzzy system PCA-ANFIS.

The Parallel-ANFIS systems use the parallel/cascaded ANFIS implementations as depicted in Figures 3 and 4.

The Parallel-ANFIS-NN systems, depicted in Figure 5, feed the normalized input variables to several ANFIS systems in parallel; these ANFIS produce estimates of the cost which are then fed to a two-layer feedforward backpropagation neural network which produces a final cost estimate by appropriately weighting the various ANFIS cost estimates.

These systems are named parallel-ANFIS-NN1 and parallel-ANFIS-NN2, for double- and triple-input systems, respectively. The Matlab commands traingdx and learngdm were chosen for the training and learning functions of the neural network, respectively. These functions train the network using batch-processing gradient descent with momentum and an adaptive learning rate. This means that for each epoch, if the performance decreases towards the goal, the learning rate is increased; if the performance increases more than a certain factor, the learning rate is decreased and the weight updates are not made. The error criterion used was the sum of squared errors. The number of neurons in the input layer of the neural network was always set equal to the number of inputs to the network which is in turn the number of ANFIS in the previous stage. The output layer consisted of a single neuron. The transfer functions tested were tansig and logsig, smooth, sigmoid-type functions commonly used in neural networks that produce real numbers as output. Figure 6 shows a typical neural network developed for the output stage. The number of membership functions was never allowed to be less than two or more than four. Various initial learning rates were tried with the best results produced with a learning rate μ=0.01, a momentum m=0.3, and logsig as the transfer function for both layers.

LLE-ANFIS feeds data transformed with the LLE algorithm to an ANFIS to predict the cost. We used $d = 3$ as the reduced dimension, $k = 3$ as the number of neighbors, and imputation to fill in gaps in the input data.

The last method used to predict the cost of engine tests is a purely neural solution. It uses radial basis function networks (RBFN; NeuralWare, 1993) to directly predict cost based on the raw data. RBFNs are similar to ANFIS in that they consist of membership

Figure 5. Parallel-ANFIS-NN systems take parallel multiinput ANFIS and feed the predicted cost from each ANFIS to a neural network

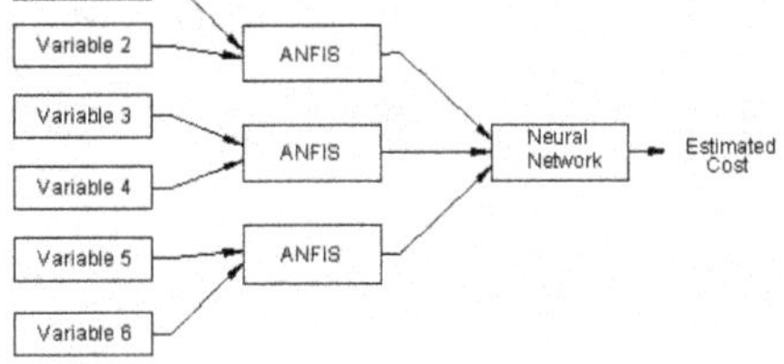

Figure 6. Two-layer feedforward network developed for the Parallel-ANFIS-NN systems

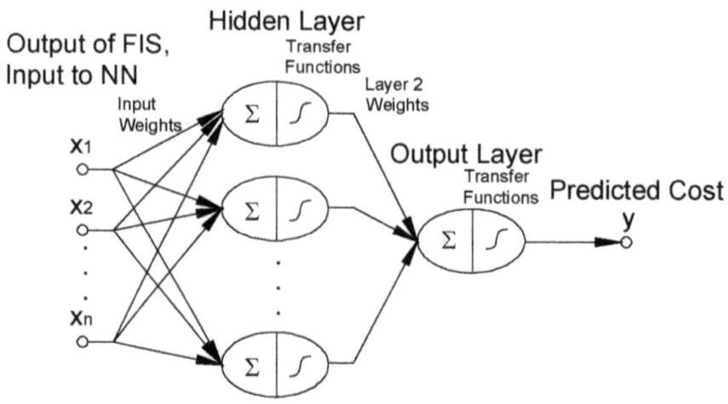

functions that are adjusted through the training stage of a neural network. They typically consist of Gaussian-type transfer functions. First, the centers of the Gaussian functions are found using a *k*-means clustering algorithm on the training data. The *k*-means algorithm groups the data sets into clusters, so that costs are associated with each cluster. After the clusters are found, the *p*-nearest neighbor algorithm is used to determine the width parameter, σ, of the Gaussian transfer function using (5). The respective centers are represented by c_k, where the subscript k represents the cluster of interest and c_{ki} is the center of the ith neighbor. These center values are stored as the neural weights in the input layer.

$$\sigma_k = \sqrt{\frac{1}{p}\sum_{i=1}^{p}\left\|c_k - c_{k_i}\right\|} \qquad (5)$$

After the σ parameter of each cluster is determined, the test data can be classified into the appropriate cluster. As with the ANFIS system, a "degree of belonging" to each membership group is obtained. This is done for each article by using (6)

Figure 7. Typical RBNF network used to predict cost of engine tests

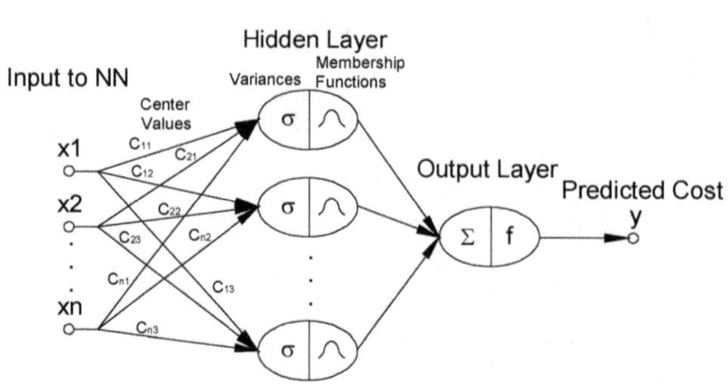

$$\phi_k = \exp\left(\frac{-\|x - c_k\|}{\sigma_k^{\ 2}}\right) \tag{6}$$

where x is the article data vector whose cost is to be predicted and k denotes the cluster. After (6) is computed, the result is normalized so that the results sum to one. Next, each normalized ϕ_k is multiplied by the calculated average cost of each cluster, and then summed into a single value. This final value is the predicted cost out of the RBFN. Figure 7 illustrates the RBFN system.

The RBFN system was developed using a set of data which applied mean, mode, or median imputation to fill missing variables in some articles. All variables in Table 1 were used.

RESULTS

In what follows we present, separately, the results for each system listed in Table 5. Before presenting the detailed results individually, we discuss the overall, comparative results in a summarized manner. We follow the discussion by particular results for the simple ANFIS, then the PCA-ANFIS, Parallel-ANFIS, Parallel-ANFIS-NN, LLE-ANFIS, and, finally, the RBFN system. In general, as system complexity increases, the accuracy in prediction increases also. We believe that all these systems would prove to be accurate if more data (i.e., more engine tests) were available for training. The performance measures used to evaluate the systems in the cost estimating suite are presented first.

System Evaluation

We would like to evaluate the cost prediction capabilities of the computational intelligence systems developed. There are many ways to measure performance, and it is up to the users to decide, based on their needs and application, which error measurement quantity is most appropriate. Oftentimes the average percentage error or root-mean-squared (RMS) error over all testing articles may be the quantities of interest. In other applications, the maximum error may be more important than an average error. Analysis of the error for each article may indeed be needed in some cases. Is it better to have a 5% error on a very expensive test than a 10% error on an inexpensive test? Clearly the absolute dollar amount should be a consideration. In developing our systems we tried to optimize so that a combination of error measures, those defined in equations (8)-(11) were minimized.

In all following formulas the subscript i denotes the article number and a "hat" over the variable denotes estimate (i.e., the output of the cost estimating system). In order to represent whether the system overestimates or underestimates the cost, the sign is used, with a negative sign indicating that the cost estimate, $\hat{C}_i$, was smaller than the actual cost, C_i. The relative error for each article is denoted by e_i, and the difference between actual and estimated cost is denoted by d_i. The error measures used are listed in what follows:

- Article cost difference

$$d_i = -(C_i - \hat{C}_i) \tag{7}$$

- Article error

$$e_i = \frac{d_i}{C_i} \qquad (8)$$

This relative error is usually given as a percentage by multiplying (8) times 100. Clearly, if the estimated cost is smaller than the actual cost, the error in (8) is negative indicating we have underestimated the cost.

- Average error

$$E = \frac{1}{N}\sum_{i=1}^{N} e_i \qquad (9)$$

- Average absolute error

$$S = \frac{1}{N}\sum_{i=1}^{N} |e_i| \qquad (10)$$

- RMS error

$$E_{RMS} = \frac{1}{N}\sqrt{\sum_{i=1}^{N} e_i^{\,2}} \qquad (11)$$

We also use (12), which gives a good indication of the dollar amount by which the total cost differs from the total estimated cost over all tests. This might be a better measure to use in selecting systems for cost estimation than the most frequently used average absolute error and RMS error measures from (10) and (11). The relative error measure weighs the errors more heavily for the expensive items, while the standard error measure weighs all errors by the same amount. We use a subscript of *R* for the relative error measure:

- Relative total error

$$E_R = \frac{\sum_{i=1}^{N} d_i}{\sum_{i=1}^{N} C_i} \qquad (12)$$

We also compute the maximum and minimum article errors which can be used to understand the range of errors obtained:

- Maximum absolute percentage error

$$e_{\max} = 100 \max_i (|e_i|) \qquad (13)$$

Table 6. Summary of quantitative results (testing only) for all systems

ANFIS System	E %	S %	E_{RMS} %	E_R %	e_{min} (%)	e_{max} %
ANFIS	1.0	37.4	18.9	2.1	4.8	64.7
PCA-ANFIS	-0.7	20.6	13.4	-36.8	0.0	63.9
Parallel-ANFIS	-28.6	44.8	23.8	-71.1	10.6	97.7
Parallel-ANFIS-NN1	-16.9	19.9	11.0	-9.11	6.0	30.3
Parallel-ANFIS-NN2	-2.5	7.0	3.9	0.8	1.4	9.7
LLE-ANFIS	-50.9	50.9	28.6	-61.3	11.4	80.8
RBFN	-9.9	14.6	11.7	-22.1	0.8	45.9
CEM[4]	-42.8	42.8	15.1	56.2	7.41	78.93

- Minimum absolute percentage error

$$e_{\max} = 100 \min_i \left(\left|e_i\right|\right) \tag{14}$$

Summary of Results

Table 6 presents summary results for all the systems discussed in this chapter; it also includes the evaluation of the cost estimating model (CEM; Lockheed Martin Stennis Operations, 2000; Rocket Propulsion Testing Lead Center, 1997, 1998). We do not know which engines were used for the development of CEM (i.e., we do not know what the training data were). The CEM results were therefore obtained on the entire set of 11 articles which almost certainly includes some, if not all, of the articles used to develop the cost estimating model and relationships used.

All errors are given as percentages. The first numerical column shows the average error from (9). This column could be misleading because overestimates tend to be cancelled by underestimates; in absolute dollar terms, however, this may indeed be desired. The absolute percentage error, computed by (10) may be preferable, and is shown in the column labeled S%. The data shown under the E_{RMS} heading, from (11), are probably the most widely accepted measure of accuracy. Under E_R we list the relative total error from (12). Error ranges are given by the last two columns.

All these measures indicate that the LLE-based system is the poorest performer. The best system is also the most complex one, the parallel-ANFIS-NN2 system with uses ANFIS with three inputs each, followed by a two-layer neural network. For this system the worst case error was less than 10%, while on an RMS sense, the errors were less than 4%. The PCA-ANFIS and Parallel-ANFIS-NN1 systems also produce very good results overall. The maximum error usually happened for one of the "outlier" (very expensive) tests.

Results were obtained both for training and for testing. The training results tell us how well the system has adapted to the "known" input data (i.e., the data that generated the configuration). This clearly should have a low error, or training should continue. Nonetheless, we wish the system to work well with "new and unseen" data (the testing set). If the network is allowed to train far too long and too well for the training set, it will tend to memorize these data, and will not be capable of generalizing to new data (Kaminsky et al., 1993). A compromise between memorization and generalization was sought. In all cases, the training results were excellent, with negligible error (much lower than 1% or on the order of a few dollars). This means that all systems developed learned the input–output relationships for the training data very well. Because all training results

Figure 8. Testing results for the simple ANFIS system using four input variables

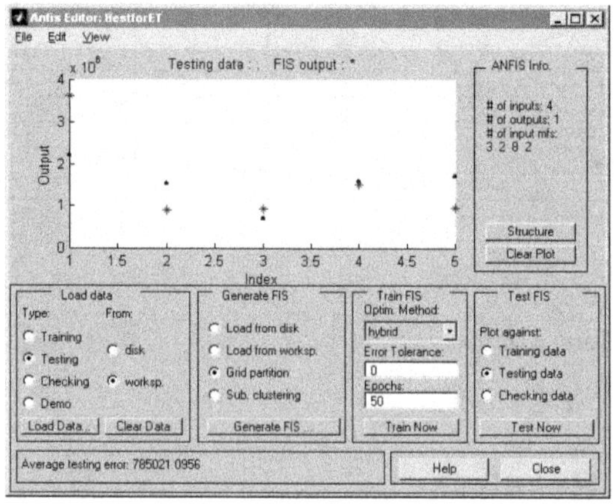

were very good and basically identical, regardless of the system used, we will not present detailed training results. These training results were used to determine the number of epochs needed for convergence of the batch processing ANFIS and NN algorithms; all systems converged in fewer than 50 epochs, with many converging in between 10 and 30 epochs.

Simple ANFIS

Figure 8 shows the testing results obtained for the simplest system, named ANFIS. In Figure 8 and on the plots that follow, the actual cost of testing the engines is shown by the dot, while the asterisk indicates the predicted value obtained with the ANFIS prototype. Remember that these 5 articles have not been seen by the network (i.e., these data were not used in the development of the systems). Clearly, only article 1 is poorly estimated (about 65% over the actual amount), while all other unseen articles are estimated with values close to their actual cost, certainly in rough order of magnitude (ROM) which is what we are after. In particular, the third and fourth testing articles have negligible estimate errors (within a few percent). The total average RMS (root mean squared) error is just under $800,000 (see bottom of Figure 8). ANFIS information is presented on the right side of the figure. In this case we see that four input variables were used with 3, 2, 8 and 2 membership functions, respectively. A single output, cost, is produced by the system. If a quick rough order of magnitude (ROM) estimate of the cost is desired, this very simple system might be preferred because it only uses a few data variables that are easily collected and present in all of NASA's test articles and works extremely fast.

PCA-ANFIS System

The results obtained using PCA on the engine test data have also been very encouraging. We obtained an RMS error of less than 500,000, but for the expensive article we still had an error of about 64%. The errors are very small for all the other articles. The results shown in Table 6 are for the original set of five testing articles. To see how the size of the training set influences results, we included a few more articles in the training set, therefore removing instances from the testing set. These extra training articles were chosen because they are scattered within the possible cost range. Doing this drastically reduced the error of the system. Clearly a significant number of articles must be available in order to be able to compute the principal component transformation matrix. We suggest that this method might be very well suited for cost prediction when a sizable training set is available

Parallel-ANFIS

The testing results obtained for the five engine test articles unseen by the Parallel-ANFIS system were not very accurate. As is almost always the case, the very expensive, high thrust engine is underestimated by a large amount, yielding an average error larger than acceptable. The other articles are all estimated with an error of approximately 10%.

Parallel ANFIS-NN

In the Parallel ANFIS-NN prototypes, several ANFIS systems work in parallel and feed their first-stage cost estimates to a neural network that merges these first-stage estimates and produces as output the final estimate of the cost. We developed and discuss here systems where each ANFIS simultaneously takes either two or three variables as inputs, namely Parallel-ANFIS-NN1 and Parallel-ANFIS-NN2. Once again, the best results were always obtained by using Gaussian type membership functions, either gaussmf, gauss2mf, or gbell in Matlab's language. The neural networks developed for the two- and three-input ANFIS were very similar to each other, and both use logsig for the transfer functions in both layers of the backprop networks.

Parallel ANFIS-NN1

Two inputs are fed to each of the four parallel ANFIS whose outputs were combined by a feed-forward backpropagation trained neural network which produced the final predicted cost. The input pairs to the first stage ANFIS are FuelFlow and Thrust, TestStand and thrust, TestDurMax and PressurantPr, and FuelFlow and OxidizerFl for ANFIS 1 through 4, respectively (refer to Table 1). We used imputation (mean, median, or mode) to fill in values for missing quantities. The variables paired in the double ANFIS used in Parallel-ANFIS-NN1 were chosen by examining the results of the single input ANFIS and choosing variables that complemented each other. For example, if one variable tends to over estimate the cost then another variable that tends to underestimate the cost would be paired with it. Several combinations of variables were tried and these four selected ANFIS produced the best results. The variable Thrust was paired twice in the double input ANFIS because it was one of the most predictive variables.

Once again, we varied the number of membership functions and their types. Gaussian membership functions worked best and the number of membership functions was always maintained between two and four. All costs were normalized to the range [0, 1] before training and testing. The intermediate prediction for each of the 4 parallel 2-

Table 7. Triple input ANFIS (first stage) testing results for each ANFIS, prior to neural network

1st Stage ANFIS Inputs	*Average %*	*RMS %*	*Min %*	*Max %*
TestStand, Thrust, DuratDd	-2.91	2.33	1.15	9.01
TestDurMax, PressuraPr, Pressurant	-9.74	15.98	26.48	36.85
FuelFlow, OidizerFl, Fuel	8.73	10.85	6.39	31.42

input ANFIS were combined by the neural network to produce the testing results shown in Table 6. That is, an average of about 17% underestimate of cost, 11% RMS error, a minimum error of about 6 percentage points, and a maximum error as large as -30%. We think it is important to note that the average sum of differences between predictions and actual costs is only $371,000 for a total cost of $10 million.

Parallel ANFIS-NN2

The ANFIS developed with three inputs achieved excellent results. Different set of triplets of inputs were tested. We selected the first stage ANFIS as shown in Table 7 where the results of each of the three first stage ANFIS (i.e., prior to the neural network merging, are also shown). The ANFIS that used TestStand, Thrust, and DuratDd attained such good results that it could stand alone as a predictor without the neural network stage

Figure 9. Normalized cost results of first-stage ANFIS using the three inputs TestStand, Thrust, and DuratDd along with a gbell membership function

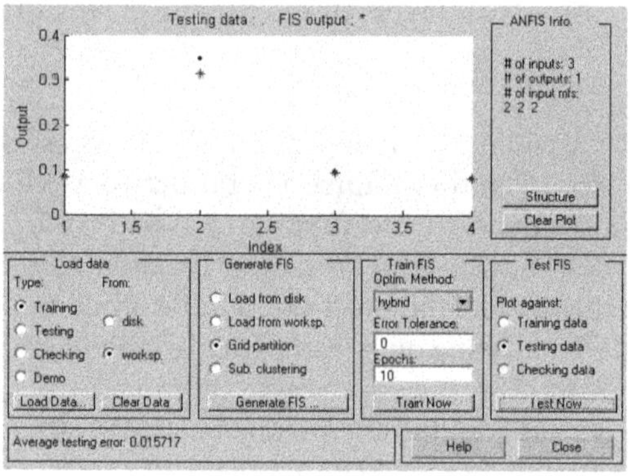

Table 8. Results of the Parallel-ANFIS-NN2 consisting of three triple-input ANFIS cascaded with a two-layer feedforward neural network

NN Cost ($)	*Actual Cost ($)*	*Overall Averages*	
1 441 500	1 590 000	% error	-2.55
5 306 200	4 935 000	RMS	3.88
1 546 200	1 713 000	S	6.99
1 562 100	1 541 000		

(see Figure 9). The FuelFlow, OxidizerFl, and Fuel ANFIS also attained very good results, even though the variables individually were not the most predictive. Our training results for the first stage (before the neural net) included a few significant errors.

Table 8 presents the neural network output results of Parallel-ANFIS-NN2 for each of the four engines in the testing set, as well as overall evaluation information. This network takes the first stage ANFIS (shown on Table 7) and merges the three estimates into a single final cost estimate. All training errors were well below 1% and all testing errors were below 10%.

LLE-ANFIS System

In this method, the LLE algorithm was used to reduce the dimensionality of the normalized data set. The new, transformed data set was then put into an ANFIS to finally predict the cost of the engine tests. The weakness of this method lies in the LLE algorithm's reliance on the k-nearest neighbor algorithm during the first step which was difficult to accomplish due to the extremely small number of points in the data set we utilized. An ANFIS was then developed from the new lower dimensional data, using grid partitioning and a linear output membership function. Several trials were performed to develop the best ANFIS by varying the number and type of membership functions. The best results were obtained using the set of eight variables shown in Table 5. We experimented with designs using different number of clusters, k, and also various LLE-reduced dimensions, d. Finally, we used $k=d=3$. The best results were obtained with a gauss2mf membership function of size 4, 3, and 3, for each transformed variable, respectively. The LLE-ANFIS system learned the training set very well, with no error, but was unable to produce good results for unseen articles. The results attained still have an average percentage error of around 66%. The first two testing set articles are both estimated to cost much less than what they actually cost to test. Interestingly, all articles' costs were underestimated, producing an estimate considerably lower than the actual cost of performing the test. This also happened when using CEM.

Radial Basis Function Network

The final method discussed uses a radial basis function network (RBFN) to predict the engine test cost directly from the raw data. Results were encouraging when we used all data available for training, but we must remember that the k-means algorithm is used for training and, as we have stated often, the training set is much too small to expect any neighborhood-based algorithm to perform well. Nonetheless, we present the results because they are certainly worth pursuing for cases where larger sets of training data are available, as is also the case for the LLE-ANFIS system.

The RBFN was developed by varying the number of clusters, k, and the number of nearest neighbors, p. The number of inputs was also varied, but the results were best

Table 9. Results for the RBFN cost estimator

RBFN Cost	*Actual Cost*	*Overall Averages*	
1 542 400	1 590 000	% error	-9.87
2 668 900	4 935 000	RMS	11.71
1 726 800	1 713 000	S	14.59
1 674 000	1 541 000		

when the full data set of eighteen variables was used with imputation algorithms used to fill in missing values. The best results were attained when both k and p were set to the maximum values of 6 and 4, respectively. Table 9 presents the predicted and actual costs for the test articles as obtained by the RBFN. The predicted cost is a weighted average of the prototype cluster costs, with the weights given by a measure of the distance to each cluster, as given by (6).

The RBFN predicted the cost of articles 1, 3 and 4 fairly accurately, but had trouble predicting article 2, the most expensive testing article in this testing set.

Comparison of Results for All Methods

A comparison of the overall results was given at the beginning of this section, in Table 6. A graphical representation of the results is given in Figure 10. The best results were obtained by the Parallel-ANFIS-NN2 system which uses a feedforward backpropagation neural network that takes the costs predicted by each of three three-input ANFIS and combines them into a single output cost. This system achieved a testing average percentage error of -2.5% with no quantity individually estimated with an error above 10%. A few of the methods developed were not effective, namely Parallel-ANFIS and LLE-ANFIS; the latter did a poor job of predicting almost all the articles. Keep in mind that the neural-based systems (the four right-most systems in Figure 10) were trained with 7 articles in the training set while the first three shown were trained with six articles only.

We would have liked to compare all our systems to results obtained with other previously developed systems described in Sundar (2001). However, very few (if any) results are available from those other methods, so strict comparisons cannot be made and final conclusions cannot be drawn. Also, as stressed earlier, many of these complex systems require a level of input data detail which is simply not available prior to

Figure 10. Standard error measures of cost prediction (percentages) for all testing results using computational intelligence methods

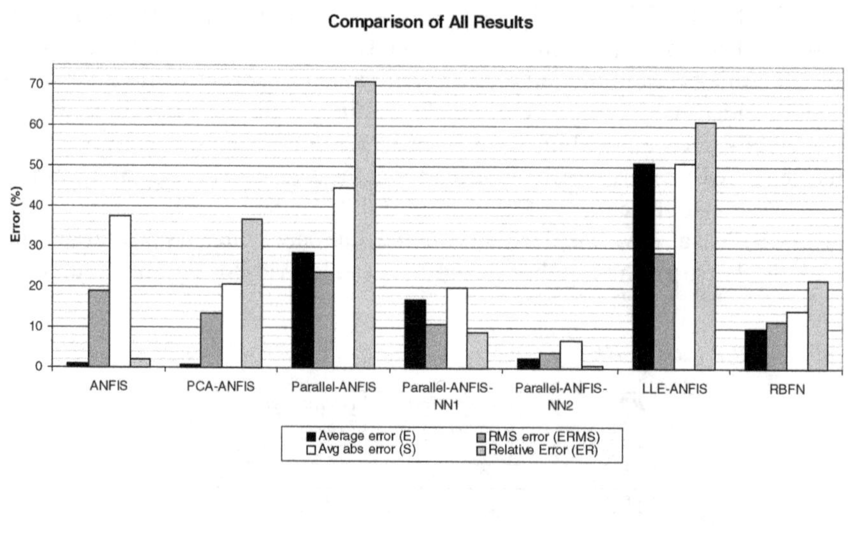

Figure 11. Comparison of all four neural methods showing actual and predicted costs of the articles in the testing set

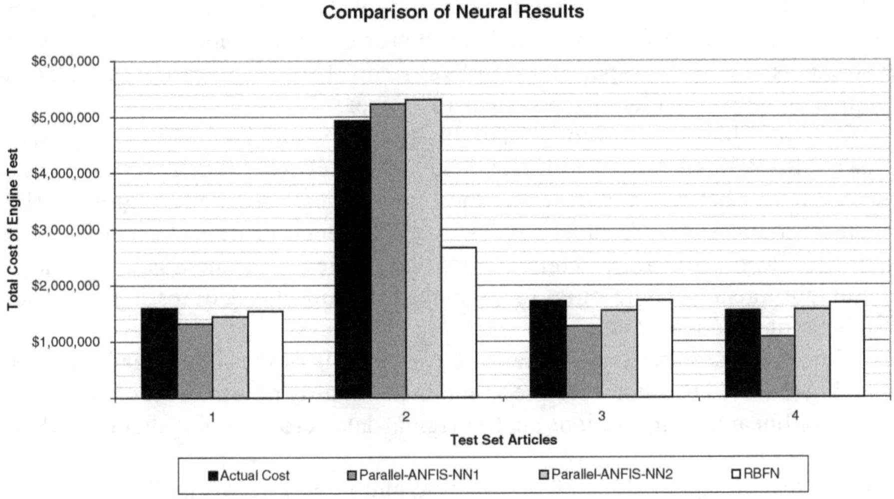

performing the tests. The CEM system (Lockheed Martin Space Operations, 2001; Lockheed Martin Space Operations, 2000; Rocket Propulsion Testing Lead Center, 1997, 1998) worked relatively well on an RMS sense, but underestimated the cost of most engine tests. The advantage of CEM is that it provides cost estimation relationships that may be quite useful and may be adjusted easily to incorporate temporal data. The other software systems could not be run with the data collected from PRDs.

The neural methods seem to be most promising. In a way, they are similar to the original methods developed at NASA and Lockheed because they seek to establish relationships among variables or functions of these variables. Unfortunately, the relationships obtained with the neural network are "hidden" and coded within the networks' weight matrices. Figure 11 shows the neural results for the four articles in the testing set and the actual costs of performing the tests.

CONCLUSION AND SUGGESTIONS FOR FURTHER WORK

We have developed several computational intelligence systems to predict the cost of testing engine and component tests based on standard data collected by NASA in their project requirement documents (PRD); only engine tests were discussed in this chapter. Our computational intelligence systems take various variables from the PRDs and use adaptive network fuzzy inference systems (ANFIS) and neural networks to combine, in a nonlinear manner, the values of these variables to produce an estimate of the cost to perform engine tests at the Stennis Space Center. Raw data were normalized and, for some of the systems, transformed with principal component analysis (PCA) or locally linear embedding (LLE) to reduce the systems' dimensionality prior to further processing.

We have also designed "specialized" fuzzy systems that work in parallel, each of which provides an estimate to a final fuzzy or neural stage which combines these results to obtain a final estimate. Our results indicate that an error of around 10%, on the average, may be expected with these parallel ANFIS systems. However, most of the test articles are estimated with considerably less than 10% error.

We have achieved very good results with a very small set of training data. The results of the RBFN, PCA-ANFIS, and both Parallel-ANFIS-NN systems are very accurate. Remember that the desire is to obtain a rough-order-of-magnitude (ROM) estimate for the cost of performing engine tests. The generalization ability of our ANFIS systems has been proven. We conclude that the project was successful at using new artificial intelligence technologies to aid in the planning stages of testing operations at NASA's Stennis Space Center.

A linear transformation—namely PCA—as well as the nonlinear locally linear embedding (LLE) algorithm were used for dimensionality reduction. It could be wise to try other nonlinear transformations on the original data before feeding them to the ANFIS systems.

Coupling the application of fuzzy logic and neural networks for modeling and optimization with the Risk Constraint Optimized Strategic Planning (RCOSP) model of Sundar (2001) is expected to yield more accurate and robust estimation of cost and an understanding of the requirements to provide rocket propulsion testing for the future. CEM, the Cost Estimating model of Lockheed Martin Space Operations (2000, 2001) and Rocket Propulsion Testing Lead Center (1997, 1998), combines complexity factors and cost estimating relationships to predict the approximate cost of performing technology development test programs. At this point, all these software pieces work independently. NASA (2001) presents analysis of PRDs and a tool (DOOR) which uses, updates, and databases PRD data. It would be very beneficial to somehow join DOORS with our cost prediction suite so that PRD data may be passed directly to the prediction systems.

In order to keep the model (decision algorithm) from becoming obsolete, some kind of date information (incremental information) must be associated with it. At the same time, we would like the decision algorithms for similar database mining queries to be reusable. An effort to homogenize all data would be valuable.

Finally, it would be of great use to be able to predict the cost of each of the three main functions that affect cost: modification, design, and fabrication, as CEM does. This can be achieved using the same type of ANFIS and neural networks that we have discussed. Unfortunately no training data are available at this moment to train such systems (i.e., we do not have access to these detailed costs).

ACKNOWLEDGMENT

We wish to thank Lockheed Martin Stennis Operations personnel for their contributions to this project. In particular, we acknowledge their effort in providing us with the required data, documents, and software.

REFERENCES

Brand, M. (2003). Continuous nonlinear dimensionality reduction by kernel eigenmaps. Retrieved November, 2003, from http://www.merl.com/reports/docs/TR2003-21.pdf

Chongfu, H. (1998, May 4-9). Deriving samples from incomplete data. In *Proceedings of the IEEE World Congress on Computational Intelligence,* Anchorage, AK.

Cohen, A. (1988). *Biomedical signal processing. Volume II: Compression and automatic recognition.* Boca Raton, FL: CRC Press.

Danker-McDermot, H. (2004). *A Fuzzy/neural approach to cost prediction with small data sets.* Master's thesis, University of New Orleans, LA.

Demartines, P., & Herault, J. (1997). Curvilinear component analysis: A self-organizing neural network for nonlinear mapping of data sets. *IEEE Transactions on Neural Networks, 8,* 148-154.

Friedrich, T. (2002). *Nonlinear dimensionality reduction with locally linear embedding and isomap.* MSc dissertation, University of Sheffield, UK.

Gering, D. (2003). Linear and nonlinear data dimensionality reduction. Retrieved November, 2003, from http://www.ai.mit.edu/people/gering/areaexam/areaexam.pdf

Granger, E., Rubin, M., Grossberg, S., & Lavoie, P. (2000, July 24-27). Classification of incomplete data using the fuzzy ARTMAP neural network. *Proceedings of the IEEE International Joint Conference on Neural Networks,* Como, Italy.

Ishibuchi, H., Miyazaki, A., & Tanaka, H. (1994, June 27-July 2). Neural-network-based diagnosis systems for incomplete data with missing inputs. *Proceedings of the IEEE International Conference on Neural Networks,* Orlando, FL.

Jang, J. S. (1993). ANFIS: Adaptive-network-based fuzzy inference system. *IEEE Transactions on Systems, Man, and Cybernetics. 23*(3), 665-684.

Jang, J. S., & Sun, C-T. (1995). Neuro-fuzzy modeling and control. *Proceedings of the IEEE, 83,* 378-405.

Kaminsky, E. J. (2000, June 26-29). Diagnosis of coronary artery disease using principal components and discriminant functions on stress exercise test data. *Proceedings of the 2000 International Conference on Mathematics and Engineering Techniques in Medicine and Biological Sciences (METMBS 2000),* Las Vegas, NV.

Kaminsky, E. (2002). *Highly accurate cost estimating model (HACEM).* (Final Report, LA BoR No. NASA Stennis Space Center.

Kaminsky, E. J., & Douglas, F. (2003, September 26-30). A fuzzy-neural highly accurate cost estimating model (HACEM). *Proceedings of the 3rd International Workshop on Computational Intelligence in Economics and Finance (CIEF'2003),* Cary, NC.

Kaminsky, E. J., Rana, S., & Miller, D. (1993, September). *Neural network classification of MSS remotely sensed data.* Report CAAC-3930, NASA, Stennis Space Center, MS.

Liou, C.-Y., & Kuo, Y.-T. (2002, November 18-22). Economic states on neuronic maps. *Proceedings of ICONIP 2002, 2* (pp. 787-791). Singapore.

Lockheed Martin Space Operations. (2001, September). NASA/Stennis space center propulsion testing simulation-based cost model. *Ninth International Conference on Neural Information Processing,* Stennis Space Center, MS.

Lockheed Martin Stennis Operations. (2000, September). A cost estimating model (CEM) and cost estimating relationships (CER) validation and evaluation analysis (Version 1). NASA Report, Stennis Space Center, MS.

NASA. (2001, July). *John C. Stennis Space Center preparation of SSC propulsion test directorate (PTD) project requirements document* (Tech. Rep. No. SOI-8080-0004), NASA-SSC. Stennis Space Center, MS.

NeuralWare. (1993). *Neural computing* (Vol. NC). Pittsburgh, PA: NeuralWare.

Rocket Propulsion Testing Lead Center. (1997, June). *A cost estimating model (CEM, Revision 1).* NASA Stennis Space Center, MS.

Rocket Propulsion Testing Lead Center. (1998, March). *A cost estimating model* (Systems Requirement Document SSC-LC-008, Decision Support System).

Roweis, S., & Saul, L. (2000). Nonlinear dimensionality reduction by locally linear embedding. *Science, 290,* 2323-2326.

Saul, L. K., & Roweis, S. T. (2003). *An introduction to locally linear embedding.* Retrieved December, 2003, from http://www.cs.toronto.edu/~roweis/lle/papers-/lleintro.pdf

Sundar, P. (2001). *Bayesian analysis of the RCOSP model.* SFFP Final Report. NASA Stennis Space Center, MS.

Takagi, T., & Sugeno, M. (1983, July 19-21). Derivation of fuzzy control rules from human operator's control actions. *Proceedings Symposium on Fuzzy Information, Knowledge Representation and Decision Analysis (IFAC),* Marseille, France (pp. 55-60).

Takagi, T., & Sugeno, M. (1985). Fuzzy identification of systems and its applications to modeling and control. *IEEE Transactions on Systems, Man, and Cybernetics, 15,* 116-132.

Tenenbaum, J., Silva, V., & Langford, J. (2000). *A global geometric framework for nonlinear dimensionality reduction science, 290,* 2319-2322.

University of New Orleans. (2000, October). *Project requirements risk analysis* (Department of Mathematics Tech. Rep.). New Orleans, LA.

Zadeh, L. (1965). Fuzzy sets. *Information Control, 8,* 338-353.

Zadeh, L. (1968). Probability measures of fuzzy events. *Journal Math Analysis and Applications. 23,* 421-427.

Zadeh, L. (1978). Fuzzy sets as a basis for a theory of possibility. *Fuzzy Sets and Systems. 1,* 3-28.

Zhou, Y. (2000). *Neural network learning from incomplete data.* Retrieved November 2003, from http://www.cs.wustl.edu/~zy/learn.pdf

ENDNOTES

1 Matlab is a trademark of The Mathworks.

2 This work was performed under grant no. NASA(2001)-Stennis-15, "Highly Accurate Cost Estimating Model (HACEM)". The contract is between the University of New Orleans (UNO), Department of Electrical Engineering, and the National Aeronautics and Space Administration (NASA), through the Louisiana Board of Regents (LA-BOR). Access to details and code are available through NASA's Technology Transfer Office: Request Highly Accurate Cost Estimating Model, NASA NTR SSC-00194, May 2003.

3 The dollar amounts used for "actual cost" are not in themselves accurate; they are NASA's posttest estimates.

4 CEM was not developed by the current authors and it is used only for comparison purpuses. Errors shown for CEM are for the entire set of 11 articles which may include CEM training data.

Chapter X

Computer-Aided Management of Software Development in Small Companies

Lukáš Pichl
University of Aizu, Japan

Takuya Yamano
International Christian University, Japan

ABSTRACT

This chapter focuses on the principles of management in software development projects and optimization tools for managerial decision making, especially in the environment of small IT companies. The management of software projects is specific by high requirements on qualified labor force, large importance of the human capital, low level of fixed costs, and highly fluctuating product demand. This yields a dynamic combinatorial problem for the management involving considerable risk factors. The key aspects addressed here are structuring of the project team, cost estimation, and error avoidance in the implementation phase of the project. Special emphasis is put on human resource and fault-tolerant management of the project cycle. Discrete faults and continuous stochastic inputs are used to test and evaluate project variants. We have developed an online simulation tool for this purpose that facilitates findings of optimal resource structures and creation of optimal network from task relations. General principles of software project management are presented along with the analysis of the software project simulation tool in a brief case study.

INTRODUCTION

The history of modern project management in general dates back to the 5th decade of the last century in connection with large military projects. About 1 or 2 decades ago, a close attention started to be paid to risk assessment and coordination of mammoth software projects (MS Windows development, etc.). Although it is fully recognized that the way of management of software projects often matters more than financial resources (and a frequent success of small software companies sold at astronomic profits to giant SW development companies demonstrates this point), relatively little is known what are the crucial factors for success. A project can be defined as a temporary endeavor undertaken to create a unique product or service (i.e., in the present case, software) or another product by using software at a large scale. It is noteworthy that a complexity limit was empirically discovered in the software development, which is as low as about 10 software engineers working on one project. Therefore, an appropriate management is crucial since most of the software projects exceed this number.

Software development and its successful management is a key issue for a number of small IT companies and, with increasing importance, also for their clients. The project management (PM) common fundamentals are integration, scope, time, cost, quality, human resource, communications, risk, procurement, delivery and service to customers. Software project management (SPM) is, in addition, characterized by unique success factors derived from the unique components of IT projects. There are specific requirements on the applicability of standards, fault-tolerance, risk management, project scheduling, code development and testing techniques. Further important issues are selection and use of third-party software and also the intellectual property rights.

It has been noted in recent surveys that most software projects suffer from inadequate management techniques that ignore the unique characteristics of this field (cf. Northwest Center for Emerging Technologies, 1999; US Government Accounting Office, 1979, 2000). The most cited reasons are poor strategic management and underestimation of human factors in particular. It is known that about one half of software projects was delayed in completion and one third was over budgeted in 1997-1999, similar to the first study conducted in 1979 on this problem by the US Government Accounting Office. This remarkably persistent problem has been gaining increasing attention in scientific literatures for about a decade (cf. Abdel-Hamid & Madnick 1991; Humprey & Kellner, 1989). Since then, books and practice guides (e.g. Bennatan, 1995; Jalote, 2002) have appeared with different levels of rigor, but the number of detailed investigations in scientific journals has been rather limited (cf. Drappa & Ludewig, 1999; Rodrigues & Bowers, 1996). There is also a nuance to be noted: Traditional PM aims to solve certain types of *problems*, while SPM is rather a *process* than a solution of a problem, and therefore it requires a different approach.

Major authorities among the professional organizations in the field of SPM are Project Management Institute (PMI), Software Engineering Institute (SEI) and IEEE Software Engineering Group. These recognize the following important factors for a successful project:

- leadership,
- communication,
- negotiating,

- problem-solving methodology,
- information sharing and training, and
- relevant technical expertise.

Coordination and cooperation are the key factors; this is within the responsibility of the administrative hierarchy that typically includes a coordinator, assistant project manager, program manager, and a software development coordinator. Each project typically involves a team, targets certain customers and relies on contractors, and must be backed by sponsors, executives, and functional managers.

The first principle of project management is that there exists no universal principle at all. Attention has to be paid to project size, project type, culture of the project team and other factors. Software projects, in addition, require a special emphasis on the communication of *technical* experts in order to guarantee code portability and program compatibility. Thus, one may raise a question whether a rigorous methodology for SPM is, in fact, possible. In this chapter, we (a) give an overview of managerial approaches in the field, and (b) address the gap in the standard SPM theory and practice, which is the lack of portable and customizable computer simulations for accurate estimation of project costs. In the early (but crucial) project phase when decisions are made so as to whether start a particular software project or not, such estimations are typically very crude. Such strategic decision making then inevitably leaves a space for cost increases, software delivery delays and even project failures.

Software companies are complex environments in which managers are faced with the decision-making problem involving uncertainty. Because of the complexity in the interactions among project tasks, resources, and people, estimates using average values of the project factors are very crude, and the errors are typically in the orders of 25%-100 % or even more. It is well known in the queuing theory that average output of a system with stochastic inputs can be substantially different from system output based only on average inputs. Many software projects at present disregard this point, or attempt to address it by using the best, mean, and the worst scenario, which still ignores the queuing structure of the project components (two blocks in a queue, each with the mean scenario, can produce a result even beyond the average worst-case scenario, for instance when a peak congestion in the queue results in a hardware damage or suspension of software service). Therefore even the overall worst-case estimates may be too optimistic and vice versa.

A deterministic algorithm can hardly be applied to estimate project costs, but the cost of false decision is typically enormous. Simulation techniques form a bridge to overcome this problem and to find the probabilistic optimum. In this work, we deal with a decision-making problem in the context of the software project management using three levels of detail, namely, (a) a decision whether to accept or refuse a new contract for a specific software project (complete computer simulation screening), (b) how to organize the project team (human aspect), and (c) what measures to take in order to optimize the cost of an accepted project with a given project team (resource optimization). Because of the importance of human factor in project management, we have decided to develop and provide a customizable, object-oriented, and free software project simulation environment that facilitates duration and cost estimates and supports decision making. Such a tool is consider more applicable than a fully deterministic optimization program with an implicit hard-encoded "general" project topology, however complex its parameterization might be.

The chapter is organized as follows. In Section 2, we review the managerial recommendations for project management, focusing on the specific features of software projects. Then we proceed to computer simulation of software projects in Section 3, discussing general design issues along with their particular implementation in the presently developed object-oriented simulation tool. Section 4 gives the simulation results for a selected case study along with discussion of their broader implications. Concluding remarks close this chapter in Section 5. We also recognize that the SPM area is, in fact, very appropriate for agent-based simulations, although it has been largely neglected in AI applications thus far.

MANAGEMENT OF SOFTWARE PROJECT

A successful project strategy is a balanced blend of development fundamentals, risk management, schedule-control, and mistake-avoidance techniques, adjusted to a certain trade-off in product quality, project cost and delivery schedule. One of important specific features in software projects is the huge range in productivity and ability of human resources. Therefore selection, organization, and motivation of the team are the key factors of SPM success or failure. In this chapter, we elaborate especially on these factors. Considering what has been outlined above, it is unlikely if not impossible to find a generally applicable SPM strategy. Instead, we focus on the development of a software simulation tool that helps to select project teams, estimate the project risks in a variety of possible scenarios, and to identify possible failures before these really occur. Here we develop a SW project simulation tool that is customizable for a particular product, human resource structure and development environment. The source code is open and the tool is free to download (Online simulation application, 2005). Let us note that there exist commercial PM tools too, e.g. MS Project 2000. Their inbuilt computer simulation features are often limited. Since no two projects are really the same, the proprietary source code of the commercial products which does not allow any modification means also a serious limitation to their applicability.

Principal functions of a general project management can be listed as (Northwest Center for Emerging Technologies, 1999):

- define scope of project
- identify stakeholders, decision-makers, and escalation procedures
- develop detailed task list (work breakdown structures)
- estimate time requirements
- develop initial project management flow chart
- identify required resources and budget
- evaluate project requirements
- identify and evaluate risks
- prepare contingency plan
- identify interdependencies
- identify and track critical milestones
- start the project and track its progress

- participate in project phase review
- secure resources as needed
- manage the change control process
- report project status
- finalization or quitting of project

In order to plan or monitor a certain project, the basic useful tools are project flow charts and network queuing diagrams for interdependent operations (visualization of tasks and their relations). Any project design should start from the final product. Therefore it is important to asses the product characteristics, size, requirements and methods of management. Project planning then means determination of available resources, selection of life-cycle model, and the design of a development strategy. Once the project starts, it needs to be tracked for costs, schedule and human efforts. When discrepancies between the plan and real state arise, a portfolio of appropriate measures should be available to handle such case. Each project can be classified into certain phases (i.e., milestones in the project tracking and project management). In case of SPM, these are:

1. software concept;
2. resource requirements;
3. architecture development;
4. detailed design;
5. implementation, programming, and debugging;
6. system integration, testing, and quality assurance; and
7. product deployment, distribution, and maintenance.

Interestingly, major mistakes in failed software project (identified ex post) appear to be very alike. It is therefore crucial to identify their emergence based on certain fingerprint patterns and eliminate them as early as possible. To that aim, one can used the so-called McConnell's Anti-Patterns, related to failures in human resource, process, product, and the technology. For instance, these are the customer-developer friction (the programmer "knows better" what the customer "should" need), "politics over substance" (e.g., prestige competition on international level in science policy and R&D), wishful thinking (withholding cooperation quietly by sticking to formal procedures), or the lack of money ("priority shift" in the middle of the project) rank among the most serious issues.

Process related mistakes include unrealistic schedules (following "optimistic variants"), contractor failure (resources in computer engineering are often stochastic), insufficient planning for phases under time pressure (e.g., complications arising in debugging of "nasty codes"—applies to the author of the code, the more to someone else). Product-related mistakes typically include lack of customers (e.g., "products for researchers in bioinformatics or nanoscience" or certain "software products for the elderly"). Technology related mistakes often include unrealistic extrapolations of available resources ("counting on the Morse law", or admiration to new platforms "preference over a CPU maker without caring for compiler availability").

The important issues to check are: What will be the total cost? How long will it last? How many developers does it need? What resources are required? What can go wrong?

And finally, the most important question for financial managers is the rentability, measured in the net present value (NPV), return on investment (ROI) or payback period. Since the required rentability can be viewed as an associated fixed cost, we do not need to consider it explicitly in what follows.

Before proceeding to the design and simulation issues in the next section, we would like to note that there exist various movements attempting to change the landscape of software development completely. One of these is eXtreme Programming (XP), a light-weight methodology for small teams, a highly iterative approach in which programmers closely interact with application users about the SW test releases in development (originally for small release applications based on certain HW or software architecture spikes). In a cycle of test scenario, user stories (bug reports, feedback from on-site customers) and incremental release version planning, the code development can be enormously accelerated. The reverse side of this methodology is high requirements on coders skills and enthusiasm for the project. In this respect, there is also an important

Figure 1. Work breakdown structure (WBS) for a sample project

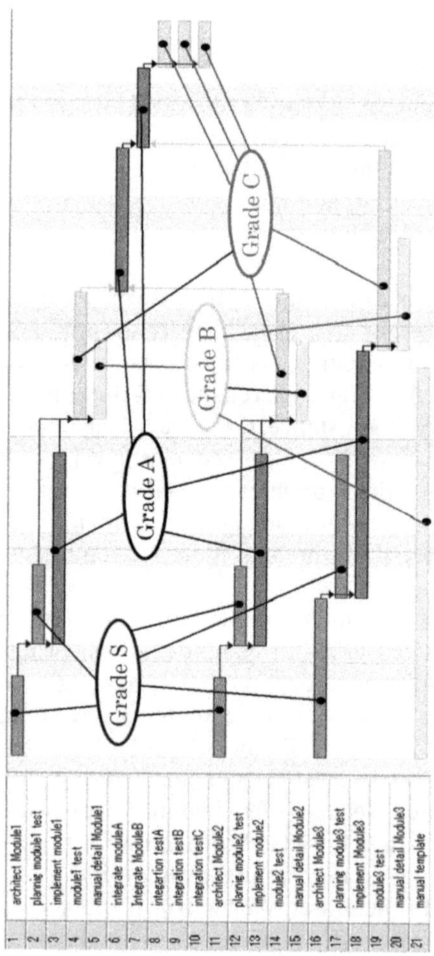

problem of measuring the programmer's output and determining appropriate rewards. One measure frequently applied is the number of lines of code (LOC) together with the number of program function points. This is certainly an informative criterion but a care should be taken when to use LOC as a motivation and remuneration basis. LOC may work well in case of standard large-size projects but is certainly inappropriate in case of XP and other lightweight SW development methods.

In the next section, we develop a general purpose simulation tool for software projects, focusing on the project structure, planning and stochastic resources (including stochastic failures).

COMPUTER SIMULATION OF SOFTWARE PROJECT

In order to facilitate the software development process in a specific way, we have developed a java-based online application with Graphical User Interface (GUI), which allows the user to define tasks, properties, resources, and team members including various attributes. The structure closely follows the principles of SPM. Java was selected because it is an object-oriented programming language with an easily implementable and well-established Web interface. Structure of project activities is outlined in Figure 1. The screen shots of the simulation environment are shown in Figure 2, starting from the front page entitled "Decision Making Simulation" in the right upper corner of the figure.

In the application program, there are four types of data: project data, task data, human resource data, and team data. These are all subject to optimization. The stochastic environment is simulated in two modes: (a) binary process that occurs with a given probability per unit of time (typically a false outcome of a certain task, for example, we set higher probability for coding mistakes on Monday mornings and Friday nights), and (b) probability distribution of some input data with a predefined range of values (data bandwidth available in external network, supercomputer CPU time available for rent, etc.). Both the discrete probabilities and continuous probability densities can be derived from histograms of real systems and input into the model by specifically tailored non-uniform random number generators. In particular, this procedure is as follows:

- Divide the range of the stochastic factor, $<x_1, x_2>$, into representative bins $\{b_i\}$.
- Create a statistical record of the stochastic factor over a suitable period of time.
- Generate probability for each bin $p_i = N_i/N$, where N_i is the number of observations falling in bin b_i and $N = \sum_i N_i$ is the total.
- Tailor a custom random number generator by using the following algorithm:
  - Repeat
  - Generate a uniform random number $r = x1 + (x_2 - x_1)\times\text{rnd}()$
  - Generate a uniform check number $c = p_m \times \text{rnd}()$ ($p_m = \max_i \{p_i\}$).
  - Determine bin $i_o(r)$ for the number r
  - If $c < p_{i_o}$ return r (and exit).
  - Until forever

Figure 2. Application interface includes project, team, member, task, resource and worker editors, and displays all data

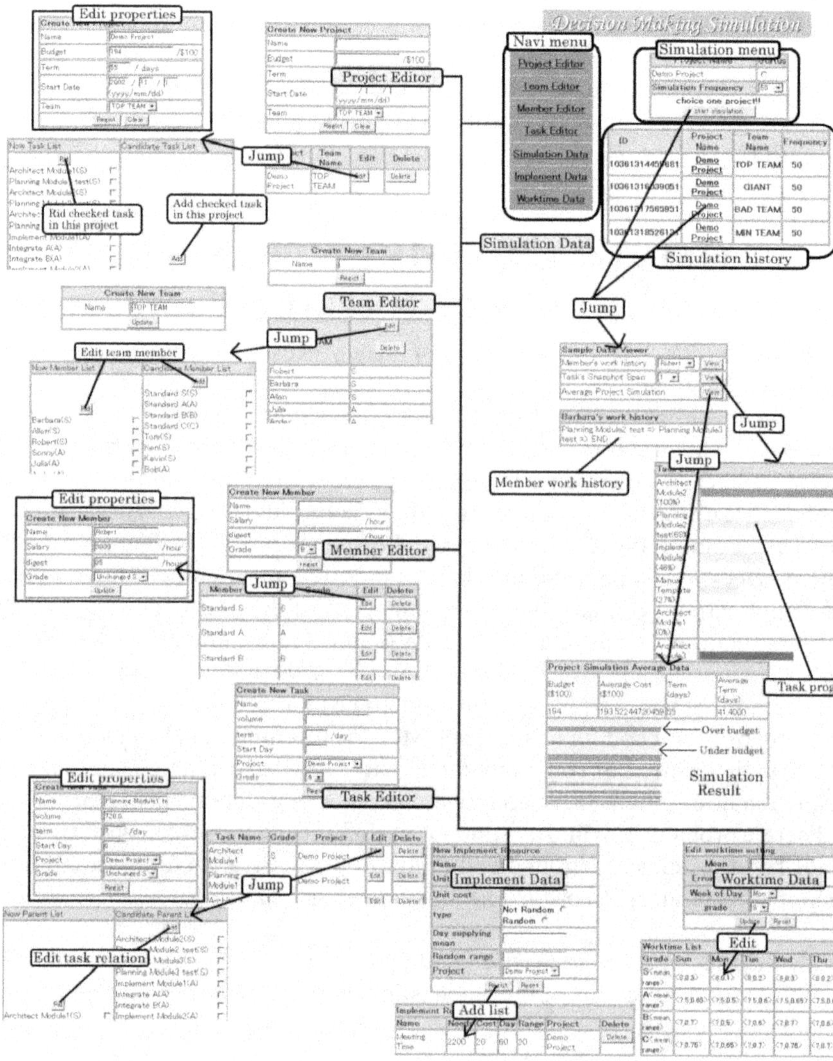

Here rnd() stands for a uniform float random number generator with values between 0 and 1 (a standard function in the libraries of most programming languages). Our simulation environment (cf. Figure 2) allows to set the relationship of tasks and structure human resources in a flexible manner. The task's determinants are time, grade, deadline and the queueing structure (standard and priority queues). Human resource (worker) determinants are skill, grade, and wage. Workers pick up tasks from the queue based on custom project team structure. Human resource is divided into four grades. Any group can take a task, if the group grade permits. Last is the project resource determinants, such as CPU time required or office supply items. Registered resources are acquired and consumed by units of days and increase the project cost. Cost of each resource is in principle time dependent, therefore various cost pricing schemes (FIFO, LIFO, opportunity costs) can be included in a straightforward manner.

Data Structures in the Simulation

The particular data structures in any SPM tool should derive from project resources and project organization. In order to design the simulation environment as general as possible, we do not hard-encode the project structure. Instead, several online editor forms allow to add project components as needed and register their mutual relations (Project, Team, Member and Task Editors in Figure 2; also Resource Editor, not shown).

The present java application stores all simulation data in a database (implemented with the MySQL relational database management system). The main database components are Member, Task, Project and Resource. Member is determined by name, identification number, wage or salary, and performance measures (A, B, C and S). Task is determined by identification, queuing schedule, progress indicator, deadline, and difficulty grade. Projects are distinguished by name, identification number, budget limit, team available, task composition and the deadline. Resources are determined by identification, number of units required by each project, unit cost, average daily supply, distribution width, and identifications of calling projects. Functional relations of the data during the course of simulation are shown in Figures 1 and 2. The simulation program is executed in discrete units by taking series of snapshots of the current progress (project, task, worker), incrementing the project immediate cost step by step. For the sake of simplicity, we implemented two particular types of random parameters: worker's fault probability p_i and a continuous randomized resource x (e.g. daily cash flow from

$$\rho(x) = \frac{1}{\sigma\sqrt{2\pi}} e^{\frac{-(x-\mu)^2}{2\sigma^2}}.$$

Generalization to a general histogram is straightforward as discussed above.

Application Data

In order to test the simulation environment, we have adopted sample model data. The respective Work Breakdown Structure (WBS) is shown in Figure 1. WBS is a useful tool to estimate project duration and workload of project participants. It is a 1D hierarchical list of project work's activities which shows inclusive and sequential relations. The 21 items listed in Figure 1 are the project activities. The labels "A", "B", "C" and "S" in the Figure show the lowest grade of the labor force qualified to deal with them. More detailed WBS in managerial applications may also distinguish the managerial level (project, task) from the technical level (subtask, work packages with definable end results, effort level). Instead of a chart, decimal catalogue-like form is sometimes used.

Next, we have created a sample case study project consisting of three modules. Each module has an architecture phase, implementation phase, integration phase and testing phase. The number of project modules and resource sharing among them is completely flexible. This is an extremely important point for the decision making support, since the entire company can be simulated in such framework by combining various modules (or projects) in one large scale simulation. Therefore the general design above and our java application tool in particular should not be misunderstood as a mere "single project simulation" unrelated to other activities in the SW company.

In particular, we implemented four sample teams: "TOP TEAM", "GIANT", "BAD TEAM" and "MINI TEAM" (see Table 1). These teams consist both of common and extra members. The project optimized here uses a stochastic resource—external supercomputer time—of 2,200 minutes in total (normal distribution with 1 hour mean and 20 minute dispersion). The flow of task relations among workers of 4 grades (S>A>B>C) in time is shown in Figure 1. Simulation is executed for each team, and the results are evaluated in the application program. Because of the general project structure that can be flexibly created using the online "Editor" forms for each project component, a universal optimization routine cannot be efficiently used, except for a full screening (gradually building teams by adding members still available; gradually including resources from the pool of resources available). Although this brute-force (full screening) approach feature was implemented in our program for the sake of completeness and suffices in case of small companies, it is not recommended in large simulations for obvious efficiency reasons. Let us note that the application performs two types of computations: (a) multiple simulation runs and the best-case, average, and worst-case analysis for each managerial

Table 1. Prototypical teams

TOP TEAM : high output, low cost					id	name	salary	outpt.	No
5	Robert	3000	35	S	1	S	2000	20	S
6	Barbara	2780	27	S	2	A	1500	20	A
9	Allen	2500	25	S	3	B	1000	20	B
11	Sonny	1800	23	A	4	C	650	20	C
12	Julia	1650	23	A					
17	Ander	1850	25	A	BAD TEAM: low output, expensive				
18	Susan	1250	25	B	7	Tom	2000	18	S
19	Diana	1300	23	B	8	Ken	2200	20	S
23	Ernie	1200	23	B	10	Kevin	1800	18	S
24	Melissa	900	26	C	14	Eva	1500	18	A
25	Nancy	800	25	C	15	Larry	1450	17	A
27	Nita	700	24	C	16	Jerry	1300	16	A
GIANT: too large team size					20	Mike	1100	22	B
7	Tom	2000	18	S	21	David	1000	20	B
8	Ken	2200	20	S	22	Eliot	1050	18	B
9	Allen	2500	25	S	26	Sander	750	23	C
12	Julia	1650	23	A	28	Anne	650	20	C
13	Bob	1500	20	A	29	Richard	600	18	C
14	Eva	1500	18	A	MINI TEAM : size is small				
15	Larry	1450	17	A	8	Ken	2200	20	S
19	Diana	1300	23	B	9	Allen	2500	25	S
20	Mike	1100	22	B	11	Sonny	1800	23	A
21	David	1000	20	B	12	Julia	1650	23	A
23	Ernie	1200	23	B	19	Diana	1300	23	B
26	Sander	750	23	C	23	Ernie	1200	23	B
27	Nita	700	24	C	24	Melissa	900	26	C
28	Anne	650	20	C	25	Nancy	800	25	C

decision (i.e., for each fixed project structure), and (b) brute-force full screening for the best project structure (small-sized projects). Because the SPM in practise is a multivariant decision making process, it is also preferable that the management modifies project structures as desired and then evaluates each variant separately, learning the most important trends and worst-case scenarios from the simulation results.

Interface and Technology

Let us briefly summarize the software project management tool developed in this work. In the simulation environment, users change and input all data with the Graphical User Interface based and Java Server Page. Logic programming is also implemented in Java. Mysql database is used to store simulation data. The interface described by Figure 2 allows the user to choose from a variety of functions in the left navigation menu of the window "Decision Making Simulation," to set the simulation properties and to check simulation progress and history. There are five editors for members, projects, teams, tasks and resources. The editor page can create and delete relations among the data. There are three main parts in Figure 2. The first one is the team member's working history. The second is a progress snapshot of all project tasks, each having one status assigned from "READY", "PROGRESS", "OVER", "END", and "NO STATUS." At last, the simulation result graph shows the total cost and indicates whether the simulation run is over the project budget or not (long and short lines indicated by arrows in the window "Simulation Result"). Work time data sheets enable editing of worker's grade and performance. The parameters are the mean and the stochastic error range. The resource editor page adds the resource data and their possible stochastic distributions for any project. Resources can be fixed or random; these are especially important to decide the need of the project and its final cost.

After multiple simulation runs, project variants are compared in order to find the optimum. This environment is used to design the best team possible for a given project (or a set of projects). The optimization is conditioned, (i.e. the Top Team in Table 1 is chosen if the project manager needs the most economical team, and the Giant team in Table 1 is chosen only when maximum speed is the criterion). Whenever a task over the deadline is found, its margin is checked, the length is edited and all other related tasks are adjusted. Thus the optimal decision making is possible with using the simulation data. Input data can be changed flexibly, including task relationships, team members, project teams, project budgets, workers ability or random input streams, and then reused for the simulation.

CONCLUDING REMARKS

In spite of various established project management models and quality management systems, such as ISO-9001, Capability Maturity Model, or Constructive Cost Model (COCOMO), SPM simulation has not received sufficient attention in academia. Also software projects in businesses often suffer from inadequate management. The complexity of software projects with various stochastic features involved implies that an object-oriented computer simulation is a very appropriate approach. In addition, because of the autonomous human factor in program coding and complexity in motivation of software developers, agent-based simulations are expected to contribute to this field in the future.

This chapter summarized principal features of software project management along with presenting a newly developed SPM simulation tool. The tool is a general purpose object-oriented simulation environment with emphasis on fault-tolerance in the development process. Randomized inputs, randomized faults, variable team structures, branching queues and idle time analysis are included (Online simulation application, 2005). The online Java program adopts flexible data structures for the teams and stores all simulation data in a dynamic database. The contribution of this work consists in developing simulation technology for the new area of SPM.

ACKNOWLEDGMENT

Lukáš Pichl acknowledges partial support by the JSPS Grant-in-Aid. We are grateful for the comments of anonymous reviewers on the background of this work.

REFERENCES

Abdel-Hamid, T. K., & Madnick, S. E. (1991). *Software project dynamics: An integrated approach.* New York: Prentice Hall.

Bennatan, E. M. (1995). *Software project management: A practitioner's approach.* New York: McGraw-Hill.

Drappa, A., & Ludewig, J. (1999). Quantitative modeling for the interaction simulation of software projects. *Journal of Systems and Software, 46,* 113.

Humphrey, W. S., & Kellner, M. I. (1989, May). Software process modeling: Principles of entity process models. *Proceedings of the 11th International Conference on Software Engineering,* Pittsburgh (p. 331).

Jalote, P. (2002). *Software project management in practice.* Adison Wesley.

Northwest Center for Emerging Technologies (1999). *Building a foundation for tomorrow: Skills standards for information technology.* Belleview, WA.

Pichl, L. (2005). Software process simulation. Retrieved March 1, 2005, from *http://lukas.pichl.cz/spm.zip*

Rodrigues, A., & Bowers J. (1996). System dynamics in project management: A comparative analysis with the traditional methods. *System Dynamics Review 12,* 121.

US Government Accounting Office. (1979). Document FGMSD-79-49. Retrieved September 2003, from *www.gao.gov:8765*

US Government Accounting Office. (2000). Document AO/AIMD-00-170. Retrieved September 2003, from www.gao.gov:8765

Chapter XI

Modern Organizations and Decision-Making Processes: A Heuristic Approach

Ana Marostica
University of Buenos Aires, Argentina

Cesar Briano
University of Buenos Aires, Argentina

ABSTRACT

This chapter explains a hybrid-decision support system (HDSS) in which a heuristic-data mining procedure (a complement of a statistic-data mining) is embedded into the original information system. For the better understanding of these concepts, these tools are presented as hybrid agents interacting in a financial environment. Structures and some important types of decisions that decision makers can adopt in a financial organization (e.g., a commercial bank) and how the suitable information is incorporated in a HDSS, are also discussed.

INTRODUCTION

Thinking is usually mentioned as the main characteristic of the intelligence of human minds, and in a certain way, of computer programs, too. From a heuristic point of view, the complex architecture of the mind when thinking uses different types of processes (such as abduction, deduction, and induction), to solve problems and to make decisions.

The main goal of this chapter is to explain a hybrid-decision support system (HDSS) in which a heuristic-data mining procedure is embedded into a common information system (DSS). For the better understanding of these concepts, these tools are presented as hybrid agents interaction in a financial environment (e.g., a commercial bank).

This chapter is organized as follows. Section 2 explains a "decision" from a heuristic point of view. Section 3 discusses a hybrid-decision support system (HDSS). Section 4 gives an illustration of decisions in a financial organization (e.g., a commercial bank), and Section 5 contains some concluding remarks and future work proposals.

WHAT IS A DECISION?

It is difficult in economic literature to find answers to direct questions such as "What is a decision in general?" Let us start with the definition found in Webster's Dictionary. There we find that a *decision,* among other meanings, is "a conclusion reached or given." Related to the specific meaning mentioned here, we can ask, "If a decision is a conclusion, which are the premises of this inference?"

Suppes (1961) detailed on the types of premises of these decision-related processes. He explained that in a decision situation, a person or group of persons (i.e., the decision makers) is faced with several alternative courses of actions but with incomplete information about the true state of affairs and the consequences of each possible action. The problem is how to choose an action that is optimal or rational, relative to the information available and according with some definite criteria of optimality or rationality. In Suppes' explanation, we have the main ingredients of what is called, in general terms, "decision theory."

Because making decisions generally occurs in a context of uncertainty, the individual must choose between several alternatives. The possible decisions may have a variety of consequences, and ordinarily the consequences are not simply determined by the decision made but also affected by the present state of things. It is supposed that the individual or group of individuals has a utility function on the possible consequences and that the decision maker has a probability function (i.e., subjective probabilities) on the possible state of the environment that expresses his or her beliefs about the true state of things. According to the expected utility hypothesis, a decision maker tries to select, with a rational choice, a possible alternative that maximized the expected utility. However, there is evidence of paradoxical behavior that do not maximize the expected utilities.

These are the main ingredients of a decision process or inference. Let us review briefly the concept of utility function related to consequences. Utility function is a numerical representation of some individual tastes and preferences. In modern times, after Pareto, utilities are considered as ordinal index of preferences (Silberberg, 1978). People are assumed to be able to rank all commodity bundles, without regarding the intensity of satisfaction gained by consuming a particular commodity bundle. More specifically, for any two bundles of goods x and y, any consumer can decide among the following three mutually exclusive situations:

- .x is preferred to y,
- .y is preferred to x, and
- .x and y are equally preferred.

Of course, only one category can apply at any specific time. If that category should change, this means that the tastes of the people, or preferences, have changed. In the third category, we say that people are indifferent between x and y. The utility function is constructed simply as an index. The utility index is to become larger when a more preferred bundle of goods is consumed.

With regard to another important element of decision-making processes, we have the subjective probabilities that a decision maker has when considering the possible states of the environment. Much work in probability theory deals with the derivation of the probabilities of certain complicated events from the specific probabilities of simpler events, with the study of how certain specified probabilities change in the light of new information, and with procedures for making effective decisions in certain situations that can be characterized in terms of specified probability distributions.

On several occasions, there are suitable probabilities that can often be assigned objectively and quickly because of wide agreement on the appropriateness of any specific probability distribution. In such a situation, people's assignment of probabilities must be highly subjective and must reflect his or her own information and beliefs. This is why, in this case, it may be convenient to represent his or her information and beliefs in terms of probability distributions. However, we have to keep in mind that in spite of the rigorous statistical treatment (De Groot, 1970), subjective probabilities are no more than "degrees of confidence" that shows the intensity of confidence a person (e.g., in our case, a decision maker) has in certain probability statement.

Now, some comments related to the controversial rationality principle. It is common to read in economic books that "rationality" is related to "the idea that people *rationally* anticipate the future and respond to what they see ahead" (Shapiro, 1999). However, in this explanation of rational expectation the important word *rationality* is not explained. Simon (1999) used to call this principle of rationality "adaptation." He argued that the outer environment determines the conditions for goal attainment. If the inner system is properly designed, it will be adapted to the outer environment, so that its behavior will be determined in large part by the behavior of the latter, exactly as in the case of the "economic man" (Simon, 1999). In this explanation, we find, again, the word *rational* without explanation. Lucas (1986), even though he does not want to argue about people being "rational" or "adaptive," and after several empirical and experimental studies, thinks that rational behavior is the end product of an adaptive process. Statisticians' optimality is, more or less, what the previous authors call "rationality" or "adaptation" (De Groot, 1970).

Because the majority of authors in the field of economics, and some related areas, either use circular types of definitions or change the name of rationality for another equivalent word, we propose a useful method: to come back to the etymology of the word *rational*. *Rational* comes from "reason" (i.e., *ratio* in Latin means "reason"). Therefore, to behave "rationally" is to behave according to reasoning. Moreover, it means to behave in a way that is suitable or even optimal for goal attainment; it is to take into account all the available information (i.e., it is always partial) for goal attainment and to choose the best possible alternative for that purpose. We think that this characterization encompasses all the main ingredients of what we mean by "rational behavior."

Now we have the main ingredients of a decision process or inference. The premises are the set of *alternatives* for decisions, the possible consequences of those alternatives, related to the expected utility hypothesis, the state of the environment, that is related to subjective probabilities, and weak preferences, that is related to the principle of rationality. The conclusion of this process is the decision itself (i.e., to adopt one of those alternatives). This is why we say that a decision is a choice among alternative course of actions. In a formal way, we have the following inference:

Alternatives $a_1, \ldots, a_n$,
Possible consequences (related to expected utility hypothesis)
Weak preferences (related to the principle of rationality or optimality)
States of the environment (related to subjective probabilities)
Therefore, Decision (a choice of the better alternative).

A HYBRID-DECISION SUPPORT SYSTEM (HDSS)

It is significant that the definition of a DSS is written from the decision-maker's perspective. It is convenient to emphasize that this type of information system is a support for the decision maker's (i.e., the user) decisions. We must remember that these types of systems can give information only for the premises of this inference whose conclusion is the decision itself.

A DSS, generally is described as having five parts (Marakas, 1999):

1. The User Interface,
2. The Model-Based Management System,
3. The Knowledge Engine,
4. The Data Management System, and
5. The User.

These five parts are the ones recognized by some authors (e.g., Marakas, 1999). All these parts correspond, more or less, to the parts we find in an information system (Marostica & Tohme, 2000), with the exception of the Model-Based Management System. This software includes different types of models (e.g., financial, statistical, management), which give the system analytical capability and appropriate administration of the software.

In information systems in general, and DSS in particular, in order to use correctly the information provided by its database or its data management software, it is necessary for the system to have heuristic tools that set first precise definitions of ambiguous variables and boundaries for vague or fuzzy variables. The architecture specified in Figure 1 shows the two parts of a hybrid-decision support system. The left part is the DSS itself, mentioned before, and the right part of the figure is a heuristic-data mining mechanism (i.e., a complement of a statistical-data mining), which is embedded into the original DSS.

If we need to set precise definitions of the variables (i.e., predicates) involved in the premises of a decision inference, we must first remember the logical criteria for good definitions. A good definition must be *clear* (i.e., the defining expression must be clearer than the defined expression), *accurate*, should not be *too narrow*, should not be *too broad*, and not be made in *negative terms*. With these criteria, we can avoid the ambiguous variables (i.e., ambiguity is a qualitative problem that certain variables have, it is more than one meaning in the same context without any specification against that). For example, in a financial context, ambiguity could arise when decisions related to a prescription that the Central Bank should vary reserve requirements in order to allow a smooth functioning of the banks could call for either an increase or a decrease in the requirements according to the circumstances.

This is why, in the information we find in a DSS, after giving precise definitions, we can check the status of each variable (i.e., predicate) to see if it is ambiguous or not by using the following algorithm:

Algorithm: AMBIGUITY

1. Evaluate type of variable in the set of alternatives
2. IF the variable is quantitative or precise, GO TO 4
3. For I = 1, 2, …, N Do
   a. Select M (I)
   b. Evaluate M (I)
   c. IF M (I) ¹ PM (I)
      Dead end
      End IF

Figure 1. A hybrid-decision support system

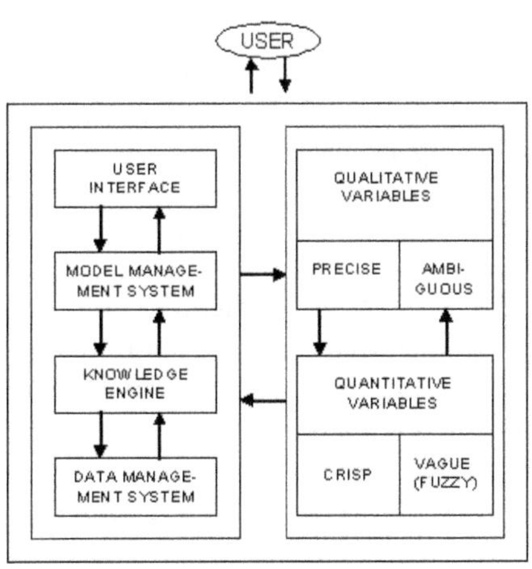

Next
4. IF there are more variables, GOTO 1
5. END

The symbol PM (*I*) represents the precise meaning of a node *I* (i.e., variable *I*). Calling AMBIGUITY, recursively performs the algorithm. SELECT is a procedure that chooses an element out from a set, such that this element obeys a set of conditions, for example, to choose precise qualitative variables instead of ambiguous ones. More details are in Marostica and Tohme (2000).

Because decision making involves the selection of the best available alternative, according to the rationality principle, sometimes the set of alternatives, which contains a solution to a decision-making problem, cannot always be defined explicitly because it contains vague or fuzzy variables. Vagueness is a quantitative problem, and has to do with representations of the world like natural languages. Decision making in finances, for instance, used natural languages where we have the problem of vagueness. In order to use fuzzy set theory as a tool for vagueness it is necessary to explain fuzzy membership functions (Zadeh, 1965). In decision inferences, we can say that the fuzzy membership function of a decision or goal in a decision problem is:

$$F(x) = A \rightarrow [0, 1] \qquad (1)$$

A, in this formula, represents a set of possible alternatives that contain a solution to a decision-making problem under consideration. *A* fuzzy decision *D* is a fuzzy set on *A* characterized by the membership function, which represents the degree to which the alternatives satisfy the specified decision goal. In general, a fuzzy decision indicates that the target should be obtained, but also quantifies the degree to which the target is fulfilled (Sousa & Kaymak, 2002).

These functions could have different shapes, such as triangular or trapezoidal. In this chapter, we are only interested in trapezoidal shapes. Since the relative membership of an element of a fuzzy set is represented in the trapezoidal shape, we can define in an informal way this type of function as follows:

Let *a, b, c,* and *d* be real numbers. Then,

$$F(x) = \begin{cases} (x-a)/(b-a) & \text{if } a \le x \le b \\ (x-d)/(c-d) & \text{if } c \le x \le d \\ 1 & \text{if } b \le x \le c \\ 0 & \text{otherwise} \end{cases} \qquad (2)$$

If we want to set boundaries to vague predicates, from a quantitative point of view, we must remember that the fuzzy sets determined by those predicates have to be analyzed, according to the information provided by experts, in several subsets of the original fuzzy set. Sometimes those subsets are called "fuzzy categories." These fuzzy categories are constructed according to the following algorithm:

Algorithm: VAGUENESS

1. Define the type of variable in the set of alternatives
2. IF the variable is qualitative or crisp, GOTO 4
3. IF the variable, or set, is fuzzy
    a. Create fuzzy subsets or fuzzy categories (given by experts)
    b. Determine the relative membership of elements of the original fuzzy set
    c. Return the relative membership of those elements
    END
4. IF there are more variables, GOTO 1
5. END.

The following algorithm performs the relationship between the DSS and the Heuristic-data mining:

Algorithm: HYBRID-DSS

1. Define the type of variable by using AMBIGUITY and VAGUENESS algorithms
2. IF the variable is an n-adic predicate where $n = 4, 5, \ldots,$
    a. Apply Reduction Principle
3. IF there are more variables, GOTO 1
4. END

Peirce's Reduction Principle (Marty, 1987) roughly says that any n- adic predicate (i.e., where $n > 3$) can be reduced to some n-adic predicates (i.e., where $n \leq 3$). Monadic, dyadic and triadic predicates are irreducible. This principle was proven in many ways for standard predicates. For fuzzy predicates, (i.e., for the common ones that are predicates which denote properties that come in degrees and they are, from a logical point of view, monadic predicates), can be proven, too.

DECISIONS IN FINANCIAL ORGANIZATIONS

Organizational decisions often have important consequences. In order to succeed, organizations (e.g., financial organizations such as commercial banks) strive to maintain a high level of performance while minimizing the occurrence of mistakes, due to either underestimating or overestimating the information coming from the environment.

We can make a taxonomy of decisions in a financial organization, such as a commercial bank, from the point of view of decision-makers. In a bank such as the National Bank of Argentina, we have decision makers who belong to the highest level (e.g., the president and vice-presidents and the board of directors). We have, as well, decision makers who belong to manager departments of the National Bank of Argentina (e.g., auditoria, international banking, commercial banking, finances, information systems). According to these divisions, we can identify some types of single or plural decisions that belong to Marakas' (1999) classification. For example, among the decisions taken by the board we find the noncollaborative type. In this type of decisions, communication among the nondecision makers is irrelevant, for example, when the Central Bank increases

Figure 2. Fuzzy categories

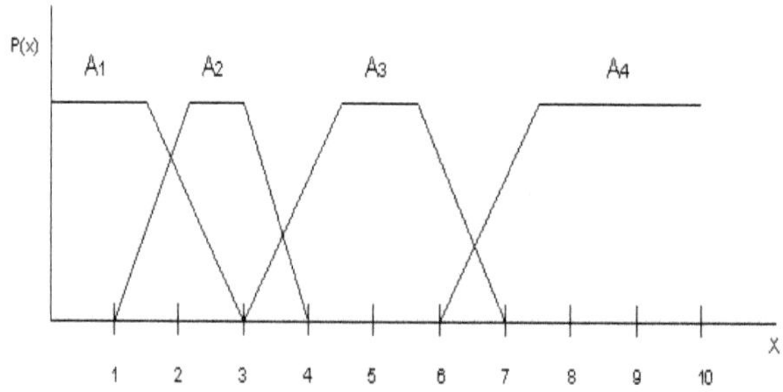

the reserve requirements for the banks. In each bank (e.g., The National Bank of Argentina), the managers in charge of information systems (i.e., the first level of managers) receiving this decision from the top level must reprogram the computers accordingly. Another type of decisions from the main board may be the ones performed by a *team*. Since a team is a formal participant that is a combination of a *group* (e.g., formal participants with multiple decision makes) and an *individual* (e.g., a concrete participant with a singular decision maker). In the decisions of a team, we have that a group shares a long-term goal but this group takes a single decision. For example, decisions related to marketing policy with the purpose of attracting more customers for the bank.

Among the decisions at the level of management departments (i.e., they should be plural), we find the *majority* type of decisions where a high stated percent of decision makers must agree. For example, in human resources (e.g., a second level manager department in the National Bank of Argentina), the decisions are related to training people for specific kind of work, legal advice for workers and so forth.

Let us suppose that at the main board level, some decision-maker must make a decision related to the marketing policy explained above. If the information is related to a country-risk index, the decision will be different if the index is very low or low or moderate or high. If the information is that the country in question is risky, the decision will be analyzed in a different way according to the country-risk index in question.

Figure 2 is an illustration of fuzzy categories where the fuzzy subsets A_1, A_2, A_3, and A_4, are subset of a fuzzy set **A**, which is related to the expression "the country is risky." These fuzzy categories set boundaries to that fuzzy set (i.e., the vagueness of the variable). In Figure 2, A_1 - A_4, are the fuzzy subsets or fuzzy category very low, low, moderate and high country risk, respectively. All this information is given by experts.

Any fuzzy subset A_i of **A** can be defined in the following way:

$$A_i = \{(x, F(x), -F(x)) : x \varepsilon A\} \tag{3}$$

Where the functions F(x): A→ [0,1] and –F(x): A→ [0,1] define the degree of membership and the degree of nonmembership respectively of an element x belonging to A, provided that the sum of F(x) and -F(x) is equal 1.0. Besides, the addition of all relative memberships is 1.0, too.

CONCLUDING REMARKS AND FUTURE WORK

A decision support system, hybrid or not, is only a "support" for the decision maker. The process of decision is only complete when the user or the human decision maker takes an actual decision. The system can give information related to the set of alternatives, the consequences of each alternative calculating the utilities, and the state of things related to specific environment with their subjective probabilities. Nevertheless, the decision is the responsibility of the user. Here we find several ways to consider the interaction between a HDSS and a human decision maker. Following Hollnagel (1991), we may have three types of human–computer interaction. The first type is the *simple interaction*, in which we can identify as independent elements the user, the computer program and the task for achieving a certain goal. The second one Hollnagel called it *hermeneutical human–computer interaction*, in which we have the user separated from the computer program plus the task. As its name indicates, the computer program serves in a hermeneutic relation to the user. It is an interpretative relation with the computer plus the task to be carried out. The third type of interaction is the *amplifying user-computer interaction*, in which there is an embodiment relation between the user and the computer program. The computer program is an augmentation of the mind of the user. They fuse the computers with the human mind (Ritchie, 1984).

This is why, based on the previous explanations, it is not odd to fuse a hybrid-decision support system with the decision maker in the decision-making process, by using the third type of relations explained above. We can call it a *hybrid agent*. In this way, we can apply the theory of multi-agent systems without problems. A key pattern of interaction in multi-agent systems is goal and task-oriented coordination (Weiss, 1999). The important concepts in a multiagent system are the idea of an *agent* in an *environment*. The *agent* (e.g., could be our hybrid agent) is the learner and decision maker. Could be heterogeneous agents as different types of decision-makers are. The environment can be understood as the things the agents interact with comprising everything outside the agents (e.g., the decision maker in a financial organization such as a commercial bank interacts with a financial world). Different agents may have different goals, actions and domain knowledge according to the type of decisions they must take (Stone, 2000).

Lucas provided the notion of an economic agent as a collection of decision rules, (i.e., rules that dictate the actions to be taken in some situations), and a set of preferences used to evaluate the outcomes arising from particular situation-action combinations (Chen, 2001). In this paper (p.137), Chen made a comparison between Lucasian agents and genetic algorithms (e.g., to decision rules correspond strings of binary ones and zeros, to decision rules review corresponds fitness evaluation). We can accept Lucas' characterization of an agent with some modifications. If we say that an agent is a collection of decision rules, you do not need to add (i.e., at least from a logical point of view) the set of preferences as a separated part. They are included in the conditions of the rules and the decisions are the actions of those rules.

We think that to improve decision support systems with heuristic tools and notions such as hybrid agents is useful. This is because the important research in genetic programs and multiagent systems in the field of organizations in general and financial ones, in particular, is nowadays not applied without restrictions. The traditional decision support systems, in turn, are applied everywhere without restrictions but they lack of intelligent tools. In the near future, a research related to this topic of hybrid agent taking decisions is promising.

ACKNOWLEDGMENT

The authors are grateful to Dr. Daniel Heymann for his explanations, examples and critical comments.

REFERENCES

Chen, S-H. (2001). On the relevance of genetic programming to evolutionary economics. In J. Aruka (Ed). *Evolutionary controversies in economics. A new transdisciplinary approach.* Tokyo: Springer.

De Groot, M. H. (1970). *Optimal statistical decisions.* New York: Mc Graw-Hill.

Hollnagel, E. (1991). The influence of artificial intelligence on human-computer interaction: Much ado about nothing? In J. Rasmussen & H. B. Anderson (Eds.), *Human-computer interaction* (Vol. 3, pp.153-202). London: Lawrence Erlbaum.

Lucas, R. E. (1986). Adaptive behavior and economic theory. In R. M. Hogarth & M. W. Reder (Eds.), *Rational choice. The contrast between economics and psychology* (pp. 217-242). Chicago: The University of Chicago Press.

Marakas, G. M. (1999). *Decision Support systems in the 21st century.* London: Prentice-Hall International.

Marostica, A., & Tohme, F. (2000). Semiotic tools for economic model building. *The Journal of Management and Economics, 4,* 27-34.

Marostica, A., Briano, C., & Chinkes, E. (2002). Semiotic-data mining procedures for a financial information system. *Proceedings of the 6th Joint Conference on Information Sciences,* Duke University, Association for Intelligent Machinery, Inc.

Marty, R. (1987). *L'Algèbre des Signes. Essai de Sémiotique Scientifique d'Apres Charles Sanders Peirce.* Amsterdam: John Benjamin.

Ritchie, D. (1984). *The binary brain.* Boston: Little, Brown.

Shapiro, A. C. (1999). *Multinational financial management.* London: Prentice-Hall International.

Silberberg, E. (1978). *The structure of economics. A mathematical analysis.* New York: McGraw-Hill.

Simon, H. A. (1999). *The science of the artificial.* Cambridge, MA: MIT Press.

Sousa, J. M. C., & Kaymak, U. (2002). *Fuzzy decision making in modeling and control.* London: World Scientific.

Stone, P. (2000). *Layered learning in multiagent systems.* Cambridge, MA: The MIT Press.

Suppes, P. (1961). Behaviorist foundations of utility. *Econometrica, 29,* 186-202.

Weiss, G. (1999). *Multiagent systems. A modern approach to distributed intelligence* (Prologue, pp.1-23). Cambridge, MA: MIT Press.

Zadeh, L. (1965). Fuzzy sets. *Information and Control, 8,* 338-353.

Section V

Policy Appraisal

Chapter XII

An Application of Multi-Agent Simulation to Policy Appraisal in the Criminal Justice System

Seán Boyle
London School of Economics, UK

Stephen Guerin
RedfishGroup, USA

Daniel Kunkle
RedfishGroup, USA

ABSTRACT

This chapter reports on a multi-agent approach to the construction of a model of the English criminal justice system. The approach is an integration of model-building with ways of enabling people to engage in strategic policy making and take into account the complex interactions of the criminal justice system. From the workings of the police to court procedures to prisons, decisions in one area of the criminal justice system can be crucial in determining what happens in another area. The purpose was to allow assessment of the impact across the whole justice system of a variety of policies.

INTRODUCTION

This chapter reports on a multi-agent approach to the construction of a model of how the criminal justice system in England operates. The model's principal purpose is to allow the impact of policy variants across the whole justice system to be assessed.

Because the model is designed to help people to think about what happens when things are changed in a deliberative manner, we provide some examples of policy changes for which the model is designed to help. We also discuss a visualization that is representative of what the model can do for different policy views.

In the next section, we describe the structure of criminal justice in England. Section 3 discusses the purpose of the project, which goes beyond the mere construction of a model. In producing the model there were at least two aspects of interest: the way in which the problem was approached, and the physical representation of a solution which we call a "model". These are discussed in Sections 4 and 5.

THE CONTEXT

The criminal justice system in England is delivered by diverse government bodies—as is true in many other countries. In England these are not part of a single government department. There are three departments involved: the Home Office which is by far the biggest financially and in terms of human resource; the Department of Constitutional Affairs; and the Crown Prosecution Service.

Each of these has its own government minister, and in the case of the first two, has a range of responsibilities outside of those that we consider in constructing a model of the criminal justice system. Thus the Home Office is also responsible for immigration and for homeland security, whereas the Department of Constitutional Affairs also has responsibility for civil and family law.

The Home Office's criminal justice responsibilities include the Police Service, the Prison Service and the Probation Service. But this is not a direct operational responsibility. Other agencies are responsible for the delivery of each service. there is little direct financial accountability (although all rely on central government funds) and only limited operational interference. Top-level targets are set for each service but how useful these are is uncertain. Operational control is divided across 42 areas of the country. Determining how things are run is a local matter.

The Department of Constitutional Affairs is responsible both for the courts and, via an executive agency, for the provision of free criminal defence services (known as Legal Aid). The courts are divided between lower and higher courts: The former are called magistrates' courts and deal with lesser offences; the latter are called the Crown Court and generally deal with more serious cases. The Crown Prosecution Service is responsible for prosecuting criminal cases. It is the least complex of the three bodies.

How the criminal justice system functions depends crucially on the way in which each of these bodies delivers services, and on the interactions between what happens in one, and what happens in another, as well as within each agency. Within each part of the system, there are thousands of individual agents who act according to sets of rules some of which are fairly proscriptive, and others which are rules of thumb, often undescribed.

Funding for the Criminal Justice System

Most of the funding for these service providers comes through the UK Treasury, although there are other flows of money that come either through local government sources or are privately funded. The UK Treasury has a system of two-yearly spending reviews, which look 3 years ahead (and which therefore overlap by a year). These take place in every government department.

Decisions in one area of the criminal justice system (CJS) may be crucial in determining what happens in another: how well the police function may make the life of courts easier or harder, the workload of prisons more or less. This has been recognized by the Treasury. Thus in the 1998 Spending Review, the Government undertook the first-ever review of the performance and management of the CJS as a whole, cutting across all three government departments. The 2002 Spending Review saw a cross-departmental review of the CJS which built on the work begun in 1998. However the Treasury did not feel that the collective CJS elements presented were sufficiently "joined up".

Thus, for the Spending Review in 2004 the Treasury has required further development of the way in which all agencies bid, so that bids take into account what the other agencies are doing and that this is mediated through some kind of model of the whole system. Our work was designed to address this need.

PURPOSE OF THE PROJECT

The primary task was to do something that would contribute successfully to the Treasury's Spending Review for 2004, and, beyond this, that could be used for assessment of future policy development across the whole of the CJS. This involved working at two levels. First, working with different groups of people (representatives of the different agencies) in the criminal justice system we tried to establish some kind of consensus around how things actually happened in the system. This entailed gathering evidence of links between the behaviour and actions of one person or group of people, and another, and through this making arguments for the best use of resources; but also establishing agreement between each set of people about all of this. This was essentially about encouraging a change in the style of working of these core government agencies.

The second level was to produce a model of the whole criminal justice system that all actors in the system would acknowledge. This entailed working with modelers and statisticians in the various government agencies and departments (i.e., more technically minded people who were interested in building better models of what happens). We acknowledge the extent of the contribution of the Criminal Justice Performance Directorate in this respect as well as various individuals in each of the departments and agencies of the CJS. Our aim was to build on existing models of the system to produce an end-to-end computer model of the criminal justice system which would provide insights particularly into questions of capacity, case flow and costs. This has the feel of a standard modeling problem.

We had to model how individuals—criminals or cases—go through the criminal justice system from the initial crime event to final disposal, culminating in receiving a prison sentence, a community sentence, including various forms of postprison supervision, or being a free member of the population. And moreover the client wanted to see these flows mapped against costed resources so that Treasury requirements would be satisfied.

PRODUCING THE MODEL

There were two distinctive parts to the project: working with the people who are actually involved in making and delivering policy in the criminal justice system, and developing an adequate model of what the system does.

Working with people involved a range of activities:

1. Determining user requirements through individual interviews and workshops, which culminated in the production of a User Requirements Report;
2. Developing ways of satisfying the client that the model was really "them", again through interviews, workshops, and culminating in a Test Suites Report; and,
3. Recording what the system does and why in terms of processes, activities and resources, which was achieved through interviews and workshops, and resulted in the production of a what was called the Modeled Processes Report.

However each of these parts was also of fundamental importance in delivering a successful model—the second part of our task. The model developed was based on agent behaviors.

To provide inputs to the model we posed the following types of question to each agency:

- What resources are used in providing services (e.g., what police and types, courts, custody suites)?
- What does each resource do, how does it makes choices, and are there different rules to choose from?
- What happens when capacity limits are threatened? How does prioritisation take place?
- What are the costs of each resource, and how does this vary as decisions are taken?

The model provides a representation of the flow of activity through the criminal justice system; this is presented both graphically and as output files in terms of, for example,

- number of crimes reported;
- number of cases tried in magistrates' courts;
- cost of various types of resource used; and,
- numbers waiting at different points in the system.

THE MODEL AS A HYBRID

We set out to produce a model in a way that would engage people in the system. To do this we adopted a multi-agent approach. However in such a short time it was never going to be possible to build a full agent model for every part of the criminal justice system. But the key question was could we produce something that would satisfy the needs of the client, and at the same time, take the client-system down the agent-based road (i.e., provide a framework that the client could readily build upon) and, what is most important, would want to build upon.

The result is a model that is a kind of hybrid between a simple system dynamics model of flows through the system—albeit with relatively complex interactions at each stage or node—and a model of individual agents behaving in ways that produce results that cannot be predicted from looking at the behaviour of groups of the same agents.

Figure 1 represents how we see the nature of what we are doing. In some parts of the system the model is more like process descriptions with high levels of agent homogeneity (super agents); in other parts we have good descriptions of activities of individual agents with significant interaction between agents. The process and activity descriptions are mutually consistent.

Using the Model

The model is structured in a way that allows the user to examine simple questions or more complex policy issues. We provide below two examples of typical policy issues that could be addressed by the model. These are,

- What happens when the number of police in the system is increased by 10,000? The effect depends on what activities these police are assigned to do, or choose to do. These can range from more patrolling to more investigation, better case preparation, better preparation for court and so forth. All these will have knock-on effects for other service providers, and all will also affect how the agents themselves work.
- What happens when sentencing powers are increased, for example from 6 months to 12 months for certain offences? It may seem obvious that this will increase the prison population, but sentencers have discretion about what they do and may choose to use the power differently. Moreover the defendants may react to longer sentences by for example appealing more, or choosing a different court for the hearing. Any of these may result in different consequences from those that might be supposed when the policy was first devised.

Figure 1. Hybrid modeling: Process and activity-based descriptions

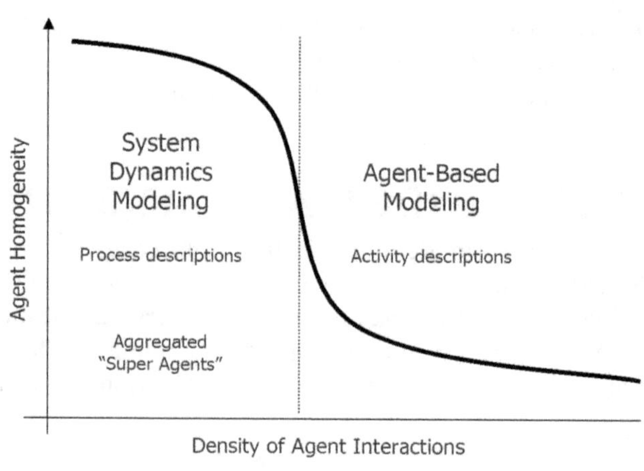

Visualizing the Criminal Justice System

We also felt it was important to provide a visualization of the system that a wide range of users could relate to—going beyond those with a technical interest in the model to those who determine policy (i.e., high-level public servants and politicians).

It was also a way of allowing the different service providers to see themselves as part of a large whole of which they are an integral part. Of course they all know that the model covers the whole system but often it is useful to have a reminder. In a way the visualization comes to represent the model as icon. It is almost as if people have something that they can touch while making their decisions.

Figure 2 shows a "screen grab" from the visualization. Our aim is that users become aware of the system and its parts. At the same time they can see the size of flows along edges between nodes; or the proportion of capacity used, or some other type of target like timeliness between two nodes; or, finally, the costs of providing services at each node (which was very important for our client audience).

The visualization is decoupled from the model. The visualization reads the log files produced by the model. This approach allows us to easily switch back and forth between different scenarios that are produced by multiple scenario runs. A second benefit is that it allows us to do early rapid prototyping to establish scope on the project while the model is being constructed. We are able to use the same visualization for outputs of "scratch-pad" throw-away prototypes in various programming languages and then plug-in the actual model data when available.

A third benefit to this approach, which can not be overstressed, is the ability to more rapidly diffuse the model and its insights throughout the organization. The visualization with the log files is a much smaller memory footprint than trying to deploy the model and all of its dependencies. Given the above benefits, one disadvantage of having a decoupled view is the inability to modify model parameters on the fly for interactive exploration by the user.

Figure 2. Visualizing the system

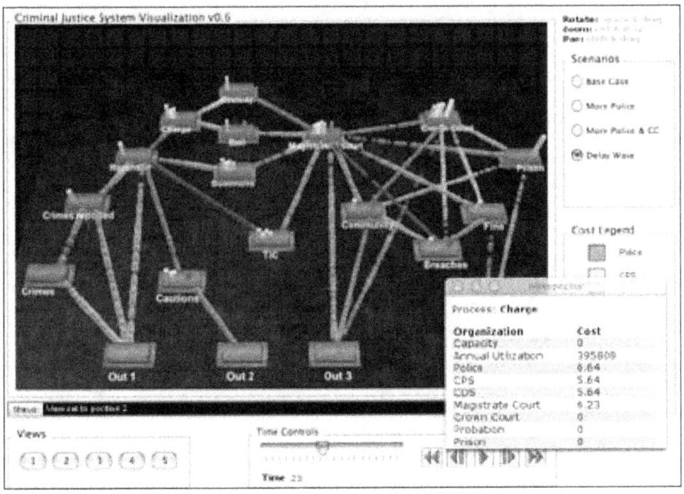

CONCLUSION

The project delivered an agent-based framework with the potential to model the impact of government policy on the criminal justice system. A core value for the client was using the model as a mechanism to drive diverse operating groups toward a coherent and consensus budget.

As well as developing the model, the project delivered two additional free-standing policy "tools", each of which was a practical application of system-wide thinking. Thus, a template for system-wide policy formulation was produced—the Systemic Impact Statement; also a high-impact demonstration of flows across the system was provided, through computer visualisation developed alongside the model.

Chapter XIII

Capital Controls and Firm's Dynamics

Alexei G. Orlov
Radford University, USA

ABSTRACT

This chapter constructs a dynamic model of a multinational enterprise (MNE) to quantify the effects of various capital control policies on a firm's debt and equity positions, innovations, and outputs at the headquarters and subsidiary. The model is calibrated to the US Foreign Direct Investment (FDI) Benchmark Survey *and the IMF's* Exchange Arrangements and Exchange Restrictions *so that it reproduces the average US FDI and technology flows to foreign subsidiaries. Both steady-state and transition analyses suggest a significant impact of capital controls on an MNE's operations. Lifting capital restrictions produces an inflow of capital and technology into the less developed countries, leading to an increase in the steady-state FDI position and production. Simulation experiments reveal that even short-term capital controls have long-lasting negative effects.*

INTRODUCTION

Despite the rapid process of globalization and financial integration that the world economy has experienced in the past several decades, many national governments choose—for short periods of time or permanently—to hinder this process of financial integration by imposing restrictions on capital mobility. Such restrictions are prevalent throughout the world: the majority of the International Monetary Fund (IMF) member nations have imposed capital controls over the past decade.

This chapter constructs and simulates a dynamic partial-equilibrium model of a multinational enterprise (MNE) that allows us to study the effects of various capital control policies on a firm's debt and equity positions, innovations, and outputs at the headquarters and subsidiary. Microeconomic considerations that lie at the heart of the model help us to arrive at important macroeconomic policy implications. Specifically, the model enables us to evaluate the costs—in terms of lost capital and output, as well as slower technological progress—of capital control policies that vary in strength and duration. We also analyze the long-term effects of short-lived capital restrictions.

Capital controls (and particularly exchange restrictions) alter the operations of US MNEs because they affect expectations about the dollar amount of profit, dividend and royalty remittance from the foreign subsidiaries back to the US parent. However, evaluating the effectiveness of capital restrictions is a difficult task since the length of the available time series data is limited (Edwards, 2000). This chapter overcomes the time-series difficulties of evaluating exchange controls—including relatively short time dimension of the available panel data on capital controls, as well as quality limitations, difficulty of isolating the effects of capital controls, and unobservable technology transfers—by examining transitional dynamics of a model of an MNE. We calibrate our model to the 1998 *US Foreign Direct Investment (FDI) Benchmark Survey* and the IMF's *Exchange Arrangements and Exchange Restrictions* so that the model reproduces the average US FDI and technology flows to foreign subsidiaries in 1998.

Our simulations show that the milder the exchange controls, the greater the rate of convergence of headquarters' capital and output and the longer it takes for the plant to reach its steady state level of production. The opposite is true for the subsidiary: the milder the restrictions, the lower the rate of convergence and the less time until it hits steady-state. During the transition and at the steady state, exchange controls induce a wedge between the headquarters' and subsidiary's capital stocks and depress the level of technology available at both the headquarters and subsidiary.

Unlike previous papers in this area, we also allow the MNE to borrow locally in each of the plants.[1] Typically, multinationals, especially those in developing countries or immature subsidiaries, start foreign operations with a limited FDI position and large local borrowings. Understanding how governmental exchange control policies affect debt versus equity financing of capital is important to developing countries that want the infusion of foreign capital, not the multinationals borrowing from local sources. Also, for countries that impose exchange controls when faced with low foreign exchange reserves, knowing how their exchange control policy affects the decision of debt versus equity flows is important for their foreign reserve position. We find that in African countries equity-financed capital would increase, local borrowing would fall, and the flow of foreign technology would intensify if these countries abolish the restrictions. However, the predicted change in these variables is minimal resulting from the fact that, although Africa can impose restrictions, they are rarely used. In Brazil, which has had on-off restrictions between the 1970s and 1990s, depending on the severity of the policy and expected length of enforcement, we find sizable movements in the FDI stock and bond issuing.

Focusing on steady state, we quantify the effects of constant exchange control policies. We find the more severe the restriction, the smaller the FDI position at the subsidiary, the larger the capital stock at home, and the smaller the innovations. We also find that constant exchange controls result in a loss of the FDI position at the subsidiary, higher capital stock at home, and a reduction in innovations. Even though the headquarters' capital stock rises, the effect of falling innovations results in lower output at the headquarters. Hence exchange controls have a negative impact on a home country's standard of living. The subsidiary's output falls as well, so a foreign country's standard of living also deteriorates. For example, applying the steady state results to African countries, which have very mild exchange controls, we find that lifting the restrictions would result in a 0.94% loss in the steady state level of headquarters capital stock, a 0.84% gain in FDI position at the subsidiary, a 1.42% increase in the level of technology, a 1.05% rise in output in a home country, and a 1.75% increase in output in the foreign country. The effects of lifting exchange controls are considerably larger for countries (such as Brazil and Malaysia) that enforce more severe restrictions.

Last, we analyze the long-term effects of temporary exchange control policies. Many countries impose exchange controls for short periods of time. Here we show that even imposing exchange controls for one year has long-lasting effects on MNE operations. The FDI position is depressed for at least 5 years, and the present discounted value loss in output at the subsidiary is at least 31% of the steady state value. For developing countries who need the inflow of capital, this illustrates that what they consider temporary controls in fact have long lasting and large effects.

The remainder of the chapter is structured as follows. The next section describes the most important recent capital control episodes. Section 3 summarizes the potential costs and benefits of capital controls and updates the reader on the recent developments in the capital controls literature. Section 4 presents the model; Section 5 outlines the solution method; Section 6 discusses model calibration. Section 7 presents model simulations for various exchange control policies; there we see the effects—short-term, long-run, and in steady state—of these policies. Section 8 quantifies the effects of exchange controls; concluding remarks are in Section 9.

CAPITAL CONTROL EPISODES

This section offers a brief historical description of how emerging economies implement capital control policies. The most frequently debated capital control episodes are Brazil in 1993–1997, Chile in 1991–1998, and Malaysia after 1997. Other important experiences include Columbia in 1993–1998, Romania in 1996–1997, Russia after 1998, Spain in 1992, Thailand in 1995–1998, and Venezuela in 1994–1996.[2]

After liberalizing capital flows in 1987–1992 by exempting foreign investors from capital gain taxes, Brazil started to tighten its capital controls on short-term capital flows once again in 1993. The objective was to introduce a larger spread between domestic and international interest rates in order to, in turn, control the aggregate demand and inflationary pressures. Brazilian capital controls were implemented also in an attempt to shift the composition of inflows toward longer-term investments. Examples of the specific implementation of capital controls in Brazil include an increase in the minimum average amortization terms for loans from 30 to 36 months and the income tax reimbursement period from 60 to 96 months. After another brief relaxation of capital restrictions in 1995, Brazil raised the tax rates on certain capital flows again in 1996. Thus, Brazil is the most prominent example of the on-off-type capital control policies.

Table 1. Chile: Most important changes in exchange arrangements during the 1990s

Date	Policy Change
April 19, 1990	New regulations liberalizing foreign exchange market operations and allowing any person to conduct freely foreign exchange transactions were introduced.
June 25, 1990	Individuals and legal entities, domiciled and resident abroad, had access to the official exchange market to remit abroad proceeds from the sale of stocks of foreign-owned corporations domiciled in Chile, as well as dividends and profits accruing from such stocks.
June 5, 1991	A reserve requirement of 20% was imposed on new foreign borrowings.
July 11, 1991	The 20% reserve requirement was extended to existing credits, except for credits with maturity of less than 6 months.
May 29, 1992	The reserve requirement on foreign currency deposits at commercial banks was increased to 30% from 20%.
August 18, 1992	Reserve requirement on external credit inflows was increased to 30% from 20%.
November 30, 1994	The ceiling on foreign exchange positions held by commercial banks was eliminated.
March 27, 1997	Foreign financial investments for amounts of less than US$100,000 were exempt from the cash reserve requirement.
April 16, 1997	The repatriation of proceeds from investments abroad, including profits, made through the formal market was exempted from the 30% reserve requirement.
October 13, 1997	The minimum amount for FDI to be exempted from the 30% nonremunerated reserve requirement was raised to US$1 million.
June 25, 1998	The unremunerated reserve requirement on capital inflows was lowered to 10% from 30%.
September 16, 1998	The unremunerated reserve requirement on capital inflows was eliminated.
May 4, 2000	The 1-year withholding requirement for foreign investments was eliminated for certain types of investments.

Source: International Monetary Fund, "Exchange Arrangements and Exchange Restrictions," Annual Reports

Table 1 summarizes the major changes in capital restrictions in Chile. Chilean authorities imposed restrictions on capital flows in 1991 in the form of an unremunerated reserve requirement. This measure required foreign lenders (with the exception of those providing trade credits) to deposit 20% of their loans in a non–interest-bearing account at the Central Bank of Chile for a period of 1 year. Starting in 1992, short-term capital movements were controlled through a 30%-reserve requirement to make non-interest-bearing deposits at the Central Bank. Chile reduced the requirements to 10% in June 1998, and subsequently lifted all controls in September of that year. The imposition of controls on the inflows of short-term capital, while attracting long-term funds, is claimed to have stabilized the Chilean economy.

The most significant changes in Malaysian capital controls since 1990 are reported in Table 2. Notably, most capital restrictions were introduced in September 1998. To a certain extent, the restrictions became milder in the subsequent years. The literature's emerging consensus is that Malaysian capital controls were largely unsuccessful (Edwards, 1999). It is thought that restricting capital outflows greatly increases the foreign investors' skepticism about possible future restrictions and thus leads to more uncertainty, volatility and capital flight. However, Edison and Reinhart (2001) find that Malaysian controls were in line with the priors of what controls are intended to achieve: greater interest rate and exchange rate stability.

Table 2. Malaysia: Most important changes in exchange arrangements during the 1990s

Date	Policy Change
November 9, 1990	Applications from nonresidents and nonresident-controlled companies to obtain any domestic financing solely for property acquisition (i.e., not for productive purposes or tourism promotion) would not be approved by the Controller of Foreign Exchange.
November 1, 1992	The guidelines on foreign equity capital ownership were liberalized. For example, companies exporting at least 80% of their production were no longer subject to any equity requirements.
February 7, 1994	Residents were prohibited to sell to nonresidents all forms of private debt securities with a remaining maturity of one year or less.
September 1, 1998	(1) A limit of RM 10,000 equivalent on the export of foreign currency by residents was introduced. Nonresidents' foreign currency export is limited to the amount brought into Malaysia. (2) A requirement to settle all imports and exports in foreign currency was introduced. (3) Nonresident sellers of Malaysian securities were required to hold on to their ringgit proceeds for at least one year. (4) Domestic credit facilities to nonresident correspondent banks and nonresident stockbroking companies, and obtaining ringgit facilities by residents from any nonresident individual were prohibited.
February 15, 1999	(1) Foreign direct investors were allowed to repatriate the proceeds from portfolio investments, subject to paying a levy. (2) A graduated system of exit taxes on capital and capital gains was introduced.
September 21, 1999	Nonresidents were allowed to repatriate proceeds from sales of securities after paying a 10% exit levy.
February 1, 2001	Nonresident sellers of Malaysian securities were allowed to repatriate profits free of levy if the profits are repatriated more than 12 months from the month the profits are realized.

Source: International Monetary Fund, "Exchange Arrangements and Exchange Restrictions," Annual Reports

BENEFITS AND RISKS OF CAPITAL CONTROLS

This section attempts to advance our understanding of reasons for and causes of establishing capital restrictions. We justify the relevance of capital controls on the basis of markets' incompleteness, provide an extensive review of the current literature, examine the pros and cons of capital control policies, and delineate the focal points of debate among researchers and policymakers. As will become evident in the ensuing subsections, the debate about the virtues and costs of capital controls is as heated as ever.

Financial (In)stability and Capital Controls

In their summary of the theoretical literature on capital liberalization, Eichengreen et al. (1999) survey the possibility that resources can be allocated more efficiently under capital restrictions than with perfect capital mobility. Asymmetric information, goes the argument, often results in suboptimal social welfare. If risk is not efficiently allocated, adverse selection and moral hazard can, at the extreme, lead to costly financial crises. Effectively, capital market liberalization can subject the economies to greater risks without offering sufficient benefits in terms of higher economic growth (Stiglitz, 2002).

Hardly anyone will dispute the fact that in a frictionless world there would be no need for capital controls. In this subsection we argue that the existence of incomplete markets could justify the imposition of capital restrictions.[3]

Freer capital mobility is associated with an increased difficulty to monitor investors' risk taking (Le Fort & Budnevich, 1998). When information is imperfect—not an unreasonable assumption by any standards—free capital mobility leads to financial crises through encouraging excessive risk-taking and moral hazard (Ulan, 2002). To this end, capital controls can limit the inflow of capital and change its composition toward longer maturities. This should be viewed as an important achievement of capital control policies, particularly in light of Cole and Kehoe's (2000) finding that lengthening the maturity of debt can significantly reduce the likelihood of a debt crisis.[4] Empirically, Calvo (1998) uses the basic accounting identities to examine the link between financial crises and sudden restrictions on capital flows; he finds that equity and long-term bond financing may help avoid a crisis.

Campion and Neumann (2003) analyze theoretically and empirically the effects of capital controls on the maturity composition, as well as the volume, of capital flows. They developed a model of asymmetric information with an explicit trade-off between debt- and equity-financed capital. Campion and Neumann's numerical computations and the model's application to the experiences of seven Latin American economies in the 1990s lead them to conclude that capital controls can, indeed, shift the composition of capital inflows from debt to equity[5] and from short-term toward longer-term maturities. The results of the fixed-effect panel regressions reported by Campion and Neumann suggest that the compositional effects of capital controls can be quite significant.

The argument of information asymmetry is elegantly formalized by McKinnon and Pill (1997) in their theoretical paper on economic liberalizations. In the context of the simplified Fisherian two-period model of borrowing and investing, McKinnon and Pill compellingly argue that during economic reforms, the free capital market can malfunction because of high uncertainty about future payoffs. It is this potential market inefficiency that could be remedied by capital controls. McKinnon and Pill remind us that many countries—both developing and industrialized—can be prone to excessive and unsustainable foreign borrowing that could lead to a sharp withdrawal of foreign assets and an economic collapse (e.g., Mexico in 1994–1995 and Argentina in late 1990s).

Perfect capital mobility tempts the developing countries to "borrow" themselves into a debt crisis. Under such circumstances, capital controls can help achieve more efficient borrowing and investment outcomes. In the words of Stiglitz (2002), "the period immediately following liberalization is one in which risk is particularly marked, as markets often respond to the new opportunities in an overly exuberant manner" (p. 224).

In their more recent work, McKinnon and Pill (1999) further extend the Fisher model to examine how different exchange rate regimes influence macroeconomic stability when moral hazard is prevalent in the banking system. The authors argue that capital controls make the economy more immune to speculative attacks and less exposed to the real economic consequences of such attacks. However, policymakers should be wary of "bad" exchange rate pegs that can exacerbate the problem of overborrowing.

McKinnon and Pill's papers summarized above exemplify how market failures and frictions render capital controls helpful in improving upon a free-market allocation of resources. The fact that some state-contingent claims cannot be purchased constitutes a significant departure from the Arrow-Debreu economy. To offer another example, a monetary authority cannot defend national currency in all states of the world. Specifically, if currency speculators act irrationally (due to imperfect information) and frantically sell the currency, a monetary authority might choose to impose exchange restrictions. Likewise, since a monetary authority cannot possibly go bankrupt, it could resort to capital controls to preclude this constraint from becoming binding.

It should also be noted that governments and monetary authorities tend to concern themselves with maximizing national—not the world's—welfare. The absence of policy coordination violates the First Welfare Theorem, and so capital controls have a potential to offer the second-best alternative and improve the competitive markets outcome.

Frenkel, Nickel, Schmidt and Stadtmann (2002) study capital controls in a modified version of the Dornbusch model of exchange rate overshooting while explicitly considering market microstructure aspects of the foreign exchange market. They find that capital controls can reduce volatility of exchange rates in the wake of a monetary shock.[6] Empirically, Edison and Warnock (2003) find that capital account liberalizations lead to the volatility of net portfolio equity flows.

Researchers and policymakers debate whether capital restrictions can help to ensure financial stability (e.g., Edwards, 1999; Errunza, 2001; Fischer, 1998; Massad, 1998). Free capital mobility, and especially short-term speculative money, is often associated with higher economic volatility and risk, which makes long-term investment less attractive (Stiglitz, 2002). As was argued previously, establishing capital controls could potentially prevent financial and currency crises (Edwards, 1999). Capital restrictions can be a particularly attractive policy tool for developing countries that face higher economic volatility—and limited ability to manage it—compared to developed economies (Stiglitz, 2002).

We acknowledge that market volatility *per se* is not destabilizing and reflects only preferences and stochastic properties of the fundamentals as well as the ways in which beliefs are formed. However, in an economy where some states of the world are noninsurable, speculative attacks can pose serious problems. With higher financial volatility, lending to firms and banks might be reduced in an attempt to cope with additional risks and prevent bankruptcies and failures. Also, the costs of portfolio adjustments (usually modeled as quadratic) can be substantial under high volatility. Finally, high volatility increases the probability of extremes, such as a depletion of foreign reserves and, thus, inability of the monetary authorities to conduct desired currency interventions.

Other Benefits of Capital Controls

Acknowledging the literature's tension between two extremes—complete financial integration and financial isolation—this and the next sections survey the benefits and costs of capital controls (over and above the theoretical relevance of capital restrictions offered in the previous subsection).[7] Passionate arguments in favor of capital controls date back to at least the 1970s (in particular, Tobin's 1974 seminal work). In his presidential address to the members of the Eastern Economic Association, Tobin (1978) writes,

National economies and national governments are not capable of adjusting to massive movements of funds across the foreign exchanges, without real hardship and without significant sacrifice of the objectives of national economic policy with respect to

employment, output, and inflation. Specifically, the mobility of financial capital limits viable differences among national interest rates and thus severely restricts the ability of central banks and governments to pursue monetary and fiscal policies appropriate to their internal economies. Likewise, speculation on exchange rates . . . have serious and frequently painful real internal economic consequences. Domestic policies are relatively powerless to escape them or offset them. (p. 154)

Thus Tobin viewed excessive international mobility of private financial capital as a big threat to national economies. To alleviate this threat, Tobin proposed a tax on foreign exchange transactions, a tax that could reduce destabilizing currency and other speculations in international financial markets. That proposition was one of the first attempts to compellingly vindicate capital controls as a means to stabilize a faltering economy.[8] Tobin himself predicted difficulties with administering such a tax:

Doubtless there would be difficulties of administration and enforcement, doubtless there would be ingenious patterns of evasion. But since these will not be costless either, the main purpose of the plan will not be lost. (p. 159)

He also predicted that distortions and allocation costs of capital controls will be small compared to the "world macroeconomic costs."

While many researchers are sympathetic to the idea of Tobin taxes (e.g., Eichengreen & Wyplosz, 1993), the taxes would have to be imposed by all countries simultaneously, or they would be ineffective (Edwards, 1999).[9] The second-best alternative to Tobin taxes is, clearly, imposing capital controls by individual countries without regard to coordination of such policies with others.

It is often argued that restrictions on capital flows help to maintain the stability of the international financial system: Speculative attacks on national currencies are less likely with the controls in place. Establishing capital controls is usually perceived as a good remedy in coping with financial and currency crises (Edwards, 1999)—especially because (short-term) capital flows tend to be strongly procyclical. Capital controls in the form of taxes on funds remitted abroad or dual exchange rates help to reduce the balance of payments deficit through preserving a stock of foreign reserves that can be used to pursue monetary sterilization policies. Indeed, capital account restrictions can decrease the vulnerability of the national economy to dangerous swings in market sentiment (Fischer, 1998; Rogoff, 2002) and help to isolate the national economy from the irrational behavior on the part of investors and from financial disturbances originated in other countries (Edwards, 1999; Massad, 1998). Stiglitz (2002) strongly believes that short-term "hot" money was partially responsible for the onset and the propagation of the Asian crisis.[10]

Eichengreen (1999) views controls on capital *inflows* as potent stabilization policies. Between 1991 and 1998, Chile forced short-term foreign investors to deposit a fraction of their funds with the Central Bank at no interest. That, in effect, was a tax on capital inflows, a tax that, according to the policy's supporters, had helped stabilize the Chilean economy. Edison and Reinhart (2001) conclude that in the case of Malaysia, capital controls helped the country to achieve exchange rate stability. On the other hand, the authors report no significant effect of capital controls on macroeconomic conditions in Thailand in 1997 and Brazil in 1999.

Cordella (2003) uses Diamond and Dybvig's (1983) model to show that foreigners can find it profitable to invest in a developing economy only in the presence of taxes on short-term capital inflows. In the context of that model, it is the reduced vulnerability of emerging markets to financial crises that may attract long-term investors. Capital controls on short-term capital can prevent bank runs and, consequently, result in higher expected returns on (long-term) investments. This reasoning is in line with Spada's (2001) argument that financial fragility of the banking sector dramatically increases the probability of a financial crisis, and that capital controls can reduce the short-term (external) indebtedness and thus improve the soundness of the financial system.

Stiglitz (2002) points out that borrowers and lenders are not alone in experiencing the effects of capital flows. Small businesses and workers in developing countries experienced particularly painful consequences of capital market liberalization manifested in lower incomes and higher insecurity. Such externality, therefore, warrants government intervention. Yashiv (1998) uses a small, open economy model with optimizing agents to study the intertemporal aspects of capital control policies. Capital controls are found to significantly enlarge the set of potential outcomes of agents' intratemporal asset allocation and intertemporal consumption patterns.

Bajo-Rubio and Sosvilla-Rivero (2001) uses a portfolio-balance model to simulate policy experiments in Spain during the period of 1986–1990. The authors conclude that capital controls would have avoided a net capital outflow amounting to an average quarterly increase in net foreign assets of 4%. Razin and Yuen (1995) extend the (stochastic) Mundell-Fleming model to study how the transmission of fiscal and trade shocks under different degrees of capital mobility may alter the Phillips Curve. The authors show that capital controls reduce the employment and output variations, but only at the expense of bigger variations in inflation rates.

Exchange rate instability and potential exchange rate appreciation are of great concern among policymakers and academics. Under flexible exchange rates, capital inflows lead to a higher exchange rate, thus making the country's exports less competitive in the international markets (Stiglitz, 2002). Capital controls are argued to be efficient in mitigating real exchange rate appreciation resulting from capital inflows, thus helping reduce current account deficits. Often, capital account liberalization leads to capital flight, which explains why national governments are so reluctant to abolish capital restrictions. Last but not least, capital controls can help the government to tax income more effectively through maintaining the domestic tax base and retaining domestic savings (Alesina, Grilli, & Milesi-Ferretti, 1994).

Risks of Capital Controls

The flip side of imposing exchange controls is the impediment to global financial integration. Obstfeld and Rogoff (1996) elegantly argue that, similar to the benefits of free trade in goods, there exist gains from free trade in (financial) capital.[11] Also, by raising domestic interest rates, capital controls make it more costly for firms to acquire capital domestically, especially for small and medium-sized firms (Edwards, 2002), and with tight restrictions, the ability of the firms to attract additional financing from abroad at a cheaper rate is severely limited (Eichengreen et al., 1999).

To add to the discussion of the real effects of capital controls, Mckenzie (2001) uses cross-sectional and panel regressions to estimate the effects of capital controls on economic growth and growth convergence. He finds that the restrictions on capital mobility have a sizable negative impact on both growth and the rate of conditional growth convergence. Combining the Dornbusch exchange rate overshooting model and the theory of capital stock formation, Frenkel et al. (2002) show that capital controls usually lead to a higher (perceived) risk associated with investing in a country. As a result, investment and the level of capital stock will be lower, which will have a negative impact on output.[12]

Latin American countries that imposed capital controls in the wake of debt crises (Argentina, Brazil, Mexico, Peru) have experienced negative output growth, high inflation and unemployment. This is due in part to the severity of the crises, and partly to the conventional wisdom that controls on capital outflows discourage macroeconomic and financial reforms, and lead to corruption, nationalization and expropriation (Dornbusch & Edwards, 1991; World Bank, 1993). In a study of Western European economies over the second half of the 20th century, Voth (2003) finds that restrictions on capital mobility in the years preceding the collapse of the Bretton Woods system led to a higher cost of equity finance and, correspondingly, had substantial negative effects on stock returns and economic growth. That capital controls are strongly associated with a higher cost of capital was also reported by Edison and Warnock (2003) for Latin American and Asian countries.

Eichengreen et al. (1999) remind us that international capital mobility enables households, firms and countries to trade intertemporally and, thus, helps smooth consumption over time. Further, through portfolio diversification and foreign direct investment, households and firms can reduce vulnerability to domestic economic disturbances (Fischer, 1998; Le Fort & Budnevich, 1998).

In a speech delivered at a seminar in Hong Kong, Stanley Fischer (1998), First Deputy Managing Director of the IMF, outlined the benefits of capital account liberalization. Recognizing that the European experience of 1993, the Latin American experience of 1995, and the Asian crisis of late 1990s raised the issue of the riskiness of capital account liberalization, Fischer claims that the benefits outweigh the potential costs of capital controls. Noting that most of the developed nations rarely use restrictions on capital mobility, he proposes an amendment to the IMF's Articles of Agreement that would ensure an orderly capital account liberalization.

Controls on capital *outflows* are generally not viewed favorably in the extant literature. For instance, Edwards (1989) and Edwards and Santaella (1993) find that, prior to many currency crises, private companies find ways to overcome (mild) capital outflow restrictions that are imposed as a preventive measure. Cuddington (1987) and Kaminsky and Reinhart (1999) also find that controls on capital outflows are usually followed by capital flight, which defeats the purpose of imposing such restrictions in the first place. Further, such policies may give a false sense of security and thus encourage both the authorities and market participants to engage in excessive risk-taking and moral hazard.

Edwards (1989) reports that half of the post-crisis countries have failed to have a significant effect on the real exchange rate or the balance of payments through capital control tightening. In addition, in two thirds of the countries under consideration, capital controls resulted in slow output growth. In sum, the debate on whether the restrictions on capital outflows are effective is still open.

Regardless of the rationale behind imposing capital controls, the actual implementation is usually politically driven and, as such, leads to corruption (Rogoff, 2002). For example, Johnson and Mitton (2003) observed that capital controls imposed in Malaysia in September 1998 benefited, in terms of the disproportionate gain in market value, companies that had strong ties to Prime Minister Mahathir. Conversely, Malaysian capital controls hurt firms that were linked to the Deputy Prime Minister Anwar, who was fired that same month.[13] Thus, Malaysian capital controls were a means to support favored firms at the expense of the firms that did not have strong political connections.

One frequently voiced concern is that restrictions on capital mobility have a tendency to be in place longer than necessary given the current macroeconomic conditions. Ulan (2002) stresses that capital controls can be justified only as a temporary measure and should not be viewed as a substitute for reforms and sound macroeconomic policies. Using a dynamic general equilibrium model, Reinhart and Smith (2002) calculate the welfare costs of procrastination in lifting the restrictions on capital inflows to be large enough to offset any potential benefits of capital controls.

Tamirisa (1999) offers another perspective on capital controls. Using the gravity-equation framework, she considers the relationship between the degree of capital mobility and the volume of trade. Theoretically, capital controls can affect trade through the domestic prices of imports, transaction costs, and the level and volatility of exchange rates. Arguing that the theoretical prediction about the effect of capital controls on trade is uncertain, Tamirisa finds empirically that capital controls significantly reduce exports into developing countries and thus represent a significant barrier to trade.

It is rarely disputed that in order for capital control policies to be effective in preventing real exchange rate appreciation and allowing for a greater autonomy of monetary policy (among other objectives) capital controls need to drive a measurable wedge between domestic and international rates of return on short-term financial instruments. Herrera and Valdés (2001) study a model of arbitrage to quantify the upper bound on the interest rate differential in the presence of Chilean-type capital restrictions. In their model, which allows for an endogenously determined investment horizon, the estimated effect of capital controls on interest rate spreads is considerably smaller than the impact computed in models with a fixed investment horizon. That capital controls might not introduce as sizable a distinction between domestic and international interest rates as previously thought certainly makes one very skeptical about the overall potency of the restrictions on capital mobility.

Regardless of how the logic of the arguments in favor of capital controls (outlined in the previous section) compares with the soundness of the counterarguments (presented in this section), financial openness may be inevitable from a pragmatic standpoint. Aizenman (2004) finds a significant positive correlation between financial and trade openness, contemporaneously and at a lag, for both developing and Organization for Economic Co-operation and Development (OECD) countries. To account for this observation, Aizenman constructs a model in which greater trade openness increases the cost of enforcing capital controls and reduces their effectiveness, thereby giving rise to the pragmatic case for financial reforms. Therefore, abandoning capital restrictions may simply be a by-product of trade integration.

THE MODEL

We consider an MNE with two plants: a headquarters in the United States and a subsidiary in a foreign country. The MNE acts as a single entity whose objective is to maximize the present value of current and future profits in terms of the headquarters' currency. To do this, the MNE decides each period how many innovations to produce and share across its plants, the capital stocks of each plant financed by debt or equity, and the amount of funds to remit from the subsidiary.

Each period the headquarters produces innovations that it shares with the subsidiary. Let $L_t(R_{t-1}, R_t)$ denote the labor demand function of the headquarters to produce R_t innovations at date t when the accumulated stock of innovations is R_{t-1}. $L_t(R_{t-1}, R_t)$ is assumed to be twice continuously (C^2) differentiable, increasing and strictly convex in R_t and non-increasing and concave in R_{t-1}. This functional form allows for many interpretations including that past innovations become obsolete ($\frac{\partial L_t(\bullet)}{\partial R_{t-1}} = 0$). Labor costs are $w_t L_t(R_{t-1}, R_t)$, where w_t is the wage rate in the developed country at date t.

The MNE starts a period with a total level of capital stock $(k_t + b_t)$ at the headquarters and $(k_t^* + b_t^*)$ at the subsidiary. k_t and k_t^* denote the equity position of the firm at the headquarters and the subsidiary, respectively; similarly, b_t and b_t^* represent the part of capital financed by debt. After production, k_t, b_t, k_t^* and b_t^* all depreciate by $\delta \times 100\%$. Prior to the end of date t, the MNE chooses an equity position and debt-financed capital to take into the next period. There are no restrictions on the inflow of capital from the headquarters to the subsidiary. The MNE purchases or sells capital at a price of p_{k_t} ($p_{k_t}^*$) in the developed (developing) country. Further, r_t (r_t^*) is the cost of borrowing (or, equivalently, the opportunity cost of capital) in the developed (developing) country. The financial, or underwriting, costs associated with debt-financed capital (but not with the equity position) are given by $g(b_t)$, where $g(b_t)$ is increasing in b_t.[14]

The total capital stock is subject to the Hayashi-type adjustment costs, $\varphi(\xi_t, \xi_{t+1})$, where $\xi_t = k_t + b_t$ (and similarly for the subsidiary). The adjustment cost function is assumed to be C^2 differentiable, decreasing and strictly concave in ξ_t and increasing and strictly convex in ξ_{t+1}. That is, $\frac{\partial \varphi(\bullet)}{\partial \xi_t} < 0$, $\frac{\partial \varphi(\bullet)}{\partial \xi_{t+1}} > 0$, $\frac{\partial^2 \varphi(\bullet)}{\partial \xi_t^2} < 0$, and $\frac{\partial^2 \varphi(\bullet)}{\partial \xi_{t+1}^2} > 0$. Convex adjustment costs ensure that (i) the value function is C^2 differentiable, (ii) the optimal policy function is C^1 differentiable, and (iii) capital stock does not instantaneously adjust to the steady state.

Output of the plant is produced, using innovations and capital, by $R_t f(k_t + b_t)$ and $R_t f(k_t^* + b_t^*)$, where $f(k_t + b_t)$ and $f(k_t^* + b_t^*)$ are the physical production of the good. The physical production function is assumed twice continuously differentiable, increasing and strictly concave in $(k_t + b_t)$. Each plant sells its output in the international market. The headquarters receives a price of p_{y_t} and the subsidiary receives a price of $p_{y_t}^*$, in the developed and developing country currency, respectively. We assume $p_{y_t} = e_t p_{y_t}^*$, where e_t is the current exchange rate of home to foreign currency (i.e., the law of one price holds).

The price of the MNE's output, p_{y_t}, could be given in a competitive market. However, more realistically, p_{y_t} depends on the MNE's output. Typically we find MNEs operating in industries with high concentration indices. Anecdotal evidence on concentration ratio and markups suggest that this is close to reality. However, if one prefers, we could assume a competitive market and the theoretical analysis remains unchanged. We assume the MNE operates as an international monopolist and, therefore, the revenue function satisfies the standard assumptions of the Cournot literature.[15]

In this chapter we consider restrictions on capital outflows.[16] Any funds the MNE remits from the subsidiary to its headquarters go through the developing country's central bank. If there are no exchange controls, then the central bank converts the subsidiary's remittance, C_t, to the developed country's currency at the exchange rate e_t. The headquarters receives e_tC_t. If the central bank imposes controls, then it either holds all of the subsidiary's remittance or converts part of the remittance and holds the remainder with no interest accrued on the amount being held at the bank. This type of capital controls is widely used by the developing countries. In essence, such an unremunerated reserve requirement is equivalent to a tax on capital outflows. When the MNE decides how much to remit from, and reinvest in, the subsidiary, it knows the remittance may encounter exchange controls, but it does not learn the severity of the control until it relinquishes the funds to the central bank.

We model various forms of exchange controls: on-off policies and policies with a constant threat of exchange controls. Let ρ_t^* represent repatriation restrictions at date t, $\rho_t^* \in [0,1]$. $\rho_t^* = 1$ means there is no repatriation restriction and $\rho_t^* = 0$ means there is no conversion at date t. Once the subsidiary relinquishes C_t to the central bank, ρ_t^* becomes known. The headquarters thus receives $\rho_t^* e_t C_t$.

The MNE's maximization problem is written as the following dynamic program[17,18]:

$$
\begin{aligned}
& V\left(k_t, k_t^*, b_t, b_t^*, R_{t-1}; C_{t-1}, \rho_{t-1}^*, I_t\right) = \\
& \max_{k_{t+1}, b_{t+1}, k_{t+1}^*, b_{t+1}^*, R_t} \; E_t\{p_{y_t} R_t f\left(k_t + b_t\right) \\
& -p_{k_t}\left[\left(k_{t+1} + b_{t+1}\right) - (1-\delta)\left(k_t + b_t\right) + \varphi\left(k_t + b_t, k_{t+1} + b_{t+1}\right)\right] \\
& -g\left(b_t\right) - w_t L_t\left(R_{t-1}, R_t\right) \\
& +\rho_t^* e_t C_t + \beta V\left(k_{t+1}, k_{t+1}^*, b_{t+1}, b_{t+1}^*, R_t; C_t, \rho_t^*, I_{t+1}\right) \mid C_{t-1}, \rho_{t-1}^*, I_t\}
\end{aligned}
\tag{1}
$$

subject to $k_{t+1} \geq 0$, $b_{t+1} \geq 0$, $k_{t+1}^* \geq 0$, and $b_{t+1}^* \geq 0$, where

$$
\begin{aligned}
& C_t = p_{y_t}^* R_t f\left(k_t^* + b_t^*\right) \\
& -p_{k_t}^*\left[\left(k_{t+1}^* + b_{t+1}^*\right) - (1-\delta)\left(k_t^* + b_t^*\right) + \varphi\left(k_t^* + b_t^*, k_{t+1}^* + b_{t+1}^*\right)\right] \\
& -g\left(b_t^*\right) + \left(1 - \rho_t^*\right) C_{t-1};
\end{aligned}
$$

$I_t = \{p_{k_t}, p^*_{k_t}, r_t, r^*_t, e_t, w_t\}$ is information about this period's wage rate, prices of capital, interest rates and exchange rate, and E_t is the expectations operator conditioned on the information of this period, as well as last period's repatriation restriction. This period the MNE makes expectations of I_{t+1} and ρ^*_t. The information set can conceivably include other variables that help predict exchange controls such as trade balances and black market premia.

Highlighted in the above framework is the fact that the MNE starts the period knowing the government's last period repatriation policy. Using last period's restriction, the MNE makes expectations about today's repatriation restriction. The expected value of the repatriation restriction affects how much capital the MNE invests in each plant, borrowing in each plant and the level of innovations produced by the headquarters. This framework links changes in a government's repatriation policy with changes in an MNE's operations.

More accurately, define $\theta = \rho^*_t + \beta\left(1-\rho^*_t\right)\rho^*_{t+1}\frac{e_{t+1}}{e_t} + \beta^2\left(1-\rho^*_t\right)\left(1-\rho^*_{t+1}\right)\rho^*_{t+2}\cdot\frac{e_{t+2}}{e_t}+\cdots$. Then $e_t E(\theta)$ is the present discounted value of a unit of foreign currency remitted at date t (today) to the home country. Exchange controls are costly in that the MNE must wait for remittance (β). They become even more costly when there is a depreciation of the local currency ($\frac{e_{t+1}}{e_t}<1$). In choosing k_{t+1}, b_{t+1}, k^*_{t+1}, b^*_{t+1} and R_t to maximize the expected present discounted value of the stream of profits, the firm considers the effects of θ_t (on marginal costs) and θ_{t+1} (on marginal revenue).[19]

SOLUTION METHOD

To study the steady-state properties of the model, we use the first-order necessary conditions for maximization. We set $k_t = k_{t+1} = k_{t+2} = k_{ss}$, $b_t = b_{t+1} = b_{t+2} = b_{ss}$, etc., and solve for the steady-state equity position of the firm at the headquarters and the subsidiary (k_{ss} and k^*_{ss}), debt-financed capital at home and abroad (b_{ss} and b^*_{ss}), and innovations produced at headquarters (R_{ss}).

Our solution of the transitional dynamics is based on the dynamic programming method. We opt for the value function iteration as our solution technique since alternative numerical methods, such as Judd's (1992) projection methods (used in Ihrig, 2000), perform poorly in models with more than two state variables. We first set up a grid for k, k^*, b, b^*, R, k', $k^{*\prime}$, b', $b^{*\prime}$, R' and calculate the return functions W for all possible combinations of the present and future state variables.[20] Using dynamic programming, we then iterate until $|V - V'| < \varepsilon$. If, in any given iteration, this condition is not satisfied, we proceed in several steps: (i) set $V = V'$; (ii) inside the k, k^*, b, b^*, R loops reset V_{old} to a large in absolute value negative number; (iii) inside all of the loops calculate $V_{new} = W + \beta V'$; if $V_{new} > V_{old}$, reset $V_{old} = V_{new}$, $V' = V_{new}$, and assign $k'_{optimal} = k'$, $b'_{optimal} = b'$, $k^{*\prime}_{optimal} = k^{*\prime}$, $b^{*\prime}_{optimal} = b^{*\prime}$, $R'_{optimal} = R'$. The process is terminated when V is within ε from V'.

At this point in the program, the four-dimensional arrays $k'_{optimal}$, ..., $R'_{optimal}$ are capable of answering questions of the following type: If $k = x_1$, $k^* = x_2$, $b = x_3$, $b^* = x_4$, and $R = x_5$ (where x_i can be any point in the grid), what are the optimal values of k', $k^{*\prime}$, b', $b^{*\prime}$, and R'? We start the transitions of debt- and equity-financed capital stocks and innovations by choosing the date-0 values of the variables and finding the corresponding date-1 values. Then we feed these new values back into the matrices contained all optimal values to find the date-2 values, and so on.[21]

CALIBRATION

We calibrate the model described in Section 2 to the average US FDI abroad that is reported in the *Survey of Current Business* and *US Direct Investment Abroad: Operations of US Parent Companies and Their Foreign Affiliates, Preliminary 1998 Estimates* (US Department of Commerce, 2000). The latter publication provides statistics on financial operations of nonbank US MNE's and their nonbank foreign subsidiaries for the fiscal year 1998. Thus, our model reproduces US MNEs' FDI and technology flows to their foreign subsidiaries in 1998.

To parameterize the model, we assume the following functional forms for the equations:

- The production function: $f(k+b) = A(k+b)^{\alpha}$.
- The inverse demand: $p_{y_t} = h\left[R_t f(k_t+b_t) + R_t f(k_t^*+b_t^*)\right] = \mu + v \cdot R_t \cdot \left[f(k_t+b_t) + f(k_t^*+b_t^*)\right]$ with $\mu > 0$ and $v < 0$. Since we assume that the MNE is an international monopolist, the price is a function of the output of both plants.
- The adjustment cost function: $\varphi(k_t+b_t, k_{t+1}+b_{t+1}) = \eta\left[(k_{t+1}+b_{t+1}) - (1-\delta)(k_t+b_t)\right]^2$, and similar for the subsidiary. The adjustment cost function is quadratic in investment; this is the same function used by Abel and Eberly (1997), Mendoza and Uribe (1996) and Ihrig (2000). The function makes it costly for the MNE to make large alterations in the plants' capital stocks and borrowing.
- Underwriting costs associated with debt-financed capital: $g(b_t) = a_b b_t$ and $g(b_t^*) = a_b b_t^*$.
- We also set $R_t - \delta_R R_{t-1} = L_t^{\gamma}$, so the labor demand function is $L_t = (R_t - \delta_R R_{t-1})^{1/\gamma}$. We assume that past innovations depreciate at the rate of $\delta_R = 0.1$ annually, which is in line with the idea that it becomes increasingly difficult to maintain the productivity level of capital unless the parts and software are updated periodically.

For β, δ, α we adopt parameter values that are standard in the macroeconomic literature. Further, by assuming a constant-returns-to-scale production function, we obtain $\gamma = 1 - \alpha$. In the rest of the calibration, we assign the values to a_b, μ, v and η, so that the model matches the observed economy. To achieve this, we solve the five optimality conditions (with respect to k', $k^{*\prime}$, b', $b^{*\prime}$, and R'), along with the supplementary equations (that define capital, labor and output) for a_b, μ, v, η, k, k', k'', b, b', b'', b^*, $b^{*\prime}$ and $b^{*\prime\prime}$ to reproduce the average 1998 US Benchmark Survey data.

SIMULATIONS

The theoretical priors about the effects of capital controls are ambiguous. For example, tightening capital restrictions can lead to a decrease in industrial production (due to lack of financing if restrictions on capital inflows are enforced) or an increase in output (due to developed competitiveness of domestic industries). It, therefore, appears that the qualitative impact of capital controls on the major variables of interest—not to mention the quantitative response—is largely an empirical question. This section highlights how key variables of the model, such as the subsidiary's FDI position (k^*), the headquarters' capital stock (k), technology (R), and outputs at headquarters and subsidiary (y and y^*) react to various exchange control policies. We consider both constant exchange control policies (such as those of US and Africa) and on-off policies (such as those enforced by Brazil).[22]

Constant Exchange Controls

Studying the transition of capital stocks and outputs allows us to explore both short-term and long-term effects of exchange controls. In Figure 1 we consider three transitions: for the economy with no exchange controls ($\theta = 1$), with relatively low exchange controls (the MNE sees 70% of the subsidiary's remitted funds, $\theta = 0.7$), and relatively severe controls (the MNE sees only 30% of the subsidiary's funds, $\theta = 0.3$). No matter the level of exchange controls, we start with the same low values of capital stocks at the headquarters and subsidiary ($k = k^* = 300$) and simulate how k and k^* evolve.

Figures 1a and 1b illustrate the transitional dynamics of the headquarters and subsidiary capital stocks for the three exchange control experiments. When $\theta = 1$ (no exchange controls), capital stocks are equal across plants in any period during the transition. When $\theta < 1$ (exchange controls are enforced), there is a wedge between the headquarters' and subsidiary's capital stocks. Focusing on Figure 1a, we observe that the headquarters has a higher rate of convergence the more severe the exchange controls. However, the steady state value of capital is greater the more mild the restriction. Between these two opposing effects, the latter dominates, so it takes longer for the headquarters to reach the steady state if restrictions are relatively mild. The situation in the subsidiary is reversed: as Figure 1b indicates, the subsidiary's capital stock converges more rapidly to the steady state for mild exchange controls. However, this effect is more than offset by the fact that the steady state value of the FDI position is greater the milder the enforcement of controls. Consequently, it takes longer for the subsidiary to attain the steady state the milder the restrictions. Similarly, the subsidiary's steady state output is higher when there are no restrictions, but it takes longer to reach the steady state.

The fact that the FDI position falls at the subsidiary and rises at the headquarters when exchange controls are enforced is easily explained. For the subsidiary, as exchange controls increase, the marginal benefit of capital in the subsidiary falls. For any given level of marginal costs, this leads to a reduction in the optimal FDI flow. The impact on the headquarters' capital stock is best understood by contrasting the two ways in which

Figure 1. Constant exchange controls

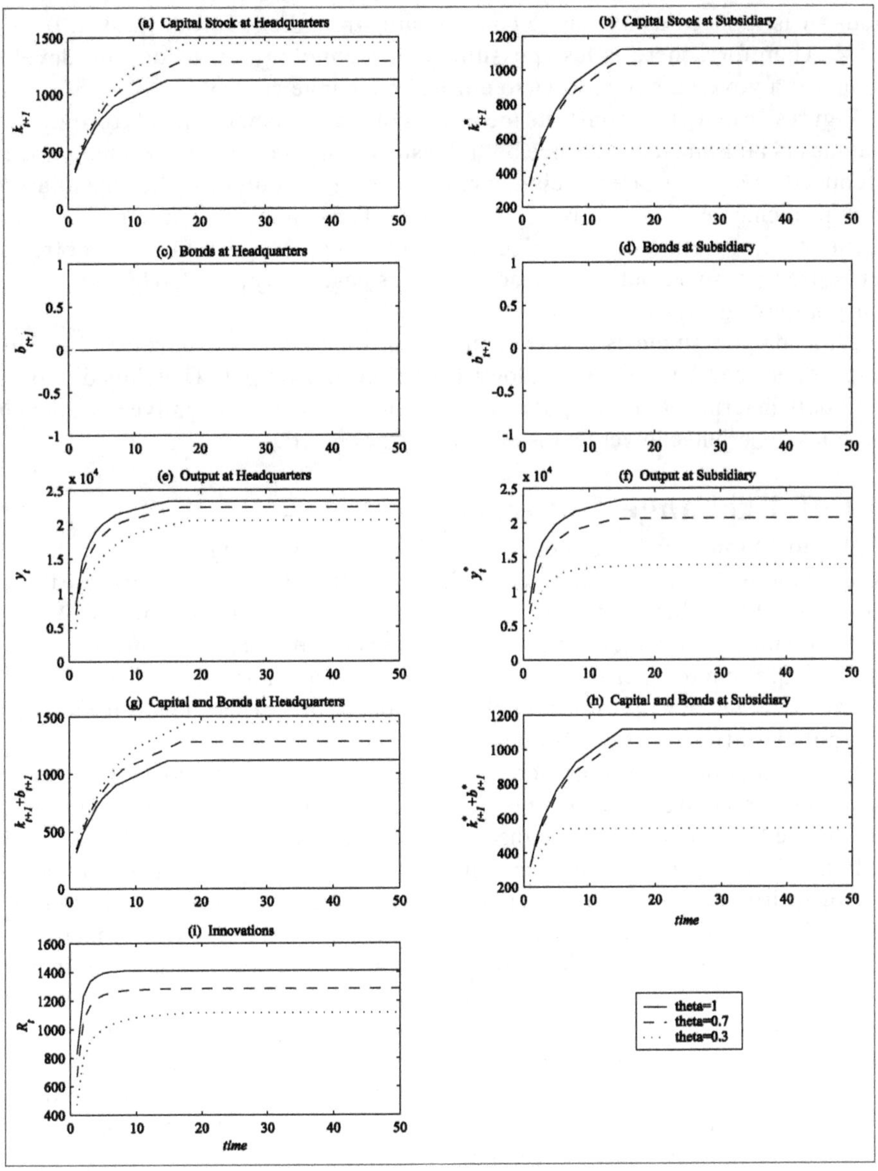

exchange controls affect capital at home. First, since innovations are shared across plants, lower level of subsidiary's capital stock negatively affects the headquarters' capital. Second, since the price is a function of output, lower capital abroad positively affects the marginal revenue of the domestic plant. It so happens that the latter effect dominates and we see the headquarters' capital stock increase as exchange controls intensify. Therefore, the MNE shifts its operation between the two plants in response to exchange control policies.

Examining the effects of exchange controls on the level of technology in Figure 1i we note that more severe exchange controls result in a lower number of innovations per period—R is reduced as exchange controls are strengthened from $\theta = 1$ to $\theta = 0.7$ to $\theta = 0.3$. Therefore, there is less possibility of technology diffusion into developing economy if a government chooses to enforce exchange controls.

Figures 1e and 1f demonstrate the effects of the exchange controls on output at the headquarters and subsidiary. Since both the subsidiary's capital stock and innovations are reduced as a result of enforcing exchange controls, output at the subsidiary falls. Although exchange controls have a positive effect on capital accumulation at headquarters, the level of technology is reduced considerably. Between these two effects, the latter is stronger, so output at the headquarters is negatively affected by the developing country imposing exchange controls.

This analysis suggests that exchange controls hinder less developed economies through depressed capital, technology diffusion and output. Developed economies benefit only in terms of more rapid capital accumulation. On a negative side, developed economies experience lower levels of technology and GDP.

On-Off Exchange Controls

We now turn to exchange control policies that vary through time. Countries, such as Brazil, have had on-off exchange controls. A simple experiment is one where the model economy fluctuates between two levels of severity of exchange controls. We start at period $t=1$ with no exchange controls ($\theta_1 = 1$). Next period exchange controls are enforced with $\theta_2 = 0.3$. From that period on, we cycle between $\theta_t = 1$ and $\theta_{t+1} = 0.3$, t = *1, 3, 5,...*. The MNE is assumed to know this cycle. The goal of this experiment is to find out how on-off policies affect the MNE's operations.

Our simulations show that there is an upward trend in transitions of capital stocks at home and abroad to their respective steady states. This transition is not smooth: peaks are associated with $\theta_t = 1$ and troughs occur when $\theta_t = 0.3$. When $\theta_t = 1$ and $\theta_{t+1} = 0.3$, the MNE believes that a present discounted value of a dollar of remittance in period t is \$1, while waiting to remit in the next period reduces the present discounted value to only 30 cents. The MNE wants to remit funds from the subsidiary, which reduces the FDI position at the subsidiary. Similarly, if $\theta_t = 0.3$ and $\theta_{t+1} = 1$, an MNE chooses to wait one period and remit the funds next period. This latter scenario increases the FDI position. Since the MNE is a monopoly, as the FDI position rises, capital stock at the headquarters falls in an attempt to keep outputs relatively constant by shifting resources across plants. Capital stock transition for $\theta = 1$ and $\theta = 0.3$ serve as "bands" on the capital transition for the capital stocks under the on-off policies. The distance between peaks and troughs is related to the adjustment costs parameter η.

The steady states for both capital stocks—at headquarters and subsidiary—are a two-period cycle. In steady state, outputs at subsidiary and headquarters, as well as innovations, also cycle between two values. This experiment suggests that on-off policies make transition less smooth. Such transition is not what the less developed countries would like to see because the on-off exchange controls cause capital flight during the periods when the controls are lifted. Less developed economies, therefore, should be aware of possible capital flight.

COSTS OF EXCHANGE CONTROLS

In this section we quantify the effects of exchange controls. We measure the loss in the steady state FDI position, output and other variables to various constant exchange control policies. We also measure the long-run impact of short-term exchange controls on the MNE.

Steady State

We evaluate the cost of exchange controls by comparing the steady state values of the capital stocks at the headquarters and subsidiary (k and k^*), innovations (R), and outputs at headquarters and subsidiary (y and y^*) for various exchange control policies. Table 3 shows the percent change of the steady state levels of these key variables from the model economy with no exchange controls ($\theta = 1$) to one with exchange controls ($\theta = 0.2, 0.3, ..., 0.9, 0.95$, and 0.99). The key findings are that the developing nation's exchange control policy lowers its FDI position, lowers innovations, increases the capital stock of the developed economy, and lowers outputs in both countries.[23]

For example, when the MNEs only see 60% of their subsidiary's remittance each period ($\theta = 0.6$), the headquarters' capital stock is 5.49% higher than with no restrictions; the FDI position of the subsidiary falls by 9.32%; innovations decline by 12.33%; and outputs at headquarters and subsidiary fall by 10.44% and 15.70%, respectively. These results suggest that a developing country's exchange control policy affects the developing as well as the developed nation. In general, countries that use exchange control policies will see FDI position rise, the flow of foreign technology intensify, and their GDP rise if these countries abolish the restrictions. A developed country will see its capital stock slightly decline, level of technology increase, and GDP rise as developing countries lift the exchange restrictions.

African countries that have exchange control policies written in their constitutions but rarely enforce them, can correspond to a value of $\theta = 0.95$. We find that lifting the

Table 3. Percentage change in the steady state levels of capital stocks, innovations, and outputs from economy with no exchange controls ($\theta = 1$)

θ	Headquarters' Capital Stock (k)	Subsidiary's Capital Stock (k)	Innovations (R)	Headquarters' Output (y)	Subsidiary's Output (y^*)
1.00	0.00%	0.00%	0.00%	0.00%	0.00%
0.99	+0.19%	–0.16%	–0.28%	–0.20%	–0.35%
0.95	+0.94%	–0.84%	–1.42%	–1.05%	–1.75%
0.90	+1.81%	–1.75%	–2.87%	–2.17%	–3.55%
0.80	+3.35%	–3.79%	–5.87%	–4.62%	–7.31%
0.70	+4.58%	–6.26%	–9.02%	–7.37%	–11.34%
0.60	+5.49%	–9.32%	–12.33%	–10.44%	–15.70%
0.50	+6.07%	–13.30%	–15.83%	–13.82%	–20.50%
0.40	+6.30%	–18.85%	–19.50%	–17.51%	–25.95%
0.30	+6.26%	–27.57%	–23.26%	–21.38%	–32.55%
0.20	+6.46%	–45.30%	–26.67%	–24.81%	–42.40%

At $\theta = 1$, $k_{ss} = k^*_{ss} = 1166$, $R_{ss} = 1409$, *and* $y_{ss} = y^*_{ss} = 2374$

exchange controls would result in a 0.94% loss in the steady state level of headquarters capital stock, a 0.84% gain in FDI position at the subsidiary, a 1.42% increase in the level of technology, a 1.05% rise in output in a home country, and a 1.75% increase in output in the foreign country. These results suggest that, although the effects of lifting the restrictions are not large, by no means will this result in an outflow of capital as some governments fear.

Ultimately, both the firms and the governments are interested in what would happen to output. To this end, a straightforward implication of the effects of exchange controls on capital stocks and innovations is that outputs at both plants decline when the host country blocks funds. The home country output falls because the effect on innovations is larger in absolute value than that on capital at the headquarters. Thus we conclude that, in terms of output gain, both countries benefit from the developing country abandoning exchange controls.

A One-Time Shock

We now study the long-term consequences of imposing exchange controls for a short period of time. Recently, Asian countries have enforced exchange controls with the intention of lifting them shortly. What is the impact of such short-term policy? To answer this question, we compare an economy with no exchange controls to one that does not have exchange controls except in period 1. We estimate the long-run welfare effects of this one-time shock as the present discounted value difference between the levels of capital stocks, innovations and outputs of a model without exchange controls and the one with a shock to exchange controls.

First we compare the economy with no exchange controls and the economy where $\theta = 0.3$ is enforced for only one period shortly after the FDI position reaches $k^* = 300$ (a relatively immature MNE). As is evident from Figure 2, even enforcing exchange controls for one period has relatively sizable and long-lasting effects on the capital stock and innovations. Figure 2b shows that the FDI position is depressed for five years after the exchange control shock, and only then does the MNE converge back to the no-controls transition path. Figures 2d and 2e illustrate that there is a sizable loss in innovations and output. We calculate the present discounted value of the loss in capital stock, innovations and output as $(\Delta x_t + \beta \Delta x_{t+1} + \beta^2 \Delta x_{t+2} + \cdots)$, where x is k^*, R, or y^*. We find that the present discounted valued loss in the FDI position is 16.7% of the steady state level and 46.5% of the current level of capital stock. Before the MNE converges to the path for the firm that does not face any exchange controls, the present discounted loss in innovations comes out to be 31.1% of the steady state level of technology or 35.6% of the current level. Finally, a total discounted loss in output at the subsidiary over the five years constitutes 30.8% of the steady state level and 58.1% of the current level of output.

If the one-time exchange control shock of $\theta = 0.3$ hits the model economy when the FDI position reaches $k^* = 1000$ (a relatively mature MNE), it would take the MNE seven years to catch up with the no-exchange-controls benchmark. We find that the present discounted loss in FDI position is 34.8 relative to the steady state level and 38.6 relative to the current level of the FDI position. Innovations are reduced by 25.2% compared with the steady state level. Also over the course of seven years, output at subsidiary falls by 38.1% (31.7%) relative to the steady state (current) level of the subsidiary's output. Thus we find that even exchange controls that are enforced for a short period of time have sizable effects on capital stock, innovations and output.

Figure 2. One-time exchange control shock at $k^{*}=300$

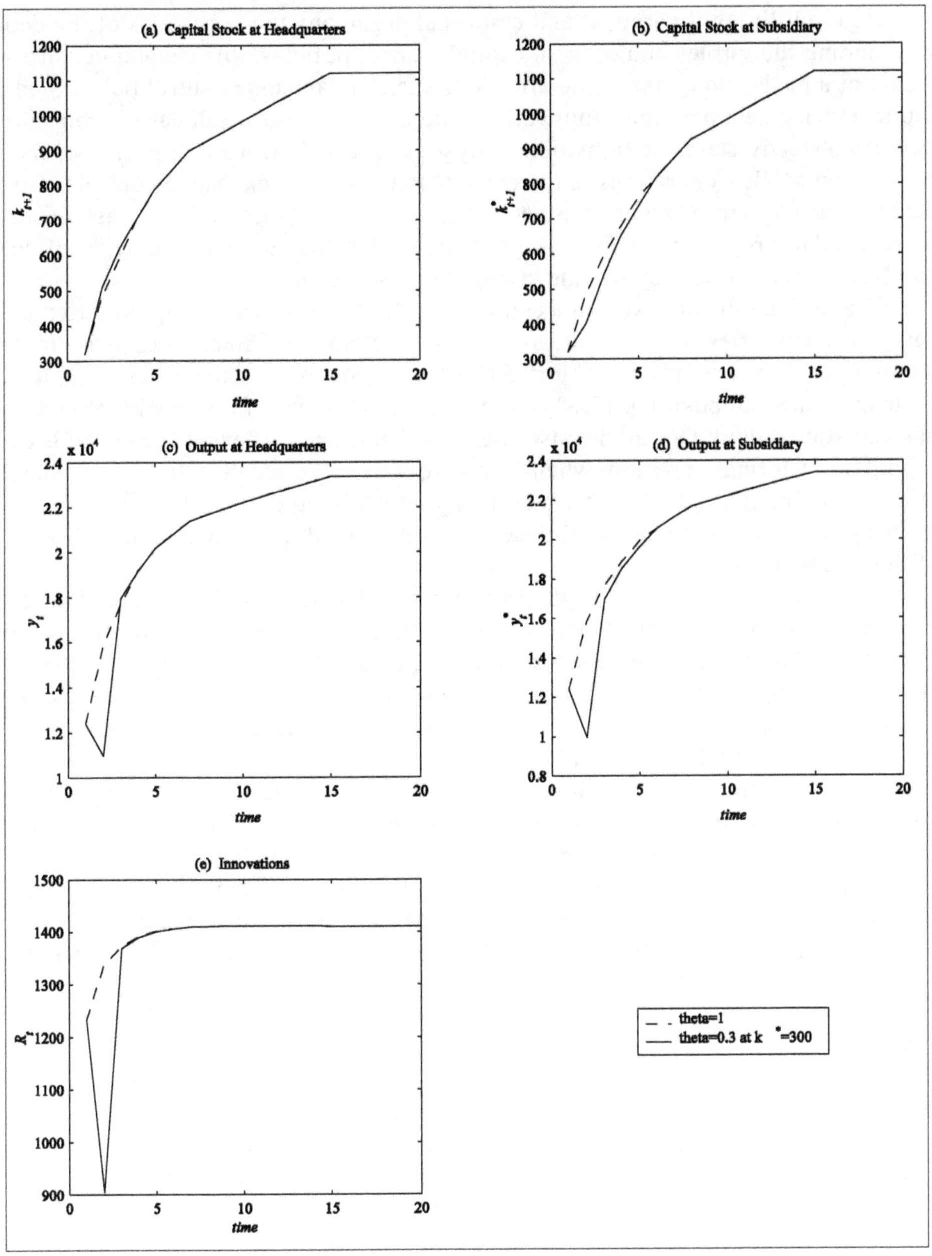

CONCLUSION

After outlining theoretical and empirical arguments on both sides of the debate surrounding the virtues and costs of capital control policies, this chapter constructs a model of an MNE to quantify the effects of various exchange control policies on the capital stocks, debt positions, innovations and outputs at the headquarters and subsidiary. Both steady-state and transition analyses suggest significant impact of exchange controls on MNE's operations in the country that enforces exchange controls, as well the MNE headquarters' country. Since MNE's actions are driven by the past, expected present and future exchange controls, governments' exchange control policies influence the firm operations as they lift and strengthen restrictions.

We find that lifting exchange controls produces an inflow of capital into the less developed countries, not an outflow as the governments sometimes fear. In fact, removing exchange controls that block 50% of remitted funds can result in 13.3% increase in steady-state FDI position, 15.8% increase in technology inflow, and 20.5% increase in stead-state output. Our model also suggests that the on-off exchange controls cause capital flight during the periods when the controls are lifted and thus such policies should be avoided. Finally, even short-term exchange controls have effects that last a minimum of five years and cost, in terms of present discounted value loss in output, at least 31% of the steady state value.

Our results are in tune with Bartolini and Drazen's (1997a) model where a government's capital control policy signals future policies with respect to capital restrictions. Their model predicts that milder policies with respect to capital outflows can help attract capital inflows. This prediction and our conclusions are consistent with the experience of many countries that have recently liberalized their capital accounts.

Conversely, Latin American countries that imposed capital controls in the wake of debt crisis—Argentina, Brazil, Mexico, Peru—have experienced negative output growth, high inflation and unemployment. Our results are broadly consistent with a bulk of the most recent empirical literature on capital controls. For example, Mckenzie (2001) uses cross-sectional and panel regressions and finds that the restrictions on capital mobility have a sizable negative impact on both growth and the rate of conditional growth convergence. In a study of European capital markets, Voth (2003) concludes that capital account liberalization facilitates economic growth.

Imposition of capital controls can, indeed, be costly in terms of lower industrial production and higher prices. This could be accounted for by the fact that domestic producers are likely to gain higher market shares and cut production with an intention to raise their prices. Further, tighter credit markets—a direct consequence of low international capital mobility—can lead to a fewer number of projects being funded. In particular, by raising domestic interest rates, capital controls make it more costly for firms to acquire capital domestically (Edwards, 1999), and with tight restrictions, the ability of the firms to attract additional financing from abroad at a cheaper rate is severely limited (Eichengreen et al., 1999).

Our model can also be used in addressing the tax price issues raised in Hines (1994). To this end, θ can be interpreted as a "tax price," which means that it is the US tax liability arising from one more dollar remitted to the US. With this interpretation, θ_t is known at date t and θ is either greater than or less than 1. Further, the model should be helpful in understanding how output and technology are affected by interest rates and exchange rates through exchange controls. This extension would require constructing a general equilibrium framework.

ACKNOWLEDGMENT

I am grateful to Jane Ihrig for numerous fruitful discussions. I also would like to thank the participants of the International Economics workshop at the University of Virginia for their helpful comments. The author alone is responsible for any errors and omissions.

REFERENCES

Abel, A. B., & Eberly, J. C. (1997). An exact solution for the investment and value of a firm facing uncertainty, adjustment costs, and irreversibility. *Journal of Economic Dynamics and Control, 21*(4-5), 831-852.

Aizenman, J. (2004). Financial opening and development: evidence and policy controversies. *American Economic Review, 94*(2), 65-70.

Alesina, A., Grilli, V., & Milesi-Ferretti, G. M. (1994). The Political Economy of Capital Controls. In L. Leiderman & A. Razin (Eds.), *Capital mobility: The impact on consumption, investment and growth* (pp. 289-321). Cambridge, UK: Cambridge University Press.

Ariyoshi, A., Habermeier, K., Laurens, B., Ötker-Robe, İ., Canales-Kriljenko, J. I., & Kirilenko, A. (2000). *Capital controls: Country experiences with their use and liberalization.* Washington, DC: International Monetary Fund.

Arrow, K. J. (1964). The role of securities in the optimal allocation of risk bearing. *Review of Economic Studies, 31*(2), 91-96.

Bajo-Rubio, O., & Sosvilla-Rivero, S. (2001). A quantitative analysis of the effects of capital controls: Spain, 1986-1990. *International Economic Journal, 15*(3), 129-146.

Bartolini, L., & Drazen, A. (1997a). Capital-account liberalization as a signal. *American Economic Review, 87*(1), 138-154.

Bartolini, L., & Drazen, A. (1997b). When liberal policies reflect external shocks, what do we learn? *Journal of International Economics, 42*(3-4), 249-273.

Calvo, G. (1998). Capital controls and capital-market crises: The simple economics of sudden stops. *Journal of Applied Economics, 1*(1), 35-54.

Campion, M. K., & Neumann, R. M. (2003). Compositional effects of capital controls—Theory and evidence. *World Economy, 26*(7), 957-973.

Cole, H. L., & Kehoe, T. J. (2000). Self-fulfilling debt crises. *Review of Economic Studies, 67*(1), 91-116.

Cordella, T. (2003). Can short-term capital controls promote capital inflows? *Journal of International Money and Finance, 22*(5), 737-745.

Cuddington, J. T. (1987). Capital flight. *European Economic Review, 31*(1-2), 382-388.

Debreu, G. (1959). *Theory of value: An axiomatic analysis of economic equilibrium.* New Haven, CT: Yale University Press.

Diamond, D. W., & Dybvig, P. H. (1983). Bank runs, deposit insurance, and liquidity. *Journal of Political Economy, 91*(3), 401-419.

Dornbusch, R., & Edwards, S. (1991). *The macroeconomics of populism in Latin America*. Chicago: University of Chicago Press.

Edison, H. J., & Reinhart, C. M. (2001). Capital controls during financial crises: The case of Malaysia and Thailand. In R. Glick, R. Moreno, & M. M. Spiegel (Eds.), *Financial Crises in Emerging Markets* (pp. 427-455). Cambridge: Cambridge University Press.

Edison, H. J., & Warnock, F. E. (2003). A simple measure of the intensity of capital controls. *Journal of Empirical Finance, 10*(1-2), 81-103.

Edwards, S. (1989). *Real exchange rates, devaluation, and adjustment: Exchange rate policy in developing countries*. Cambridge, MA: MIT Press.

Edwards, S. (1999). How effective are capital controls? *Journal of Economic Perspectives, 13*(4), 65-84.

Edwards, S. (2000). Capital flows, real exchange rates, and capital controls: Some Latin American experiences. In *Capital flows and the emerging economies: theory, evidence, and controversies* (NBER Conference Report series, pp. 197-246). Chicago: University of Chicago Press.

Edwards, S. (2002). Capital mobility, capital controls, and globalization in the twenty-first century. *Annals of the American Academy of Political and Social Science, 579*(0), 261-270.

Edwards, S., & Santaella, J. A. (1993). Devaluation controversies in the developing countries: Lessons from the Bretton Woods era. In M. Bordo & B. Eichengreen (Eds.), *A retrospective on the Bretton Woods System: Lessons for international monetary reform* (pp. 405-455). Chicago: University of Chicago Press.

Eichengreen, B. (1999). *Toward a new international financial architecture: A practical post-Asia agenda*. Washington, DC: Institute for International Economics.

Eichengreen, B., & Wyplosz, C. (1993). The unstable EMS. *Brookings Papers on Economic Activity, 0*(1), 51-143.

Eichengreen, B., Mussa, M., Dell'Ariccia, G., Detragiache, E., Milesi-Ferretti, G. M., & Tweedie, A. (1999). Liberalizing capital movements: Some analytical issues. In *Economic Issues, 17*. Washington, DC: International Monetary Fund.

Errunza, V. (2001). Foreign portfolio equity investments, financial liberalization, and economic development. *Review of International Economics*, 9(4), 703-726.

Fischer, S. (1998). Capital-account liberalization and the role of the IMF. *Princeton Essays in International Finance, 207,* 1-10.

Frenkel, M., Nickel, C., Schmidt, G., & Stadtmann, G. (2002). The effects of capital controls on exchange rate volatility and output. *International Economic Journal, 16*(4), 27-51.

Gallego, F. A., & Hernandez, F. L. (2003). Microeconomic effects of capital controls: The Chilean experience during the 1990s. *International Journal of Finance and Economics, 8*(3), 225-253.

Herrera, L. O., & Valdés, R. O. (2001). The effect of capital controls on interest rate differentials. *Journal of International Economics, 53*(2), 385-398.

Hines, J. R., Jr. (1994). Credit and deferral as international investment incentives. *Journal of Public Economics, 55*(2), 323-47.

Ihrig, J. E. (2000). Multinationals' response to repatriation restrictions. *Journal of Economic Dynamics and Control, 24*(9), 1345-1379.

Johnson, S., & Mitton, T. (2003). Cronyism and capital controls: Evidence from Malaysia," *Journal of Financial Economics, 67*(2), 351-382.

Judd, K. L. (1992). Projection methods for solving aggregate growth models. *Journal of Economic Theory, 58*(2), 410-452.

Kaminsky, G. L., & Reinhart, C. (1999). The twin crises: The causes of banking and balance of payments problems. *American Economic Review, 89*(3), 473-500.

Le Fort, G., & Budnevich, C. (1998). Capital account regulation and macroeconomic policy: two Latin American experiences. In G. K. Helleiner (Ed.), *Capital account regimes and the developing countries* (pp. 45-81). London: Macmillan Press.

Massad, C. (1998). The liberalization of the capital account: Chile in the 1990s. *Princeton Essays in International Finance, 207,* 34-46.

Mckenzie, D. J. (2001). The impact of capital controls on growth convergence. *Journal of Economic Development, 26*(1), 1-24.

McKinnon, R. I., & Pill, H. (1997). Credible economic liberalizations and overborrowing. *American Economic Review, 87*(2), 189-193.

McKinnon, R. I., & Pill, H. (1999). Exchange-rate regimes for emerging markets: Moral hazard and international overborrowing. *Oxford Review of Economic Policy, 15*(3), 19-38.

Mendoza, E. G., & Uribe, M. (1996). *The syndrome of exchange-rate-based stabilizations and the uncertain duration of currency pegs.* Board of Governors of the Federal Reserve System, International Finance discussion paper 548.

Obstfeld, M., & Rogoff, K. (1996). *Foundations of international macroeconomics.* Cambridge, MA: MIT Press.

Razin, A., & Yuen, C.-W. (1995). *Can capital controls alter the inflation-unemployment tradeoff?* NBER working paper No. 5239.

Reinhart, C. M., & Smith, R. T. (2002). Temporary controls on capital inflows. *Journal of International Economics, 57*(2), 327-351.

Rogoff, K. S. (2002). Rethinking capital controls. *Finance and Development, 39*(4), 55-56.

Santos, M. S. (1994). Smooth dynamics and computation in models of economic growth. *Journal of Economic Dynamics and Control, 18*(3-4), 879-895.

Santos, M. S., & Vigo-Aguiar, J. (1998). Analysis of a numerical dynamic programming algorithm applied to economic models. *Econometrica, 66*(2), 409-426.

Schmidt, R. (2001). Efficient capital controls. *Journal of Economic Studies, 28*(2-3), 199-212.

Spada, P. (2001). Capital controls on inflows: A remedy to financial crises? *Rivista di Politica Economica, 91*(11-12), 133-181.

Stiglitz, J. (2002). Capital market liberalization and exchange rate regimes: Risk without reward. *Annals of the American Academy of Political and Social Science, 579*(0), 219-248.

Survey of Current Business. (2000, July). *US multinational companies: Operations in 1998.* Bureau of Economic Analysis (US Department of Commerce).

Tamirisa, N. T. (1999). Exchange controls as barriers to trade. *IMF Staff Papers, 46*(1), 69-88.

Tobin, J. (1974). *New economics one decade older. The Eliot Janeway Lectures in Historical Economics in Honor of Joseph Schumpeter,* Princeton, NJ: Princeton University Press.
Tobin, J. (1978). A proposal for international monetary reform. *Eastern Economic Journal, 4,* 153-159.
Ulan, M. K. (2002). Should developing countries restrict capital inflows? *Annals of the American Academy of Political and Social Science, 579*(0), 249-260.
US Department of Commerce, Bureau of Economic Analysis. (2000). *US direct investment abroad: Operations of US parent companies and their foreign affiliates, preliminary 1998 estimates.* Washington, DC: US Government Printing Office.
Voth, H.-J. (2003). Convertibility, currency controls and the cost of capital in western Europe, 1950-1999. *International Journal of Finance and Economics, 8*(3), 255-276.
World Bank. (1993). *Latin America: A decade after the debt crisis.* Washington, DC.
Yashiv, E. (1998). Capital controls policy: An intertemporal perspective. *Journal of Economic Dynamics and Control, 22*(2), 219-245.

APPENDIX A: DERIVATIVES OF THE OPTIMAL POLICY FUNCTION

Letting $W\left(k_t, k_{t+1}, \rho_t^*\right)$ be the return function, we can rewrite the dynamic program (1) more generally[24]:

$$V\left(k_t; \rho_{t-1}^*, I_t\right) = \max_{k_{t+1}} E_t\left\{W\left(k_t, k_{t+1}, \rho_t^*\right) + \beta V\left(k_{t+1}; \rho_t^*, I_{t+1}\right) \mid \rho_{t-1}^*, I_t\right\}.$$

Differentiation with respect to the choice variable (k_{t+1}) obtains:

$$\frac{\partial E_t\left[W\left(k_t, k_{t+1}, \rho_t^*\right) \mid \rho_{t-1}^*, I_t\right]}{\partial k_{t+1}} + \beta \frac{\partial E_t\left[V\left(k_{t+1}; \rho_t^*, I_{t+1}\right) \mid \rho_{t-1}^*, I_t\right]}{\partial k_{t+1}} = 0.$$

Define the optimal policy function as $k_{t+1} \equiv g\left(k_t; \rho_{t-1}^*, I_t\right)$. Now plug $g(\bullet)$ into the first-order condition and totally differentiate with respect to k_t:

$$\frac{\partial^2 E_t\left[W(\bullet) \mid \rho_{t-1}^*, I_t\right]}{\partial k_{t+1} \partial k_t} + \frac{\partial^2 E_t\left[W(\bullet) \mid \rho_{t-1}^*, I_t\right]}{\partial k_{t+1}^2} \frac{\partial g(\bullet)}{\partial k_t} +$$

$$\beta \frac{\partial^2 E_t\left[V(\bullet) \mid \rho_{t-1}^*, I_t\right]}{\partial k_{t+1}^2} \frac{\partial g(\bullet)}{\partial k_t} = 0. \tag{A1}$$

Solving for $\frac{\partial g(\bullet)}{\partial k_t}$ gives the first derivative of the optimal policy function:

$$\frac{\partial g(\bullet)}{\partial k_t} = -\frac{\dfrac{\partial^2 E_t\left[W(\bullet)|\rho_{t-1}^*, I_t\right]}{\partial k_{t+1}\partial k_t}}{\dfrac{\partial^2 E_t\left[W(\bullet)|\rho_{t-1}^*, I_t\right]}{\partial k_{t+1}^2} + \beta\dfrac{\partial^2 E_t\left[V(\bullet)|\rho_{t-1}^*, I_t\right]}{\partial k_{t+1}^2}} > 0.$$

$V(\bullet)$ is twice continuously differentiable for this class of stochastic models and standard assumptions.25 This implies $g(\bullet)$ is differentiable of class C^1 (Santos & Vigo-Aguiar, 1998).

Strict concavity of $W(\bullet)$ and convexity of the state space ensure that $V(\bullet)$ is strictly concave (Santos, 1994): $\frac{\partial^2 E_t\left[V(\bullet)|\rho_{t-1}^*, I_t\right]}{\partial k_{t+1}^2} < 0$. Furthermore, since the production function is increasing and concave in k_t, and adjustment costs are decreasing and concave in k_t and increasing and convex in k_{t+1}, we know that $\frac{\partial^2 E_t\left[W(\bullet)|\rho_{t-1}^*, I_t\right]}{\partial k_{t+1}\partial k_t} > 0$ and $\frac{\partial^2 E_t\left[W(\bullet)|\rho_{t-1}^*, I_t\right]}{\partial k_{t+1}^2} < 0$. The last three inequalities guarantee $\frac{\partial g(\bullet)}{\partial k_t} > 0$.

To obtain the second derivative of the optimal policy function, we totally differentiate (A1) with respect to k_t:

$$\begin{aligned}
&\frac{\partial^3 E_t\left[W(\bullet)|\rho_{t-1}^*, I_t\right]}{\partial k_{t+1}\partial k_t^2} + \frac{\partial^3 E_t\left[W(\bullet)|\rho_{t-1}^*, I_t\right]}{\partial k_{t+1}^2\partial k_t}\frac{\partial g(\bullet)}{\partial k_t} \\
&+\frac{\partial^3 E_t\left[W(\bullet)|\rho_{t-1}^*, I_t\right]}{\partial k_{t+1}^2\partial k_t}\frac{\partial g(\bullet)}{\partial k_t} + \frac{\partial^3 E_t\left[W(\bullet)|\rho_{t-1}^*, I_t\right]}{\partial k_{t+1}^3}\left(\frac{\partial g(\bullet)}{\partial k_t}\right)^2 \\
&+\frac{\partial^2 E_t\left[W(\bullet)|\rho_{t-1}^*, I_t\right]}{\partial k_{t+1}^2}\frac{\partial^2 g(\bullet)}{\partial k_t^2} + \beta\frac{\partial^3 E_t\left[V(\bullet)|\rho_{t-1}^*, I_t\right]}{\partial k_{t+1}^2\partial k_t}\frac{\partial g(\bullet)}{\partial k_t} \\
&+\beta\left[\frac{\partial^3 E_t\left[V(\bullet)|\rho_{t-1}^*, I_t\right]}{\partial k_{t+1}^3}\left(\frac{\partial g(\bullet)}{\partial k_t}\right)^2 + \frac{\partial^2 E_t\left[V(\bullet)|\rho_{t-1}^*, I_t\right]}{\partial k_{t+1}^2}\frac{\partial^2 g(\bullet)}{\partial k_t^2}\right] = 0.
\end{aligned}$$

After rearranging terms and noting that $\frac{\partial^3 E_t\left[W(\bullet)\mid \rho_{t-1}^*, I_t\right]}{\partial k_{t+1}\partial k_t^2} =$ $\frac{\partial^3 E_t\left[W(\bullet)\mid \rho_{t-1}^*, I_t\right]}{\partial k_{t+1}^3} = 0$ (due to the assumptions we put on $f(k_t)$ and $\varphi(k_t, k_{t+1})$) and $\frac{\partial^3 E_t\left[V(\bullet)\mid \rho_{t-1}^*, I_t\right]}{\partial k_{t+1}^2 \partial k_t} = 0$ (since $V\left(k_{t+1}, \rho_t^*\right)$ is independent of k_t), we have:

$$\frac{\partial^2 g(\bullet)}{\partial k_t^2} = -\frac{\beta \frac{\partial^3 E_t\left[V(\bullet)\mid \rho_{t-1}^*, I_t\right]}{\partial k_{t+1}^3}\left(\frac{\partial g(\bullet)}{\partial k_t}\right)^2}{\frac{\partial^2 E_t\left[W(\bullet)\mid \rho_{t-1}^*, I_t\right]}{\partial k_{t+1}^2} + \beta \frac{\partial^2 E_t\left[V(\bullet)\mid \rho_{t-1}^*, I_t\right]}{\partial k_{t+1}^2}}.$$

Since $\frac{\partial^2 E_t\left[W(\bullet)\mid \rho_{t-1}^*, I_t\right]}{\partial k_{t+1}^2} < 0$

and $\frac{\partial^2 E_t\left[V(\bullet)\mid \rho_{t-1}^*, I_t\right]}{\partial k_{t+1}^2} < 0$, $sign\left[\frac{\partial^2 g(\bullet)}{\partial k_t^2}\right] = sign\left[\frac{\partial^3 E_t\left[V(\bullet)\mid \rho_{t-1}^*, I_t\right]}{\partial k_{t+1}^3}\right]$.

Assumptions on $f(k_t)$ and $\varphi(k_t, k_{t+1})$ ensure the existence of $\frac{\partial^3 E_t\left[V(\bullet)\mid \rho_{t-1}^*, I_t\right]}{\partial k_{t+1}^3}$.

APPENDIX B: MATLAB CODE FOR DYNAMIC PROGRAMMING

for $k = k_{\min} : k_{\max} : step$

⋮

for $R = R_{\min} : R_{\max} : step$

for $k' = k'_{\min} : k'_{\max} : step$

⋮

for $R' = R'_{\min} : R'_{\max} : step$

$W\left(k, k^*, b, b^*, R, k', k^{*\prime}, b', b^{*\prime}, R'\right) = \ldots$ % $W(\cdot)$ is the return function

```
        end
         ⋮
      end
    end
  ⋮
  end
  while 0~=1
   V = V'; % initialize the iteration
   for k = k_min : k_max : step
    for k* = k*_min : k*_max : step
     for b = b_min : b_max : step
      for b* = b*_min : b*_max : step
       for R = R_min : R_max : step
        template=zeros(n,n,n,n,n);  % n is the number of points in the grid
        y = squeeze(W(k,k*,b,b*,R,:,:,:,:,:)) + βV;
        y_max = max(max(max(max(max(y)))));
        [y_max index1] = max(max(max(max(max(y,[],2),[],3),[],4),[],5),[],1);
        [y_max index2] = max(max(max(max(max(y,[],1),[],3),[],4),[],5),[],2);
        [y_max index3] = max(max(max(max(max(y,[],1),[],2),[],4),[],5),[],3);
        [y_max index4] = max(max(max(max(max(y,[],1),[],2),[],3),[],5),[],4);
        [y_max index5] = max(max(max(max(max(y,[],1),[],2),[],3),[],4),[],5);
        V'(k,k*,b,b*,R) = y_max;
        template(k,k*,b,b*,R) = 1;
       K'_optimal(logical(template))=K'(index1)
       K*'_optimal(logical(template))=K*'(index2)
       B'_optimal(logical(template))=B'(index3)
       B*'_optimal(logical(template))=B*'(index4)
       R'_optimal(logical(template))=R'(index5)
       end
      end
     end
    end
   end
   if abs(V - V)' < ε, break, end
  end
  K_transition(1) = ...; B_transition(1) = ...; K*_transition(1) = ...; B*_transition(1) = ...; R_transition(1) = ...;
% start the transition
  for i=2:n+1
```

$$K_{transition}(i) = K'_{optimal}(find(k == K_{transition}(i-1)), find(k^* == K^*_{transition}(i-1)),$$
$$find(b == B_{transition}(i-1)), find(b^* == B^*_{transition}(i-1)), find(R == R_{transition}(i-1)));$$
$$B_{transition}(i) = B'_{optimal}(find(k == K_{transition}(i-1)), find(k^* == K^*_{transition}(i-1)),$$
$$find(b == B_{transition}(i-1)), find(b^* == B^*_{transition}(i-1)), find(R == R_{transition}(i-1)));$$
$$K^*_{transition}(i) = K^{*'}{}_{optimal}(find(k == K_{transition}(i-1)), find(k^* == K^*_{transition}(i-1)),$$
$$find(b == B_{transition}(i-1)), find(b^* == B^*_{transition}(i-1)), find(R == R_{transition}(i-1)));$$
$$B^*_{transition}(i) = B^{*'}{}_{optimal}(find(k == K_{transition}(i-1)), find(k^* == K^*_{transition}(i-1)),$$
$$find(b == B_{transition}(i-1)), find(b^* == B^*_{transition}(i-1)), find(R == R_{transition}(i-1)));$$
$$R_{transition}(i) = R'_{optimal}(find(k == K_{transition}(i-1)), find(k^* == K^*_{transition}(i-1)),$$
$$find(b == B_{transition}(i-1)), find(b^* == B^*_{transition}(i-1)), find(R == R_{transition}(i-1)));$$

end

ENDNOTES

1 Bartolini and Drazen (1997a, 1997b) and Ihrig (2000) do not distinguish between debt- and equity-financed capital.

2 A detailed account of these and other capital control episodes can be found in Ariyoshi et al. (2000).

3 The term "incomplete markets" describes an economy where not all risks are insurable. This is the opposite of the admittedly extreme assumption put forth by Arrow (1964) and Debreu (1959). When markets are incomplete, firms, individuals and governments cannot make asset trades that hedge them against all adverse contingencies. Indeed, moral hazard and imperfect international contract enforcement, among other factors, prevent any country from fully insuring itself against all risks.

4 Cole and Kehoe (2000) use a dynamic, stochastic general equilibrium model to derive the government's optimal policy in response to the threat of a debt crisis. They argue that the country's fundamentals place it inside the "crisis zone," and that the "crisis zone" can be reduced if the debt's structure is shifted toward longer maturities.

5 This conclusion is echoed by Gallego and Hernandez's (2003) firm-level study of Chilean capital controls.

6 However, since a country that imposes capital controls is likely to be considered a higher-risk economy, a decrease in investment may follow and the economy would have to incur a (temporary) cost of lower real output.

7 At the risk of sounding trivial, we note that costs of capital controls correspond to the benefits of financial integration, and benefits of capital controls justify the impediments to financial integration.

8 In 2001, Germany's chancellor Gerhard Schröder and the former French prime minister Lionel Jospin proposed that the European Union take the lead in calling for a global Tobin tax to reduce currency speculation and volatility.

9 Schmidt (2001) advocates a modified version of Tobin tax whereby wholesale foreign-exchange payments are subject to taxation. Such tax could be imposed unilaterally by any country without any regard to coordination and would affect transactions in domestic and one or more foreign currencies. Among the potential benefits of the foreign-exchange-payment tax are the opportunity to increase foreign reserves, the possibility to tax short-term (more volatile) capital flows at a higher rate, and low implementation costs.

10 It should be noted that certain short-term flows, such as trade credits and instruments that enabled investors to hedge, can be quite desirable (Rogoff, 2002).

11 However, Stiglitz (2002) points out that capital markets are characterized by substantial risks and incomplete information, which make them markedly distinct from goods markets. Consequently, the benefits of trade liberalization might not be directly extended to the capital account liberalization.

12 Notice how this logic is diametrically opposite to the gist of Cordella's (2003) argument summarized in the previous subsection.

13 In Johnson and Mitton's (2003) study, the "political connections" effect is large and statistically significant even after controlling for firms' leverage.

14 If there were no underwriting costs, we would expect the Modigliani-Miller property to hold in this model. Given our setup, however, $g(b_t) > 0$ implies that all capital in steady state should be financed with equity.

15 That is, the revenue function of each plant is twice continuously differentiable in the output of the plant, strictly concave in the output of the plant, and marginal revenue of a plant is decreasing in the other plant's output. In addition, the own effects on marginal revenue are greater than the cross effects.

16 The model can easily be extended to also consider capital controls that limit the inflow of capital.

17 Our framework also allows one to price the firm since $V(\bullet)$ can be calculated precisely up to a constant transformation $(1-\rho_{t-1}^{*})C_{t-1}$.

18 The derivatives of the underlying optimal policy function are presented in Appendix A.

19 The optimization problem boils down to solving a system of second-order difference equations in k, k^*, b, b^* and R.

20 Here we adopt the following conventional notation: $k \equiv k_t$, $k' \equiv k_{t+1}$, $k'' \equiv k_{t+2}$, etc.

21 Appendix B contains a MATLAB code that vectorizes this element-by-element intuition.

22 We set $b_t = b_t^* = 0$ since debt finance is more costly than equity finance due to the underwriting costs $g(b_t) > 0$. Such simplification allows us to rewrite the problem as a 6-dimensional program instead of 10-dimensional.

23 Exchange control policies do not affect the steady state bond holdings in that bonds are not held at headquarters or subsidiary regardless of the value of θ.

24 For simplicity, this Appendix describes a one-subsidiary case with debt-financed capital set to the steady state value of zero. An extension of this analysis to a two-subsidiary case with nontrivial debt finance is tedious but conceptually straightforward.

[25] The assumptions include (i) convexity of a state space, (ii) boundedness, continuity, and C^2 differentiability and α-concavity of $W(\bullet)$, (iii) the existence of an interior optimal solution to the dynamic programming problem, and (iv) boundedness of the stochastic process.

Section VI

Organizational Theory and Inter-Organizational Alliances

Chapter XIV

A Physics of Organizational Uncertainty: Perturbations, Measurement and Computational Agents

W. F. Lawless
Paine College, USA

M. Bergman
Penn State Worthington Scranton, USA

N. Feltovich
University of Houston, USA

ABSTRACT

Of two contradictory approaches to organizations, one builds a plausible story to advance knowledge, and the second resolves the interaction into a physics of uncertainty to make predictions. Both approaches lend themselves to computational agent models, but the former is based on information derived from methodological individualism operating within a stable reality, the latter on interaction uncertainty within a bistable reality. After case studies of decision making for Department of Energy (DOE) Citizen Advisory Boards, we relate the lessons learned to an agent model (EMCAS). We conclude that simple interactions can produce complex stories of organizations, but poorly anchored to reality and of little practical value for decision making. In contrast, with a physics of uncertainty we raise fundamental questions about the value of consensus to instrumental action. We find that by not considering uncertainty in the interaction, the former model instantiates traditional beliefs and cultural values, the latter instrumental action.

INTRODUCTION: ORGANIZATIONAL SCIENCE

According to organizational theorists (Werck & Quinn, 1999), the state of theory is poor and little advanced from the time of Lewin (1951). There are at least two broad but incommensurable theories attempting to move theory forward: Traditional methodological individualism, which tries to fashion results into a consistent story of organizational processes (Macal, 2004), and the mathematical physics of uncertainty, which focuses on predicting organizational outcomes. We review the traditional theory of organizations along with our new theory of the mathematical physics of organizations, apply it to two field tests, and then apply the lessons learned to a review of the EMCAS (Electricity Markets Complex Adaptive Systems) agent model designed by the DOE's Argonne National Laboratory (www.dis.anl.gov/CEEESA/EMCAS.html). Afterwards, we review future research directions and conclude with a discussion of where the results of the traditional model and our model agree and disagree.

Methodological individualism, the traditional model of organizations (Nowak & Sigmund, 2004), assumes that interactions between agents generate stable information, *I*, that an optimum set of perspectives, beliefs, or knowledge, *K*, subsume other beliefs, and that the aggregate perspectives of individual members is the organization (i.e., an organization is what its members believe). This approach is static (Von Neumann & Morgenstern, 1953), but when repeated generates computational models of dynamics and evolution. The best example is game theory, typically used to promote the advantages of cooperation over competition. Bounding this view, the normative social welfare model of Arrow (1951) indicates that cooperation to achieve a rational consensus as preferences multiply becomes impossible without the imposition of either a dictator or democratic majority rule. From a different direction, Nash's (1950) possibility of consensus increases as the differences between two cooperating parties sufficiently diminish to compromise over the remainder. In agreement with Arrow and Nash, May (2001, p. 174) concluded that as the heterogeneity of beliefs decreased, a system mathematically becomes easier to control but if it becomes more rigid, it also becomes unstable, requiring a reduction in feedback to maintain control. Thus, in the traditional model of organizations, stability arises from the convergence of consensus-seeking for decisions; a command decision making hierarchy or dictatorship to influence the process; and hierarchical limits to information, *I*, or censorship. Generally, efficiency increases with centralized command for well-defined solutions to problems (Lawless & Grayson, 2004b). For example, Unilever has concluded that its primary barrier to efficiency is having two CEO's (www.wallstreetjournal.com, 1/3/2005). However, this method of governance also reduces the organizational forces of innovation, motivating adaptations such as restructures and mergers.

In sharp contrast, random exploration among competing organizations and beliefs in democracies generates stable environments and innovation (Fama, 1965; May, 1997). Yet, proving that democracy works so that it can be rationally applied to hierarchical organizations set within democracies or even to computational agent systems is a hard problem. From a review of the mathematics, Luce and Raiffa (1967) concluded that methodological individualism was unlikely to capture the essence of organizations. From a review of group psychology, Levine and Moreland (1998) concluded that aggregating self-reported preference data from the members of a group fails to capture its critical processes. Phenomenologically, Campbell (1996), the founder of social convergence theory, concluded that convergence processes could not validate democratic processes. As examples of the problems with convergence methods and human choices, after his review of game theory, Kelley (1992) concluded that even when the payoff matrices of a game converged to perfectly match previously stated preferences, human participants in the presence of other players transformed their preferences into a set of unpredictable choices. In 1922, at the beginning of his career, Allport strenuously claimed there was no difference between an aggregation of individuals and a group composed of the same individuals, but ended his career by concluding the transformation of individuals into group members was the major unsolved problem in social psychology (Allport, 1962). Tversky and his colleagues (Shafir, Simonson, & Tversky, 1993) found no relationship between decisions and subsequent justifications for decisions. Polyani (1974) found that while society enshrined certain decisions by judges as precedents, society mostly ignored the justifications of judges for their decisions. Even undermining the traditional meaning of an "individual," to explain why the traditional assessments of individuals consistently produce poor results (Baumeister, 1995), Eagly and Chaiken (1993) concluded that questions put to individuals could be worded to achieve any desired self-reports.

Methodological Individualism

Methodological individualism is based on the normative assumption that cooperation has a greater value to social welfare than does competition, but its supporters also recognize that this assumption is arbitrary (Nowak & Sigmund, 2004), that cooperation is not cost free and must either be coerced (Axelrod, 1984; Hardin, 1968) or deception used (Suskind, 1999) to dampen spontaneous organizational forces. Determined minorities can easily subvert the social welfare benefits of consensus-seeking to their own purposes, giving them dictatorial power over majorities, impelling even long-time advocates like the European Union to reject this decision process for its new constitution (WP, 2001, p. 29); for example, minorities in the European Union used consensus-seeking to establish a Precautionary Principle that promotes nonscientific control over scientifically determined risks (Von Schomberg, 2004), consequently increasing the probability of mistakes. For example, in 2002, the embargo of British beef by France under the Precautionary Principle after the discovery of bovine spongiform encephalopathy was declared illegal by the European Court of Justice. And while the Precautionary Principle does not apply in the United States, mistakes based on risk perceptions are still possible. For example, a study of risk perception by Slovic and colleagues with questionnaires led to his prediction in 1991 that the negative images associated with a nuclear waste repository at Yucca Mountain in the United States would harm the Las Vegas economy by reducing tourism; however, after Slovic's research was criticized, 10 years later he admitted that even with the repository still under construction, tourism continued to make Las Vegas the fastest growing community in the US (Slovic et al., 2001, pp. 102-103).

But as a consequence of overvaluing cooperation, some have come to believe that competition reflects a "toxic excess of freedom" (Dennett, 2003, p. 304). Yet competition generates knowledge, K, in an open political competition even when only one side of an issue is presented (Coleman, 2003). Instead of the Precautionary Principle, the European Union's Trustnet (2004) concluded that disagreement (competition) in public among scientists provides the public with a critical tool to work through scientific uncertainty in solving a public problem. In politics, competition drives social evolution by forcing losers to revise strategies and sometimes even to adopt from the winners policies previously inimical to their expressed self-interests. For example, the democrats in power under President W. J. Clinton adopted social welfare reform, and the republicans in power under President G. W. Bush adopted education reform (Lawless & Castelao, 2001). Business reactions to competitive threats also drive social evolution. For example, in 2004, to fight against a growing threat from Symantec, Microsoft shifted its business strategy to acquire Giant, a small software company that makes products to protect against spyware and junk mail; to fight against the erosion of its video-rental market by giant retailers selling massive numbers of cheap DVD's, Blockbuster has made a hostile merger offer for Hollywood Entertainment; and Siemens and General Motors are attempting to reduce Germany's generous benefits to laid-off workers to jump start the sputtering German economy in order to help their own businesses (i.e., "Hartz IV" rule changes proposed by the German State would allow greater rates of firing, less benefits to laid-off workers, and shorter terms of benefits; see www.bundesregierung.de).

Mathematical Physics of Uncertainty

Computational models of uncertainty in the interaction developed in response to the problems with methodological individualism. By adapting the Heisenberg Uncertainty Principle, Bohr (1955) and Heisenberg (1958) were the first to apply bidirectional uncertainty to the social interaction. After Bohr critiqued their theory of games, Von Neumann and Morgenstern (1953, p. 148) concluded that if correct, a rational model of the interaction is "inconceivable." In part the reason can be attributed to the traditional "meaning" of rational (p. 9) and in part to the traditional definition of social reality. First, a rational perspective or understanding of a social process is based on a cognitive or mental convergence process that resolves contradictions by marginalizing them to reduce cognitive dissonance (e.g., Axsom & Lawless, 1992). Second, traditional reality is stable so that the information, I, generated by the interaction is accessible to all parties of the interaction. Campbell (1996) rejected the first, and game theorists have slowly modified the second (Luce & Raiffa, 1967).

The Bohr-Heisenberg model is the only bidirectional uncertainty model we are aware of, but it can be extended to include fuzzy logic (Zadeh, 2003). It rejects both the traditional meanings of *rational* and *social* reality. With it we have made substantial progress towards a new theory of organizations. In a surprise to Air Force educators, we found in a study of USAF combat fighter pilots that K of air combat maneuvering was irrelevant but experience in the management of energy, E, during combat was critical (Lawless, Castelao & Ballas, 2000). We extended this result to find associations that indicate the more competitive was a nation, the more energy it spent, the more scientific wealth it generated, the better its human health, the freer its people, the more trust in its politicians, and the less corruption it experienced (Lawless, Castelao, & Abubucker, 2000); and in a subsequent qualitative study, we observed that the more democratic a country, the more quickly it responded to natural disasters and the more disaster resistant its population became (Lawless & Castelao, 2001). For example, since 1900, no modern democracy is among the top 10 lists of nations that have suffered from the worst natural disasters (i.e., fatalities measured for floods, droughts, and earthquakes; however, in 1923 Japan suffered one of the worst disasters from an earthquake when it was not a democracy, but in 1993 when it was a democracy, it lost only 200 to a major tsunami, fully recovering in 5 years). In the next study, we theorized that the management and moderation of conflict generated by competition promoted social evolution (Lawless & Schwartz, 2002), and recently we theorized that the relatively lower *E* state of organizations implied a low generation of *I*, motivating the need of perturbations initiated by competitors to generate *I* (Lawless & Grayson, 2004b), supporting an idea about organizational restructuring first proposed by Lewin (1951) more than 50 years ago.

Justification of Bidirectional (Quantum) Uncertainty or Bistable Reality

The difficulty of understanding bidirectional, conjugate, or interdependent uncertainty in the interaction causes many questions to be raised about going forward with our project (Axtell, 2002). To answer some of these questions, we present a brief justification for borrowing quantum mathematics for computational models of organizations.

1. From the perspective of biological physics, the eye is a quantum *I* processor (French & Taylor, 1979), meaning that quantum reality is reduced to classical information; in agreement, Bekenstein (2003) has proposed that stable social reality is a quantum illusion.
2. Luce (1997) concluded that the quantum model of different *E* levels proposed by Bèkèsy in the 1930's and Stevens in the 1940's was an adequate alternative to traditional signal detection receiver operating characteristic (ROC) curves. From quantum mechanics as suggested by Penrose, where *E* and time, *t*, uncertainties (ΔE and Δt) are interdependently related by $\Delta E \Delta t \geq h$, with *h* as Planck's constant and $E = h\omega$, then $\Delta E \Delta t \geq h$ gives $\Delta(h\omega)\Delta t \geq h$, leading to $\Delta\omega\Delta t \geq 1$. Thus, signal detection or object acquisition by the brain with 40 Hz gamma waves should occur on average no less than 25 msec while working memory tasks with theta waves at 5 Hz should take no less than 200 msec, illustrating *Et* interdependence in the human brain (i.e., with gamma waves at 40 Hz, $\Delta\omega\Delta t \geq 1$ leads to $\Delta t \geq 0.025$ s; and with theta waves of 5 Hz, $\Delta\omega\Delta t \geq 1$ leads to $\Delta t \geq 0.2$ s), agreeing beautifully with data from Hagoort and colleagues (Hagoort et al., 2004, Figure 2, p. 440; similarly, shortening by 1/2 the time for a digital voice track doubles its energy, i.e., $\Delta\omega \geq 1/\Delta t = 1/(1/2) = 2$ Hz; in Kang & Fransen, 1994).
3. Tajfeld (1970) discovered that the boundaries of in-groups and out-groups arise spontaneously. But humans can focus attention on only one topic at a time (Cacioppo, Bernston & Crites, 1996), the flaw of multitasking theories (Wickens, 1992). According to Schama (1995), out of interdependent uncertainties between boundaries arises "social memory," the incommensurable histories of competing groups. In the command center of one of these competing groups, full attention can be directed to either a business strategy or its execution (e.g., Gibson, 1986); similarly, it can be directed to either reducing uncertainties in the internalities or externalities of an organization, the critical job of a CEO (Drucker, 2004).
4. Competing histories arise because the measurement of social systems (Bohr, 1955), just like quantum systems, produces only classical *I* that is incapable of being used to reconstruct an organization's prior state (e.g., Levine & Moreland, 1998).

Because measurements are being taken by different humans at different points across time, I sums into different perspectives, world views or beliefs, giving rise to different cultures. While organizations arise as means to leverage scarce sources of E into technologies that individuals cannot perform alone (Ambrose, 2001), once the drive by organisms to seek sources of E for survival (Eldredge, 2004) becomes the function of a formal organization, organizations serve as force drivers for the random explorations that evolve society.

5. Yet despite the limits of logical positivism established by Kuhn's (1970) model of the tension between competing schools of science, as a matter of practice, organizational science hews to the thesis of logical positivism that an optimum convergence of K or beliefs is theoretically possible.
6. But even if logical positivism produced a consensus that ended any notion of competing beliefs, and even if there were no supporting physics in item 2 previously, social scientists have known for some time that measurement of social phenomena, whether psychological, social, political, or economic, affects the data collected (e.g., Carley, 2003; Lipshitz, 1997), alone justifying the need for a new theory of generating I from groups; that is, perturbation theory (Lawless & Grayson, 2004b). In 2004, the Department of Defense formalized this idea in its proposal to gain information with combat raids to characterize unknown enemy groups by "fighting for intelligence" (Boykin, 2004).

Perturbation Model: Organizational Structure as Prelude to Measurement

Assume that organizational structures seek a minimum E state across both physical and K space, where $K = f(location)$, with $\Delta K = I$ (Shannon's I), and where perfect K implies that $\Delta K \rightarrow 0$ (Conant, 1976). Then $\partial E/\partial K = F$; that is, the forces in an organization reflect varying E levels as one moves across its K landscape; keeping E constant, $F \rightarrow 0$ as K uncertainty increases (e.g., as ambiguity rises, the volume on a stock exchange slows or stops; in Insana, 2001). The potential E surface (E^{PES}) reflects the functional, hierarchical and geo-cultural-intellectual differences across an organization (Sallach, 2002):

$$E^{PES}(x,y) = min_{z,R\text{-}org}\ E^{TOT}(x,y,z,R_{org}) \quad (1)$$

A recruit moves across the E surface of an organization, R_{org}, until F approaches zero or where E^{TOT} is the ground state and PES the minimum total E in physical space along the z coordinate of the organizational hierarchy. Knowing that it takes E to recruit or to merge two organizations into a new one indicates that an organization represents a lower E level than an aggregation (Figure 1; e.g., after mergers, organizations often restructure in an attempt to reduce costs and personnel; in Andrade & Stafford, 1999).

The growth rate of an organization, P, is contingent on available E:

$$\Gamma_P = n_R n_M\, v\, \sigma_{RM}\, exp(-\Delta A/k_B T). \quad (2)$$

where n_R and n_M are the numbers of targeted outsiders (R) and organization members (M) interacting together (e.g., recruits; potential merger targets); K flow, v, is the rate of

Figure 1. The binding E to form a group or break it up. Shown here, two followers (2A) bind together with each other and to one leader (B) to form a group (A_2B).

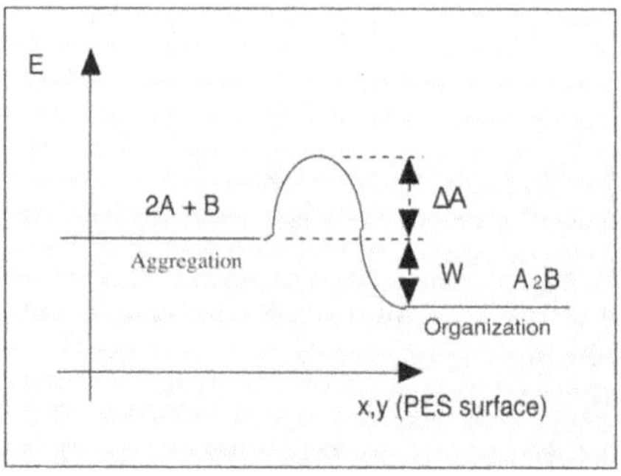

change of I in the interaction; σ_{RM} is the interaction cross-section between agents interacting like coupled harmonic oscillators but under the influence of differences between the vocal, brain or interaction frequencies of outsiders, ω_R and members, ω_M, where ω_R is a driver that transforms an organization, increasing rapidly (resonance) from a random exploration that converges as frequencies "match"; that is, $\sigma_{RM} = f(\omega_M{}^4/(\omega_R{}^2 - \omega_M{}^2)^2)$; $exp(\bullet)$ is the probability that sufficient free E, ΔA, is available to overcome the barriers to an interaction—the more ΔA required for an activity, the less likely it occurs; k_B is Boltzman's constant and T temperature, $T = (\partial E/\partial K)_V$, for a constant volume, V; and k_BT represents the average distribution of an activity such as revenue directed at the target interaction; e.g., all things being equal, the greater the average revenue generated by a new product or idea, the lower the barrier to the interaction.

Frequency, ω, provides other information. If the average distance between agents implies organizational wave length, λ (where $\lambda = f(1/\omega)$), at the E minimum, the more cooperation among agents, systems, and humans, the less I density and more K homogeneity that exists (e.g., fewer of Schama's competing beliefs), with the likelihood K remains localized as inversely proportional to an organization's success (Arrow, 1962). The converse occurs under perturbations from competition, reproducing the reliable observation that organizations under threat become physically closer (i.e., a threat to an organization increases E, reducing λ). In addition, the more well-organized an organization, like a city, that is attacked, the more likely it pulls together versus a disorganized organization (Glaeser, 1996). For example, the stock price of the comparatively well-run Dutch/Shell Group fell then quickly recovered in 2004 after news that it revised downward its oil and gas reserves, but the \$32 price for US Airways stock has fallen and stayed below \$5 with news that it was under competitive assault from Southwest Airlines.

But why does a group stick together? The advantages to joining a successful group are reduced expenditures to assure E for survival in exchange for membership: social loafing (Latane, 1981); enhanced skills from audience effects (Zajonc, 1998); better health from greater interaction density (House, Landis & Umberson, 1988) and protected belief systems (Rosenblatt et al., 1990). Economists consider one of the main advantages of joining a group to be the gains from specialization within the group (e.g., Ambrose, 2001). However, this I can be hidden even to the organization.

Perturbations energize an attacked organization, illuminating its structures and responses to attack, producing *I*. For example, the main goal of the Afghanistan Campaign was to disrupt the enemy and hinder its ability to execute another attack, but the first strikes also served to "produce intelligence that would allow the United States to understand and counter the enemy" (Feith, 2004, A21). But if the *E* in the attack is too low, the attack may be thwarted or its *I* content poor; if the *E* of attack is too high, the attacker may be disabled or dismembered, again producing poor *I* content. If each unit of an organization can be characterized by how it was built and the organization resides in a stable state at its lowest *E*, reversing the process by an attacker going from low to high *E* should produce a profile or spectrum of the organization, with breakup occurring at a resonance characteristic of the structure (imagine using Dooley's, 2004, discourse analysis inside of an organization as an attack against it intensifies; at a characteristic point, our speculation is that after perturbations of increasing intensity, at some point an incremental additional perturbation aimed at an organization from outside generates an unusually large response inside of the organization—resonance—as the organization begins to break apart). But using perturbations to produce *I* raises the measurement problem.

Perturbation Model: The Measurement Problem

In our perturbation model (Lawless & Grayson, 2004b), instead of disturbances that must be avoided or resolved from the traditional perspective, the perturbation of an organization generates bidirectional feedback that becomes the primary source of *I* for both the attacked and attacker. In our model, there is no need to determine the value of cooperation or competition. Instead, observers neutral to an attack contribute to the solution of an ill-defined problem reflected in the attack by choosing or selecting a winner, as in the courtroom, or by buying a car from a dealer, or by watching or listening to a media channel (2). Thus, we avoid the unsolvable problem of determining preferences or normative values in methodological individualism by measuring the result of a perturbation. For example, the outcome of the Southwest Airline's low-fare maneuver in 2004 against US Airways in Philadelphia was predatory, but beneficial to consumers; the inability of AT&T Wireless to enact phone number portability made it prey for a merger; and in the 2003 Iraq War, the plan for multiple attacks to get "inside of the enemy's decision cycle" (Franks, 2004, p. 466) executed by the coalition forces caused the Iraqi troops to panic and its military organizations to break apart (Keegan, 2004).

We replace the unsolvable "normative" problem of values with a difficult but ultimately solvable one—the measurement problem: Measuring an interdependent or bistable phenomenon such as a human organization produces classical *I* that cannot recreate the original phenomenon (Lawless & Grayson, 2004a). In the bistable model, uncertainties between acting and observing are interdependent, as they are between individuals and organizations, and between two organizations contemplating a merger. Reducing uncertainty in the observable of interest increases the uncertainty in its conjugate factor. That is, the more that is known about say a plan to merge, the less that can be known simultaneously about its execution; or the more known about the costs to merge, the less that can be known simultaneously about the time involved in completing the merger. These uncertainties are illustrated in Figure 2 (with $v = \Delta K/\Delta t$, and given the

Figure 2. (3) and (4). The measurement problem from the perspective of a merger target (parallel uncertainty relations exist for the acquiring organization). For example, ***Strategy****: After AT&T Wireless put itself on the auction block in early 2004 and Cingular made the first offer, AT&T Wireless did not know whether bids would be received from other players such as Vodafone, or how much more would be offered;* ***Execution****: Cingular expected that AT&T Wireless would execute a strategy with momentum by choosing the best bid by the deadline it had set, an expectation that turned out to be incorrect;* ***Energy****: AT&T Wireless did not know whether Cingular or Vodafone would increase their bids to an amount it considered sufficient;* ***Time****: Although the bidders believed incorrectly that the deadline was firmly established, AT&T Wireless was uncertain of the time when the bids would be offered. Finally, although power goes to the winner, it was not easy to determine who won and who lost in this auction. AT&T Wireless was unable to enact number portability and became the prey, but its CEO exacted a superior premium for his company and stockholders; although the merger on paper made Cingular the number one wireless company in the United States, it may have overpaid for the merger; and during the uncertainty of regulatory review (both the length of the regulatory review period and the regulatory decision), with AT&T Wireless losing customers as competitors exploited the regulatory uncertainty, it was unknown how costly the eventual merger would be based on the assets remaining once the merger had been consummated.*

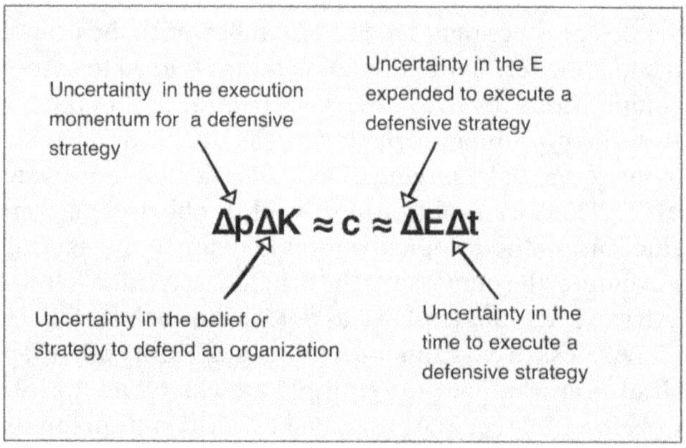

inertial effects of j for reactance, $j\,\Delta v\Delta K = j \bullet(\Delta K/\Delta t)\ \Delta t/\Delta t\ \Delta K = j \bullet(\Delta K/\Delta t)^2\,\Delta t$, giving $\Delta p\Delta K = \Delta t\Delta E \geq c$; from Lawless & Grayson, 2004b).

In sum, if "methodological individualism is all about accessible I, the mathematical physics of organizational behavior is all about information that is mostly inaccessible to an organization and its outsiders. To uncover this hidden I about an organization requires that it be disturbed, an idea traceable to Lewin (1951). But if social reality is bistable (interdependent), measurement produces classical information that cannot recover the character of the organization, the essence of the measurement problem (Figure 2). A common perturbation in economics is a price war between competing organizations; for our case studies below, a familiar perturbation on the Citizen Advisory Boards (herein called "Boards") providing cleanup advice to DOE is the conflict caused by incommensurable views, interpretations or beliefs. Although *cooperation* rules attempt to dampen conflict, *competition* rules harness it by driving random searches among multiple sources of information for the idea that withstands all challenges (i.e., stochastic resonance). From a bistable perspective, the primary difference between the two styles of decision making is that consensus-seeking methodologically converts an organization into accessible individuals, consequently devaluing neutral observers; in contrast, the competition between two or more opponents under majority rule exploits bistability by converting neutral members into judges.

The Case Study of a Measurement Problem: DOE Citizen Advisory Boards

Recently, we applied this model in a field test among Citizen Advisory Boards working to help the Department of Energy (DOE) make cleanup decisions at its sites across the United States (Lawless, Bergman, & Feltovich, 2005). In comparing the two Boards with the largest budgets of about $1 billion each, the Hanford Board used consensus-seeking and the Savannah River Site (SRS) Advisory Board used majority rule (Table 1). In our earlier study, we had found that the Hanford Advisory Board relied primarily on values while the SRS Board attempted to accelerate the cleanup (Table 2).

As one example of what we had found, both DOE sites had to consider shipments of transuranic (Tru) wastes to their respective sites for interim storage before eventual transport to the Tru waste repository at the Waste Isolation Pilot Plant (WIPP) in New

Table 1. Citizen Advisory Boards (CAB's) associated with DOE sites

Active CAB's (N = 9)	Decision Process	Inactive SSAB's (N = 3)	Decision Process
Fernald	CR	Pantex	CR
Hanford	CR	Sandia	CR
Idaho (ID)	CR	Monticello	MR
Nevada Test Site	MR		
Northern New Mexico	MR		
Oak Ridge (OR)	MR		
Paducah	MR		
Rocky Flats Plant	CR		
Savannah River Site (SRS)	MR		

Table 2. Expectations for CR and MR (Bradbury, Branch, & Malone, 2003; Lawless et al., 2005)

	CR	MR
Pros	Consensus rules promote substantive issues, cooperative relationships, accountability, values (e.g., fairness) and information disclosure.	Majority rules promote compromise and instrumental action; e.g., accelerating cleanup safely.
Cons	Instead of accelerating cleanup, reiterating values wastes time.	Energy required to resolve conflicts.

Figure 3. Transuranic (Tru) wastes are being shipped via trucks (TRUPACT II containers; above left) to the repository in a salt formation at WIPP near Carlsbad, NM (www.wipp.ws). Tru wastes are contaminated with uranium 233 or elements beyond uranium on the periodic table in concentrations greater than 100 nCi/g. These isotopes have half-lives that range greater than 20 years, but consist mostly of Plutonium-239 with a half-life of about 24,000 years.

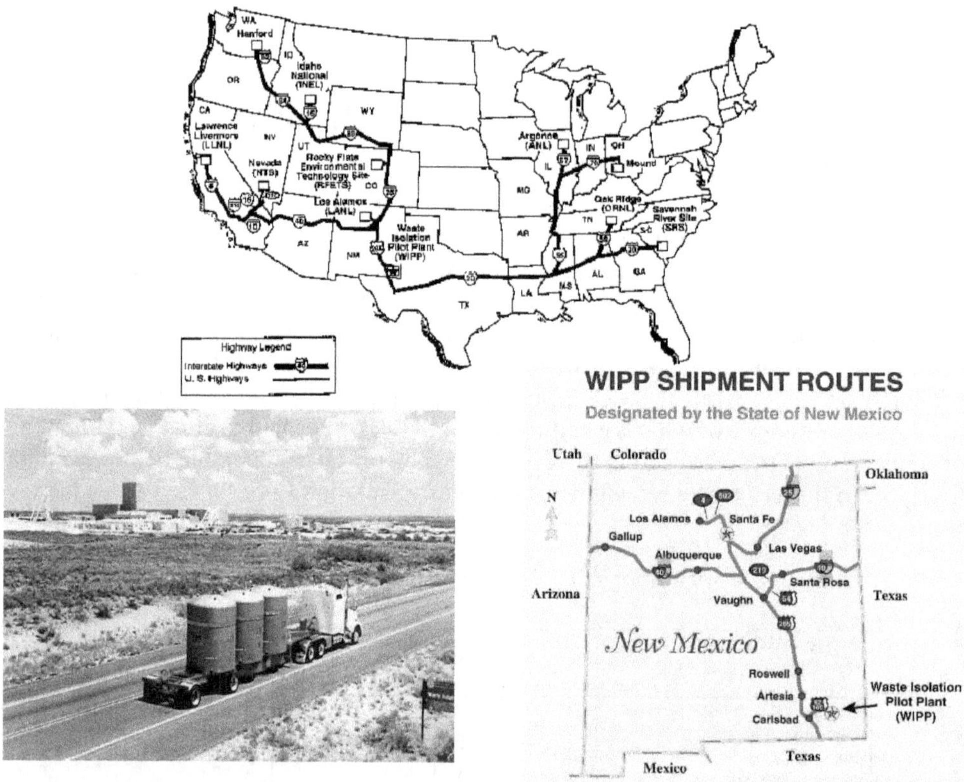

Mexico (see Figure 3). In response, the consensus-seeking Hanford board concluded that "the recent shipments of Tru wastes from Battelle Columbus (BCK) and Energy Technology Engineering Center (ETEC) to Hanford caused grave concern to the Hanford Advisory Board (Board)" (HAB, 2002). In contrast, the majority-rule SRS Board concluded that due to the considerable taxpayer savings, the relatively low risk, and the use of funding external to SRS for the activity, the SRS CAB recommends that DOE-SR accept the [offsite] TRU waste shipments from Mound as long as the following conditions are met: 1. DOE receives approval to ship more TRU waste volume from SRS [to WIPP, in NM] than received from Mound. The SRS CAB preference is to see at least twice the volume (SAB, 2000).

Differences in the field as a result of these two decisions were dramatic. Prior to 2003, with the inventory of Tru wastes at Hanford at about twice that of SRS, shipments of Tru waste to the Tru waste repository at WIPP from both sites were about 1% of their respective inventories (see DOE, 2003). However, today, Hanford has made only 2,500 shipments compared to 10,934 shipments by SRS (Lawless et al., 2005). But would this finding for two Boards hold for all Boards?

Assistant Secretary of Energy Roberson (2002) called for an acceleration of the cleanup in 2002, including Tru wastes destined for WIPP. In response, DOE Scientists developed 13 recommendations to accelerate the disposal of Tru wastes (Table 3). In 2003, these recommendations were submitted to representatives of all of the Boards for their approval.

As an example of what the recommendations would mean if enacted, the eighth recommendation (bolded in Table 3) indicates that some waste currently classified as Tru waste, requiring it to be packaged and sent to the Tru waste repository at WIPP for its ultimate disposition, might be left at the individual sites if a scientific risk analysis indicated that it could be safely buried *in situ*. If implemented, the decision would save money and time, but it would leave a long-lived waste in near-surface disposal.

The measurement problem requires a prediction of how an organization acts to a perturbation such as the request by DOE scientists that Boards support their recommendations to accelerate the disposition of Tru wastes. Figure 4 illustrates mathematically the effects of interdependence on uncertainty. For example, as uncertainty in strategy

Table 3. Recommendations by DOE scientists to accelerate Tru waste disposition

- DOE characterize TRU waste as required to reduce risk and minimize transportation and handling of waste while making confirmation process cost effective
- Therefore, to meet Site Specific needs, DOE allocate and coordinate resources complex-wide to optimize shipping to maximize the receiving capacity of WIPP
- DOE in concert with stakeholders and regulators initiate an ongoing program to identify, correct and revise those requirements that interfere with the safe, prompt and cost effective management of TRU waste
- DOE identify volumes and disposition pathways for all potential TRU waste streams
- DOE in consultation with stakeholders and regulators initiate action to assure that WIPP has the capacity to accommodate all of the above listed TRU waste
- DOE accelerate TRU waste container design, licensing and deployment
- DOE streamline TRU waste management by accepting demonstrated process knowledge for TRU waste characterization
- **DOE, in consultation with stakeholders and regulators, reexamine the categorization of TRU waste using a risk-based approach**
- DOE identify the inventory of orphan TRU waste and assign a corporate team to identify a path forward
- DOE evaluate the concept of one or more locations to characterize TRU waste for WIPP disposal
- DOE finish its analyses and make a decision with adequate public involvement regarding where to characterize TRU waste for disposal
- DOE expedite the design, fabrication and certification of container transport systems Arrowpak and TRUPACT III and accelerate the adoption of rail transport as appropriate
- DOE revitalize its efforts in coordinating its transportation issues with States and Tribes and assist in updating and disseminating information to the public about transportation risks and safety and provide public participation opportunities on transport issues

Figure 4. The measurement problem from the perspective of DOE for its Transuranic wastes. In response to DOE Assistant Secretary Roberson (2002), ***Strategy****: Could DOE's sites respond with an aggressive plan to accelerate Tru wastes to WIPP (e.g., SRS planned to dispose of all of its Tru wastes by 2006)?* ***Execution****: Could accelerating Tru waste shipments occur when shipments are contingent on new containers for large objects (TRUPACT III) and high-activity Tru (ARROWPAK for Plutonium-238 wastes)?* ***Energy****: Are sufficient funds available to accelerate the acquisition and licensing of containers to accelerate Tru waste shipments?* ***Time****: Could new containers be licensed in a timely fashion?*

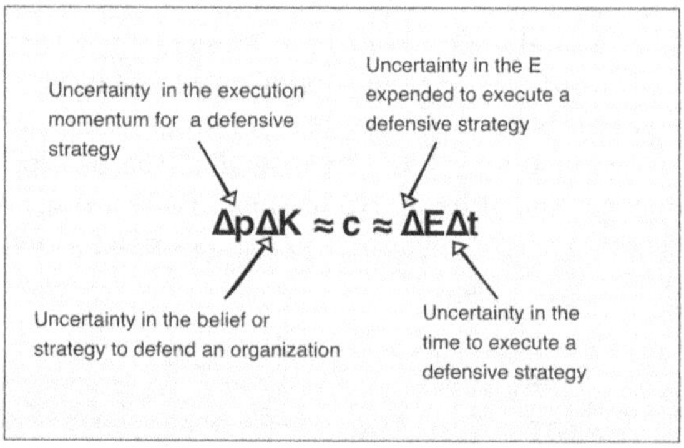

increases (e.g., more emphasis on values), uncertainty in execution decreases, and similarly for E and t.

The request by the DOE scientists amounted to a perturbation felt across all of the Boards over four domains. Figure 4 takes the perspective of DOE. Shifting to the perspective of the Boards, Figure 4 becomes:

- **Strategy Uncertainty:** Would Boards believe in the plan?
- **Execution Uncertainty:** Would the Boards vote for the plan?
- **Energy Uncertainty:** Would Boards expend effort in support?
- **Time Uncertainty:** Would support by the Boards be timely?

Based on our prior research (Lawless et al., 2005), we expected that majority rule Boards would adopt the measures to accelerate Tru waste disposition at their respective sites, that consensus-rule Boards would take longer to make this decision, and that ultimately the focus by consensus rule Boards on values would produce less complex decisions than those by majority-rule Boards.

At the SSAB Transuranic Workshop in Carlsbad, New Mexico, in January 2003, representatives (N=105) from all of the Boards discussed the recommendations by the DOE scientists and reached unanimity. The representatives from each of the Boards were expected to return to their respective sites and present these recommendations to their own Boards for a consensus vote. The result (Figure 5): Five of nine Boards approved these Tru waste recommendations (*Majority Rule Boards*: SAB [SRS], Oak Ridge,

Figure 5. Mathematical interdependence of uncertainty: ***A****. Majority rule (MR) Boards bring opposing views together to seek the best decision (ΔK low; Lawless & Schwartz, 2002), producing instrumental action (Δv high; shown: 4 MR Boards agreed, not shown: 1 MR Board did not).* ***B****. After expressing multiple views (ΔK high; Bradbury et al., 2003), consensus-rule (CR) Boards mostly did not accept the requests on Tru wastes by DOE Scientists (Δv -> 0; shown: 1 CR Board accepts; not shown: 3 CR Boards did not).* ***C****. Conflict on MR Boards is intense (ΔE -> ∞; e.g., Hagoort, 2003; Lawless et al., 2000b) but among few participants and thus short-lived (shown: Δt = 0.5 hours).* ***D****. Instead of instrumental action, CR Boards repeatedly restate values with many speakers over long and uncertain periods of time (shown: Δt = 2 hours), suggesting a lack of interest in many observers (ΔE -> low; Hagoort et al., 2004).*

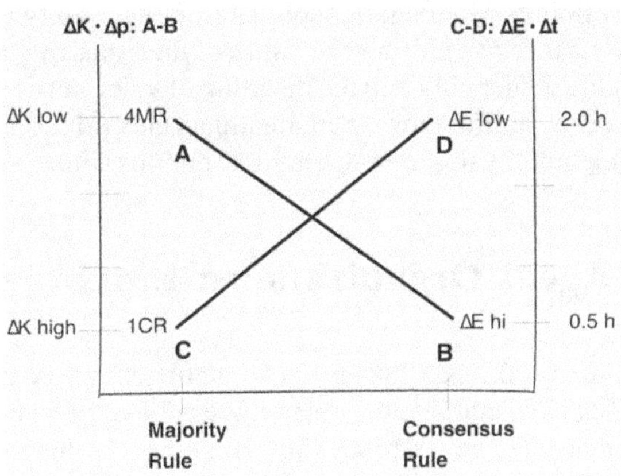

Northern New Mexico; Nevada Test Site; *Consensus Rule Boards*: Idaho); four of the nine Boards disapproved (*Majority Rule Boards*: Paudcah; *Consensus Rule Boards*: Hanford, Fernald, Rocky Flats), giving $\chi^2(1)=2.74, p<.05$.

The interdependence observed in Figure 5 agreed with predictions. The time to complete consensus seeking was much longer than for majority rule (and the energy expended was less). More importantly, majority rule Boards mostly adopted the recommendations by DOE scientists, while consensus rule Boards mostly rejected them, possibly reflecting that as participants sought consensus, they became more motivated to reach "understanding" as claimed in a recent evaluation of these Boards (Bradbury et al., 2003) rather than motivate their respective sites to take instrumental action to cleanup their sites. The tradeoff observed was that consensus-rule Boards were more focused on values whereas majority rule Boards were more focused on accelerating cleanup.

DISCUSSION: FIELD EXPERIMENTS

From a practical perspective, normative social scientists have long argued that cooperative decision making (consensus) improves social welfare more effectively than the competition used as part of truth seeking in a democracy. In a recent evaluation of its policy on consensus (Bradbury et al., 2003), the Department of Energy (DOE) encouraged its Citizen Site Specific Advisory Boards "to work toward consensus" in order to be "fair," thereby improving American democracy. But no empirical evidence was collected from the field by DOE to validate its policy (Lawless et al., 2005). In contrast, the literature and field data contradicted DOE: consensus seeking retarded cleanup; the coercion necessary to seek consensus reduced trust; and consensus-seeking favored risk perception rather than scientifically determined risk. In contrast, and as the first application of the mathematical physics of uncertainty between organizations, we have found that the competition of ideas driven by truth seeking encouraged by majority rule significantly accelerated DOE's cleanup and improved trust.

Jones (1990) speculated that nothing could be known about the interaction, only its starting and ending points. Mathematical physics of uncertainty does not contradict Jones, but goes much further by limiting the value of these starting and ending points. It indicates that the value of meaning and the meaning of value act as a veil that, because we are organisms alive in a culture awash in meanings and values, cannot be removed no matter how exacting our physics or mathematics, but this ambiguity can be managed (Choo, 1998).

Extensions to Agent Organizations: EMCAS—An Agent Model

Chen, Tai and Chie (2002, p. 1238) propose that agent based models may reveal important features of financial market phenomena. We believe the same may be true about organizational phenomena. However, Macy (2004) cautions us that agent models will be dismissed as "toys" if their choices and behaviors are not empirically valid. Our interpretation of Macy is that when agents attempt to address phenomena in computational environments, models must be as constrained by social and physical reality as are humans or robots. This ecological validity can be accomplished by reverse engineering phenomena.

We apply these ideas and lessons learned to a well-established model. Briefly, EMCAS agents (herein, we treat EMCAS and its predecessor agent models as one) model the complexities in the electricity power generation and distribution industry (North, 2001). We review predictions by the EMCAS model along with relevant field results from the power industry. This review is important not only because EMCAS is designed to explore public policies in electricity markets, but also as Dignum and Weigand (2002) have noted, knowledge, *K*, is an organization's most important asset, and how an organization reacts to this *K* is important to its competitiveness and to whether or not it survives (Lawless & Grayson, 2004b).

EMCAS builds on the "repast" model, itself derived from swarm models at the Sante Fe Institute (see http://www.wiki.swarm.org/wiki/Main_Page). EMCAS is designed to simulate the power industry as it moves from very stable, centrally controlled monopolies to deregulated, highly competitive but also analytically intractable systems of consumers, multiple organizations and regulatory agencies. EMCAS agents are stylized, well-defined, and, according to the authors, rational learning agents that use the "best estimator for tomorrow's [electricity] prices" (North, personal communication, 2004; North et al., 2003, p. 256). Uncertainty is programmed into EMCAS by applying probability distributions to the interactions between agents and organizations (North et al., 2002). Its designers envision EMCAS as an extension of game theory (MI), based on the results of a power market simulation game run by humans and from extensive interviews of the human players and power industry experts. Claims for EMCAS include the notion that deregulation of the power industry has been disruptive, citing the example of California (Thomas et al., 2003), that the low prices for natural gas generation were increasing its market share (Macal & North, 2002), and that regulators must carefully monitor natural gas supplies (North, 2001), citing as an example Com-Ed in Illinois (ANL, the creator of EMCAS, is located in the Com-Ed market). Further, the claim was made that "EMCAS and its component agents are currently being subjected to rigorous quantitative validation and calibration" (North et al., 2002).

The field evidence contradicts the claims made for EMCAS. First, North (2004; also, North et al., 2003) claimed that the EMCAS agents should use the best available forecast tools to predict market behavior, but as Kahneman and Tversky (1979) pointed out, human agents do not use the best available tools and are often irrational—reflected at any moment on any stock market, including the electricity power market, as the struggle between buyers expecting rising values and sellers expecting falling values produces an efficient market (e.g., Fama, 1965). Second, the California power market was deregulated only at the wholesale level but not the retail level, making its electricity market "dysfunctional" according to the Federal Energy Regulatory Commission (see www.ferc.gov; also, see Bushnell, Mansur, & Saravia, 2004). Third, in Illinois, the electricity generated by natural gas for 2002 was only 4.8% of its total market (the national rate is about 16% and steady over the past few years; see DOE/EIA 0226, 2004/09), and its prices of natural gas in 2002 were over two times that of coal and more for nuclear, the two primary sources in Illinois (DOE/EIA State profile, 2002, Illinois; Illinois Commerce Commission at www.icc.state.il.us/ec/electricity.aspx), both mostly ignored in the results for the EMCAS model—currently, the operational costs over the life of an electricity generation plant in the Unites States averages $1.71 per kWh for nuclear, $1.85 for coal, and $4.06 for natural gas (see online.wsj.com). Fourth, no validation results have yet been published for EMCAS.

But the critical flaw, as we have demonstrated, is that the substantial bias interjected into EMCAS with interviews of human players and experts was not constrained by field results—to reiterate, Eagly and Chaiken (1993) have noted that questions can elicit any desired response, game theory preferences and choices do not match (Kelley, 1992), and once decisions have been made, justifications do not agree with decisions (Shafir et al., 1993). Thus, to be useful, subjectivity must be constrained by field results; e.g., in a contrast of domestic market futures for the 2004 United States presidential election of play money futures against real money futures, the former predicted a landslide for Kerry while the latter predicted a close Bush win (e.g., compare presidentialmarket.org with www.biz.uiowa.edu/iem/markets; also see Berg & Rietz, 2003); illustrating subjective denial, GM and Ford blamed their loss of market share over the past year on high energy prices and declines in consumer spending and personal income, when over the same period sales for Japanese cars surged and rose overall for the United Sstates (see online.wsj.com); and at a time when competition in the EU is deteriorating, the EU has drafted a constitution to make its 25 nation bloc more competitive, but its length and complexity (ΔK high) make enactment less likely (Wim Kok, Nov. 3, 2004; europa.eu.int/

comm/enlargement/communication). Finally, unlike EMCAS, before manipulating variables to address policy issues, Bushnell and his colleagues (2004) first made their Nash-Cournot model match power consumption across regions of the United States.

On other critical issues, EMCAS is silent. It ignores the need for real-time pricing of electricity to better affect consumer demand (e.g., www.euci.com); it ignores the effects of divestitures and mergers as monopolies "unbundle" electricity services or combine to gain others (e.g., Exelon, the "best-in-its-class" and a Chicago utility with the largest capitalization in the US, proposed in December 2004 a merger with New Jersey's PSE&G to expand its nuclear power generation to gain economies of scale, significant cost savings, and more efficiency); and it ignores the need for R&D as deregulation impels electricity providers to become more competitive—today, the power industry invests in R&D at one of the lowest rates for any industrial sector (Fairley, 2004). The result is that the EMCAS model could have been tested and validated from the beginning with field data, but instead it has already produced a recommendation for policy that was incorrect and unjustified.

CONCLUSION

What we have found in this study of organizations is inconclusive on our part due to the incomplete trail of data (see Figure 5), but the results for organizational science provide a path forward in the laboratory, the field, and with agent models. For computational agent models, the path forward is becoming clearer. Without resorting to stories, we were able to build on Lewin's (1951) insights regarding perturbations by empirically constraining agents and organizations with social and physical effects. Our results illustrate the danger of the subjective approach of Bradbury and her colleagues with human organizations and North and his colleagues with computational agents as organizations. Otherwise, the results reported above for the Iowa US presidential futures market become an insuperable challenge to agent models. We have noted several reasons why physics models have not worked with human agents—human agents generate substantial uncertainty in interviews, preferences and justifications—making the rational path from individual to organization problematic.

But we have provided a model that constrains these uncertainties and illustrates how to exploit them with the mathematical physics of uncertainty borrowed from quantum theory. We did this by replacing the apparently unsolvable "normative" problem of arbitrarily elevating the value of cooperation with a difficult but ultimately solvable one—the measurement problem: Measuring an interdependent or bistable phenomenon such as a human organization produces classical *I* that cannot recreate the original phenomenon; as centers of cooperation, organizations are low *I* producers, motivating the need for perturbations to generate *I*; however, the more resistant (inertia) an organization or system is to perturbations, the less *I* it produces from mundane perturbations.

In closing, we agree with Giddens (1979) who wrote "the structural properties of social systems are both the medium and the outcome of the practices that constitute those systems" (p. 69). It is this interdependence that our results illuminate. Taken as a whole, we have found that in contrast to consensus-seeking, truth-seeking constrains risk perception. We extended this finding to computational agents by concluding that a model increases risk perception and moral hazard when it is not valid for the social and physical environment.

ACKNOWLEDGMENT

The first author would like to thank the reviewers for their helpful comments and suggested changes. The first author also thanks James A. Ballas Information Technology Division, Naval Research Laboratory (NRL), Washington, DC, where most of this research was conducted with funds from Office of Naval Research through an American Society of Engineers Education (ASEE) grant.

REFERENCES

Allport, F. H. (1962). A structuronomic conception of behavior: Individual and collective. *Journal of Abnormal and Social Psychology, 64,* 3-30.

Ambrose, S. H. (2001). Paleolithic technology and human evolution. *Science, 291,* 1748-53.

Andrade, G., & Stafford, E. (1999). *Investigating the economic role of mergers* (Working paper No 00-006). Cambridge, MA: Harvard University Press. Retreived July 29, 2005, from *http://ssrn.com/abstract=47264*

Arrow, K. J. (1951). *Social choice and individual values.* New York: Wiley.

Arrow, K. J. (1962). Economic welfare and the allocation of resources for invention. In R. Nelson (Ed.), *The rate and direction of inventive activity.* Princeton University Press.

Axelrod, R. (1984). *The evolution of cooperation.* New York: Basic.

Axsom, D., & Lawless, W. F. (1992). Subsequent behavior can erase evidence of dissonance-induced attitude change. *Journal of Experimental Social Psychology, 28,* 387-400.

Baumeister, R. F. (1995). Self and identity: An introduction. In A. Tesser (Ed.), *Advanced social psychology* (pp. 51-97). New York: McGraw-Hill.

Bekenstein, J. D. (2003, August). Information in the holographic universe. Retrieved from www.sciam.com

Berg, J. E., & Rietz, T. A. (2003). Prediction markets as decision support systems. *Information Systems Frontiers, 5*(1), 79-93.

Bohr, N. (1955). Science and the unity of knowledge. In L. Leary (Ed.), *The unity of knowledge* (pp. 44-62). New York: Doubleday.

Boykin, W. G. (2004, October 26). *Fighting for intelligence.* Retrieved from http://www.ausa.org

Bradbury, J. A., Branch, K. M., & Malone, E. L. (2003). *An evaluation of DOE-EM public participation programs (PNNL-14200).* Richland, WA: Pacific Northwest National Laboratory.

Bushnell, J., Mansur, E. T., & Saravia, C. (2004). Market structure and competition: A cross-market analysis of US Electricity deregulation. *CSEM WP, 126.*

Cacioppo, J. T., Berntson, G. G., & Crites, S. L., Jr. (Eds). (1996). Social neuroscience: Principles, psychophysiology, arousal and response. In E. T. Higgins & A. W.

Kruglanski (Eds.), *Social psychology handbook of basic principles* (pp. 72-101). New York: Guilford.

Campbell, D. T. (1996). Can we overcome worldview incommensurability/relativity in trying to understand the other? In R. Jessor & R.A. Shweder (Eds.), *Ethnography and human development* (pp. 153-172). Chicago: University of Chicago Press.

Carley, K. M. (2003). Dynamic network analysis In R. Breiger, K. Carley, & P. Pattison, *Dynamic social network modeling and analysis* (Workshop summary and papers, pp. 133-145). National Research Council of the National Academies, The National Academies Press, Washington, DC.

Chen, S.-H., Tai, C.-C., & Chie. B.-T. (2002). Individual rationality as a partial impediment to market efficiency. *JCIS,* 1163-1116.

Choo, C. W. (1998). *The knowing organization: How organizations use information to construct meaning, create knowledge, and make decisions.* New York: Oxford University Press.

Coleman, J. J. (2003). The benefits of campaign financing. Retrieved October 10, 2003, from *www.cato.org/pubs/briefs/bp-084es.html*

Conant, R. C. (1976). Laws of information which govern systems. *IEEE Transaction on Systems, Man, and Cybernetics, 6,* 240-255.

Dennett, D. C. (2003). *Freedom evolves.* New York: Penguin.

Department of Energy. (2003, October). *Top-to-bottom review of environmental management program.* Report to Congress, Washington, DC.

Dignum, V., & Weigand, H. (2002). Towards an organization-oriented design methodology for agent societies. In V. Plekhanova (Ed.), *Intelligent agent software engineering* (pp. 191-212). Hershey, PA: Idea Group Publishing.

Dooley, K. (2004), The semantic evolution of the Journal NDPLS. *The14th Annual International Conference, Society for Chaos Theory in Psychology and Life Sciences,* Marquette University, July 16.

Drucker, P. F. (2004, December 30). The American CEO. *Wall Street Journal,* p. A8.

Eagly, A. H., & Chaiken, S. (1993). *Psychology of attitudes.* Ft. Worth, TX: Harcourt.

Eldredge, N. (2004). *Rethinking sex and the selfish gene.* New York: Norton.

Energy Information Administration (2004). *Electric Power Monthly,* September. Report DOE/EIA-0226. Retrieved July 29, 2005, from *www.eia.doe.gov/cneaf/electricity/epm/emp_sum.html*

Fairley, P. (2004, August). The unruly power grid. *IEEE Spectrum,* 22-27.

Fama, E. F. (1965, September-October). Random walks in stock market prices. *Financial Analysts Journal, 51*(1), 75-80.

Feith, D.J. (2004, August 7). Op-ed: A war plan that cast a wide net. *Washington Post,* p. A21.

Franks, T. (with McConnell, M.) (2004). *American soldier.* New York: Harper-Collins.

French, A. P., & Taylor, E. F. (1979). *An introduction to quantum physics (MIT introduction to quantum physics.* Cambridge, MA: MIT Press.

Gibson, J. J. (1986). *An ecological approach to visual perception.* Hillsdale, NJ: Erlbaum.

Giddens, A. (1979). *Central problems in social theory.* London: MacMillan.

Glaeser, E. L. (1996). Why economists still like cities. *City Journal, 6*(2), 70-77.

HAB. (2002, February 7). HAB Recommendation 142. Acceptance of offsite Tru wastes.

Hagoort, P. (2003). How the brain solves the binding problem for language: A neurocomputational model of syntatic processing. *NeuroImage, 20,* S18-S29.

Hagoort, P., Hald, L., Bastiaansen, M., & Petersson, K. M. (2004). Integration of word meaning and world knowledge in language comprehension. *Science, 304*, 438-441.
Hardin, G. (1968). The tragedy of the commons. *Science, 162*, 1243-1248.
Heisenberg, W. (1958/1999). Language and reality in modern physics. In *Physics and philosophy: The revolution in modern science* (pp. 167-186). New York: Prometheus.
House, J. S., Landis, K. R., & Umberson, D. (1988). Social relationships and health. *Science, 241*, 540-545.
Insana, R. (2001). *The message of the markets*. New York: HarperCollins.
Jones, E. E. (1990). *Interpersonal perception*. New York: Freeman.
Kahneman, D., & Tversky, A. (1979). Prospect theory: An analysis of decision under risk. *Econometrica, 47*, 263-292.
Kang, G. S., & Fransen, L. J. (1994). Speech analysis and synthesis based on pitch-synchronous segmentation of the speech waveform (NRL Report 9743). Washington, DC.
Keegan, J. (2004). *The Iraq War*. New York: Knopf.
Kelley, H. H. (1992). Lewin, situations, and interdependence. *Journal of Social Issues, 47*, 211.
Kok, W. (2004, November 3). Enlarging the European Union: Achievements and challenges. Retrieved July 29, 2005, from *europa.eu.int/comm/enlargement/communication*
Kuhn, T. (1970). *The structure of scientific revolutions*. Chicago: University of Chicago Press.
Latane, B. (1981). The psychology of social impact. *American Psychologist, 36*, 343-356.
Lawless, W. F., Bergman, M., & Feltovich, N. (2005). Consensus-seeking versus truth-seeking. *ASCE Practice Periodical of Hazardous, Toxic, and Radioactive Waste Management, 9*(1), 59-70.
Lawless, W. F., & Castelao, T. (2001, Summer). The University as decision center. *IEEE Technolgy and Society Magazine, 20*, 6-17.
Lawless, W. F., Castelao, T., & Abubucker, C. P. (2000). In C. Tessier et al. (Eds.), *Conflicting agents: Conflict management in multi-agent systems* (pp. 279-302). Boston: Kluwer.
Lawless, W. F., Castelao, T., & Ballas, J. A. (2000). Virtual knowledge: Bistable reality and the solution of ill-defined problems. *IEEE Systems Man, and Cybernetics, 30*(1), 119-126.
Lawless, W. F., & Grayson, J. M. (2004a). A conjugate model of organizations, autonomy, and control. In *Interaction between humans and autonomous systems over extended operation* (AAAI Tech. Rep. SS-04-03, pp. 116-121). Stanford.
Lawless, W. F., & Grayson, J. M. (2004b). A quantum perturbation model (QPM) of knowledge and organizational mergers. In L. van Elst, V. Dignum, & A. Abecker (Eds.), *Agent-mediated knowledge management* (pp. 143-161). Berlin, Germany: Springer-Verlag.
Lawless, W. F., & Schwartz, M. (2002). The social quantum model of dissonance. From social organization to cultural evolution. *Social Science Computer Review (Sage), 20*(4), 441-450.
Levine, J. M., & Moreland, R. L. (1998). Small groups. In D. T. Gilbert, S.T. Fiske, & G. Lindzey (Eds.), *Handbook of social psychology* (Vol. 2, pp. 415-469). McGraw-Hill.

Lewin, K. (1951). *Field theory in social science.* Boston: Harper.

Lipshitz, R. (1997). Naturalistic decision making perspectives on decision errors. In C. E. Zsambok & G. Klein (Eds.), *Naturalistic decision making* (pp. 49-59). Mahwah, NJ: Erlbaum.

Luce (1997). Several unresolved conceptual problems of mathematical psychology. *Journal of Mathematical Psychology, 41*, 79-87.

Luce, R. D., & Raiffa, H. (1967). *Games and decision.* New York: Wiley.

Macal, C. (2004), *Closing comments.* Agent 2004 Conference on Social dynamics: Interaction, reflexivity and emergence, Argonne National Lab, University of Chicago.

Macal, C. M., & North, M. J. (2002). *Simulating energy markets and infrastructure interdependencies with agent-based models.* Presented at Agent 2002, University of Chicago, October 7-9.

Macy, M. (2004). *Social life in silico: From factors to actors in the new sociology.* Chicago: Argonne National Lab, University of Chicago.

May, R. M. (1973/2001). *Stability and complexity in model ecosystems.* Princeton University Press.

May, R. M. (1997). *Science, 275,* 793-796.

Nash, J. F., Jr. (1950). The bargaining problem. *Econometrica, 18,* 155-162.

North, M. (2001). Technical note: Multi-agent social and organizational modeling of the electric power and natural gas markets. *Computational and Mathematical Organization Theory, 7*(4), 331-337.

North, M. (2004, October 27). Personal communication (e-mails).

North, M., Conzelmann, G., Koritarov, V., Macal, C., Thimmapuram, P. & Veselka, T. (2002, April 15-17,). *E-Laboratories: Agent-based modeling of electricity markets.* American Power Conference, Chicago.

North, M. J., Thimmapuram, P. R., Cirillo, R., Macal, C., Conzelmann, G., Boyd, G., Koritarov, V., & Vseekla, T. (2003, October). *EMCAS: An agent-based tool for modeling electricity markets.* Presented at Agent 2003, University of Chicago, IL.

Nowak, M. A., & Sigmund, K. (2004). Evolutionary dynamics of biological games. *Science, 303,* 793-799.

Polanyi, M. (1974). *Personal knowledge.* Chicago: University of Chicago Press.

Roberson, J. H. (2002, April 10). DOE Assistant Secretary for Environmental Management, Statement before the Subcommittee on Strategic Committee on Armed Services, US Senate.

Rosenblatt, A., Greenberg, J., Solomon, S., Pyszczynski, T., & Lyon, D. (1990). Evidence for terror management theory. *Journal of Personality and Social Psychology, 57,* 681-690.

Sallach, D. L. (2002). *Modeling emotional dynamics: Currency versus fields.* American Sociological Association, University of Chicago.

Savannah River Site Citizens Advisory Board (SAB). (2000, September 26). SAB Recommendation 130. Mound tru waste shipments to SRS.

Schama, S. (1995). *Landscape and memory.* New York: Random House.

Shafir, E., Simonson, I., & Tversky, A. (1993). *Cognition, 49,* 11-36.

Slovic, P., Layman, M., Kraus, N., Flynn, J. Chalmers, J., & Gesell, G. (2001). Perceived risk. In J. Flynn, P. Slovic, & H. Kunreuther (Eds.), *Risk, media and stigma* (pp. 87-106). London: Earthscan.

Suskind, L. S., & Thomas-Larmer, J. (1999). *The consensus building handbook*. Thousand Oaks, CA: Sage.

Tajfel, H. (1970). Experiments in intergroup discrimination. *Scientific American, 223*(2), 96-102.

Thomas, W. H., North, M. J., Macal, C. M., & Peerenboom, J. P. (2003). *From physics to finances: Complex adaptive systems representation of infrastructure interdependencies*. Naval Surface Warfare Center Technical Report.

Trustnet. (2004). *Draft: Trustnet 2: Towards inclusive governance of hazardous activities*. European Commission—Science, Research, Development, Fifth Framework Programme of the European Atomic Energy Community (EURATOM) for research in the fields of nuclear energy (1998-2002). Retrieved July 29, 2005, from *http://www.trustnetinaction.com/article.php3?id_article=185*

Von Neumann, J., & Morgenstern, O. (1953). *Theory of games and economic behavior*. NJ: Princeton University Press.

Von Schomberg, R. (2004). The normative dimensions of the precautionary principle and its relation to science and risk management decisions. In T. Achen (Ed.), *Microscopic modification and big politics*. Sweden: Vadstena.

Weick, K. E., & Quinn, R. E. (1999). Organizational change and development. *Annual Review of Psychology, 50*, 361-386.

Wickens, C. D. (1992). *Engineering psychology and human performance* (2nd ed.). Columbus, OH: Merrill.

WP (White Paper). (2001). European governance (COM (2001) 428 final; Brussels, 25.7.2001). Brussels, Belgium.

Zadeh, L. A. (2003, October 6). Computing with words and perceptions, a paradigm shift in computing and decision analysis. Retrieved from *becat.engr.uconn.edu/IEEE_CSMC_2003*

Zajonc, R. B. (1998). Emotion. In D. T. Gilbert, S. T. Fiske, & G. Lindzey (Eds.), *The handbook of social psychology*. Boston: McGraw-Hill.

Chapter XV

Reducing Agency Problem and Improving Organizational Value-Based Decision-Making Model of Inter-Organizational Strategic Alliance

Tsai-Lung Liu
I-Shou University, Taiwan
Tajen Institute of Technology, Taiwan

Chia-Chen Kuo
I-Shou University, Taiwan

ABSTRACT

This chapter employs a cross-theory perspective by combining the four theories of agency theory, resource-dependent theory, resource-based theory, and knowledge-based theory, intending to explore the impact of inter-organizational strategic alliance on organizational value-based decision-making model and intellectual capital. Drawing the related variables upon making the literature review, analysis and inference, it infers 18 propositions and builds up a conceptual model. As a result, it is found that different formation factors of inter-organizational strategic alliance not only have significanty impact on an agency problem, but also have positive or negative impact on core resource and core knowledge strategic alliance. It is also found that when there is an inter-organizational agency problem, it will further increase the agency cost, and impact on the organizational value-based decision of inter-organizational strategic alliance in the future. Furthermore, the authors hope that researchers understanding through the governance mechanisms of inter-organizational core resource alliance and core knowledge strategic alliance are more matured, it will be more effective to prevent the appearance of agency problem and reduce agency cost and will be more helpful to the increase of organizational intellectual capital and the creation of organizational value.

INTRODUCTION

As there is a tendency towards global economization, many researchers are concerned about the issue of inter-organizational strategic alliance. First, when citing resource-dependent theory to study the issue of strategic alliance, Boyd (1990) found that when external environment uncertainty is raised, an inter-organizational merger is encouraged, ensuring the acquisition of rare resource. Second, the problem of how an organization uses the mechanism of strategic alliance to increase asset return ratio, reduce cost and raise organizational efficiency can be studied from a transaction cost perspective (Hennart, 1988; Oliver, 1991; Williamson, 1981). Third, some researchers adopt the perspective of strategic behavior theory to explore how the mechanism of inter-organizational strategic alliance increases organizational competitive advantage (Davlin & Bleackley, 1988; Kanter, 1990; Porter, 1990). Fourth, the perspective of unified theory has been taken to integrate internalization theory, market failure and transaction cost theory, proving organizational strategic alliance to be the best choice of business operation model (Contractor, 1990). Fifth, from the perspective of network theory, some researchers explore how an organization merges with other organizations through network relationship alliance so as to obtain competitive advantage (Jarill, 1988; Johanson & Mattson, 1987).

After literature reviews related to inter-organizational strategic alliance can be derived, it is clearly understood that most of the researchers have agreed with the argument that if an organization adopts appropriate strategic alliance, it is helpful to the reduction of operation cost, enlargement of economic scale, development of new product, acquisition of low capital cost, increase of profit and after-tax earnings, and improvement of financial performance (Auster, 1989; Contractor & Lorange, 1988; Souder & Nassar, 1990). Besides, strategic alliance enables the development of new market and new product, and the increase of market share and sales growth ratio in terms of marketing performance (Badaracco, 1991; De La Sierra, 1995; Harrigan, 1987). Furthermore, through the resource integration and synthetic organizational development of strategic alliance, an organization can undertake some general research and development (R&D) projects, obtain new knowledge or new technology and increase its competitive capability (De La Sierria, 1995; Gulati, 1999; Harrigan, 1987; Porter, 1990).

As we know, most of the researchers in the past agreed with the argument that strategic alliance can improve an organizational performance. But after examination of the evolution indicator of strategic alliance performance from the literature, this chapter finds that most of the literature uses either subjective or objective methods to measure the strategic performance. Thus, many controversial arguments on this issue are found:

1. **Objective measurement indicator:** Although the indicators of profit ratio, growth ratio, market share and so forth, can clearly and definitely measure the organizational performance, they cannot explain how strategic alliance contributes to such an organizational performance. As to some performance measurement indicators, such as acquisition or growth of resource and technology, numerical measurement cannot be made easily.
2. **Subjective measurement indicator:** Although its adoption enables us to know the organizational performance more clearly than the adoption of objective measurement indicator, it may bring forth wrong research method or design and create information error.

Hence, this chapter is organized first to discuss different arguments against the perspective for strategic alliance and the evolutionary performance measurement methods of strategic alliance as found in the past research. After that, this chapter employs a cross-theory perspective by combining the four theories of agency theory, resource-dependent theory, resource-based theory, and knowledge-based theory, intending to explore the impact of inter-organizational strategic alliance on organizational value-based decision-making model and intellectual capital. Subsequently, this chapter endeavors to explore the following important issues:

1. The content and formation factors of inter-organizational strategic alliance
2. The content of agency theory and the problem of agency cost
3. The content of core resource strategic alliance, core knowledge strategic alliance, and intellectual capital
4. How different formation factors of inter-organizational strategic alliance affect agency problems, core resource alliance, and core knowledge alliance
5. How an agency problem affects the value-based decision-making model of inter-organizational strategic alliance
6. How inter-organizational core resource and core knowledge strategic alliance affect an agency problem
7. How inter-organizational core resource and core knowledge strategic alliance affect the value-based decision-making model of inter-organizational strategic alliance

LITERATURE REVIEW

Content and Formation Factors of Inter-Organizational Strategic Alliance

When an organization is confronted with the international, industrial, and market transition environmental influences, it is hard for the organization to maintain long-term, sustainable, and competitive advantages if its business continues to adopt the past strategies and proceed with steady steps. Thus, a business always has to face uncertainties or encounter perilous phases in its life cycle. In the 1990s, strategic alliance seemed to be an efficient means for business to achieve growth, create competitive advantage, pursue transformation, or upgrade organizational goals. To face the coming of the new era and environmental changes, especially on the organizational development process, organizations today find it hard to survive by the competition style of single combat. Only through cooperation in the form of strategic alliance can organizations conduct organizational efficiency, acquire useful resources, and increase competitive advantage (Gulati, 1999).

The reasons for an organization to have the intention to build up inter-organizational alliance relationship can be traced back to these motivations of organization, such as risk dispersion, entry to new market, enlargement of economic scale, acquisition of new technology, and technological complementarity. It also enables the intermember resource complementarity and sharing, and integration of resource capabilities (Baranson, 1990). Inter-organizational interaction and cooperation by strategic alliance not only helps enhance the exchangeability and acquisition of resources with each other, but also increases organizational competition (Dyer & Singh, 1998). However, the management of such alliances of rival firms always gives rise to greater problems of obtaining relevant information, alliances between competitors blur the distinction between competition and cooperation (Porter & Fuller, 1986).

Regarding the issue of what the formation factors of inter-organizational strategic alliance are, it is always a common but important issue to many researchers. Viewing the context of formation factor of inter-organizational strategic alliance, it is meant by the main reason why organization wants to walk on the way to strategic alliance. Simply speaking, this is because of the mutual demand of inter-organizational resource dependence. After literature reviews can be derived, the following 20 formation factors summarized, explaining the motivations of inter-organizational strategic alliance:

1. degree of organizational suffering from industrial competition (Harrigan, 1987)
2. industrial growth rate (Boyd, 1990)
3. degree of industrial concentration (Lamar, 1994)
4. degree of product standardization (Harrigan, 1988)
5. market demand uncertainty (Harrigan, 1988)
6. degree of government's support for strategic alliance (Davlin & Bleackley, 1988)
7. law limitation of target market (Alice, 1990)
8. degree of technological intensiveness (Harrigan, 1988)
9. speed of technological innovation (Wu, 1987)
10. cost of technological development (Kogut, 1988)
11. task knowledge ambiguity (Butler & Carney, 1986)
12. time pressure (Maynard, 1996)
13. resource complementarity (Brouthers, Brouthers., & Wilkinson, 1995)
14. goal commitment and capacity (Feng & Cheng, 1997)
15. absolute scale (Geringer, 1988a)
16. past cooperation experience (De La Sierra, 1995)
17. business competition position (Shan & Visudtibhan, 1990)
18. importance of R&D (Hladik, 1988)
19. degree of marketing intensiveness (Kobrin, 1988)
20. intention of business expansion (Shan & Visudtibhan, 1990)

Each of these 20 influential formation factors of strategic alliance has a different implication for the formation of strategic alliance. Principally, this chapter focuses on these five formation factors: (1) degree of industrial competition (Harrigan, 1987); (2)

market demand uncertainty (Harrigan, 1988); (3) task knowledge ambiguity (Butler & Carney, 1986); (4) resource complementarity (Brouthers et al., 1995); and (5) goal commitment and capacity (Feng & Cheng, 1997) in exploring the future implications for the formation of strategic alliance. Finally, this chapter stresses the issue of how an inter-organizational strategic alliance affects organizational value-based decision-making models and intellectual capital.

Content of Agency Theory and Problem of Agency Cost

If a principal has an agent who always tries to seek his and her own self-interests before taking action, under these circumstances there is an agency relationship between the principal and the agent (Jensen & Meckling, 1976). Then, in the cases of search for an individual's self-interest, financial rationale boundary and risk evasion, agency problem may occur (Eisenhardt, 1989). Because there may be goal conflict and asymmetric feelings among inter-organizational members, the principal has to make the best and the most effective decision before signing contract in order to prevent the raise of agency cost.

Generally speaking, the asymmetric situation created to an agent is due to the opportunist behaviors of self-interest consideration, adverse selection (hidden information), and moral hazard. Adverse selection refers to the misrepresentation of ability by the agent. Adverse selection arises because the principal cannot completely verify these skills or abilities either at the time of hiring or while the agent is working. Moral hazard refers to lack of effort on the part of the agent that is the agent's shirking behavior (Eisenhardt, 1989). Furthermore, hidden information is meant by the principal's inability to appoint a representative and to make an ex ante evaluation, whereas moral hazard is meant by the principal's lack of efforts to make an ex post evaluation. Therefore, if the principal and the agent have inconsistent ideas about the firm's goal, cognitive difference on risk, information asymmetry, and uncertain information between them, these problems will increase the agency cost of principal. According to the argument of Jensen and Meckling (1976), agency cost is divided into three types: (1) the principal's monitoring cost; (2) the agent's bonding cost; and (3) the principal's residual loss or opportunity cost. This chapter concludes that the main reason for the problem of agent cost is the existence of goal conflict or inconsistency, asymmetric uncertain information, and self-interest consideration and cognitive difference on risk between the principal and the agent.

Content of Core Resource Strategic Alliance

There are many resources in our environment. For survival, organization has to acquire the resources from the environment. Due to the uncertainties in the environment, there are inter-organizational conflict, dependence and uncertainty within the organization (Pfeffer & Salanick, 1978). Therefore, it is clear to know the importance of building up the mechanism of inter-organizational core resource strategic alliance.

Coyne (1986) found that the core resource of a firm comes from the four parts of function, culture, position, and regulation. Organizational core resource is composed of value, rarity, inimitability, irreplaceability, and resource. It is divided into tangible capital resource, human capital resource and organizational capital resource. Organization must be able to accumulate resources and create competitive advantage (Barney, 1991). Through the complementarity of unique resource and sustainable cooperation in inter-organizational alliance, competitive advantage can be created to both parties (Kogut, 1988). Core resource alliance also helps raise the organizational legitimate position, obtain market power, acquire new technology, enter new market at high speed and achieve more investment choices and opportunities in the future (Eisenhardt & Schnoonhoven, 1996).

According to the viewpoints on core resource alliance in the past studies, this chapter argues that an organization should adopt the mechanism of resource strategic alliance. An organization should first examine the internal conditions of resource and the combination with external resource. Then it can expand resource by undertaking efficient and sustainable development in order to secure the characteristics of core resource, such as the appropriation, value, heterogeneity, complementarity, isolation, irreplacebility of resource and so forth, and build up sustainable and competitive advantage.

Content of Core Knowledge Strategic Alliance

Quintas, Lefrere, and Jones (1997) proposed that knowledge management is adopted through appropriate management process in order to explore, use, deliver, and absorb internal and external organizational knowledge, and to satisfy the present and future organizational demands. Organizational knowledge is a kind of spiral process from tacit to explicit and from explicit to tacit, where organization can undertake spiral sharing of knowledge and creation process (Nonaka & Takeuchi, 1995).

Knowledge includes articulated (explicit) knowledge and tacit knowledge. Articulated knolwedge is a kind of knowledge that can be expressed in detailed description or words, computer program, patent or figure. Tacit knowledge is a kind of word-free knowledge embedded in the brains and memories of individuals (Hedlund, 1994). Simonin (1999) highlights that the critical role played by task knowledge ambiguity is a barrier of the process of knowledge diffusion in strategic alliance. Szulanski (1996) points out that unproveness will have negative impacts upon knowledge receiver in the future. Therefore, the factors of casual ambiguity of tacit knowledge and unproveness are the determinative factors of gaining knowledge, especially if there is moderator factors of uncertain information of great difference of characteristics among alliance partners and great ambiguity of task knowledge contingency. Thus, if the principal and the agent have inconsistent ideas over inter-organizational goal, cognitive difference on risk, and uncertain information between them, these problems will increase the uncertainty with gaining knowledge of principal within parties of strategic alliance.

As the development of new key product technology is gradually getting more complicated for the difficulty of controlling the core resource, it drives business to adopt strategic alliance and undertake core knowledge sharing in order to produce new research technology (Ohame, 1989). In fact, there are many researchers discussing the content of knowledge management. It is known that the formation of knowledge is a dynamic process of tacit knowledge acquisition. It is especially difficult for an organization to create, acquire, or share from other people tacit knowledge such as know-how, innovation ability and so forth. But it is easier for an organization to obtain or imitate from other people explicit knowledge such as standard operation manuals, operation processes, business documents and so forth. Hence, to explain the content of core knowledge alliance from the perspective of this chapter, if there is a high degree of intra-industry competition, high market demand uncertainty, high task knowledge ambiguity, low resource complementarity, and great conflict over goal in organization, it should seek for organizational core knowledge alliance to carry out the exchange activity of know-how, core technology, innovation capability and so forth, which are hard to be imitated by competitor and are of unique tacit knowledge.

Furthermore, through the establishment of the mechanisms long-term trust, mutual commitment and cooperation, both parties tend to interact frequently for achievement of common specific strategic goals. For example, trust and commitment are believed to be the behavior of knowing other partners that would benefit oneself but do not lead to opportunistic behavior (Anderson & Narus, 1990). If the extent of cognitive uncertainty of the alliance member and the possibility for favorable results of international strategic alliance are high, trust can be established to maintain good relationship with alliance (Cyril & Tomkins, 2001). Especially that if the ambiguity of task knowledge is great, it refers that it is hard for one partner of alliance to transfer clearly the explicit or tacit knowledge to another. In sum, when the alliance partners have great difference in their characteristics (e.g., goal inconsistency and self-interest behavior), it means that the conflict contingency will be gradually increased among partners.

Content of Intellectual Capital

The concept of intellectual capital can be traced back to the source of resource-based or knowledge-based perspective (Bontis, 1999). The resource-based view emphasizes how to create internal resources for gaining organizational sustainable competitive advantage (Barney, 1991; Wright & McMahan, 1992). This is especially referring to the resource, like the knowledge of employee and the technical and physical technological system, management system, value concept, and norm (Leonard-Barton, 1992). It also includes intangible human capital and organization capital (Snell, Youndt, & Wright, 1996). Relatively, the knowledge-based view emphasizes the knowledge being the main source of the organizational system (Spender, 1996; Tsoukas, 1996). Knowledge is the key resource of organization if knowledge can be managed and adopted effectively, and it will become an importance source for creation of organizational value (Grant, 1996).

The content of intellectual capital includes human capital, structural capital, and relationship capital. Human capital (Bontis, 1999; Johnson, 1999), it refers to the knowledge, technical skill and experience that employee possesses. Regarding structural capital, it can help and support human capital effectively, such as routine, mechanism and structure (Bontis, 1999). As to relationship capital, it includes the knowledge of organization in connection with the external environment. It also includes the social relationship knowledge of internal organization (Johnson, 1999).

In summary, this chapter tries to define the meaning of intellectual capital in such way that organization tries to create the human capital of knowledge, technical skill, and social interaction experience, the structural capital of inter-organizational route, mechanism, structural culture and resource, and the relationship capital of knowledge alliance network relationship through members internally and stockholders externally.

DEVELOPMENT OF PROPOSITIONS

Formation Factors of Inter-Organizational Strategic Alliance, Agency Problem, Core Resource Alliance and Core Knowledge Alliance

Strategic alliance is an inter-organizational relationship on the basis of a contract or agreement in which, through common resource adoption and organizational management, a common goal can be achieved (Parkhe, 1991). According to Grossman and Shapiro (1987), it is found that under the environment of intensive competition, general firms have no intention to carry out common R&D alliance actively. As found in this chapter, an organization has a fear that if R&D is co-implemented, the other party may not be honest, and may steal the organizational resource and knowledge. Besides, when the market is in the situation of high demand uncertainty, it means that general organizations cannot effectively and correctly forecast the future market potential and demand. Hence, there is high asymmetric situation and goal inconsistency among organizations. Under these circumstances, an organization should develop an internalization mechanism to prevent from taking any operation risk after inter-organizational strategic alliance.

Moreover, to explain the issue of task knowledge alliance, this chapter follows Simonin's (1999) study's findings that highlight the critical role played by knowledge ambiguity as a full mediator of tacitness, prior experience, complexity, cultural distance, and organizational distance on knowledge transfer. When the degree of knowledge ambiguity associated with a partner's competence is high, chances of effectively repatriating and absorbing the competence are rather limited. These significant effects are further found to be moderated by the firm's level of collaborative know-how, its learning capacity, and the duration of the alliance (Simonin, 1999). Hence, if a high negative degree of task knowledge ambiguity associates with a partner's competence and great conflict over goal in interorganization, it should seek through organizational learning alliance with complementarity of rare knowledge to carry out the exchange activities of know-how, core technology, innovation capability and so forth, which are hard to be imitated by competitor and are of unique tacit knowledge. This chapter also argues that although some moderator factors of information uncertainty of great difference of characteristics among alliance partners (e.g., goal commitment, goal reciprocality, relative scale, and past cooperation experience), and great negative degree of ambiguity of task knowledge have negative impacts on obtaining relevant information and the benefit or performance of strategic alliance, an organization can establish long-term organizational learning governance mechanisms (e.g., knowledge innovation and technological innovation) to cope with the internal or external transitional environment. Because the existing rare knowledge or technological innovation increased by each of the alliance members not only can help alliance members adapt to the unknown transitional environment, but also can create innovation capacity and increase the competitive advantage.

On the other hand, if there is exists a high positive degree of task knowledge ambiguity associates with a partner's competence, there is low conflict over goal in interorganization. For example, some alliances often occur because a target organization has been unable to handle new technology or product innovation. In sum, when task knowledge ambiguity is found within an organizational operation, it implies that the tacit task knowledge is high. If the degree of knowledge ambiguity associates with a partner's competence is negative, it is not easy for an organization to understand or undertake inter-organizational transfer rare knowledge. Thus, goal inconsistency, asymmetry, self-interest and opportunist behavior can be happened in process of inter-organizational strategic alliance. In contrast, if the degree of knowledge ambiguity associates with a partner's competence is positive, it is easy for an organization to understand or undertake inter-organizational transfer rare knowledge.

The main concept of resource-based theory applied on the issue of strategic alliance refers to an acquisition of resource complementarity and transferability, and rare and appropriate asset through strategic alliance so as to create sustainable competitive advantage (Hamel & Prahalad, 1993; Ohame, 1989). Besides, the main concept of resource-dependent theory applied on the issue of strategic alliance is an acquisition of resource efficiency and adaptation to uncertain or complicated environment through inter-organizational exchange and mutual relationship (Boyd, 1990; Zuckeman & D'Aunno, 1990). This chapter reminds an organization that not all resources can create efficiency. Due to the emphasis of cooperation in inter-organizational strategic alliance, this chapter highly stresses the creation of rare resource complementarity to cope with the quickly emerging markets and transitional environment. This chapter argues that if the complementarity of rare resource is built among partners, mutual supplementing effect can be created to solve the problem of insufficient resources of partners. For instance, the creation of know-how method, knowledge and technological sharing can bring more benefits to partners. Just because of the complementarity of resource and imperfection of transfer, asymmetry situation will appear to the dyadic interaction in inter-organizational activities. Thus, when low degree of rare resource complementarity is found among organizations, it has deep impact on agency problem or strategic alliance. Over this point, low rare resource complementarity among organizations refers to no demand of long-term cooperation or alliance on each other. On the other hand, a high degree of rare resource complementarity means that organizations can adopt strategic alliance method to create the resource advantage of each party and achieve strategic synthesis. In sum, this chapter infers that if an organization owns higher complementarity of rare resource, it will get more sustainable competitive advantages and be of greater help to value creation in the future. Through unique inter-organizational rare resource complementarity, long-term successful cooperation can be strengthened.

Regarding the issue of goal commitment and capacity, Geringer (1988) argued that the commitment and capacity of intermember goal and policy have impact on the intention of strategic alliance. It implies that inter-organizational commitment and capacity is a kind of intangible contract or agreement signed by both parties on the basis of reciprocal trust and honesty. It is also an important formation factor of strategic alliance. Therefore, it is clearly known that different formation factors of inter-organizational strategic alliance have profound impact on and close relationship with agency problem, core resource alliance and core knowledge alliance. To sum up the previous discussions, this chapter infers Proposition 1, Proposition 2, Propositions 3, and the subpropositions of each of the three propositions as follows:

- **Proposition 1:** Different formation factors of inter-organizational strategic alliance have significant impact on an agency problem.

- **Proposition 1-1:** When the degree of intra-industry competition and market demand uncertainty are high, it means that there is great inter-organizational conflict over the goal, serious asymmetric situation, much consideration of self-interest and opportunist behavior and high agency cost.
- **Proposition 1-2:** When the inter-organizational task knowledge ambiguity is high negative degree, the complementarity of rare knowledge, the complementarity of rare resource and the goal commitment and capacity are low, it means that there is great inter-organizational conflict or inconsistency over the goal, serious information asymmetry and uncertainty, much consideration of self interest and opportunist behavior, cognitive difference on risk and high agency cost.
- **Proposition 2:** Different formation factors of inter organizational strategic alliance have positive or negative impact on core resource strategic alliance.
- **Proposition 2-1:** When the degree of intra-industry competition and market demand uncertainty are high, it means that there is serious inter-organizational agency problem. Thus, organization has less intention of core resource strategic alliance. Relatively, when the degree of intra-industry competition is low, there is less inter-organizational agency problem. Thus, organization has the intention of core resource strategic alliance.
- **Proposition 2-2:** When the inter-organizational task knowledge ambiguity is high negative degree, there is serious inter-organizational agency problem. Thus, organization has less intention of core resource strategic alliance. Relatively, when the inter-organizational task knowledge ambiguity is low negative degree, there is less inter-organizational agency problem. Thus, organization has the intention of core resource strategic alliance.
- **Proposition 2-3:** When the inter-organizational rare resource complementarity and the goal commitment and capacity are low, there is serious inter-organizational agency problem. Thus, organization has less intention of core resource strategic alliance. Relatively, when the inter-organizational rare resource complementarity and the goal commitment and capacity are high, there is less inter-organizational agency problem. Thus, organization has the intention of core resource strategic alliance.
- **Proposition 3:** Different formation factors of inter-organizational strategic alliance have positive or negative impact on core knowledge strategic alliance.
- **Proposition 3-1:** When the degree of intra-industry competition and market demand uncertainty are high, there is serious inter-organizational agency problem. Thus, organization has less intention of core knowledge strategic alliance. Relatively, when the degree of intra-industry competition and market demand uncertainty are low, there is less inter-organizational agency problem. Thus, organization has the intention of core knowledge strategic alliance.
- **Proposition 3-2:** When the inter-organizational task knowledge ambiguity is high positive degree, there is less inter-organizational agency problem. Thus, organization has the intention of core knowledge strategic alliance. Relatively, when the inter-organizational task knowledge ambiguity is low positive degree, there is serious inter-organizational agency problem. Thus, organization has less intention of core knowledge strategic alliance.
- **Proposition 3-3:** When the inter-organizational rare resource complementarity and the goal commitment and capacity are low, there is serious inter-organizational

agency problem. Thus, an organization has less intention of core knowledge strategic alliance. Relatively, when the inter-organizational rare resource complementarity and the goal commitment and capacity are high, there is less inter organizational agency problem. Thus, an organization has the intention of core knowledge strategic alliance.

Agency Problem and Inter-Organizational Strategic Alliance Value-Based Decision-Making Model

Agency problem occurs whenever the existence of individual's consideration of self-interest. Besides, sometimes between the principal and the agent there are (a) inconsistency or conflict over goal; (b) asymmetric situation of both parties; and (c) cognitive difference on risk and agency performance (Bergen, Dutta, & Walker, 1992; Eisenhardt, 1989; Stump & Heide, 1996). Hence, if an inter-organizational agency relationship exists, there are four agency problems, namely self-interest behavior, inconsistency or conflict over goal, asymmetric situation, and cognitive difference on risk. It refers that each party can seek for the maximum interest for one's own and creates the motivations for the seeking of hidden information.

An inter-organizational agency problem also brings about a worse agency relationship and increases the agency cost to both parties. Due to the lack of inter-organizational reciprocity or trust, the agreement or contract is only a kind of formal document that does not have real meaning or implication. Hence, this chapter infers the following three aspects made that focus to explain why trust or reciprocity plays the important role within the inter-organizational strategic alliance: (a) *Boundary rationality*. When a person has incomplete information and is unable to handle uncertain information, he or she can still forecast the future transaction condition and make the right choice of contract or governance mode to minimize its agency cost. Thus, the manager will have higher risk in the decision making in the future. (b) *Opportunist behavior*. When two persons consider self interests and have inconsistent ideas over the firm's goal, they may have opportunist behavior, causing impact on achievement of firm's goal. It implies that when inter-organizational trust or commitment mechanism cannot be set up, organization should adopt trust and commitment. (c) *Information asymmetry and information uncertainty*. Under the circumstances of information incompleteness, it is for easy for a party owning more information to create opportunist behavior, moral hazard and adverse selection, which result in alliance failure. When both parties cannot fully forecast or control the transaction complexity due to the vicissitudinous environment, information uncertainty and information asymmetry, the manager is unable to make right decisions for the limitation of boundary rationality. As a result, there will be high cooperation cost. Hence, it implies that when the degree of information asymmetry and information uncertainty is high, an organization should adopt the trust or reciprocity mechanism to reduce agency problem and obtaining relevant information for or critical information to an organization and especially to an alliance.

In sum, this is the main reason why an organization cannot increase the three kinds of intellectual capital and organizational value, namely human capital, structural capital, and relationship capital, and cannot effectively achieve a decision-making model of inter-organizational strategic alliance. From the perspective of this chapter, if there is any inter-organizational agency problem, it will negative impact on the organizational value-based decision-making model of inter-organizational strategic alliance. To sum up the above discussions, this chapter infers Proposition 4 and its subpropositions as follows:

- **Proposition 4:** When there is an existent inter-organizational agency problem, high agency cost will be created, such as the principal's monitoring cost, the agent's bonding cost, the principal's residual loss or opportunity cost, which will have adeep impact on the value-based decision-making model of inter-organizational strategic alliance. Relatively, if the mechanisms of inter-organizational trust and reciprocity are adopted in the formation of strategic alliance, it will positively decrease or solve the agency problem and is helpful to organizational value-based decision-making model of strategic alliance.
- **Proposition 4-1:** When there is an existent inter-organizational self-interest consideration or opportunist behavior and information asymmetry and uncertainty, it cannot effectively increase the intellectual capital, including human capital, structural capital and relationship capital, and cannot create organizational value.
- **Proposition 4-2:** When there is an existent inter-organizational conflict or inconsistency over the goal, or cognitive difference on risk, it cannot effectively increase the intellectual capital, including human capital, structural capital, and relationship capital, and cannot create organizational value.

Core Resource, Core Knowledge and Agency Problem

Inter-organizational core resource alliance enables an organization to rise to a legitimate position and obtain market power, new technology, quick entry to new markets, and more investment choices and opportunities (Esenhardt & Schoonhoven, 1996). Viewing this issue from a knowledge-based perspective, if there are more inter-organizational social interactions, it will be followed by more frequent information exchange, language communication, know-how sharing, and better cooperation atmosphere in various kinds of alliances (Dyer & Singh, 1998; Lane & Lubatkin, 1998). This chapter argues that if inter-organizational core resource alliance and core knowledge alliance can be established by strategic alliance, it not only creates in both parties a greater consistency over goal and a higher degree of information asymmetry and uncertainty reduction, but also prevents the principal and the agent from considering their self-interests or having opportunist behavior of financial rationale. Thus, if there is inter-organizational interaction of strategic alliance, it will help both parties prevent from encountering an agency problem and increase of agency cost. To sum up the above discussions, this chapter infers Proposition 5 and Proposition 6 as follows:

- **Proposition 5:** When there is a matured governance mechanism of inter-organizational core resource strategic alliance, it can avoid agency problem and reduce agency cost more effectively.
- **Proposition 6:** When there is a matured governance mechanism of inter-organizational core knowledge strategic alliance, it can avoid agency problem and reduce agency cost more effectively.

Value-Based Decision-Making Model of Core Resource and Core Knowledge of Inter-Organizational Strategic Alliance

To meet the approach of the era of knowledge economy, knowledge-intensive organizations are gradually rising up and further developing rapidly. Therefore, there are more and more organizations emphasize more attention to their business operation and management of knowledge and intellectual capital (Druck, 1993). According to Handy (1989), the intellectual capital of a company has estimated usually greater than the book value by three to four times. The estimation of Edvinsson and Malone (1997) even gives the highest organizational intellectual value by multiplying the physical and financial capital by five to six times. Hence, being inseparable from internal organizational procedure, knowledge or intellectual capital plays an important role (Lynn, 1999; Tovstiga, 1999).

Viewing this issue from a resource-based perspective, if an organization can obtain useful resource with other people the transfer of internal and external resource, it is helpful to link asset capabilities to produce heterogeneity and performance (Yiannis & Spyros, 2001). This chapter argues that if organization can alliance with other organization to produce core resource and core knowledge strategic alliances, internally it can help increase the organization's (a) human capital, such as personnel and technical knowledge and experience; (b) structural capital, such as the structural effectiveness and development, rationalization of operation procedures; and (c) relationship capital, such as intermember social interaction, and sharing of resource and knowledge. To sum up the above discussions, this chapter infers Proposition 7 and Proposition 8, as follows:

- **Proposition 7:** When there is a matured governance mechanism of core resource strategic alliance, it not only helps increase organizational intellectual capital including human capital, structural capital and relationship capital, but also helps develop a value-based decision-making model of strategic alliance.
- **Proposition 8:** When there is a matured governance mechanism of core knowledge strategic alliance, it not only helps increase organizational intellectual capital including human capital, structural capital and relationship capital, but also helps develop a value-based decision-making model of strategic alliance.

CONCEPTUAL MODEL

According to Propositions 1 through 8 and their subpropositions inferred previously, this chapter proposes a conceptual model, showing the impact of inter-organizational strategic alliance on an organizational value-based decision-making model and intellectual capital. This model is shown in Figure 1.

Figure 1. Conceptual model of impact of inter-organizational strategic alliance on organizational value-based decision-making model and intellecutal capital

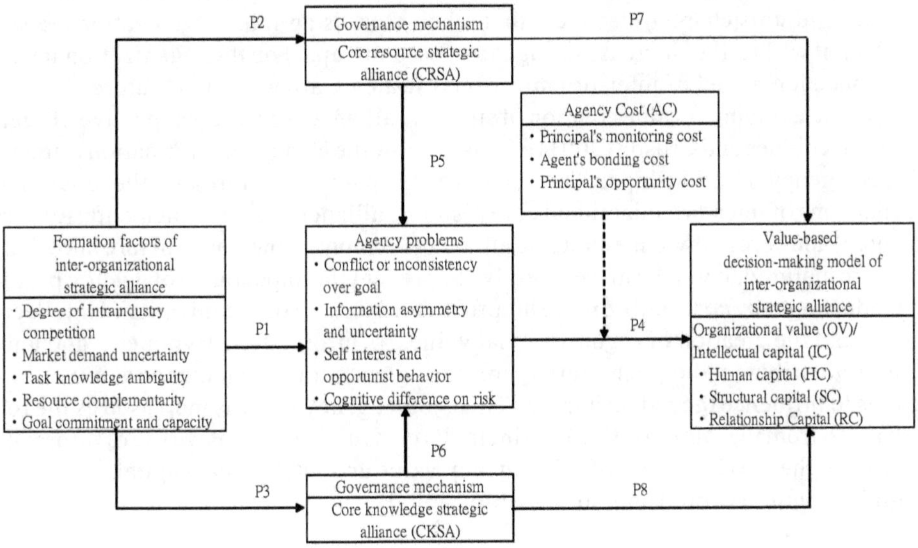

DISCUSSION AND IMPLICATIONS

The main purpose for employment of organizational theory is to explore (a) the purposes of an organizational existence; (b) the organizational boundary; and (c) the organizational control, coordination, and governance. Relatively, the purpose of strategic management is to seek for the uniqueness of an organization, which includes choice, commitment, and action. Through these three properties, the uniqueness of an organization can be adopted to create organizational value and generate profit.

Reviewing the literatures related to inter-organizational strategic alliance, this chapter examines the resource-dependent theory, transaction cost theory, strategic behavior theory, unified integration theory and network theory perspectives to study the related research issues of the financial performance, marketing performance, competitive capability and so forth, of an organization after strategic alliance. Most of the past researchers agreed with the argument that strategic alliance can improve an organizational performance. However, it is found that most of the past literature uses subjective or objective method to measure the strategic performance. Thus, there are many controversial arguments created on some issues related to strategic alliance.

Dissimilar to the past researches, this chapter adopts a cross-theory perspective by combining the four theories of agency theory, resource dependence theory, resource-based theory and knowledge-based theory, intending to explore the impact of inter-organizational strategic alliance on organizational value-based decision-making model and intellectual capital. This chapter infers 18 propositions and builds up a conceptual model. It is expected that the study will have the following implications:

First, this chapter finds that different formation factors of inter-organizational strategic alliance have significant relative impact on agency and also have positive or negative relative impact on core resource and core knowledge strategic alliance.

Second, this chapter discovers that when there is an inter-organizational agency problem, it will further increase the agency cost and impact on the organizational value-based decision model of inter-organizational strategic alliance in the future.

Third, explaining value creation of strategic alliance from the perspective of agency theory, Jacobides and Croson (2001) evaluated how the change of information utilization affects agency relationships. This chapter discovers that through the governance mechanisms of inter-organizational core resource alliance (i.e., complementarity of rare resource) and core knowledge strategic alliance (i.e., complementarity of rare knowledge) are more matured, it will be more effective to prevent the appearance of agency problem and reduce agency cost, and be more helpful to the increase of organizational intellectual capital and the creation of organizational value. As information asymmetry and uncertainty redistribute value, penetrated monitoring encourages agents to take inefficient actions to influence the redistribution. Thus, joint agency value is increased as the focus is changed from the minimization of principal's costs and the extensive use of information benefits to the maximization of joint agency value and intellectual capital (e.g., human capital, structural capital and relationship capital).

REFERENCES

Alice, J. A. (1990). Cooperation in R&D. *Technovation, 10*(5), 319-332.

Anderson, J. C., & Narus, J. A. (1990). A model of distributor firm and manufacturer firm working partnerships. *Journal of Marketing, 54,* 42-58.

Auster, E.R. (1989, March-April). International corporate linkages: Dynamic forms in changing environments. *Columbia Journal of World Business Review,* 143-154.

Badaracco, J. L. (1991). *The knowledge link: How firm compete through strategic alliances.* Boston: Harvard Business School Press.

Baranson, J. (1990). Transnational strategic alliance: Why, what, where and how. *Multinational Business, 2,* 54-61.

Barney, J. B. (1991). Firm resources and sustained competitive Advantage. *Journal of Management,* 99-120.

Bergen, M., Dutta, S., & Walker, O. C. (1992). Agency relationships in marketing: A review of the implications and applications of agency and related theories. *Journal of Marketing, 56,* 1-24.

Bonits, N. (1999). Managing organizational knowledge by diagnosing intellectual capital: Farming and advancing the state of field. *International Journal of Technology Management, 18*(5/6/7/8), 433-462.

Boyd, B. (1990). Corporate linkage and organizational environment: a test of the resource dependence model. *Strategic Management Journal, 11,* 419-430.

Brouthers, K. D., Brouthers, L. E., & Wilkinson. J. J. (1995). Strategic alliances: Choose your partners. *Long Range Planning, 28*(3), 18-25.

Butler, R. J., & Carney, M. (1986). Strategic and strategic choice: The case of telecommunications. *Strategic Management Journal, 7,* 161-177.

Contractor, F. J. (1990). Contractual and cooperative forms of international business: Towards a unified theory of model choice. *Management International Review, 30*(1), 31-54.

Contractor, F. J., & Lorange, P. L. (1988). Whey should firm corporate? Strategy and economics basis for cooperative ventures. In F. J. Contractor & P. Lornages (Eds), *Cooperative Strategies in Inter National Business* (pp. 1-28). MA; Toronto: D. C. Health /Lexington.

Coyne, K. P. (1986, January-February). Sustainable competitive advantage—What it is, what it isn't. *Business Horizons, 29*, 54-61.

Cyril, T. (2001, March). Interdependencies, trust and information in relationships, alliance and networks. *Accounting, Organizational and Society, Oxford,* 61-76.

Davlin, G., & Bleackley, M. (1988). Strategies alliance—Guidelines for success. *Long Range Planning, 21*(5), 18-23.

De La Sierra, M. C. (1995). *Managing global alliances—Key steps for successful collaboration.* New York: Addison Wesley.

Druck, P. (1993). *Post-capitalist society*. Oxford, UK: Butterworth-Heinemann.

Dyer, J. H., & Singh, H. (1998). The relational view: Cooperative strategy and sources of inter-organizational competitive advantage. *Academy of Management Review, 23*(4), 660-679.

Edvinsson, L., & Malone, M. S. (1997). *Intellectual capital: Realizing your company's true value by finding it's hidden roots.* New York: Harper Business.

Eisenhardt, K. M. (1989). Agency theory: An assessment and review. *Academy of Management Review, 14*(1), 57-74.

Eisenhardt, K. M., & Schoonhoven, C. B. (1996). Resource-based view of strategic alliance formation: Strategic and social effects in entrepreneurial firm. *Organization Science, 7*(2), 136-150.

Feng, G. M., & Cheng, G. C. (1997). The impact of formation condition on international joint venture business performance. *Sun Yat-Sen Management Review, 5*(5), 537-552.

Geringer, J. M. (1988a, Autumn). Selection of partners of international joint ventures. *Business Quarterly,* 31-36.

Grant, R. M. (1996). Prospering in dynamically competitive environments: Organizational capacity as knowledge integration. *Organization Science, 7,* 375-387.

Grossman, G. M., & Shapiro, C. (1987, June). Dynamic R & D Competition. *Economic Journal,* 372-387.

Gulati, R. (1999). Network location and learning: The influence of network resource and firm capabilities on alliance formation. *Strategic Management Journal, 20,* 397-420.

Hamel, G., & Prahalad, C. K. (1993, March-April). Strategy as stretch and leverage. *Harvard Business Review,* 75-84.

Handy, C. B. (1989). *The age of unreason*. London: Arrow Books.

Harrigan, K. R. (1987). Strategic alliance: Their new role in global competition. *Columbia Journal of World Business, 22*(2), 67-69.

Harrigan, K. R. (1988). Joint ventures and competitive strategy. *Strategic Management Journal, 9,* 141-158.

Hedlund, G. (1994). The model of knowledge management and the form of corporation. *Strategic Management Journal, 15,* 73-90.

Hennart, J. F. (1988). A transaction cost theory of equity joint ventures. *Strategies Management Journal, 9,* 361-374.

Hladik, K. J. (1988). R & D and international joint ventures. In F. J. Contractor & P. Lorange (Eds), *Cooperative strategies in international business* (pp. 29-55). New York: Lexington.

Jacobides, M. G., & Croson, D. C. (2001). Information policy: Shaping the value of agency relationships. *Academy of Management Review, 26*(2), 202-223.

Jarill, J. C. (1988). On strategic network. *Strategic Management Journal, 9,* 31-41.

Jensen, M. C., & Meckling, W. H. (1976). Theory of the firm: Managerial behavior, agency cost and ownership structure. *Journal of Financial Economics, 3,* 305-360.

Johanson, J., & Mattson, G. (1987). Internationalization in industrial system—A network approach compared with the transaction cost approach. *International Studies of Management and Organization, 17*(1), 34-48.

Johnson, J. L. (1999). strategic integration in industrial distribution channels: Managing the inter-firm relationship as a strategic asset. *Journal of Academy of Marketing Sciences, 27,* 4-18.

Johnson, W. H. (1999). An integrative taxonomy of intellectual capital: Measuring the stock and flow of intellectual capital components in the firm. *International Journal of Technology Management, 18*(5/6/7/8), 562-575.

Kanter, R. M. (1990, July-August). How to compete. *Harvard Business Review,* 1-2.

Kobrin, S. J. (1988). Trends in ownership of US manufacturing subsidiaries in developing countries: An inter-industry analysis. In F. J. Contractor & P. Lorange (Eds), *Cooperative strategies in international business* (pp. 34-48). New York: Lexingion Books.

Kogut, B. (1988). Joint ventures: Theoretical and empirical perspective. *Strategic Management Journal, 9,* 319-332.

Lamar, C. (1994). Telecommunications: The best of times, the worst of times. *Executive Speeches, 8*(5), 34-37.

Lane, P. J., & Lubatkin, M. (1998). Relative absorptive capacity & inter-organizational learning. *Strategic Management Journal, 19*(5), 461-477.

Leonard-Barton, D. (1992). Core capabilities and core rigidities: A paradox in managing new product development. *Strategic Management Journal, 13,* 111-125.

Lynn, B. E. (1999). Culture and intellectual capital management: A key factor in successful icm implementation. *International Journal of Technology Management, 18*(5/6/7/8), 590-603.

Maynard, R. (1996). Strategic the right match. *Nation's Business, 84*(5), 18-20.

Nonaka, I., & Takeuchi, H. (1995). *The knowledge creating company.* New York: Oxford University Press.

Ohame, K. (1989, March-April). The global logic of strategic alliance. *Harvard Business Review,* 143-154.

Oliver, C. (1991). Network relations and loss of organization autonomy. *Human Relations, 44*(9), 943-690.

Parkhe, A. (1991). Inter-firm diversity, organization learning and longevity in global strategic alliance. *Journal of International Business Studies, 22*(4), 579-601.

Pfeffer, J., & Salancik, G. (1978). *The external control of organizations: A resource dependence perspective.* New York: Harper & Row.

Porter, M. E. (1990). *The competitive advantage of nations*. New York: Free Press.

Porter, M. E., & Fuller, M. B. (1986). Coalitions and global strategy. In M. E. Porter (Ed.), *Competitive in global industries* (pp. 315-343). Boston: Harvard Business School Press.

Quintas, P., Lefrere, P., & Jones, G. (1997). Knowledge management: A strategic agenda. *Long Range Planning, 30*(3), 385-391.

Shan, W., & Visudtibhan, K. (1990). Cooperative strategic in commercializing an emerging technology. *European Journal of Operational Research, 47,* 172-181.

Simonin, B. L. (1999). Ambiguity and the process of knowledge transfer in strategic alliance. *Strategic Management Journal, 20,* 595-623.

Snell, S. A., Youndt, M. A., & Wright, P. M. (1996). Establishing a framework for research in strategic human management: Merging resource theory and organizational learning. In J. Shaw, P. Kirkbride, & K. Rowland (Eds.), *Research in personnel and human resource management* (Vol. 14, pp. 61-90). CT: JAI Press.

Souder, W. E., & Nassar, S. (1990, March-April). Choosing on R&D consortium. *Research Technology Management,* 35-41.

Spender, J. C. (1996, Winter). Making knowledge the basis of a dynamic theory of the firm (Special issue). *Strategic Management Journal, 17*, 45-62.

Stump, R. L., & Heide, J. B. (1996). Controlling supplier opportunism in industrial relationships. *Journal of Marketing Research, 33*(4), 431- 441.

Szulanski, G. (1996). Exploring internal stickiness: Impediments to the transfer of best practice with the firm. *Strategic Management Journal, 17,* 27-44.

Tovstiga, G. (1999, Winter). Profiling the knowledge worker in the knowledge-intensive organization: Emerging role (Special issue). *International Journal of Technology Management Journal, 17,* 11-25.

Tsoukas, H. (1996, Winter). The firm as a distributed knowledge system: A constructionist approach (Special issue). *Strategic Management Journal, 17,* 11-25.

Williamson, O. E. (1981, December). The modern corporation: Origins, evolution, attributes. *Journal of Economic Literature, 19,* 1537-1568.

Wright, P. M., & McMahan. G. C. (1992). Theoretical perspectives for strategic human resource management. *Journal of Management, 15,* 295-320.

Wu, C. S. (1987). *Strategic alliances in global technological competition: Cases of computer and telecommunication industries*. Unpublished doctoral dissertation, University of California, Los Angeles.

Yiannis, E. S., & Spyros, L. (2001). An examination into the causal logic of rent generation: Contrasting porter's competitive strategy framework & the resource- based perspective. *Strategic Management Journal, 22,* 907-934.

Zuckerman, H. S., & D'Aunno, T. A. (1990). Hospital alliances: Cooperative strategy in a competitive environment. *Health Care Management Review, 15*(2), 21-30.

About the Authors

Shu-Heng Chen is a professor in the Department of Economics of the National Chengchi University, Taipei, Taiwan. He now serves as the director of the AI-ECON Research Center, National Chengchi University, the editor- in-chief of the *Journal of New Mathematics and Natural Computation (World Scientific)*, the associate editor of the *Journal of Economic Behavior and Organization*, and a member of the editorial board of the *Journal of Management and Economics*. He also served as an associate editor of *IEEE Transactions on Evolutionary Computation*. Dr. Chen holds a M.A. degree in mathematics and a Ph.D in economics from the University of California at Los Angeles. He has more than 150 publications in international journals, edited volumes, and conference proceedings. He has been invited to give keynote speeches and plenary talks on many international conferences. He is also the editor of the volume "Evolutionary Computation in Economics and Finance" (Plysica-Verlag, 2002), "Genetic Algorithms and Genetic Programming in Computational Finance" (Kluwer, 2002), and the co-editor of the volume "Computational Intelligence in Economics and Finance" (Springer-Verlag, 2003), "Multi-Agent for Mass User Support" (Springer-Verlag, 2004), and "Applications of Artificial Intelligence in Finance and Economics" (Elsevier, 2004). His research interests are mainly on the applications of computational intelligence to the agent-based computational economics and finance. Details of Shu-Heng Chen can be found at http://www.aiecon.org/ or http://www.aiecon.org/staff/shc/E_vita.html.

Lakhmi C. Jain, M.E., PhD, is director/founder of the Knowledge-Based Intelligent Engineering Systems (KES) Centre, located in the division of information technology, engineering, and the environment. He is a fellow of the Institution of Engineers Australia. He has initiated a postgraduate stream by research in the knowledge-based intelligent engineering systems area. He is the founding editor-in-chief of the *International Journal of Knowledge-Based Intelligent Engineering Systems* and served as an associate editor of the *IEEE Transactions on Industrial Electronics*. Dr. Jain was the technical chair of the ETD2000 International Conference in 1995 and publications chair of the Australian and New Zealand Conference on Intelligent Information Systems in 1996. He also initiated the first International Conference on Knowledge-Based Intelligent Electronic Systems in 1997, which is now an annual event. He served as the vice president of the Electronics Association of South Australia in 1997. He is the editor-in-chief of the International Book Series on Computational Intelligence, CRC Press, USA. His interests focus on the use of novel techniques such as knowledge-based systems, artificial neural networks, fuzzy systems, and genetic algorithms and the application of these techniques.

Chung-Ching Tai is currently a PhD student in the Department of Economics, National Chengchi University in Taiwan. He is currently a member of AI-ECON research center. He finished his master thesis in 2001. His research interest are agent-based modeling, double auction market, and experimental economics.

* * *

M. Bergman received her PhD in economics from the University of Houston. The topic was *Foundations and Applications of Agent Based Modeling in Economics*. Her main research interests are relating risk and perception in decision making. In addition, she is interested in methodological advances in both agent-based modeling and economic experiments. The intersection between the artificial agent and the human agent is also of great interest. She is currently an assistant professor of economics at Penn State Worthington Scranton.

Siddhartha Bhattacharyya is an associate professor in the Information and Decision Sciences Department of the College of Business Administration at the University of Illinois at Chicago, USA. His research interests include agent-based models, evolutionary computation, and data mining. His research appears in *Annals of Operations Research, Complex Systems, Computational Statistics and Data Analysis, Decision Sciences, Evolutionary Computation, European Journal of Operational Research, IEEE Transactions, INFORMS Journal on Computing, Information Sciences, Information Technology and Management* and other publications.

Paul W. Box is currently a regional analyst with Australia's Commonwealth Scientific and Industrial Research Organization (CSIRO) Centre for Arid Zone Research in Alice Springs. He received his PhD in geography from the University of Florida in 1997 and was at Utah State University's Department of Geography and Earth Resources before working at CSIRO. He has been active with the Swarm Development Group since its first public release and has worked for integration of agent-based models with geographic information systems.

Seán Boyle is an economist with a detailed knowledge of the public policy environment in the UK. He has experience of working at senior level with public and private sector managers, civil servants and politicians (both local and national). His main government work has been with the UK Department of Health and the NHS. He has researched and written extensively on a range of policy issues concerning the finance and provision of health care in the UK: these include the economic evaluation of the use and allocation of resources, public-private partnerships, modelling elective and emergency health care and performance measurement.

Cesar Briano is associate professor of information systems at the Department of Informatics at the School of Economics, University of Buenos Aires, Argentina. Professor Briano was also subdirector of the Department of Informatics (1998-2001). He is a consultant for the study of information systems at the School of Economics, University of Buenos Aires. He is also consultant for projects in information systems for international banks, such as the Banco Mundial (World Bank). Professor Briano holds his master's degree in informatics from the University of Buenos Aires, and is co-author with Dr. Ana Marostica of specialized articles in information and economic sciences both in the United States and in Europe.

Holly Danker-McDermot received both her BS and MS degrees in electrical engineering from the University of New Orleans in 2002 and 2004, respectively. In May of 2001 she was awarded the Electrical Engineering Outstanding Achievement Award. In May of the following year she was received the Electrical Engineering Robert Lee Chandler Outstanding Graduate Student Award.

Freddie Douglas, III is the chief, systems integration officer in the program development directorate at NASA's John C. Stennis Space Center (SSC) in Bay St. Louis, Mississippi. In this position he is responsible for the management and operations of the two primary functions of the systems integration office, which includes the execution of system projects that assist functional organizations improve and be successful in the execution of their respective missions; the conduct of requested or emergent independent assessments; leadership of the center's integrated management council; he is the executive secretary of the Center Program Management Council and provides program analysis support to the center's programs and projects. Mr. Douglas joined NASA at the Marshall Space Flight Center in Huntsville, Alabama, in 1983 as a professional intern. In 1989 he transferred to the Stennis Space Center. Born in Houma, Louisiana, Mr. Douglas received a bachelor's degree in mechanical engineering from Southern University and A&M College in Baton Rouge, a master's of science degree in engineering management, with minors in statistics and operations research from the University of Alabama in Huntsville, and a master's of science degree in engineering and management from the Massachusetts Institute of Technology (Systems Design and Management Program). He also completed NASA's APPL Accelerated Leadership Option. Mr. Douglas has authored and co-authored numerous technical publications. He has received awards including the NASA Astronaut's Silver Snoopy and the *Dollars and Sense* magazine's "America's Best & Brightest Business and Professional Men and Women" in 1994. He is an officer in the United States Naval Reserve, where he is an engineering duty officer and holds the rank of lieutenant commander.

N. Feltovich is currently associate professor of economics at University of Houston in Houston, Texas, USA. He earned his BS in mathematics at Virginia Tech and his PhD in economics at University of Pittsburgh under Alvin Roth (now at Harvard University). His main area of specialization is in the area of imperfect rationality: its measurement, its determinants and its consequences. He has written several published papers in game theory, experimental economics, industrial organization, behavioral economics and statistics.

Nicholas S. Flann received his PhD in computer science in 1992 from Oregon State University, where he studied symbolic approaches to reinforcement learning. Flann has worked in the development of intelligent behaviors for autonomous robotic vehicles and in intelligent tutoring systems for young children. Flann is currently an associate professor in computer science at Utah State University, USA. Flann's current research interests include modeling of morphogenesis using the Cellular Potts model of cells and computational models of the evolution body plans.

Stephen Guerin is currently president of RedfishGroup. His work centers on the design and visualization of agent-based modeling systems. He recently worked as a senior software developer at BiosGroup and participated as a member of Stuart Kauffman's research group. Over the last 5 years, Stephen has created complexity science-based applications for Fortune 100 and government clients including NASDAQ, El Paso Energy, Honda R&D, Air Products, Amgen, Eli Lilly, Walgreens, Southwest Airlines, Veritas and the UK Home Office.

Serge Hayward, works for the Department of Finance, Ecole Supérieure de Commerce de Dijon, France His research interests include computational economics and finance, financial modeling and forecasting, and financial markets & instruments. He is an active member of the Technical Committee in Computational Finance & Economics, IEEE Computational Intelligence Society; the Society for Computational Economics, and the New England Complex Systems Institute.

Edit J. Kaminsky is currently an associate professor and the associate chair of the Department of Electrical Engineering at the University of New Orleans, LA, USA. She has received numerous service and teaching awards over the last 10 years and is a member of the honor societies Tau Beta Pi and Eta Kappa Nu. She is an active volunteer in the IEEE and is currently the chair of the IEEE New Orleans Section. She is also a member of SWE and ASEE. Her research interests include digital communications, underwater acoustic communications, fuzzy systems, neural networks, sonar systems and biomedical signal processing.

Satoshi Kishino is assistant professor of system information engineering in the Faculty of Engineering, Musashi Institute of Technology, Tokyo. He received his BEng from MIT, Tokyo, and MEng in Industrial Engineering in 1969 from Nagoya Institute of Technology. He has published many technical papers, mainly on production planning and wavelet analysis, and has performed several case studies on signal processing. He has also worked on computer control of actual systems. He is a member of the Japan Industrial Management Association (Editorial Staff, 1972-1975), Japan Society of Business Mathematics, Japanese Society for Quality Control, Information Processing Society of Japan and The Information and Systems Society.

Daniel Kunkle is currently a PhD student in the College of Computer and Information Science at Northeastern University, focusing in the areas of data mining and machine learning. He received his MS in computer science at Rochester Institute of Technology (RIT) in 2003, focusing on evolutionary search & optimization and emergent behavior in computation. He received a BS with highest honors in information technology RIT in 2001. His master's thesis explores methods of classifying one-dimensional cellular automata based on dynamical complexity. In 2002, he consulted with the Laboratory for Applied Computing at RIT, developing evolutionary methods for optimizing the halftone printing of continuous-tone images. In the summer of 2001 he was an intern for Stephen Guerin at BiosGroup developing systems for the visualization of complex systems.

Chia-Chen Kuo is a doctoral candidate in graduate school of management at I-Shou University, Taiwan, majoring in organizational and strategy research and minoring in human resources and organizational behavior research. Her current research interests include organizational and strategy research (e.g., strategy formulation and implementations, strategic planning and decision processes, competitive strategy and cooperative strategy) and human resources and organizational behavior research (e.g., performance improvement of human resources practices, impact of the employment relationship on outcomes critical to the organization and its applicants, the individuals and groups within an organizational context and internal processes and practices, such as individual personality characteristics, individual emotion and decision making, group composition characteristics, group decision making and leadership).

W. F. Lawless received his PhD in social psychology and game theory from Virginia Tech in 1992. His research is in organizations and decision-making. He is a professional mechanical engineer in nuclear waste management, past and current member of the Department of Energy (DOE) Savannah River Site Citizens Advisory Board (1994-2000; 2003-current), the co-technical lead for its Consolidated Incinerator Facility Focus Group (2000-03); a member of the European trustnet hazardous decision group (2002-current); past member DOE Mixed Wastes Tribal and Stakeholders Working Group (1995-6) and a DOE nuclear waste management whistleblower, 1983.

Tsai-Lung Liu studied his undergraduate education in department of international trade at Feng Chia University, Taiwan. In the master program, his major was business management and minor was financial management at Azusa Pacific University, USA. In addition to his nearly 13 years' working experience in the business field, he has accumulated much interests and ideas in the areas of operational management, marketing management, financial management and human resources management. Currently, he is the lecturer of Department of Marketing and Distribution Management at Tajen Institute of Technology, Taiwan. He also is a doctoral candidate in graduate school of management at I-Shou University, Taiwan. His current research interests include strategic alliance, organizational decision processes, corporate diversification, marketing mix strategy and consumer behavior.

Ana Marostica is a professor of mathematical logic for information and expert systems at the Doctorate Department in the School of Economics, University of Buenos Aires,

USA. Dr. Marostica was the logician of an international group of investigators in artificial intelligence with headquarters in the University of Goettingen (1989-1992). She is now the head of an interdisciplinary group of researchers working on the logical-heuristic representations of decision-maker agents in economic field with headquarters in the University of Buenos Aires. Her research interests include the logical-heuristic structure of scientific reasoning and cognitive sciences applied to Economics. She holds a PhD from Indiana University at Bloomington and is the author of many journal articles both in the United States and in Europe.

Tsutomu Mishina is a professor in the Department of Management Science and Engineering at Akita Prefectural University, Japan. He received his PhD in industrial engineering from the University of Oklahoma. He has previous work experience in the electronics industry where he mainly designed strategic business models. His current research includes financial engineering and its applications to corporate strategy.

Yuriy Nevmyvaka is a PhD candidate at Carnegie Mellon University. He received his BA from Middlebury College and his MS from Carnegie Mellon University. He also holds a diploma from Institute d'Etudes Politiques de Paris (Sciences-Po). His research interests include general market microstructure issues, automated market making, efficient trade execution, financial engineering, machine learning and optimization techniques. He has authored a number of academic papers and book chapters. Among his professional experiences are positions at Lehman Brothers, Credit Suisse and in the hedge fund industry.

Alexei G. Orlov is an assistant professor of economics at the College of Business and Economics of Radford University, USA. A native of Moscow, Russia, he received his PhD from the University of Virginia in 2002. His research spans the fields of macroeconomics, international finance, economic growth and computational economics, with the specific topics of interest including capital controls, intellectual property and costs of recessions. As a part-time instructor at the University of Virginia, an assistant professor at Radford University and a visiting assistant professor at Virginia Tech, he has taught a variety of courses, ranging from the undergraduate mathematical economics and international economics to the graduate-level managerial economics.

Lukáš Pichl received his PhD degrees from the Graduate University of Advanced Studies Japan (National Research Institutes) in 2000, and from the Charles University, Prague, in 2003. Since 2001, he has been affiliated as an assistant professor with the Department of Computer Software, University of Aizu, Japan. Research interest of Dr. Pichl in computational intelligence ranges from behavioural aspects of artificial societies to machine learning in networked database systems. He participates in Japan-US and Japan-Germany international cooperation programs supported by the Japan Society for Promotion of Science (JSPS). Dr. Pichl is a member of ACM, IEEE, and IEICE.

Yuya Sasaki is currently a graduate student of the Department of Economics, Utah State University, USA. He has worked on evolutionary dynamics and aggregate effects of bounded rationality in contexts of several economic situations, particularly with computational tools of agent-based modeling in which cognitive structures are embedded in artificial agents. His current research interest lies in an attempt to address the computational issues of agent-based macroeconomic modeling from an analytic point of view.

Duane J. Seppi is a professor of Financial Economics in the Tepper School of Business at Carnegie Mellon University, USA. He received his PhD from the University of Chicago Graduate School of Business. He teaches classes on stochastic processes for option pricing and on Monte Carlo simulation. His research interests include modeling spot and option prices for energy and other commodities and market microstructure issues such as futures manipulation, limit orders, and market liquidity. His work has appeared in the *Review of Financial Studies, the Journal of Finance, the Journal of Financial Economics* and other leading finance and economics journals.

Katia Sycara is a professor in the School of Computer Science at Carnegie Mellon University, USA, and director of the Laboratory for Agents Technology and Semantic. She holds a BS in applied mathematics from Brown University, MS in electrical engineering from the University of Wisconsin and PhD in computer science from the Georgia Institute of Technology. She holds an honorary doctorate from the University of the Aegean (2004). She has authored more than 250 technical papers dealing with multiagent systems, software agents, Web services, the semantic web, human-agent interaction, negotiation, and machine learning. Professor Sycara is one of the contributors to the development of DAML-S/OWL-S, a language for semantic web services. From 2001-2003 she served as Invited Expert of the W3C (the World Wide Web Consortium) Working Group on Web Services Architecture. She is a member of the Scientific Advisory Board of France Telecom and a member of the Scientific Advisory Board of the Greek National Center of Scientific Research "Demokritos" Information Technology Division. Professor Sycara is a fellow of the American Association for Artificial Intelligence and the recipient of the 2002 ACM/SIGART Agents Research Award. She is a founding editor-in-chief of the journal *Autonomous Agents and Multi Agent Systems* and on the editorial board of an additional six journals.

Chiu-Che Tseng joined Texas A&M University, USA, as an assistant professor for a little over 2 years. Dr. Tseng received his BS in information and computer engineering from Chung-Yuan Christian University in Taiwan, his MS in computer science from the University of Memphis, Memphis Tennessee, and his PhD in computer science engineering from the University of Texas at Arlington. Prior to joining Texas A&M University-Commerce, he worked in the telecommunication industry for over 4 years as a software engineer, focusing on the firmware and device driver development for real-time embedded system.

Ayako Watanabe received her MS from Ochanomizu University, Japan, in 1992, where she has become affiliated with the Department of Information Sciences as a research associate since 1994. She is interested in applications of artificial intelligence for physically handicapped people and visualization of dynamical processes in quantum theory. Dr. Watanabe received her PhD from Ochanomizu University in 2004.

Senlin Wu is a PhD candidate of management information systems in the Information and Decision Sciences Department of the College of Business Administration at the University of Illinois at Chicago, USA. He graduated from Tsinghua University, China, with a master's degree in management information systems in 1996 and then worked several years in the banking industry. His current research is about the methods of threshold variable selection in the mixture model, which can be applied on the economic and marketing dataset to improve the accuracy of classification and prediction. He is also interested in the research of the mechanism of the double auction market.

Takuya Yamano received his MS degrees from the University of Tokyo in 1998 and from Tokyo Institute of Technology in 2000. After acquiring his PhD from the Tokyo Institute of Technology in 2003, he was a postdoctoral researcher with the Max Planck Institute in Dresden, Germany, and a visiting fellow with the New England Complex Systems Institute and Interdisciplinary Center for Bioinformatics in Leipzig. He is currently a special postdoctoral researcher of the Japan Society for the Promotion of Science. Dr. Yamano research interest includes generalized entropy, queuing processes and development of new complexity measures.

Christopher Zapart obtained an MSc by Research degree in pattern analysis and neural networks from the Neural Computing Research Group, Aston University, UK, in 1996. This was followed by several years of PhD research at Aston University and several more years working in London as an IT consultant for a major global oil company. He is a founder and director of a scientific research company Advanced Financial Trading Solutions Ltd., UK, performing independent research in computational finance and artificial intelligence, publishing papers in leading journals, presenting at conferences and collaborating with international research centres. His research interests are in applying artificial intelligence techniques such as neural networks, fuzzy logic and genetic algorithms to problems in computational finance and experimental physics.

Index

S

T

U

V

W

Z

www.ingramcontent.com/pod-product-compliance
Lightning Source LLC
LaVergne TN
LVHW062115200926
848484LV00007B/1673
* 9 7 8 1 5 9 1 4 0 6 4 9 5 *